Counseling Troubled Boys

The Routledge Series on Counseling and Psychotherapy with Boys and Men

SERIES EDITOR

Mark S. Kiselica
The College of New Jersey

ADVISORY BOARD

VOLUMES IN THIS SERIES

Counseling Troubled Boys: A Guidebook for Professionals
Mark S. Kiselica, Matt Englar-Carlson, and Arthur M. Horne

COUNSELING TROUBLED BOYS

A Guidebook for Professionals

Mark S. Kiselica, Matt Englar-Carlson, and Arthur M. Horne
EDITORS

Routledge
Taylor & Francis Group
New York   London

Routledge
Taylor & Francis Group
270 Madison Avenue
New York, NY 10016

Routledge
Taylor & Francis Group
2 Park Square
Milton Park, Abingdon
Oxon OX14 4RN

© 2008 by Taylor & Francis Group, LLC
Routledge is an imprint of Taylor & Francis Group, an Informa business

Printed in the United States of America on acid-free paper
10 9 8 7 6 5 4 3 2 1

International Standard Book Number-13: 978-0-415-95547-8 (Softcover)

Library of Congress Cataloging-in-Publication Data

Counseling troubled boys : a guidebook for professionals / [edited by] Mark S. Kiselica, Matt Englar-Carlson, Arthur M. Horne.
    p. ; cm. -- (The Routledge series on counseling and psychotherapy with boys and men ; v. 1)
    Includes bibliographical references and index.
    ISBN 978-0-415-95547-8 (softcover : alk. paper)
    1. Teenage boys--Counseling of. 2. Boys--Counseling of. 3. Problem youth--Counseling of. 4. Adolescent psychology. I. Kiselica, Mark S. II. Englar-Carlson, Matt. III. Horne, Arthur M., 1942- IV. Series.
    [DNLM: 1. Adolescent Psychology. 2. Counseling--methods. 3. Mental Health Services. WS 462 C855 2007]

HV1423.C68 2007
362.74'86--dc22

2007024858

Visit the Taylor & Francis Web site at
http://www.taylorandfrancis.com

and the Routledge Web site at
http://www.routledge.com

To Otto and Winnie Kiselica—my dear parents,
loving mentors, and best friends (MK).

For the teachers, coaches, and especially my parents, Jon and Laura,
who supported and encouraged me when I was a boy (MEC).

Dedicated to my friend and coauthor, Mark Kiselica (AH).

Contents

Series Editor's Foreword

During the late 1970s and throughout the 1980s and 1990s, a handful of mental health professionals began to focus their research investigations and clinical services on the unique challenges associated with helping boys and men. The work of these pioneers was largely focused on understanding and addressing the social construction of gender roles, men's sexism and homophobia, the problems associated with traditional masculinity and the male socialization process, men's gender role conflicts, male help-seeking behaviors, and institutional barriers to providing services to boys and men.

The efforts of these dedicated individuals have raised awareness about the special needs of boys and men and fostered the development of gender-sensitive approaches to helping these populations. However, to date no publisher has produced a book series that captures this burgeoning body of knowledge about the emotional and psychological lives of boys and men and the process of counseling them in a male-friendly manner. The purpose of the Routledge Series on Counseling and Psychotherapy With Boys and Men is to respond to this gap in the professional literature by developing the most comprehensive set of books on helping boys and men that has ever been assembled. I am proud to launch this exciting new series with the present volume, *Counseling Troubled Boys: A Guidebook for Practitioners*.

The idea for this project emerged amid one of the many conversations Matt Englar-Carlson, Arthur "Andy" Horne, and I have enjoyed during our reunions at professional conferences. At one of those reunions, which occurred at the annual convention of the American Psychological Association in Washington, DC, in August 2005, Matt, Andy, and I met for dinner at a restaurant, where I shared with them my vision for creating a new series of books in which highly respected scholars and practitioners would share their ideas about doing gender-sensitive counseling and psychotherapy with boys and men. Just as I expected, Matt and Andy were thrilled with the idea. We decided to create the first book for the series, and we agreed that this initial volume should be focused on troubled boys who are often misunderstood or overlooked by society.

As we explain in the preface to this book, we made a deliberate attempt to balance our concern for the many adjustment difficulties of boys with a recognition of the many strengths boys have and how to utilize those strengths in counseling and psychotherapy. My intention as the editor of this series is to recruit a team of renowned experts in the field to produce other books that reflect this balanced perspective on understanding and helping boys and men. I am pleased to report that numerous authorities on the subjects of boys, men, and masculinity have responded to my invitations to write books for the series with great enthusiasm. As a result, my esteemed colleagues on the advisory board for the series and the fine editorial staff at Routledge are now entertaining many outstanding book proposals for the series that have been sent to me by potential authors who are eager to contribute their expertise to this series. I am honored and grateful for their support of my vision.

I hope you enjoy *Counseling Troubled Boys*, and I welcome your feedback on this and the forthcoming volumes in the series.

Mark S. Kiselica, Editor
The Routledge Series on Counseling and
Psychotherapy With Boys and Men
The College of New Jersey
May 14, 2007

Preface: The Struggles and Strengths of Boys and How We Can Help Them

During the late 1990s and the early part of the 21st century, there was an explosion of interest regarding the well-being of boys in the United States. The topic became the focus of numerous newspaper and magazine articles throughout the country. For example, the cover story of the August 22, 1999, edition of the *New York Times Magazine* was titled "The Troubled Life of Boys," and the July 30, 2001, edition of *U.S. News & World Report* featured the headline "Boys: The Weaker Sex? Why Girls Do Better in the Real World." Around the same time, the trade book market was flooded with publications lamenting the disturbed emotional lives of boys, including the well-known volumes *Real Boys: Rescuing Our Sons From the Myths of Boyhood* (Pollack, 1999); *Lost Boys: Why Our Sons Turn Violent and How We Can Save Them* (Garbarino, 1999); and *Raising Cain: Protecting the Emotional Life of Boys* (Kindlon & Thompson, 1999). Collectively, these and many other publications played a major role in raising awareness about the special problems experienced by boys and in generating extensive discussions about how to reduce the risks that young men face.

Concern for the well-being of boys is certainly warranted because legions of boys struggle with a host of adjustment difficulties during childhood and adolescence. Consider, for example, the following health, educational, and social statistics pertaining to boys:

- 1,915 males age 19 or younger were murdered in 2005 (U.S. Department of Justice, Federal Bureau of Investigation, 2006).
- In 2001, 272 boys between the ages of 5 and 14 years and 3,409 boys between the ages of 15 and 24 years committed suicide,

accounting for 86% of all youth suicides that year (Centers for Disease Control and Prevention, 2007; U.S. Census Bureau, 2003).

- The suicide rate among gay boys is extremely high, possibly accounting for 30% of all adolescent suicides (Borowsky, Ireland, & Resnick, 2001).
- Eight percent of all boys are the victims of some type of nonfatal crime at school or while going to or from school (U.S. Census Bureau, 2003).
- 425,387 boys were the victims of child abuse or neglect in 2005 (U.S. Department of Health and Human Services, Administration on Children, Youth and Families, 2007).
- Sixteen percent of men report that they were the victims of child sexual abuse (Baker & King, 2004).
- Each year, more than 170,000 young men aged 15–19 years father a child; the vast majority of their children are born out of wedlock (Kiselica, in press).
- 9.5 percent of all males aged 3–17 have a learning disability, and 10.2% have been diagnosed with attention deficit hyperactivity disorder (ADHD; U.S. Census Bureau, 2007).
- Young men drop out of school at higher rates than women; by age 19, 76% of men finished high school compared to 83% of women. Young men also lag behind women in terms of college attendance; at age 19, 50% of women were attending college, but only 39% of men (U.S. Department of Labor, 2007).
- 74.3 percent of all delinquency offenses are committed by boys (U.S. Census Bureau, 2007).
- Every year, tens of thousands of boys are arrested for running away from home (Darnay et al., 2003).

We contend that the interaction of a number of biological and social factors accounts for these problems. Compared to girls, boys enter the world hard-wired to be more active, yet our educational systems expect boys to remain still throughout most of the school day (Gurian & Stevens, 2007). Boys' brains, particularly the neurological structures responsible for reading acquisition, tend to develop at a later age, placing many boys at risk to fall behind in their academic development (Sax, 2001). Parents are more likely to use physical punishment with their sons than their daughters, thereby modeling for boys that violence is an acceptable way to deal with problems (Garbarino, 1999). Society gives boys the message that they must be tough and self-reliant, discouraging them from expressing vulnerability and from seeking help when they are in distress (Courtenay, 2001; Levant, 1992). The media bombards boys with the message that sex in the absence of a caring relationship and contraceptive use is OK, and that girls and women are objects for their sexual gratification, which are disturbing signals that can foster exploitive and high-risk sexual behavior in young men (Brooks, 2003).

And father absence, a serious social problem associated with the high divorce rate, the awarding of child custody to mothers, and fathers abandoning their children, has resulted in more and more boys being raised in father-absent homes where they often hunger for the loving, steady guidance of their fathers (Heesacker, Baker, & Romelus, 2005). In the face of these circumstances, it is not surprising that so many boys feel badly about themselves, are confused about what it means to be a man, and struggle to fit in and find their way in life.

Compared with the lives of their economically advantaged counterparts, the lives of boys who are raised in poverty are especially bleak. According to Evans (2004), impoverished boys "are exposed to more family turmoil, violence, separation from their families, instability and chaotic households" (p. 77). They "experience less social support, and their parents are less responsive and more authoritarian" (p. 77). They

> are read to relatively infrequently, watch more TV, and have less access to books and computers. Their parents are less involved in their school activities. The air and water the poor consume are more polluted. Their homes are more crowded, noisier, and of lower quality. Low-income neighborhoods are more dangerous, offer poorer municipal services, and suffer greater physical deterioration. Predominantly low-income schools and day care are inferior. (p. 77)

As exposure to the number of these factors increases, so too do the odds that a young man will experience academic difficulties, drop out of school, engage in delinquent behavior and substance abuse, and become an adolescent father or a victim of child sexual abuse (Thornberry, Wei, Stouthamer-Loeber, & Van Dyke, 2000). Consequently, boys who are raised in a world of poverty desperately need the dedicated assistance of skilled professionals who understand their needs and can help them to cope with the harsh conditions of their worlds.

Unfortunately, the clinical assumptions and practices established in some mental health, medical, educational, and social service organizations located in both poor and well-to-do communities are neither male sensitive nor male friendly (Kiselica, 2003; Romo, Bellamy, & Coleman, 2004). Many practitioners are unable to diagnose serious depression in boys because they do not understand that acting-out behaviors and substance abuse mask depression in some young men who are considering suicide (Cochran & Rabinowitz, 2000). There has also been a historical underreporting and misdiagnosis of the terror of child sexual abuse in boys because of the mistaken, widespread assumption that only girls are victimized (Camino, 2000). Frequently, boys who are referred for help, especially youngsters demonstrating hyperactivity, substance abuse, aggression, and oppositional behavior, are deemed poor candidates for counseling, in spite of the fact that there are empirically supported strategies for treating these behaviors (Kapalka, 2007; Newman, Horne, & Webster, 1999; Sheidow & Henggeler, in press). Too often, the problems of gay boys go undetected due to an absence of gay-affirming practices

(Stone, 2003), as do the concerns of gifted and talented boys because of a lack of awareness of the special challenges and needs of this population (Kerr & Cohn, 2001). It is common for well-meaning practitioners to become frustrated in their attempts to help boys because they do not understand how to adapt their traditional models of counseling and psychotherapy to fit the relational style and emotional baggage of boys (Kiselica, 2003). Consequently, they may erroneously conclude that boys are "resistant" to getting help, when their problems with establishing a therapeutic connection with boys are actually the result of a mismatch between how boys form close relationships and the manner in which helping professionals relate to boys (Kiselica & Horne, 1999). Due to these assumptions and practices, some professionals unintentionally alienate rather than help a substantial number of boys who are referred for assistance (Beymer, 1995; Kiselica, 2003; Romo et al., 2004).

One of the major shortcomings of the burgeoning literature on boys and how we can best help them is the dearth of information on male strengths. The massive attention that has been devoted to the problems of boys has fostered the promulgation of inaccurate deficit models of male development (Kiselica, 2006). Although raising awareness about the problems of boys has helped professionals to better understand the special challenges and problems boys experience during the journey to manhood, it also has overshadowed crucial information about the overall well-being and resiliency of boys (Kiselica, Englar-Carlson, & Fisher, 2006). In spite of the many problems boys experience, including the common ones that were listed earlier, the best available data show that American boys are doing much better than commonly depicted (Nichols & Good, 2004). Specifically, these data verify that boys, as a whole, are fairly well adjusted, engage in a wide range of prosocial behaviors, and approach the world with both the desire and the ability to make and sustain positive relationships (Kiselica & O'Brien, 2001; Lindberg, Boggess, Porter, & Williams, 2000; Lindberg, Boggess, & Williams, 2000; Nichols & Good, 2004). Showing concern for the hardships of boys is certainly laudatory, but we must be careful not to exaggerate and sensationalize the problems boys have, or else we run the risk of ignoring the important lessons we can learn from boys who are doing well in life. Studying, understanding, and reporting on the many strengths of boys and incorporating our knowledge of male assets into our clinical work represent useful ways we can help all boys, especially those who are troubled.

The purpose of this book is to address these issues by presenting the latest information about male development, the strengths of boys, and male-oriented approaches to helping. We have gathered many of the nation's leading authorities on counseling boys to explain the difficulties that boys experience and how to build upon male strengths to help boys live happy, well-adjusted lives.

This book is divided into two parts. Part 1, "Understanding and Establishing Rapport with Boys," opens with a chapter by John M. Robertson and David S. Shepard that is focused on the developmental challenges of boys. Robertson and Shepard demonstrate that gender-sensitive counseling with boys must include a keen understanding of the male socialization process and its impact on the psychological development of boys. In chapter 2, Mark S. Kiselica, Matt Englar-Carlson, Arthur M. Horne, and Mark Fisher utilize a positive psychology framework to identify how healthy aspects of traditional masculinity can be considered potential building blocks for promoting strengths and well-being in boys. In chapter 3, Mark S. Kiselica and Matt Englar-Carlson draw from the findings of extensive empirical research on hard-to-reach adolescent fathers to propose a male-friendly approach to establishing rapport with boys in individual counseling and psychotherapy. Part 2 of this book, "Helping Special Populations of Boys," begins with chapter 4 by Joseph M. Cervantes and Matt Englar-Carlson, in which they describe the sobering hardships of boys from impoverished families and the unique considerations associated with assisting these youths. In chapter 5, Mark S. Kiselica and Gerald Novack discuss the therapeutic process of helping boys and young men who have been sexually abused. Mark C. Fleming and Matt Englar-Carlson examine the diagnosis and treatment of boys who are depressed and suicidal in chapter 6. Based on his many years of research with out-of-control boys, George M. Kapalka explains multifaceted strategies for counseling boys with attention deficit hyperactivity disorder in chapter 7. The team of Le'Roy E. Reese, Arthur M. Horne, Christopher D. Bell, and John Harvey Wingfield employ an ecological model in chapter 8 to consider the factors that lead to the formation of aggression in boys, and they endorse multiple levels of intervention with this population. In chapter 9, Mark S. Woodford explains why the rate of substance abuse is higher in boys than in girls, and he describes the motivational interviewing model as the foundation for helping boys who abuse drugs and alcohol. Chapter 10, written by Mark S. Kiselica, Maryann Mulé, and Douglas C. Haldeman, is devoted to understanding gay boys and a gay-affirming process of helping them. In the final chapter of this book, William Ming Liu, Samuel J. Shepard, and Megan Foley Nicpon discuss the unique adjustment difficulties of gifted boys and the special considerations associated with counseling these young men.

We have designed this project to be a practical and scholarly guide for mental health, educational, social service, and medical professionals who want to render gender-sensitive services to boys and adolescent males. Consequently, this book includes numerous instructive case studies illustrating how to engage young men in counseling and psychotherapy in a male-friendly manner. In addition, throughout the book, the chapter authors explain how both healthy and unhealthy conceptions of masculinity and other important demographic and contextual variables, such as race, ethnicity, socioeconomic status, and culture, affect the adjustment of boys and the process of counseling them. It is our fervent hope that this information will enhance the efforts of practitioners to empathize with boys who are in psychic pain, help troubled

boys to feel comfortable in counseling by affirming and building upon
their strengths, and foster their fullest potential during the journey to
manhood.

REFERENCES

Baker, D., & King, S. E. (2004). Child sexual abuse and incest. In R. T. Francoeur & R. J. Noonan (Eds.), *International encyclopedia of sexuality* (pp. 1233–1237). New York: Continuum.

Beymer, L. (1995). *Meeting the guidance and counseling needs of boys.* Alexandria, VA: American Counseling Association.

Borowsky, I. W., Ireland, M., & Resnick, M. D. (2001). Adolescent suicide attempts: Risks and protectors. *Pediatrics, 107,* 485–493.

Brooks, G. R. (2003). *The centerfold syndrome: How men can overcome objectification and achieve intimacy with women.* San Francisco: Jossey-Bass.

Camino, L. (2000). *Treating sexually abused boys: A practical guide for therapists & counselors.* San Francisco: Jossey-Bass.

Centers for Disease Control and Prevention. (2007). *Suicide: Fact sheet.* Retrieved April 20, 2007, from http://www.cdc.gov/ncipc/factsheets/suifacts.htm

Cochran, S. V., & Rabinowitz, F. E. (2000). *Men and depression: Clinical and empirical perspectives.* San Diego, CA: Academic Press.

Courtenay, W. H. (2001). Counseling men in medical settings: The six-point HEALTH plan. In G. R. Brooks & G. E. Good (Eds.), *The new handbook of psychotherapy and counseling with men: A comprehensive guide to settings, problems, and treatment approaches* (pp. 59–91). San Francisco: Jossey-Bass.

Darnay, A. J., Lazich, R., Fisher, H. S., Magee, M. D., Piwowarski, J., & Schmittroth, L. (2003). *Social trends and indicators: USA: Vol. 4. Crime & justice.* Detroit, MI: Gale Research.

Evans, G. W. (2004). The environment of childhood poverty. *American Psychologist, 59,* 77–92.

Garbarino, J. (1999). *Lost boys: Why our sons turn violent and how we can save them.* New York: Free Press.

Gurian, M., & Stevens, K. (2007). *The minds of boys: Saving our sons from falling behind in school and life.* San Francisco: Jossey-Bass.

Heesacker, M., Baker, J. O., & Romelus, A. M. (2005, August). Development of an empirically derived measure of father hunger. In J. M. Robertson (Chair), *The* Frontline *PBS documentary* Country Boys: *Theoretical and practical implications for psychologists.* Symposium conducted at the annual convention of the American Psychological Association, Washington, DC.

Kapalka, G. M. (2007). *Parenting your out-of-control child: An effective, easy-to-use program for teaching self-control.* Oakland, CA: New Harbinger.

Kerr, B. A., & Cohn, S. J. (2001). *Smart boys: Talent, manhood, & the search for meaning.* Scottsdale, AZ: Great Potential Press.

Kindlon, D., & Thompson, M. (1999). *Raising Cain: Protecting the emotional lives of boys.* New York: Ballantine.

Kiselica, M. S. (2003). Transforming psychotherapy in order to succeed with boys: Male-friendly practices. *Journal of Clinical Psychology: In Session, 59,* 1225–1236.

Kiselica, M. S. (2006, August). Contributions and limitations of the deficit model of men. In M. S. Kiselica (Chair), *Toward a positive psychology of boys, men, and masculinity.* Symposium presented at the annual convention of the American Psychological Association, New Orleans, LA.

Kiselica, M. S. (in press). *When boys become parents: Examining the hidden crisis of adolescent fatherhood in America.* Piscataway, NJ: Rutgers University Press.

Kiselica, M. S., Englar-Carlson, M., & Fisher, M. (2006, August). A positive psychology framework for building upon male strengths. In M. S. Kiselica (Chair), *Toward a positive psychology of boys, men, and masculinity.* Symposium presented at the annual convention of the American Psychological Association, New Orleans, LA.

Kiselica, M. S., & Horne, A. M. (1999). Preface: For the sake of our nation's sons. In A. M. Horne & M. S. Kiselica (Eds.), *Handbook of counseling boys and adolescent males* (pp. xv–xx). Thousand Oaks, CA: Sage.

Kiselica, M. S., & O'Brien, S. (2001, August). Are attachment disorders and alexithymia characteristic of males? In M. S. Kiselica (Chair), *Are males really emotional mummies? What do the data indicate?* Symposium and paper presented at the annual convention of the American Psychological Association, San Francisco, CA.

Levant, R. F. (1992). Toward the reconstruction of masculinity. *Journal of Family Psychology, 5,* 379–402.

Lindberg, L. D., Boggess, S., Porter, L., & Williams, S. (2000). *Teen risk-taking: A statistical report.* Washington, DC: Urban Institute.

Lindberg, L. D., Boggess, S., & Williams, S. (2000). *Multiple threats: The co-occurrence of teen health risk behaviors.* Washington, DC: Urban Institute.

Newman, D. A., Horne, A. M., & Webster, C. B. (1999). Bullies and victims: A theme of boys and adolescent males. In A. M. Horne & M. S. Kiselica (Eds.), *Handbook of counseling boys and adolescent males* (pp. 313–340). Thousand Oaks, CA: Sage.

Nichols, S. L., & Good, T. L. (2004). *America's teenagers—myths and realities: Media images, schooling, and the social costs of careless indifference.* Mahwah, NJ: Erlbaum.

Pollack, W. (1999). *Real boys: Rescuing our sons from the myths of boyhood.* New York: Henry Holt.

Romo, C., Bellamy, J., & Coleman, M. T. (2004). *TFF final evaluation report.* Austin: Texas Fragile Families Initiative.

Sax, L. (2001). Reclaiming kindergarten: Making kindergarten less harmful for boys. *Psychology of Men and Masculinity, 2,* 3–12.

Sheidow, A. J., & Henggeler, S. W. (in press). Multisystemic therapy with substance using adolescents: A synthesis of the research. In N. Jainchill (Ed.), *Understanding and treating adolescent substance use disorders.* Kingston, NJ: Civic Research Institute.

Stone, C. B. (2003). Counselors as advocates for gay, lesbian, and bisexual youth: A call for equity and action. *Journal of Multicultural Counseling and Development, 31,* 143–155.

Thornberry, T. P., Wei, E. H., Stouthamer-Loeber, M., & Van Dyke, J. (2000, January). Teenage fatherhood and delinquent behavior. *Juvenile Justice Bulletin.* Retrieved June 25, 2007, from http://www.ncjrs.org/html/ojjdp/jjbul2000_1/contents.html

U.S. Census Bureau. (2003). *Statistical abstract of the United States: 2003.* (122nd ed.). Washington, DC: Author.

U.S. Census Bureau. (2007). *Statistical abstract of the United States* (126th ed.). Retrieved April 20, 2007, from http://www.census.gov/prod/www/statistical-abstract.html

U.S. Department of Health and Human Services, Administration on Children, Youth and Families. (2007). *Child maltreatment: 2005.* Washington, DC: Government Printing Office.

U.S. Department of Justice, Federal Bureau of Investigation. (2006). *Expanded homicide data: Table 2.* Retrieved April 20, 2007, from http://www.fbi.gov/ucr/05cius/offenses/expanded_information/data/shrtable_02.html

U.S. Department of Labor. (2007). *America's youth at 19: School enrollment, training, and employment transitions between ages 18 and 19 summary.* Retrieved May 11, 2007, from http://www.bls.gov/nls/

Acknowledgments

Each day that I worked on this book, I said a small prayer of thanks for my beautiful family and their support of me. To Sandi, Andrew, Christian, and Sasha, I thank you for your understanding and patience regarding every moment I have had to devote to my professional duties, including my work on this book, which I consider in many ways to be an expression of my love for all of you. To my precious parents, Otto and Winnie Kiselica, please know I am always inspired by you and the admirable example you have set for me. To John, Mary, Patty, and Matt, you are all wonderful siblings, and I thank you for supporting me my entire life.

I am fortunate to be a member of a wonderful kinship network that extends far beyond the realms of my biological family and includes dozens of professionals from the American Counseling Association and the American Psychological Association, especially Division 51, the Society for the Psychological Study of Men and Masculinity, who have affirmed my desire to help troubled boys and their families. I thank all of you—especially those of you who have helped me to see the light in all living things—for your support and encouragement and for the important lessons you have taught me about boys, men, and masculinity.

My kinship network also includes two very special people—my good buddies and coeditors of this book, Andy Horne and Matt Englar-Carlson. Our friendship and how it was formed is a very special story. Long before I started publishing my own work, Andy Horne was one of the nation's leading authorities on counseling aggressive boys and their families, and on addressing the problem of bullying in our nation's schools. I first met Andy at the 1991 annual convention of the American Counseling Association during the early days of my career in academe when I was laying the foundation for a multifaceted agenda for studying, understanding, and helping teenage fathers. Andy and I had been recruited to serve on a panel discussing gender issues in counseling, and we instantly formed a friendship during that experience, which was fueled by our passion for helping troubled boys and our desire to have people think more complexly about boys and men. Ever since then, we have participated in numerous projects and symposiums sponsored by professional groups concerned about men's issues, which led us to discover Matt Englar-Carlson, who emerged as a new authority on counseling and psychotherapy with men during the early 2000s. Matt invited Andy and me to serve on some of his conference symposiums when Matt was starting his career in higher education, and through these forums, I realized that Matt has a keen grasp of the professional literature on men and many innovative ideas for male-sensitive counseling. More importantly, during my very first conversation with Matt, I experienced the exact same chemistry with him that I share with Andy, and I immediately realized that I had made another great friend. This book is an outgrowth of my friendships with Andy and Matt, which are priceless to me. I am proud and lucky to be able to say you guys are my buddies!

I am privileged to be a faculty member of the College of New Jersey. I thank my colleagues in the Department of Counselor Education— Peggy Abromaitus, Charleen Alderfer, Debbie Caroselli, Marion Cavallaro, MaryLou Ramsey, Atsuko Seto, and Mark Woodford—and Bill Behre, Dean of the School of Education, as well as my students for your support of this project.

I am grateful to the many professionals who contributed their expertise to the development of this book, including the esteemed members of the advisory board for the Routledge Series on Counseling and Psychotherapy with Boys and Men, whose input has shaped the direction of this series, and the chapter authors, whose competent work advances our understanding about boys and their strengths and struggles. I want to express a special thanks to Dana Bliss of Routledge, who guided this book through every stage of its development, and to his coworkers, George Zimmar and Charlotte Roh, for their respective roles in launching this project and moving it toward its completion. Thanks also to Robert Sims, who did a fine job as the project editor of this book. It has been an enjoyable experience to work with all of you.

And to the boys and men—the hundreds of boys and men I have counseled, taught, and coached—thank you for helping me to understand your ways of relating to the world, your many splendid qualities, your hardships, your pain, and your accomplishments. It has been an honor to share in your experiences, which have informed and inspired my work as a scholar, teacher, practitioner, and advocate.

Mark Kiselica
Ewing, New Jersey

Hope is a state of mind, not of the world.... Either we have hope or we don't; it is a dimension of the soul, and it's not essentially dependent on some particular observation of the world or estimate of the situation.

Hope ... is not the same as joy that things are going well, or willingness to invest in enterprises that are obviously heading for success, but rather an ability to work for something because it is good, not just because it stands a chance to succeed. The more propitious the situation in which we demonstrate hope, the deeper the hope is.

Vaclav Havel

The process of editing and writing chapters in this book provoked strong feelings within me. It is the sheer vulnerability and potential in boys and teenage males that touches me and stirs my passion to simply offer assistance in the ways that I can. In contemporary American society, there are many deleterious avenues open to boys that can easily lead to poor outcomes in one's youth or later as an adult. At the same time, boyhood is an amazing time of exploration and excitement. It is my sincere wish that the perspectives and ideas offered within this book encourage practitioners, and boys themselves, to realize the ability and promise of being a responsible and healthy male.

First and foremost, I want to thank my coeditors, Mark Kiselica and Andy Horne. As the junior member of the team on this book, I have known their professional work for many years. In their own way, Mark and Andy both served as influential role models in helping form my own professional identity and interests. Their 1999 book, *Handbook of Counseling Boys and Adolescent Males: A Practitioner's Guide*, was a landmark publication in the field. My own copy is worn out from reading and referring to it so much! What an honor to be invited on board this book project and to work with them. There was a synergy of creative ideas when the three of us got together to develop this book. Being in their presence has really helped me become a more thoughtful practitioner. Beyond their considerable expertise and experiences in helping boys and adolescent males, Mark and Andy share an incredible passion for their work. Their dedication and energy were infectious, and it was easy to become engrossed in the book.

Second, I would like to thank all of the contributors to the book. Assembling the contributors for this book was like drawing up an all-star team of people we would be honored to work with.

I would like to thank my colleagues in the Department of Counseling at the California State University, Fullerton, for their support and creation of a healthy family atmosphere at work. It is an honor to be on this faculty. Specifically, I want to thank two of the contributors in this book, David Shepard and Joseph Cervantes, for their work on this project and for their continued friendship. I also want to acknowledge the departmental leadership of Jeffrey Kottler and his ability to elevate the importance of relationships, collegiality, and living a good balanced life over academic competition and workaholism. That is a difficult thing to do in the academic setting.

Much of the scholarly work on which this book is based comes from my colleagues from the American Psychological Association (APA)

Division 51, the Society for the Psychological Study of Men and Masculinity, whose members have been great mentors, colleagues, and wonderful friends. So much of what we know about working with boys has come from this dynamic group of men and women. I also want to acknowledge my colleagues and friends from the American Counseling Association (ACA) who have been supportive of me throughout my career. I think it is important to recognize that I have two professional homes—APA and ACA—and that I benefit from active memberships in both groups. I wish more members in these groups would move beyond professional boundaries and collaborate on our common interests.

I need to give my thanks and appreciation to my cycling friends who understand that riding a bike is the perfect counterpoint to our fast-paced modern lives. Cycling is my therapy, and my cycling companions are my therapists. So thank you to Tyler Myers, Jeffrey Kottler, Chris Kane, Juan Cagampang, and Mark Stevens for riding the hills and suffering with me. Cycling continually reminds me that the greatest accomplishment comes from the unique satisfaction of feeling the most pain.

My final acknowledgments are to my parents, Laura and Jon Carlson; my siblings, Kirstin, Karin, Kali, and Ben; and especially my wife, Alison, and my son, Jackson. A substantial project like this book is only possible with dedicated time to complete the work. I am aware of how this project meant spending time away from those whom I love. I am grateful for the endless love and support.

Matt Englar-Carlson
Huntington Beach, California

My friend and coauthor, Mark, has described in his acknowledgment our developing connection from years ago. My friendship for Mark matches the level of friendship he has described, and I am most thankful for the alliance we have had for almost 2 decades; I have appreciated the ongoing kindness and thoughtfulness he has provided. Beyond friendship, though, Mark has been the most influential contributor to the development and refinement of work with boys, adolescent males, and men that I know of, and in the process he has influenced me greatly in my thinking, writing, and work with boys and men. I acknowledge him for his wonderful contributions to the field, and I am grateful for his being a friend and colleague.

Matt Englar-Carlson has also been so very influential in my developing beliefs and abilities in working with men. Matt has brought a youthfulness and vigor to projects we three have engaged in to help advance knowledge and understanding of the development of boys and men; his energy and enthusiasm have been addictive, and he has shared freely of ideas and wisdom. Matt and Mark contributed to an ideal team for a project such as ours, for all our interactions are positive, affirming, creative, and energizing.

My friend and colleague, Dave Jolliff, has been with me on the journey of working with men and men's issues for more than 3 decades. His quiet wisdom, his dependable support, and his clinical acumen are powerful. His humor and creativity have led us to some of the most interesting and engaging work one could ever ask for. We've done workshops and training in many cities, states, and countries, and each time the work is a learning and growing experience. One can't ask for more than that out of a friend and colleague.

I have been graced with the opportunity of working with some of the most outstanding leaders in the field of men and masculinity. From the early days of attempting to develop a division of interest within the American Psychological Association, to today, the members and leaders of Division 51 have been a wonderful group for inspiration, creativity, growth, and wisdom. Appreciation is expressed to both the senior and/or long-term members, and the younger, newer members of the association, for the ongoing cumulative development of knowledge and awareness.

To the students and faculty at Indiana State University who contributed to the early work on men's issues, and then to the students and faculty at the University of Georgia, who have provided ongoing support and cooperation for various projects developed to work with boys and adolescent males, I thank you. Without the ongoing support and enthusiastic encouragement (and more than the occasional teasing as well), the projects could not have flourished.

Doing quality work costs money. Appreciation is given to the U.S. Department of Education Institute for At-Risk Youth for the 7 years they funded our research, and to the Centers for Disease Control and Prevention National Center for Injury Prevention for funding our Multi-Site Violence Prevention Program GREAT Schools and Families; without the financial resources provided, the work would never have happened.

Finally, though I am officially retired, the hours of labor are more extensive than they were preretirement, and I give my thanks to my family for being so understanding of the fact that to me the work isn't work, but an opportunity to be fully engaged and to have some hope of actually providing a positive impact on the lives of the young people of our community and country. Thanks for your support and understanding. Particularly, appreciation is expressed to Gayle for her high rate of tolerance and her ongoing support and understanding. I guess that is what 40+ years of living with this guy has led to, and I am most fortunate for having you as the focus of my life.

Andy Horne
Athens, Georgia

About the Editors

Mark S. Kiselica, Ph.D., HSPP, NCC, LPC, is a professor of counselor education at the College of New Jersey. He is the author, coauthor, or coeditor of over 100 professional publications, most of which are focused on the subjects of counseling boys and men, especially teenage fathers, and on the process of confronting racism. He is a fellow and former president of Division 51 of the American Psychological Association (APA), the Society for the Psychological Study of Men and Masculinity; a former consulting scholar for the Country Boys Community Engagement Outreach Campaign; and a member of the APA Working Group to Develop Guidelines for Psychological Practice With Boys and Men. He is also a member of the National Advisory Board for the Quality Improvement Center on Non-Residential Father Involvement in Child Welfare. Dr. Kiselica is the editor of the Routledge Series on Counseling and Psychotherapy with Boys and Men. He resides in Newtown, Pennsylvania, with his wife, Sandi, and their children, Andrew, Christian, and Sasha.

Matt Englar-Carlson, Ph.D., is an associate professor of counseling at California State University, Fullerton. He holds graduate degrees in health psychology education and counselor education, and received his Ph.D. in counseling psychology from the Pennsylvania State University. A former elementary school counselor, his main areas of scholarly interest focus on men and masculinity. In reference to boys and male adolescents, he is interested in training counselors to understand how masculinity influences well-being, interpersonal relationships, and the process of counseling. An additional theme in his scholarly work is exploration of the positive psychology of men and the integration of masculinity with social justice work. Dr. Englar-Carlson resides in Huntington Beach, California, with his wife, Alison, and son, Jackson.

Arthur (Andy) M. Horne, Ph.D., is Distinguished Research Professor Emeritus of Counseling Psychology and director of the Educational

Policy and Evaluation Center at the University of Georgia. He is a fellow of APA Division 51, the Society for the Psychological Study of Men and Masculinity; fellow and past president of the Division of Group Psychology and Psychotherapy; and a fellow of the Division of Family Psychology and the Society of Counseling Psychology; as well as past president and fellow of the Association for Specialists in Group Work. He has coauthored and coedited more than a dozen books and more than 100 papers and articles, primarily focusing on group counseling and therapy; violence and aggression reduction in children, schools, and families; and promoting healthy male development. Andy lives in Athens, Georgia, with his wife, Gayle, and they celebrate their children and grandchildren who live in other parts of the country.

Contributors

Christopher D. Bell, M.S., is a doctoral candidate in the Counseling Psychology Program at the University of Georgia. He has clinical experience working with child and adolescent males who have been identified as having moderate to severe behavioral disorders, and research and consultation experience in developing and implementing school- and family-based bullying and aggression reduction programs.

Joseph M. Cervantes, Ph.D., ABPP, is a diplomate in clinical and family psychology, American Board of Professional Psychology, and professor, Department of Counseling, California State University, Fullerton. His research interests include counseling boys and their families, children's spirituality, and psychological issues related to immigration with Latina/o children and families.

Mark Fisher, M.A., NCC, is a counselor at New Horizon Treatment Services of Trenton, New Jersey. He specializes in providing crisis counseling and helping people who have relationship difficulties. He also has an interest in strengths-based counseling with individuals struggling with sexual identity and sexual orientation issues.

Mark C. Fleming, Ph.D., CRC, LPCMH, holds a joint appointment as a licensed psychologist at the Center for Counseling and Student Development and as an assistant professor in the Department of Individual and Family Studies at the University of Delaware. His areas of clinical expertise involve multicultural issues and the developmental and psychological issues of adolescent boys and men. He maintains a private clinical and consultation practice, where he provides therapy and training with an emphasis on treating developmental traumas in men and boys.

Megan Foley Nicpon, Ph.D., is the supervisor of psychological services for the Assessment and Counseling Clinic at the Belin-Blank Center for Gifted Education and Talent Development and an adjunct assistant professor in the Counseling Psychology Program at the University of Iowa. Dr. Foley Nicpon specializes in providing assessment and counseling services for children and adolescents, and she is the project manager for the Javits-funded Iowa Twice-Exceptional Project (2005–2008), which focuses on gifted students with disabilities. Her research and clinical interests include the psychosocial and emotional needs of gifted and talented students, twice-exceptionality, pediatric psychology, and the assessment of attention deficit hyperactivity disorder.

Douglas C. Haldeman, Ph.D., is a counseling psychologist in Seattle, Washington. He maintains a full-time psychotherapy practice, with a special focus on the gay, lesbian, bisexual, and transgender community. He also specializes in relationship counseling with heterosexual, gay, and lesbian couples. Dr. Haldeman is a member of the Board of Directors of the American Psychological Association, and he comments frequently in the media on a variety of issues related to professional psychology and social policy. He has written numerous articles and chapters on the ethical and competent treatment of lesbian, gay, and bisexual clients in psychotherapy, and is a nationally recognized expert on men's issues.

George M. Kapalka, Ph.D., ABPP, is board certified in several areas of clinical practice, including clinical psychology, psychopharmacology, and learning disabilities. He is an associate professor of psychological counseling at Monmouth University. He conducts research in the areas of management and education of children with attention and behavioral disorders, childhood trauma, and pediatric psychopharmacology. He is the author of over 100 professional publications and presentations, and he is the editor of the *New Jersey Journal of Professional Counseling*. Dr. Kapalka maintains a part-time private practice and heads a state-approved independent Child Study Team, and he is a member of the medical staff at Meridian Health Systems' Brick Hospital.

William Ming Liu, Ph.D., is the program coordinator for the Counseling Psychology Program at the University of Iowa. His research interests are in men and masculinity, social class and classism, and multicultural competencies. He is an associate editor for the *Psychology of Men and Masculinity*, and he is on the editorial boards of *The Counseling Psychologist* and *Cultural Diversity and Ethnic Minority Psychology*.

Maryann Mulé is a graduate student in the Counselor Education Program at the College of New Jersey. Ms. Mule's research is centered on lesbian, gay, bisexual, and transgender issues, with a particular focus on the process of helping young gay boys.

Jerry Novack, M.A., NCC, CPT, is a master's-level Clinician, a certified personal trainer and sports fitness specialist. He has published articles and book chapters concerning integrated approaches to wellness, and lectured on integrated wellness, counseling the terminally ill client, and multidisciplinary helping approaches. He has a particular interest in using integrated wellness approaches with boys and men.

Le'Roy E. Reese, Ph.D., is an associate professor at the Morehouse School of Medicine in the Department of Community Health and Preventative Medicine, where he conducts community-based health research focused on the development of healthy lifestyles and the reduction of risk behavior among youth and their families in underresourced communities. Prior to coming to Morehouse, Dr. Reese was a senior scientist at the Centers for Disease Control and Prevention's National Center for Injury Prevention and Control, where he conducted violence prevention research.

John M. Robertson, Ph.D., is a licensed psychologist who conducts a full-time private practice for adolescent boys and men in Lawrence, Kansas. He also is senior staff psychologist and coordinator of research, emeritus, at University Counseling Services, Kansas State University. He is a past president of the Society for the Psychological Study of Men and Masculinity, Division 51 of the American Psychological Association; and has presented workshops and published research on various aspects of providing psychotherapy for males.

David S. Shepard, Ph.D., is an associate professor of counseling at California State University, Fullerton. He is the author or coauthor of numerous articles and book chapters on male development and on counseling men, as well as the coauthor of an introductory textbook on the field of counseling. He is a member of Division 51 of the American Psychological Association, the Society for the Psychological Study of Men and Masculinity. Dr. Shepard has been a psychotherapist in private practice in West Los Angeles for over 2 decades, where he specializes in individual counseling with men and couples counseling.

Samuel J. Shepard is a doctoral student in counseling psychology at the University of Iowa. He currently works at the Belin-Blank International Center for Gifted Education and Talent Development, where he conducts research, assessment, and counseling with gifted children and adolescents. He is also a member of a research team that focuses on the psychological study of men and masculinity.

John Harvey Wingfield, Ph.D., is a postdoctoral fellow at the Prevention Research Center at the Morehouse School of Medicine. His main area of interest is self-regulation in health behavior, with a particular concern for the role of culture in health behavior maintenance. He is a member of the American Psychological Association, the American Public Health Association, the Society for Prevention Research, and Psychologists for Social Responsibility.

Mark S. Woodford, Ph.D., LPC, NCC, MAC, is an associate professor and chairperson of the Department of Counselor Education at the College of New Jersey. His research interests are in the fields of substance abuse and family counseling, and his work as a scholar reflects a focus on systemic prevention and early intervention for addressing substance abuse among adolescents and young adults. His current scholarship is focused on the interplay of gender issues and substance abuse and addiction.

Part 1

Understanding and Establishing Rapport With Boys

1

The Psychological Development of Boys

JOHN M. ROBERTSON AND DAVID S. SHEPARD

"How can you stand to work with boys? They're angry. They don't talk. They're aggressive. And they refuse to deal with their emotions." Most counselors who work with boys and male adolescents have heard some version of that question many times. How indeed? The standard answer from one of the present authors (JMR) is straightforward: "Because a boy's choices can determine the direction of his entire life—choices about risks, relationships, roles, occupations, and values. If choices that reduce risk and enhance life can be encouraged, well, why *not* work with boys?"

This chapter provides an introductory overview of the development of boys from birth through adolescence. We begin with the childhood struggle to disconnect from the primary caregiver, become a separate individual, and face the loss of connection with the caregiver. We summarize the relative contributions of neurobiological development and cultural socialization that influence gender role behavior. We then examine adolescent development by reviewing the wide range of demands young boys face during this period of their lives: They must cope with substantial changes in their bodies, they must learn how to think and reason, they must respond to the demands of masculine role expectations, and they must make decisions about the wide variety of behavioral risks they face. And finally, we offer some brief overarching guidelines about ways in which counselors can assist young men as they move through these changes.

We have attempted to (a) ground this chapter in current research on male development, and (b) provide a comprehensive overview, incorporating object relations, neurobiological, and gender role socialization

3

perspectives. Nevertheless, we must acknowledge the particular influence of scholarship conducted by researchers connected with the New Psychology of Men movement in men's studies; we count ourselves among the scholars and clinicians aligned with the goals of the New Psychology of Men—that is, a gender-aware examination of male psychology that identifies those ways in which developmental and social forces construct the various options boys and men have when defining or expressing their own masculinity. The New Psychology of Men has become a "large tent" of scholarly writings, some of which are rigorously designed empirical research studies, and some of which are speculative models informed by theoretical precedents and clinical observations; the first section below reflects the latter.

THE SEPARATION–INDIVIDUATION TRAUMA OF EARLY CHILDHOOD

Many New Psychology of Men theorists have begun their examination of boyhood development by drawing on psychoanalytic or object relations models of childhood that emphasize the development of the self. Specifically, William Pollack (1995, 1998a) has proposed that the separation–individuation experience involves psychological trauma for boys that is both normative in male development and consequential for adult men's capacities for intimacy and vulnerability to depression. The structure of Pollack's model is founded on Margaret Mahler's ideas regarding the separation–individuation process with a specific focus on the rapprochement phase between the ages of 16 and 24 months. The developmental journey Mahler and her colleagues (Mahler, Pine, & Bergman, 1975) described is, of course, a well-known one, repeated in the human development textbooks that many therapists and counselors read in graduate school (e.g., Broderick & Blewitt, 2006; Newman & Newman, 2006).

This journey begins with an infant fused in a symbiotic relationship with the primary caregiver (typically, the mother), followed by the infant's growing awareness of the boundaries between self and other. In the rapprochement phase, the child begins to tentatively explore the surrounding world. These short forays away from the mother depend on the child's confident knowledge that the mother is close by to protect him or her from harm. This secure bond is crucial to the child's capacity to explore as an individual. During the rapprochement stage, the child will often return in clinging fear to the arms of the awaiting mother, relaxing in the comfort of dependency while summoning up the courage to go out for another test of survival. This process of oscillation continues until the child has developed a requisite sense of individuation, has internalized the mother as a secure object, and experiences the self as an individual capable of braving the world alone (in the limited means available to a toddler, of course).

For example, Dylan was 3 years old, and his mother loved to invite various community groups into their home for socials and planning meetings. Dylan was highly curious about all these adult visitors, but also in frequent need of contact with his mother. So he would hang around the edges of the conversations, watching people and playing with his own toys in a corner. Every once in a while, however, he would jump up and boldly cross in front of the other adults to make contact with his mother. He would hold onto her wrist or leg for a few moments, and then rush back to his toys. Sometimes he would need to touch her only for a moment. If he felt especially in need of contact, he would jump into her lap for a few moments before wanting to "get down" and return to his playthings.

Mahler's developmental arc (Mahler, Pine, & Bergman, 1975) has the disadvantage, however, of not differentiating between male and female development, and the work of explaining these processes has been left to others. In writings highly relevant to much of the thinking on male development, Chodorow (1978) theorized that boys are pressured into breaking free of the dependency bond with the mother so that they begin to develop their male identities in accordance with the traditional male role norms of self-reliance and autonomy. Father and mother both contribute to this separation from mother. In their desire to be good parents, they encourage their sons to disconnect from the dependency relation with the primary caregiver. Both parents are, after all, influenced by culturally sanctioned definitions of masculinity, and those constructs include the message that dependency is inconsistent with being a man.

To illustrate the importance of this dynamic, consider the presenting issue brought by Susan and Tom to their counselor. Their 3-year-old son, Barry, was waking up several nights a week, saying, "I'm scared. Big noise." Susan and Tom argued intensely in the middle of the night about what to do. Neither of them ever heard a noise. Susan wanted to get up and comfort Barry back to sleep, whereas Tom argued that the boy should conquer his fears on his own, saying, "I don't want Barry to be called a scaredy cat by other boys." Because Tom generally had the upper hand in power struggles with Susan, the frightened boy was falling back asleep on his own, night after night. Over the course of about a month, the crying had worsened until the episodes lasted about 30 minutes, and occurred two or three times a night. During the day, the little guy had become more demanding of physical reassurance, and was protesting being left alone in a room. At one point, the counselor asked if the couple remembered any frightening events that may have occurred prior to the change in behavior. They recalled a sudden storm several months earlier during which a microburst had hit their home, breaking several windows. This led to a discussion that normalized the boy's reactions, and also emphasized ways in which they both might comfort him. One can only speculate about the long-term emotional consequences for boys like Barry when they are forced to outgrow these fears alone.

According to Chodorow (1978), this separation process may be started prematurely for many male children, depriving them of an attachment to the primary caregiver who can provide soothing, security, and empathic understanding throughout childhood. Female children, on the other hand, are permitted to experience this closeness longer and with more support because of its consistency with female role norms.

Pollack's thesis (1995, 1998a) is that this early separation process for males not only is unnecessary for a healthy development of the self, but also becomes a traumatic experience of abandonment for which little boys are ill prepared. Wrote Pollack,

> We never stop to wonder what it must feel like for a young boy to lose his connection to mother. Such an enforced separation from the most cherished, admired, and loved person in his life must come as a terrible loss—all the more so in a family structure in which girls of the same age are encouraged to remain bonded and where fathers are often unable or unwilling to assuage their son's fall from the maternal safety net with an equally nurturant form of caregiving. Men's traumatic experience of abandonment in boyhood, though not consciously remembered, forever casts a shadow on their relationships. It is a sadness without a name, a yearning without clear object. (1998a, pp. 155–156)

According to Pollack (1995), the pressure on parents or caregivers to "toughen up" their sons by limiting their dependency on the female caregiver has significant implications for male development and adult emotional health. Boys learn to fear intimate connection, lest the pain of the repressed abandonment trauma is reactivated.

> Having experienced a sense of hurt in the real connection to their mothers … many boys, and later men, are left at risk for empathic disruptions in their affiliative connections, doomed to search endlessly … and yet fend women off because of their fear of retraumatization. (Pollack, 1995, p. 41)

Although Pollack (1995) claimed that this type of experience is normative for boys, research on attachment in children suggests that the majority of boys probably do not experience the type of separation trauma that Pollack has described because most boys have secure attachment styles (Kiselica & O'Brien, 2001). Nevertheless, we concur with Pollack that this form of trauma does occur in at least some boys, and when it does, it can have a detrimental impact on their development.

There may be another negative consequence for boys arising out of the dynamic Pollack has described. Blazina and Watkins (2000) have suggested that the abandonment experience leads to the development of internal conflicts between yearnings for closeness and repressed feelings of abandonment, as well as conflicts between dependency needs and the male role norm of self-reliance. The latter conflict may be reinforced by parents who respond to their sons' expression of dependency needs with disapproval, and in some case harsher punishments. For example, with the family described in the previous vignette, Tom would frequently respond to 3-year-old Barry's anguished pleas of "Where's Mommy?" with a "She's busy now. Go play by yourself. Be a big boy." Tom's well-meaning response, designed to both protect his tired wife and teach Barry about self-reliance, nevertheless may be a wounding experience for his son.

One of the present authors (JMR) witnessed a poignant example of this dynamic at a soccer field for boys who were 5 and 6 years old. Given the "beehive" nature of soccer at this age, most of the boys were in a pack, following the ball around wherever it went. Slower boys were not getting a chance to kick the ball. At one point, a young boy was about to kick the ball, then quickly stepped aside and said to a boy on the other team, "You kick it, David. It's your turn!" His father was outraged. "What are you doing?" he screamed from the bleachers. "You're acting like a girl. You've got to be aggressive." The boy immediately ran crying from the field toward his father. But his father turned him back toward the field, saying, "Get back out there. You've got to fight for the ball." In extreme cases like this one, the strict enforcement of traditional masculinity roles leads to a sense of abandonment, and tends to extinguish behavior that reaches toward emotional connection with a caregiver.

Blazina and Watkins (2000) suggested that these kinds of experiences are psychic wounds, as boys grapple with their needs for dependency and closeness versus their fears of expressing these vital needs. These conflicts can persist internally throughout adulthood; the male psyche may thus be under chronic stress, with the consequence of needing continual emotional support (Blazina & Watkins, 2000). The narcissistic striving for externally shoring up the self experienced by many men (e.g., some men's need for constant attention) thus begins with this early childhood separation from the primary caregiver.

THE LOSS OF CONNECTION

Jeremy was anxious about his first day at preschool. His mother had told him about all the fun things he would do. Nevertheless, at the moment she left him behind in the classroom, Jeremy started crying. Another boy, clearly much less anxious, began chanting, "Crybaby, crybaby, you are a crybaby." Jeremy's painful separation from his mother is what Bergman (1995) described as a "turning away from connection" (p. 74). Building on the self-in-relation theories of female development proposed by Jordan and colleagues at the Stone Center in Wellesley, Massachusetts (Jordan, Kaplan, Miller, Stiver, & Surrey, 1991), Bergman noted that both boys and girls have a primary desire for connection. Healthy child development occurs within the context of a self-in-relation, that is, a self that experiences a state of connectedness to the primary caregiver characterized by consistent nurturance, empathic attunement, and permission for dependency. The separation from the primary caregiver at around age 3 begins a process for boys in which their male identity becomes focused on difference from others rather than relation to others. As boys develop, they learn to compare themselves to other boys, deriving their confidence from achievement, success over others, and feelings of specialness. As self-esteem becomes dependent on success in competition with other boys, sustaining feelings of well-being and self-confidence becomes increasingly difficult. Moreover, all of these goals conflict with mutual relating, and although boys yearn for this connectedness, they gradually learn to avoid it and forgo opportunities to practice how to be in relationships. Noted Bergman, "With a growing sense of competence in the world, a boy experiences a parallel sense of incompetence in the process of relationship" (p. 75).

This process can be observed in most cities during Pee Wee Football practices and games. Beginning in the first grade, boys quickly learn to compare themselves with each other, as they watch their coaches decide which boys are the strongest or fastest. Officially designed to teach such values as sportsmanship, teamwork, and self-respect, the unspoken reality is that boys also learn to rate themselves against the skills of other boys. Shepard (2005) proposed that the need to feel special requires boys to self-monitor their position vis-à-vis other boys; are they being responded to with admiration or disapproval? These persistent self-in-comparison cognitions leave boys in a precarious state of emotional vulnerability, as the possibility of feeling incompetent or inferior becomes as ever present as the potential to feel special.

This section reviewed recent thinking about the painful and enduring consequences of boys' premature breaking away from a state of connectedness with their primary caregivers. Some caveats are in order: One is a reminder that these ideas are largely theoretical. As clinicians, it makes intuitive sense to us that boys pay a price for learning to disavow their normal human strivings. However, Pollack's and other authors' contention that men are vulnerable to psychological distress because of a pivotal, normative separation–individuation sequence in early childhood development is not supported by any data we have seen, regardless of its explanatory power. The second caveat is that these ideas regarding early childhood male development do not take into account cultural differences in child-raising practices. For example, what are the psychological ramifications for boys raised in cultures that emphasize collectivism more than the individualism of Eurocentric societies?

Caveats aside, object relations approaches to conceptualizing early childhood development have critical implications for counseling men, in that they suggest the value of helping men and boys connect difficulties with grieving a present-day loss to an unconscious fear of experiencing a long-buried grief from their earliest years. By emphasizing how *young* boys are when they first learn to repress basic human yearnings and needs, these models normalize the intense difficulty many boys and men have in crying or in displaying other emotional responses to loss.

THE CONTRIBUTIONS OF NEUROBIOLOGY

Any discussion of the research literature on male development must address an important question: Have researchers in this field overemphasized the role of parenting influences and socialization experiences, while underemphasizing the influence of genetics and any inherent gender role proclivities with which both sexes are born? The nature versus nurture debate regarding sex role development has been ongoing at least from the Freudian era, when Sigmund Freud proposed a mixed model of psychological development that included both innate biological tendencies and environmental factors. The current argument is sometimes framed as the "essentialist" perspective (fixed, inherent sex role tendencies) versus a social constructionist view in which masculine or feminine gender behaviors are defined by the dominant discourses within a particular culture (Smiler, 2004).

According to Daniel Siegel (1999), a pioneer in the field of interpersonal neurobiology, this debate may have been largely resolved. He summarized research showing that nature influences nurture; that is to say, genetic instructions for development are present at birth, but these biological and psychological processes must be activated during the early months of life (Siegel, 1999). Thus, the relationship between the infant and the primary caregiver is critically important in human development. From this relationship, the infant learns lifelong lessons about the self, relationships, and the world. Subsequent interactions with both genders are interpreted through the lens of this primary relationship (Schore, 1994, 2003).

Research now shows that this early learning is indelible. It is neurological and measurable. The developing person's capacities are affected in many areas—the ability to regulate intense emotion, the likelihood of making secure relationships with others, and the development of a unique personality. The earliest and primary relationship with a caregiver can facilitate healthy developmental processes, or inhibit them (samples of work in this area include Eisenberg, 1995; Helmeke, Ovtscharoff, Poeggel, & Braun, 2001; Schore, 1994; Trevarthen, 1993).

This general understanding of development is now shared by researchers in several academic disciplines, including neurobiology, developmental psychology, developmental neurochemistry, and infant psychiatry. The explosion of research in these areas has resulted in literally thousands of studies, many of them using brain-imaging techniques such as functional magnetic resonance imaging (fMRI) and positron emission topography (PET). Moreover, findings from these efforts point to the conclusion that the impact of a primary caregiver on an infant includes not only a person's behaviors but internal physiological events as well. Brain researchers are now examining ways in which the role of the primary caregiver is crucial not only in sustaining life, but also in beginning socialization processes. This latter function begins during the last half of the second year, and continues throughout childhood. Events that occur during this period are "indelibly imprinted into the structures that are maturing in the first years of life" (Schore, 1994, p. 3).

Schore (1994) substantiated this assertion in a four-part summary of abundant evidence from the neurosciences. First, "The growth of the brain occurs in critical periods and is influenced by the social environment" (Schore, 1994, p. 10). He cited work reporting that the human brain grows from 400 grams at birth to about 1,000 grams in just the first 12 months of life, and continues its rapid growth until 18 to 24 months of age. During this period, the most rapidly growing portions of the brain are the very structures most susceptible to social influences. Second, "[T]he infant brain develops in stages and becomes hierarchically organized" (p. 13). For example, one stage of brain development that begins at the end of the first year and ends in the middle of the second year of life involves the maturing of a cortical structure that is essential to basic social functioning. It is located at the top of the limbic system. Third, "[G]enetic systems that program brain development are activated and influenced by the postnatal environment" (p. 16). To illustrate, Schore cited research showing that the variety of RNA sequences and the quantity of protein in the rapidly expanding brain of the infant are affected directly by environmental events such as social isolation. Fourth, "[T]he social environment changes over the stages of infancy and induces the reorganization of brain structures" (p. 18).

Parents have noted for millennia that infant functioning is dominated by intense and demanding emotions. Developmental affective neuroscientists have discovered the neurological explanation for these observations by identifying the dominant role of the right hemisphere in emotional development (Chiron et al., 1997). Right hemisphere dominance continues from about the 25th week of gestation until the left hemisphere begins a growth spurt some time during the second postnatal year (Trevarthen, 1996). This body of neurobiological research suggests that boys and girls begin life with similar capacities for emotional experiences. Evidence for this assertion lies in the fact that emotional regulation operations (i.e., monitoring the intensity, frequency, and duration of an emotion) are carried out in the right orbit frontal cortex of the developing brain in both sexes (Cavada & Schultz, 2000; Elliott, Dolan, & Frith, 2000; Hariri, Bookheimer, & Mazziotta, 2000; Matsuzawa et al., 2001; Schore, 2000, 2001). It is important to note that this brain structure does not mature until the middle of the second year of life, leaving significant time for the early impact of the social world on the developing infant brain (Schore, 2003; Trevarthen).

Put another way, boys (and girls) are emotionally driven beings during the first 2 years of life. As boys develop, the right hemisphere continues, on an unconscious level, to store emotional information, to regulate emotional interactions and process emotional information, to control empathic abilities, and to influence the capacity for self-reflection (Schore, 2003). The emotional influence of the right hemisphere does not disappear as the abilities of the left hemisphere "take over" the conscious management of life; nevertheless, as we have discussed previously in this chapter, boys often restrict vulnerable emotions, may speak a less emotional vocabulary than do girls, and tend to value aggression and competitiveness as hallmarks of masculinity.

Thus, socialization processes become important in understanding how most boys' infant neurological blueprints become modified over time to manifest in these more masculine-typical behaviors. Male infants learn early that some behaviors are rewarded, and others are scorned. Given that most early interactions with primary caregivers are a function of the right hemisphere, it would appear that young boys are required to "unlearn" the importance of right brain functions after those forms of interaction have been dominant for the first 2 years of life. Later in their development, the influence of socialization experiences with peers, parents, teachers, and media images becomes prominent. These forces deemphasize right brain skills such as empathizing, reflecting on one's inner life, using subtle socioemotional cues in friendships, and utilizing nonverbal imagery to enhance one's understanding of various opinions, judgments, and beliefs. Because these right brain skills are dominant and functional during the first 2 years of life, it seems unreasonable to argue that they simply lose their relevance or disappear on their own, or to assert that boys automatically experience a reduced ability to use them skillfully. It seems more likely that boys learn to minimize their use of right hemisphere knowledge over time as they respond to countless and readily identifiable directives to avoid intuition, emotional expression, or the artful use of socioemotional information (Rutter & Rutter, 1993; Siegel, 1999).

In sum, findings from neurological science support the perspective that the development of identity, affect regulation, and interpersonal skills begins very early and occurs in the right hemisphere; that these implicit and affective processes dominate human development during the first 2 years of life; and that brain structures corresponding to these abilities are activated and affected over time by the software of human interaction and socialization. Put another way, much of what a culture regards as "gender-appropriate behavior" is learned, beginning with the interactions between infant and caregiver, and continuing through childhood. The evidence from neuroscience is that learning affects brain structures, beginning with the experiences between the infant and the primary caregiver, and, over time, the additional experiences that teach "proper" gender role behavior. Humans certainly are born with genetic hardware that defines maleness and femaleness (e.g., reproductive systems and some hormonal functioning), but the power of socialization processes in defining culturally appropriate cognition, affect, and behavior is profound. In the next section, we will expand on how gender role socialization affects boys' psychological development.

ADOLESCENCE

Jason slumped into the chair in front of me (JMR). He clearly did not want to be talking to a psychologist. He leaned forward so that his long hair completely covered his face. He was dressed in black with lots of metal hanging from his clothing. He started the conversation abruptly.

"Let me tell you something, dude. I hate psychos."

I couldn't help myself. I laughed. Hard. "You know what?" I responded. "I think I'm going to like you."

Jason continued to lean forward, but lifted one hand and parted his hair so that he could see me with one eye. "Don't game me, man. I don't like no gamers."

"I don't either," I responded. "I like talking to people who say what they think."

It took three or four sessions for Jason to believe me, but once he did, he began to talk. Like many troubled adolescents, Jason desperately wanted to tell his stories and have them taken seriously. Unfortunately, some adults see the tattoos, the piercings, or the brightly colored hair and find themselves hesitant to initiate a conversation. Disdain comes more easily than empathy. But we can have better empathy for boys like Jason if we have an understanding of adolescence and the challenges a boy faces during this developmental period.

Defining Adolescence

Just what is this stage of life we call *adolescence*? It certainly is not a precisely defined stage of life. When an age range is used to define adolescence, professional organizations vary in their estimates. The Centers for Disease Control, for example, use ages 10–24 (Eaton et al., 2006), and an American Psychological Association document sets ages 10–18 as parameters (Gentry & Campbell, 2002). A more useful approach is to think of adolescence as a set of changes that occur over a short period of time.

When Octavio first visited his psychologist, he was 13 years old and no more than 5 feet 6 inches tall. Although slightly built, he was very proud of his ball-handling skills on a basketball court. His hair was cut short, and his face looked too young for the regular use of a razor. Although he was brought to the office by his mother to address "his depression," he took therapy seriously and worked hard to address his own emotions following the unexpected death of his father. An earnest and talkative young man, Octavio often leaned forward into the conversation, looking directly into his therapist's eyes. After six sessions, he reported that he was feeling much better, and asked to stop therapy. He agreed to return if the need arose.

Nearly 2 years later, a high school counselor sent Octavio back to see his therapist. But the young man was now nearly impossible to recognize. He was still thin, but about 4 inches taller, and layered in several T-shirts under an Oakland Raiders sweatshirt that would fit comfortably on a 300-pound man. His baggy pants sagged from his waist, revealing several inches of plaid boxers. His hair was long and stringy under a black and silver ball cap turned sideways. Especially prominent was a large earring shaped like a teardrop. He shuffled into the office with headphones around his neck, the pulsing hiss of the music audible from across the room. His eyes were half-closed. What had happened?

A starting point for understanding some of the stressors Octavio had been facing is Steinberg's (1996) set of adolescent transitions. In effect, these developmental changes can function as a practical definition of adolescence itself:

- Biologically, it begins when puberty arrives, and ends when a person feels ready for the adult responsibilities of sexual reproduction.
- Emotionally, it begins when a child deliberately begins to detach from his or her parents, and ends with an identity separate from one's parents'.
- Cognitively, it begins as more abstract and advanced reasoning skills emerge, and ends when a person can consider various hypotheses, look at several possibilities, see ideas from the perspectives of other persons and cultures, and examine evidence in drawing reasonable conclusions.
- Interpersonally, the shift is from a preadolescent focus on family interactions through the adolescent primacy of peer relationships to a postadolescent attachment with another adult in a serious romantic commitment.
- Socially, it begins with an exploration of various forms of work and life goals, and ends with the arrival of adult responsibilities and privileges.
- Educationally, it typically begins with enrollment in junior high classes and continues until the educational process ends.
- Legally, it begins with the term *juvenile* and ends with the designation of *adult*.
- Culturally, it may mean moving through some socially sanctioned rite of passage, and being accepted as an adult.

Given the breadth of these changes, Octavio's behavior becomes more understandable. Even in the best of times, an adolescent like Octavio will feel anxious, confused, and unappealing as he tries to master these many developmental challenges. But imagine how complicated and intense these feelings and challenges must be when a boy suffers a significant loss, as Octavio did when his father died.

It is critically important to note that the eight developmental transitions mentioned earlier typically are expressed in ways that are consistent with a young man's cultural identity. More than a third of all North

American adolescents (37%) come from backgrounds other than European American (Gentry & Campbell, 2002), making room for a wide range of cultural expressions to mark an adolescent's passage into adulthood. Octavio's parents had emigrated from Mexico, presenting the therapist with an additional layer of information to consider in working with him. Research has shown that parental death in a Mexican family reduces the family investment in both education and health services for the children. About 20% of bereaved children will drop out of school at some point, in part, to care for the remaining members of the family (Gertler, Martinez, Levine, & Bertozzi, 2003). Knowledge of these factors would alert a counselor to some of the pressures Octavio was likely to face at home.

In terms of understanding male adolescents, several of the transitions noted by Steinberg (1996) merit more detailed attention: physical development; cognitive development, including the formation of a masculine identity; and the development of behavioral patterns in a world filled with risks.

Physical Development

Physical changes may be the most visible indications of adolescence for boys (cf. Hofmann & Greydanus, 1997; McAnarney & Kreipe, 1992; Newberger, 2000). The pituitary gland releases growth hormones, and boys can reach a peak growth rate of up to 4 inches a year. The hands, head, and feet get larger first, followed by the limbs and torso. Shoulders broaden. The larynx enlarges, and the voice deepens. The muscle:fat ratio reaches about 3:1 by late adolescence. Testes may begin to enlarge by 10 years of age, but some not until age 13. Pubic hair appears, and changes from fine and light to coarse and dark over the course of a year. The penis begins growing larger as early as age 10, but may not begin until 14. Facial and underarm hair appears about 2 years after the appearance of pubic hair, and increases in density over several years. The skin becomes rougher as the sweat glands enlarge. Oiliness develops, and acne can follow. Changes occur in the male breast, as circumference increases and the nipples become more prominent. Internal sexual organs enlarge and mature. The seminal vesicles develop, and the prostate and bulbourethral glands begin to generate seminal fluid. The first ejaculation of seminal fluid occurs between the ages of 12 and 14 for most boys, but they tend not to report their very first ejaculations because they feel "perplexed" by the event (Stein & Reiser, 1994).

Cognitive Development

It appears that many of the stereotypical behaviors of male adolescence are influenced by changes in cognitive processing. Gentry and Campbell (2002) cited the work of several researchers in confirming that young men do indeed argue just for the sake of arguing (Walker & Taylor, 1991), jump rather quickly to conclusions and think in more self-centered ways (Jaffe, 1998), tend to look for discrepancies and contradictions in the comments and behavior of adults (Bjorklund & Green, 1992), and express their thoughts in overly dramatic ways (Jaffe). It is worth nothing that although these behaviors can be highly annoying to parents and other adults, they have a positive and constructive purpose. Adolescent thinking does tend to morph into adult thinking. Young men are learning to examine ideas critically, understand new perspectives and philosophies, and develop their own views of issues. Yet, because these higher-level skills in analysis and decision making occur over a period of years for male adolescents, the experience can be annoying for adults and quite unnerving for adults and the adolescents themselves.

When Octavio returned to his therapist, his appearance was not the only thing that had changed. He also thought differently. Earlier, he had been willing to think with his therapist about various ways of understanding his father's death, and to express his profound grief at the loss. He was willing to look collaboratively at how life was going to be different for him, and how he might adjust. But on his return visit, he was less a seeker and more a debater. At times, he seemed ready to challenge every question and observation his therapist would make. He would offer his own opinions quickly and energetically, not for discussion, but to challenge. His therapist was now dealing with a young man whose thinking processes were still entirely normal, but very different from what they were 2 years earlier. To keep Octavio engaged, his male therapist had to change his approach and tactics.

Another facet of cognitive development deserves a brief comment. Julian was sent to his counselor because of being disruptive and distracting in class. After consulting with Julian's teacher, his counselor administered a series of cognitive assessments, and identified a learning disorder. Like many young men who become disruptive, Julian was coping with the frustration of not being able to learn as effectively as his friends. Compared to young women, young men appear to have higher reported rates of learning disabilities involving dyslexia, reading comprehension, and written language (for a review of some of this literature, see Fletcher, Lyon, Fuchs, & Barnes, 2007). A young man with a learning disability may find adolescence especially challenging, as he struggles to grasp fully the information he needs to be effective in his reading, writing, memorizing, speaking, and reasoning. Further, there is some evidence that young men with learning disabilities are more likely than their peers to face emotional distress, engage in violence, or consider suicide (Svetaz, Ireland, & Blum, 2000).

Gender Role Socialization Models

Gender role socialization models presume that boys develop male identities through learning processes, as they internalize cultural norms and values regarding what it means to be a man (Addis & Mahalik, 2003).

Parents, teachers, and peers are the primary sources of learning, and they shape boys' gender role identities by modeling, encouraging, and discouraging certain behaviors and attitudes (Bandura, 1977; Levant, 1996; Maccoby, 1990). As Levant (1996) pointed out, boys adopt these values and behaviors to the extent that parents and other authoritative figures themselves have been socialized to subscribe to specific definitions of masculinity (Levant, 1995). Socialization is thus both transgenerational and fluid, as definitions of masculinity evolve over time. In the 1950s, for example, the notion of a "sensitive male" wasn't a widely discussed model for a young man to consider. Now it is. Moreover, much of the current thinking in gender role socialization processes emphasizes the degree to which male gender role norms are social constructions, neither fixed ideologies nor, as discussed later in this chapter, innate tendencies born out of human evolutionary requirements for the preservation of the species.

Some authors have summarized these constructions as rules, or as a Boy Code (David & Brannon, 1976; Pollack, 1998b). Although there is cultural variability in the understanding, acceptance, and enforcement of these rules, four dictums summarize much of what boys in the dominant North American culture are taught. Boys (a) should be stoic and not show weakness by sharing pain or displaying grief; (b) should demonstrate daring, bravado, and an attraction to violence; (c) should strive to achieve dominance and power over others; and (d) should not express tender feelings such as dependence, warmth, and empathy.

Another approach to understanding the socialized expectations of men is the concept of "scripts" (Mahalik, Good, & Englar-Carlson, 2003). To illustrate, there is the strong-and-silent script, the tough-guy script, the "give-'em hell" script, the playboy script, the homophobic script, the winner script, and the independent script. Some scripts are important for some males but not for others. Because these scripts, or role norms, differ across cultures and contexts, it has become common in the male gender role research arena to use the word *masculinities*, rather than *masculinity*, in exploring the various male ideologies with which men can identify (Tager & Good, 2005). This theory might be extended to include scripts for adolescent males: the jock script, the nerd script, the gangsta script, the stoner script, the preppy script, the country boy script, and so on.

The power of these scripts or codes to influence both boys and men is illustrated by an experience one of the present authors (JMR) had while hiking up a mountain with his son and another adult male friend. The terrain became unexpectedly treacherous at one point, with loose gravel covering a steep rock formation. My son slipped and fell, cracking a bone in his arm, though that wasn't known until much later. At the age of 8, he was in tears, saying over and over, "It hurts." Looking to the two grown-up men for comfort, the boy heard my friend say, "Don't cry. You're fine. You must be strong because it's a long way to the bottom of the mountain." My son then heard his father give him some conflicting advice: "Go ahead and cry. It's OK to cry, because it hurts. We'll get you to a doctor to fix your arm." It is no wonder that boys find the expectations of the Boy Code to be not only strong but also baffling and confusing.

Attempts to conform to the fourth rule of the Boy Code noted above (the prohibition against expressing vulnerable emotions) may have the most insidious and enduring impact on boys' development, because it inhibits gaining experience in the language of emotion, and reduces the opportunities to gratify any yearnings for closeness and intimacy that may develop. As many boys are dissuaded by peers, parents, and media messages from verbalizing vulnerable feelings (e.g., sadness, shame, fear, and vulnerability), they internalize prohibitions against displaying these feelings, lose opportunities to practice identifying and articulating tender emotions, and become unable to receive emotional support when needed. Arguably, this process may lead to impaired abilities to communicate tender feelings as an adult, thus limiting fully experienced intimate connections with partners. Although the neurological findings noted above indicate that boys and girls begin life with the potential to develop similar levels of emotional awareness and competency, boys learn rather early that expressing tender feelings is not valued, thus reducing the appeal of becoming fully emotionally expressive. Further, such expressions can spark ridicule and aggressive attacks. For many boys, the preferred solution is to learn how to keep tender feelings hidden, whether that means maintaining a consciously constructed façade or a more out-of-awareness instinctual suppressing of vulnerable emotions. Indeed, over time, it may be increasingly difficult for some boys to identify those situations (e.g., intimate conversations at home) in their lives where tender emotions can be safely expressed.

Levant's 1995 review of the literature on male socialization suggests that socialization processes inhibiting emotional language development may start well before boys experience the Boy Code of male behavior that is enforced in schools, playgrounds, and backyards. For example, when boys are toddlers, a time when fathers are often becoming more actively involved with them, fathers generally do not speak the same emotional language that they would to their daughters. Words that might convey sadness or fear are avoided, depriving sons not only of witnessing their primary male role models expressing difficult emotions but also of having the opportunity as little boys to practice this kind of language. As boys enter the school-age years, parents may enforce the Boy Code with obvious commands (e.g., "Big boys don't cry," and "Don't act like a girl."), as well as more subtle displays of negative reinforcement (e.g., a negative glance thrown a son's way when he starts to evince feelings; Levant, 1995).

It is also important to keep in mind that the suppression of vulnerable emotions like sadness, fear, and embarrassment can be especially problematic as a young man's hormones are generating emotions that are new, confusing, and quite intense. When these emotions are expressed ineffectively, the consequences can be extraordinarily harmful for the young man and the rest of society. Difficulty with expressing emotions has been empirically associated with anger, hostility, and aggression, as well as alcohol and cannabis use (Jakupcak, Tull, & Roemer, 2005; Monk & Ricciardelli, 2003). These consequences have become the focus of significant social and policy discussions (e.g., Garbarino, 2000; Horne & Kiselica, 1999). In addition, young men who differ from the predominant culture around them face particularly difficult emotions. Those who are gay, physically disabled, chronically ill, or members of ethnic minorities or unpopular religious groups find themselves facing an especially difficult emotional passage through adolescence.

When counseling male adolescents, one of the present authors (JMR) defines emotions for male adolescents in ways that emphasize their adaptive and functional roles. As emotions are defined more as tools and skills, productive discussions can follow, even in clinical settings. Emotional competency becomes more appealing when it is operationalized as a set of abilities for young men that increases their skills at interacting with peers, makes them more effective in dealing with problematic teachers and parents, provides them with a larger capacity to enjoy music and athletics, gives them more success in resolving conflicts, and connects them more closely with romantic partners. In this way, young men learn how to *think* more about their emotions, and can learn to say more than "I'm OK" when asked how they're feeling.

Enforcing the Rules of Masculinity

The messages imparted to boys in early life are hammered home by peers as boys transverse the elementary and high school years. The pejorative *sissy* may no longer be in much use in 21st-century schools, but it has been replaced by *fag* and *gay* as equally powerful messages regarding acceptable masculine behavior. Two qualitative studies on male adolescence illustrate the power of shaming language in enforcing the Boy Code. For example, Pascoe (2003) described the experiences of Kevin, a 15 year old at a California high school. Kevin is frustrated because he does not have a girlfriend but sees himself as someone girls would be attracted to. "I like to dance. I like to bring flowers, I'm just a romantic.... I imagine myself singing, like serenading her ... all the guys are like, 'Dude, you're gay!'" (Pascoe, 2003, p. 1435).

Homophobic language was also the currency of shame and role norm enforcement among boys interviewed by Plummer (2001) in an Australian school. The actual words are different in Australia, but the meanings are the same. Not being tough risked being called *faggot*. The worst word a boy could be called was *poofter*. Plummer reported that his interviewees did not believe these terms implied a boy had a homosexual orientation, but rather saw homophobic criticism as the primary enforcer of maintaining masculine codes of behavior. Violations included being academic and studious, timid, slow to mature physically, artistic, prone to crying when physically hurt, and not playing in team sports.

Two themes that emerged from these studies are especially worth noting because of their wider implications for how boys develop a masculine identity. First, shame plays a powerful role in making violations of male role norms emotionally painful. Kaufman (1985) described shame as a feeling of worthlessness and helplessness, "a piercing awareness of ourselves as fundamentally deficient in some vital way as a human being" (p. 8). Krugman (1995) has suggested that shaming may be a useful social mechanism in preparing boys for combat, and in pressuring boys and men to mask vulnerability and suppress fear and anxiety. However, few boys will need to face actual war situations, and the lessons in hiding vulnerable feelings instead lead to compromised capacities for connection and intimacy. Moreover, Krugman observed that as male norms push boys to act aggressively with each other, self-esteem and competitiveness become linked. In every competitive situation, some boys will inevitably lose, and the pain of shame and humiliation, along with swelling rage intermingled with welling tears, can be excruciating (Krugman, 1995). Boys learn to tough it out, rather than display their shame, fear, sadness, and even physical pain. One can watch any junior high school football or basketball game to see this in action. These boys embrace athletic competition and aggression, risking humiliation on a regular basis. Some boys may not be athletes, but still engage in competitive activities (e.g., informal sports). Others may opt out of these role norms, reducing the risk of shame but experiencing instead feelings of not "measuring up" as men. In either case, boys are learning to restrict their emotionality, in a process Levant (1995) called "the Ordeal of Emotional Socialization" (p. 236).

Second, these stories of boys' adolescent experiences, as well as the stories reported by Pollack (1998b) in his popular book, *Real Boys*, point out that despite the painful risks of violating male role norms, many boys do so anyway. In Pascoe's (2003) study, for example, Kevin was a football player who also got involved in high school theater. Oliver engaged in two sports, not just because of their competitive, traditionally masculine environments, but also because of the range of connections and emotions that two sports allowed him to permissibly experience. Jeff was an 18-year-old football player who rejected his "jock" identity and the pressure to develop a muscular body shape because he wanted to construct his own identity, not one dictated by high school male role norms (Pascoe, 2003).

In the examples above, Kevin was engaging in what Pascoe (2003) termed "Jock Insurance": Participating in a stereotypically masculine activity prevented him from being ridiculed for his more feminine-associated interests (p. 1428). Another good example of jock insurance can be seen in the film *American Pie* (Weitz, Zide, Perry, Moore, & Weitz, 1999), as the adolescent male character Oz (actor Chris Klein) who secretly likes to sing is able to get away with joining the high school choir because he is also a highly regarded school lacrosse player.

Behavioral Risks for Adolescent Males

The National Risk Behavior Survey in 2005 (Eaton et al., 2006) demonstrates the wide variety of risks faced by male adolescents. Beginning in 1991, this biannual survey has examined risk behaviors that contribute to social problems, disabilities, and deaths of adolescents in the United States. The four leading causes of death among American young people are vehicle accidents (30%), unintentional injuries (14%), homicide (15%), and suicide (11%; Eaton et al.). It would seem apparent that the death rate from these causes is higher because of behavioral choices made by young men who adhere to traditional masculine socialization expectations that reinforce these behaviors.

The worktof Mahalik and colleagues (2002) provides a larger context for understanding the behavioral risks that adolescent males take. Mahalik has developed the Conformity to Masculine Norms Inventory (Mahalik et al., 2002), which consists of an empirically developed set of 11 categories of traditional masculine norms for men. These expectations are also in the background for adolescent males as they make choices about their behavior. Themes from this inventory include the importance of winning, risk taking, dominance over others, violence, "playboy" attitudes, self-reliance, having power over women, physical toughness, and the pursuit of status.

It is useful to keep these adult male norms in mind while reviewing the survey findings that follow. The 2005 National Youth Risk Behavior Survey (Eaton et al., 2006) makes it abundantly clear that male adolescents who engage in behavior consistent with these traditional gender role demands increase their chances of dying early from accidents, unintentional injuries, homicide, and suicide.

The following percentages report only on the behavior of *male* adolescents in grades 9 through 12.

Safety Behavior

During the 30 days preceding the survey, 27.2% of male adolescents had ridden in a car with someone who had been drinking alcohol; 11.7% had driven a vehicle after drinking; 27.5% acknowledged drinking at least 5 drinks within a 2-hour period; 29.8% had carried a weapon at least once (gun, knife, or club); 9.9% had carried a gun; 10.2% had carried a weapon to school; and 61.8% had played on a sports team, with 24.4% seeing a doctor or nurse for an injury that occurred while playing.

During the 12 months immediately preceding the survey, 86.1% of male adolescent bicycle riders had never or rarely worn a helmet; 38.4% of motorcycle riders had never or rarely worn a helmet; 12.5% had never or rarely worn a seat belt while a passenger in a vehicle; 43.4% reported having been in a physical fight; 9.0% had experienced dating violence (being hit, slapped, or physically hurt on purpose by their girlfriends), with 4.2% saying that they had been physically forced to have sexual intercourse; 31.4% had their cars, clothing, or books deliberately damaged or stolen while on school property at least once; 20.4% had felt so sad or hopeless every day for at least 2 weeks in a row that they had stopped engaging in some of their usual activities; and 12.0% had seriously considered suicide.

Sexual Behavior

Young men also suffer significant consequences from choosing to engage in unprotected sexual behavior. The costs of producing unintended pregnancies and contracting sexually transmitted diseases or an HIV infection are high, both for the young men and for society at large. The Youth Risk Behavior Survey identified the levels of risk behavior among adolescent males: 47.9% have had sexual intercourse at least once, with 16.5% reporting intercourse with four or more persons; 33.3% indicated they were currently sexually active (intercourse with one or more persons during the preceding 3 months); 30% had not used a condom during their most recent intercourse, and 85.4% of their female partners had not used birth control; and 27.6% had used alcohol prior to their most recent sexual intercourse.

Use of Drugs and Alcohol

Similarly, significant numbers of male adolescents use drugs known to have health risks, and incur all the hazards associated with the procurement, preparation, and use of these substances. In the survey, 55.9% of male adolescents have tried cigarettes at least once; 31.7% smoked a cigarette on at least 20 of the preceding 30 days; 19% use cigars, and 13.6% use smokeless tobacco; 40.9% have tried marijuana, 8.4% have tried cocaine, 7.2% have tried ecstasy, 6.3% have tried methamphetamine, and 3.3% have tried heroin; marijuana had been used at least once during the preceding 30 days by 22.1% of the sample, and cocaine by 4.0%; and illegal steroid use during the previous 30 days was 4.8%. A particularly striking finding is the early age at which many of these behaviors begin. By the time they reach 13 years of age, 18.3% of male adolescents have already used cigarettes, 29.2% have already used alcohol, 11% have used marijuana, and 8.8% have had sexual intercourse.

Models of Optimal Adolescent Development

Given the wide range of risks noted in the previous section, it is important to acknowledge the attention that has been given to defining optimal adolescent development. In addition to the increased interest in "positive psychology" among many practitioners (e.g., Peterson & Seligman, 2004; Snyder & Lopez, 2002), organized groups within the mental health professions have devoted considerable effort to defining the elements of a mature and effective passage through childhood and adolescence (ICDL-DMIC Diagnostic Classification Task Force, 2005; PDM Task Force, 2006). These models are extensive, multiauthored, often empirical, and developed with an eye toward clinical applications.

To illustrate the breadth of these models, consider the aspects of adolescent development addressed by just one of these projects (PDM Task Force, 2006): capacity for regulation, attention, and learning; capacity for relationships and intimacy; quality of internal experience (level of confidence and self-regard); affective experience, expression, and communication; defensive patterns and capacities; capacity to form internal representations; capacity for differentiation and integration; self-observing capacity (psychological mindedness); and the capacity to construct or use internal standards and ideals (sense of morality).

In this particular model, each of the nine areas includes not only a definition of optimal performance for children and adolescents, but also a description of the range of possible developmental expressions. Professionals who work with young men can gain much from these models, as they delineate various levels of emotional, cognitive, and social functioning.

Surviving Adolescent Development

Given the risks and dangers to adolescent males, what helps them move toward optimal performance, and how do counselors help? Although the rest of the present book offers numerous answers to this question, some general protective factors can be noted at the outset. Young men are more likely to avoid harming themselves and others when they have at least one stable, competent, and caring adult in their lives (Garbarino, 1999); when they have found spiritual or religious ways of interpreting the world that are constructive and prosocial (Garbarino); when they are helped to develop academic skills in school (Seidman, Abner, & French, 2004); when they have at least one warm and stable parent (Lerner & Galambos, 1998; Mason, Cauce, Gonzales, & Hiraga, 1994); and when they become adept at identifying and understanding emotions in themselves and others (Garbarino).

It is a challenge to translate these protective factors into counseling strategies that work. One of the present authors (JMR) devotes about one third of his private practice to male adolescent clients. Most of these young men have engaged in several of the high-risk behaviors noted above, and many are in trouble with school officials or the court system. Over time, various approaches have seemed to work more effectively in generating discussions with young men moving through adolescence. The following ideas offer a supportive approach to many of the central developmental tasks of male adolescence.

Attention

Boys in trouble really do want to tell their stories. They both want and need someone to pay attention to them. Consistent with the increasing independence that comes with adolescence, they want their own perspectives to be heard. They want less telling and more listening. When this does *not* occur, an effective and understandable response is silence: brooding, glowering silence. But this stereotypical sullenness tends to give way when it becomes clear that the counselor will take a young man's ideas and experiences seriously. Indirectly, of course, a male counselor who responds in this way to an adolescent is also modeling the reality that adult men can relate to other men in ways that are attentive, facilitative, and respectful.

Strengths

Young men in trouble expect judgment. They hear adults comment critically on their behavior or their experiences with illegal behavior, and react strongly to common epithets such as *wasted potential, bad kid,* or *disaster waiting to happen.* It can help to talk with young men about what they see as their strengths, skills, accomplishments, and goals. At one level, this strengths-based emphasis is congruent with the socialized masculine expectation to be competent, strong, and successful. At a more practical level, it speaks directly to the self-judging and self-comparing themes that inhibit an adolescent from accurately identifying natural abilities that can be molded into marketable adult skills.

Genuineness

Credibility must be earned by those who counsel adolescents. This requires honesty, consistency, reliability, and a determination to follow through. Adolescents develop highly effective radar systems that quickly detect phony, incomplete, or deceptive comments. Correctly identifying such information is highly functional for young men, as it provides an effective defense against exchanges with adults who tend to be dismissive, manipulative, or judgmental. A further benefit of being genuine with an adolescent is the effect such modeling can have on the young man's developing views about the value of authenticity in his own interactions with others.

Timing

Adolescents must trust before they will agree to discuss information that is sensitive, shaming, or painful. They will not accept self-serving "You can trust me" statements from counselors. It is crucial to give a young man control over the timing of these difficult discussions. Follow him, and he will take you where he needs to go, and he will talk when the time is right. Developmentally, this approach is mindful of the egocentrality of adolescence and the need to assert increasing levels of autonomy. It also happens to be congruent with the norm in many masculinities that men must take responsibility for directing and managing their own affairs.

Normalizing

A distressing and often unasked question among male adolescents is some version of "Am I normal?" Sensing the presence of this unasked question in the background and responding to it in a respectful way can be deeply relieving to a young man. Because he may be embarrassed that you think he doesn't know something, it is especially important to avoid being patronizing or belittling. Effectively letting a young man know that others have had similar questions, similar experiences, and similar doubts can give him an opening to explore his own uncertainties.

Activities

An activity may help some boys to relax and confide their problems. Playing chess, shooting baskets, and listening to an adolescent's favorite music present numerous openings for a counselor to ask questions or make observations. Given the socialized expectation that males connect by "doing things" rather than by "sharing feelings" together, a mutual activity creates an atmosphere that is both familiar and comfortable. Depending on the privacy of the location, taking a walk with an adolescent near the office can lead to interactions that feel more like conversations than interviews.

CONCLUSION

In this review of current thinking about boys' psychological development, we described a separation–individuation process that may prematurely disconnect young boys from their caregivers, leaving psychic wounds that can persist throughout adult life. Moreover, we suggested that the infant and toddler's neurobiological development in the first 2 years of life is significantly devoted to learning interpersonal skills and gender-role-associated behaviors. We reviewed the literature on normal growth processes, emphasizing the challenges boys face as they mature into adolescence. Next, we addressed the impact of socialization on adolescent development, highlighting how boys are taught to conform to rules of male behavior, and how boys navigate these difficult shoals to define their own masculine identities.

We noted the dark side of adolescent development, the aggressive and hostile emotions that at times seem to dominate an adolescent's psychological life, as well as the risky and self-destructive behaviors some boys pursue. Finally, we offered some practical suggestions on how clinicians can help their young male clients "survive" adolescent development.

When an understanding of male development informs counseling boys and adolescents, the question noted at the beginning of this chapter becomes easier to address: "How can you stand working with adolescent boys?" The short answer: because young men really do want to make their lives better. It is true that working with adolescents in counseling settings can be demanding, puzzling, and even exasperating. But it also is intensely rewarding to see a troubled young man walk into the office with a tentative smile and say, "I brought my grades with me. Do you want to see them?" Or, "I've decided to stop smoking. Can you help?" Or, as Octavio, the young man noted above, said at the return visit to his therapist, "My girlfriend is pregnant. Should I drop out of school and get a job?" In counseling rooms, choices are made that can influence a man's life for decades.

REFERENCES

Addis, M. E., & Mahalik, J. R. (2003). Men, masculinity, and the contexts of help seeking. *American Psychologist, 58,* 5–14.

Bandura, A. (1977). *Social learning theory.* Englewood Cliffs, NJ: Prentice Hall.

Bergman, S. J. (1995). Men's psychological development: A relational perspective. In R. F. Levant & W. S. Pollack (Eds.), *A new psychology of men* (pp. 68–90). New York: Basic Books.

Bjorklund, D. F., & Green, B. L. (1992). The adaptive nature of cognitive immaturity. *American Psychologist, 47,* 46–54.

Blazina, C., Pisecco, S., & O'Neil, J. M. (2005). An adaptation of the Gender Role Conflict Scale for Adolescents: Psychometric issues and correlates with psychological distress. *Psychology of Men and Masculinity, 6,* 39–45.

Blazina, C., & Watkins, C. E., Jr. (2000). Separation/individuation, parental attachment, and male gender role conflict: Attitudes toward the feminine and the fragile masculine self. *Psychology of Men & Masculinity, 1,* 126–132.

Broderick, P. C., & Blewitt, P. (2006). *The lifespan: Human development for helpers and professionals* (2nd ed.). Upper Saddle River, NJ: Merrill Prentice-Hall.

Cavada, C., & Schultz, W. (2000). The mysterious orbit frontal cortex: Foreword. *Cerebral Cortex, 10,* 203.

Chiron, C., Jambaque, I., Nabbout, R., Lounes, R., Syrota, A., & Dulac, O. (1997). The right brain hemisphere is dominant in human infants. *Brain, 120,* 1057–1065.

Chodorow, N. (1978). *The reproduction of mothering.* Berkeley: University of California Press.

David, D., & Brannon, R. (1976). *The forty-nine percent majority: The male sex role.* Reading, MA: Addison-Wesley.

Eaton, D. K., Kann, L., Kinchen, S., Ross, J., Hawkins, J., Harris, W. A., et al. (2006). Risk behavior surveillance: United States, 2005. National Center for Chronic Disease Prevention and Health Promotion, Centers for Disease Control and Prevention. *Morbidity & Mortality Weekly Report 2006, 55*(SS-5), 1–108.

Eisenberg, L. (1995). The social construction of the human brain. *American Journal of Psychiatry, 152,* 1563–1575.

Elliott, R., Dolan, R. J., & Frith, C. D. (2000). Dissociable functions in the medial and lateral orbit frontal cortex: Evidence from human neuroimaging studies. *Cerebral Cortex, 10,* 308–317.

Fletcher, J. M., Lyon, G. R., Fuchs, L. S., & Barnes, M. A. (2007). *Learning disabilities: From identification to intervention.* New York: Guilford.

Garbarino, J. (2000). *Lost boys: Why our sons turn violent and how we can save them.* New York: Vintage Anchor.

Gentry, J. H., & Campbell, M. (2002). *Developing adolescents: A reference guide for professionals.* Washington, DC: American Psychological Association.

Gertler, P., Martinez, S., Levine, D., & Bertozzi, S. (2003). Losing the presence and presents of parents: How parental death affects children. Berkeley: Haas School of Business, University of California. Retrieved April 5, 2007, from http://faculty.haas.berkeley.edu/levine/Papers/Presence%20and%20Presents%20of%20P

Hariri, A. R., Bookheimer, S. Y., & Mazziotta, J. C. (2000). Modulating emotional responses: Effects of a neocortical network on the limbic system. *NeuroReport, 11,* 43–48.

Helmeke, C., Ovtscharoff, W., Jr., Poeggel, G., & Braun, K. (2001). Juvenile emotional experience alters synaptic inputs on pyramidal neurons in anterior cingulate cortex. *Cerebral Cortex, 11,* 717–727.

Hofmann, A. D., & Greydanus, D. E. (1997). *Adolescent medicine.* Stamford, CT: Appleton & Lange.

Horne, A. M., & Kiselica, M. S. (1999). *Handbook of counseling boys and adolescent males: A practitioner's guide.* Thousand Oaks, CA: Sage.

ICDL-DMIC Diagnostic Classification Task Force. (2005). *Interdisciplinary Council on Developmental and Learning Disorders diagnostic manual for infancy and early childhood mental health disorders, developmental disorders, regulatory-sensory processing disorders, language disorders, and learning challenges.* Bethesda, MD: Interdisciplinary Council on Development and Learning.

Jaffe, M. L. (1998). *Adolescence.* New York: Wiley.

Jakupcak, M., Tull, M. T., & Roemer, L. (2005). Masculinity, shame, and fear of emotions as predictors of men's expressions of anger and hostility. *Psychology of Men & Masculinity, 6,* 275–284.

Jordan, J. V., Kaplan, A. G., Miller, J. B., Stiver, I. P., & Surrey, J. L. (1991). *Women's growth in connection: Writings from the Stone Center.* New York: Guilford Press.

Kaufman, G. (1985). *Shame: The power of caring.* Rochester, VT: Schenkman.

Kiselica, M. S., & O'Brien, S. (2001, August). Are attachment disorders and alexithymia characteristic of males? In M. S. Kiselica (Chair), *Are males really emotional mummies? What do the data indicate?* Symposium conducted at the annual convention of the American Psychological Association, San Francisco.

Krugman, S. (1995). Male development and the transformation of shame. In R. F. Levant & W. S. Pollack (Eds.), *A new psychology of men* (pp. 91–128). New York: Basic Books.

Lerner, R. M. & Galambos, N. L. (1998). Adolescent development: Challenges and opportunities for research, programs, and policies. *Annual Review of Psychology, 49,* 413–446.

Levant, R. F. (1995). Toward a reconstruction of masculinity. In R. F. Levant & W. S. Pollack (Eds.), *A new psychology of men* (pp. 229–251). New York: Basic Books.

Levant, R. F. (1996). The new psychology of men. *Professional Psychology: Research and Practice, 27,* 259–265.

Maccoby, E. E. (1990). Gender and relationships: A developmental account. *American Psychologist, 45,* 513–520.

Mahalik, J. R., Good, G. E., & Englar-Carlson, M. (2003). Masculinity scripts, presenting concerns, and help seeking: Implications for practice and training. *Professional Psychology: Research and Practice, 34,* 123–131.

Mahalik, J. R., Locke, B., Diemer, M., Ludlow, L., Scott, R., Gottfried, M., et al. (2003). Development of the Conformity to Masculine Norms Inventory. *Psychology of Men & Masculinity, 4*(1), 3–25.

Mahler, M. S., Pine, F., & Bergman, A. (1975). *The psychological birth of the human infant.* New York: Basic Books.

Mason, C. A., Cauce, A. M., Gonzales, N., & Hiraga, Y. (1994). Adolescent problem behavior: The effects of peers on the moderating role of father absence and the mother–child relationship. *American Journal of Community Psychology, 22,* 723–743.

Matsuzawa, J., Matsui, M., Konishi, T., Noguchi, K., Gur, R. C., Bilker, W., et al. (2001). Age-related changes of brain gray and white matter in health infants and children. *Cerebral Cortex, 11,* 335–342.

McAnarney, E. R., & Kreipe, R. W. (1992). *Textbook of adolescent medicine.* New York: W. B. Saunders.

Monk, D., & Ricciardelli, L. A. (2003). Three dimensions of the male gender role as correlates of alcohol and cannabis involvement in young Australian men. *Psychology of Men & Masculinity, 4,* 57–69.

Newberger, E. H. (2000). *The men they will become: The nature and nurture of male character.* New York: Perseus.

Newman, B. M., & Newman. P. R. (2006). *Development through life: A psychosocial approach* (9th ed.). Belmont, CA: Thomson Brooks/Cole.

Pascoe, C. J. (2003). Multiple masculinities? Teenage boys talk about jocks and gender. *American Behavioral Scientist, 46,* 1423–1438.

PDM Task Force. (2006). *Psychodynamic diagnostic manual.* Silver Spring, MD: Alliance of Psychoanalytic Organizations.

Peterson, C., & Seligman, M. E. P. (2004). *Character strengths and virtues.* New York: Oxford University Press.

Plummer, D. C. (2001). The quest for modern manhood: Masculine stereotypes, peer culture and the social significance of homophobia. *Journal of Adolescence, 24,* 15–23.

Pollack, W. S. (1995). No man is an island: Toward a new psychoanalytic psychology of men. In R. F. Levant & W. S. Pollack (Eds.), *A new psychology of men* (pp. 33–67). New York: Basic Books.

Pollack, W. S. (1998a). The trauma of Oedipus: Toward a new psychoanalytic psychotherapy for men. In W. S. Pollack & R. F. Levant (Eds.), *New psychotherapy for men* (pp. 13–34). New York: Wiley.

Pollack, W. S. (1998b). *Real boys: Rescuing our sons from the myths of boyhood.* New York: Henry Holt.

Rutter, M., & Rutter, M. (1993). *Developing minds: Challenge and continuity across the life span.* New York: Basic Books.

Schore, A. N. (1994). *Affect regulation and the origin of the self: The neurobiology of emotional development.* Hillsdale, NJ: Lawrence Erlbaum.

Schore, A. N. (2000). The self-organization of the right brain and the neurobiology of emotional development. In M. D. Lewis & I. Granic (Eds.), *Emotion, development, and self-organization* (pp. 155–185). New York: Cambridge University Press.

Schore, A. N. (2001). The effects of relational trauma on right brain development, affect regulation, and infant mental health. *Infant Mental Health Journal, 22,* 201–269.

Schore, A. N. (2003). *Affect dysregulation and disorders of the self.* New York: Norton.

Seidman, E., Abner, J. L., & French, S. (2004). Restructuring the transition to middle/junior high school: A strengths-based approach to the organization of schooling. In K. Maton, C. Schellenbach, B. Leadbeater, & A. Solarz (Eds.), *Promoting strengths-based policies for children, youth, families, and communities.* Washington, DC: American Psychological Association.

Shepard, D. S. (2005). Male development and the journey towards disconnection. In D. L. Comstock (Ed.), *Diversity in development: Critical contexts that shape our lives and relationships* (pp. 133–160). Belmont, CA: Thomson Brooks/Cole.

Siegel, D. J. (1999). *The developing mind: Toward a neurobiology of interpersonal experience.* New York: Guilford.

Smiler, A. P. (2004). Thirty years after the discovery of gender: Psychological concepts and measures of masculinity. *Sex Roles, 50,* 15–26.

Snyder, C. R., & Lopez, S. J. (2002). *Handbook of positive psychology.* New York: Oxford University Press.

Stein, J. H., & Reiser, L. W. (1994). A study of White middle-class adolescent boys' responses to "semenarche" (the first ejaculation). *Journal of Youth and Adolescence, 23,* 373–384.

Steinberg, L. (1996). *Adolescence* (4th ed.). New York: McGraw-Hill.

Svetaz, M. V., Ireland, M., & Blum, R. (2000). Adolescents with learning disabilities: Risk and protective factors associated with emotional well-being: Findings from the National Longitudinal Study of Adolescent Health. *Journal of Adolescent Health, 27,* 340–348.

Tager, D., & Good, G. E. (2005). Italian and American masculinities: A comparison of masculine gender role norms. *Psychology of Men & Masculinity, 6,* 264–274.

Trevarthen, D. (1993). The self born in intersubjectivity: The psychology of an infant communicating. In U. Neisser (Ed.), *The perceived self: Ecological and interpersonal sources of self-knowledge* (pp. 121–173). New York: Cambridge University Press.

Trevarthen, D. (1996). Lateral asymmetries in infancy: Implications for the development of the hemispheres. *Neuroscience and Biobehavioral Reviews, 20*, 571–586.

Walker, L. J., & Taylor, J. H. (1991). Family interactions and the development of moral reasoning. *Child Development, 62*, 264–283.

Weitz, C., Zide, W., Perry, C., & Moore, C. (Producers), & Weitz, P. (Director). (1999). *American pie* [Motion picture]. Universal City, CA: Universal Pictures.

2

A Positive Psychology Perspective on Helping Boys

MARK S. KISELICA, MATT ENGLAR-CARLSON,
ARTHUR M. HORNE, AND MARK FISHER

Mental health professionals, social scientists, and members of the media rarely proclaim the beauty of boys and men and their ways of relating to the world. Instead, when the subject of boys is discussed in the professional literature, the popular press, or public forums, the conversation is usually focused on either the bad things that men and boys do or how the male socialization process scars boys and men for life, leaving them chronically flawed and in dire need of fixing (Kiselica, 2006b). Although the intense attention devoted to these issues has generated a greater awareness about some of the serious social problems that are mainly perpetrated by males (e.g., violent crime) or primarily suffered by boys and men (e.g., suicide), it has also discouraged an understanding and appreciation for the many good things that boys and men do (e.g., caring for family members) and the great strengths associated with traditional masculinity (e.g., healthy self-reliance; Kiselica, 2006b). However, over the past several years, there has also been an increased interest in positive psychology (see Seligman & Csikszentmihalyi, 2000; Snyder & Lopez, 2007), whose purpose is to foster well-being and resiliency in people through the study of strengths and virtue over disease, weakness, and damage, and the application of therapeutic strategies that are designed to build in people what is right rather than solely focusing on repairing what is wrong (Aspinwall & Staudinger, 2003; Seligman &

31

Csikszentmihalyi, 2000). Nevertheless, approaches to counseling that focus explicitly on the positives of clients are rather rare (Seligman, Rashid, & Parks, 2006). Even rarer is a helping perspective that looks at the strengths and contributions of boys. Consistent with a positive psychology perspective, the purpose of this chapter is to identify traditional male strengths that can be the foundation for a happy, well-adjusted life in boys.

Although we are strong proponents of promoting positive aspects of masculinity, such as courage and personal sacrifice, we acknowledge that several other aspects of traditional masculinity are dysfunctional, especially when they are rigidly practiced. For example, findings from over 25 years of research on gender role conflict in men has demonstrated that certain features of traditional masculinity, such as extreme emotional constriction, homophobia, and an overemphasis of competition and success, are associated with a wide range of adjustment difficulties in men (O'Neil, 2006). Because this is the case, we contend that an effective application of a positive psychology of masculinity with boys involves helping young men to distinguish healthy forms of masculinity from unhealthy ones. Thus, our approach to promoting the well-being of boys includes teaching them about noble forms of masculinity while steering them away from traditional notions of masculinity that can do them harm.

Drawing from the work of Levant (1995), who observed that there are several attributes of traditional masculinity that are valuable for male development; Kiselica, Englar-Carlson, and Fisher (2006), who proposed a positive psychology model of boys, men, and masculinity; and Horne, Jolliff, and Roth (1996), who designed a model of optimal male development through the life span, we describe an approach to counseling and psychotherapy with boys that accentuates the following healthy behaviors and traditions of boys and men: (a) male relational styles; (b) generative fatherhood; (c) male ways of caring; (d) male self-reliance; (e) the worker–provider tradition of husbands and fathers; (f) male daring, courage, and risk taking; (g) the group orientation of boys and men; (h) the humanitarian service of fraternal organizations; (i) men's use of humor; and (j) male heroism. We acknowledge that this list of strengths is a representative rather than an exhaustive inventory of male assets and that some of these strengths overlap to some degree. We also recognize that the strengths discussed in this chapter are social constructions that are neither male specific (e.g., many women have worker–provider roles) nor based on biologically determined sex differences between men and women, and therefore can be considered *human* strengths. Nevertheless, we have emphasized the ways that males demonstrate these strengths and how mental health professionals can consider each strength as a building block for promoting wellness and honorable manhood in boys.

POSITIVE MASCULINITY IN BOYS AND MEN

It is a refreshing and inspirational experience to know a truly good boy or man who embraces and lives a positive masculinity. In his moving description of such a man, Levant (1995) lauded the following qualities of traditional masculinity, which are worth celebrating:

> A man's willingness to set aside his own needs for the sake of his family; his ability to withstand hardship and pain to protect others; his tendency to take care of people and solve their problems as if they were his own; his way of expressing love by doing things for others; his loyalty, dedication, and commitment; his stick-to-it-ive-ness and will to hang in until a situation is corrected; and his abilities to solve problems, think logically, rely on himself, take risks, stay calm in the face of danger, and assert himself. (p. 232)

We agree with Levant (1995) that these qualities and traditions are valuable and a source of self-esteem and pride for men. Further, it is clear that the foundation for these qualities is established during boyhood and adolescence. Yet, we are surprised that mental health professionals rarely discuss the notion of promoting these characteristics and traditions as a way to bolster the psychological health of boys. What are these attributes and customs? And how can counselors foster their development in boys?

Male Relational Styles

It is a joy to watch young boys when they get together to play. Typically, as they gather around each other, one of the boys asks the others, "What do you want to do?" In response, the other boys name some activity, such a playing a sport or an electronic game, and then the group jumps into action, having fun together. Kiselica (2001, 2003a, 2003b, 2006a) observed that the sharing of these types of action-oriented activities is a common way for boys and men to develop friendships. Thus, compared to girls, who establish intimacy through personal discussions and self-disclosure, boys enjoy intimacy and thriving friendships through shared physical activities (Buhrmester, 1996; McNelles & Connolly, 1999). Although there may be fewer exchanges of intimate emotions among males hanging out as a group of buddies than when a group of females socializes, boys and men nevertheless form strong bonds and get to know each other quite well through this manner of socialization.

Other writers have shared similar observations about male relational styles. For example, several scholars from the Stone Center of Wellesley College remarked that men tend to relate to others through instrumental activities (e.g., Clinchy & Zimmerman, 1985; Surrey, 1985), and Levant (1995) argued that boys and men have high levels of action empathy, which is the ability to take action based on how a person sees things from another's point of view.

Unfortunately, many social scientists have been guilty of judging male friendships against the standard type of intimate relationships that women tend to construct. Women tend to place a high value on talk, and for a relationship to become more intimate, there must be a willingness to verbally and mutually share very personal details about one's inner life with another. From the idealized feminine standard, men's friendships may seem impoverished due to the lack of verbal intimacy. If male friendships are examined from the point of view of men, however, rather than from a feminine model, male friendships may be characterized by a "covert style of intimacy" (Swain, 1989) featuring the development of emotional closeness through self-disclosure that occurs within the context of shared activities (Camarena, Sarigiani, & Petersen, 1990).

One of the problems with the treatment of boys and men in counseling and psychotherapy is that, as conceptions of intimacy have become more feminized (Cancian, 1987), there has been a tendency for mental health professionals to pathologize boys and men for having an action-oriented approach to the world (Kiselica, 2001). In particular, there is a belief that the action orientation of boys and men is a sign that they are emotionally handicapped, in spite of the fact that the extant research on gender differences in emotion shows that males and females are more alike than different in their emotions (Wester, Vogel, Pressly, & Heesacker, 2002). We cannot emphasize strongly enough that boys and men are *not* emotional mummies. On the contrary, they are capable of experiencing and expressing very powerful emotions, such as joy, sorrow, happiness, and anger (Kiselica, 2001; Kiselica & O'Brien, 2001). Furthermore, the action orientation of boys and men is a beautiful sight to behold! Visit a schoolyard, and witness the fun boys experience in chasing each other. Drop in on boys when they are clustered around an X-Box, and notice how often they laugh and talk with each other as they react to what is happening on the screen. Go to a boys' basketball game, and watch how teammates can pump each other up before the start of the contest. Walk through a neighborhood on a spring day, and notice the nice conversations fathers have with their sons while playing a game of catch with a baseball. Hang out with a bunch of men as they play cards or bowl together, and you will see lots of good-natured ribbing. Run to the scene of a house fire, and watch how firemen launch into coordinated action as they fight and extinguish the flames, saving their fellow human beings and their belongings in the process. These are all male styles of relating to the world, and they deserve our appreciation.

As therapists, we must respect and support these forms of expression, for they are important keys to the development of friendships in boys and men. Furthermore, when we see boys in counseling and psychotherapy, we will be able to join them successfully if we utilize male-friendly practices in which we match the process of therapy to male relational styles, such as enthusiastically challenging boys to *take action* to solve their problems, and talking to boys about their concerns while participating in action-oriented activities, such as playing catch with a ball or walking side by side together (Kiselica, 1995, 1996, 1999, 2001, 2003a, 2003b, 2006a; Kiselica, Rotzien, & Doms, 1994; Kiselica, Stroud, Stroud, & Rotzien, 1992).

Generative Fatherhood

Historically, psychologists neglected to study the important role of fathers in their children's lives, while focusing on the alleged inadequacies of fathers as parents (Rohner & Veneziano, 2001). Many behavioral scientists prior to the 1960s and 1970s assumed that fathers were relatively unimportant in the development of their children (Cabrera, Tamis-LeMonda, Bradley, Hofferth, & Lamb, 2000). Fathers were thought to be peripheral to the job of parenting because children spent most of their time with mothers. Fortunately, over the past several decades, many psychologists who study child development and family relations have shifted their perspectives on father–child relations in a positive direction. For example, in the 1970s, Michael Lamb and his colleagues started a new trend of organizing findings from emerging research documenting that fathers contribute to their children's development in beneficial ways. Lamb's classic volume on the subject, *The Father's Role in Child Development*, is now in its fourth edition (Lamb, 2003). Similarly, Hawkins and Dollahite (1996) and their associates have devoted considerable attention to the ways that fathers care for the next generation through positive father work, or *generative fathering*, which refers to the way a father responds readily and consistently to his child's developmental needs over time (see also Dollahite & Hawkins, 1998). Fathering thus becomes not only a way for men to provide for and protect their children but also a means to contribute to the development of a new generation of men. Being a "good" father becomes an important aspect of identity for many men and a way of contributing to social welfare.

In a related review of the literature on father–child relations, Kiselica (1995) concluded that fathers (a) stimulate the physical development of infants through proximal, vigorous, and arousing forms of play; (b) promote autonomous, imaginative, and confident behavior in boys, and well-socialized, friendly, and dependable behavior in girls, through the application of consistent, authoritative discipline and physical contact with their children; and (c) foster the cognitive skills and academic functioning of children through various forms of physical and social stimulation. Simply put, much of what is good about men has to do with their contributions to their children's well-being.

Teaching boys about generative fatherhood is an excellent way to prepare boys for one of their most important potential roles in life: being a loving father. In a series of prior publications pertaining to this idea, Kiselica and his colleagues (Kiselica, 1995, 1996; Kiselica, Rotzien, & Doms, 1994) described a psychoeducational course on fatherhood for boys. The purpose of this course is to help boys clarify their conceptions about being a man and a father, and to learn effective parenting skills and responsible sexual behavior. One of the central topics permeating all three topics is the notion that a good father cares for his children and the mother of his child. Teaching boys these subjects can help them to understand what it takes to be a caring parent and to develop a vision of the type of father they would want to be. In addition, it can arm them with a sense of competence and confidence about becoming fathers in the future.

Male Ways of Caring

Generative fathering is just one of the many ways males show that they care about others. Boys and men protect their loved ones and their friends. Protecting others can take the form of standing up to bullies or invading armies that might harm a family member or friend. Protecting others can also mean facing grave dangers until one's family is safe, such as a boy I (MK) once counseled, who escorted and guarded his brothers and sisters through a dangerous neighborhood as they walked to and from school. Showing concern can take the form of running errands and fixing things, or comforting a distraught wife or child simply by holding her. When a good man provides for his family, he is willing to work until he drops. He will work under deplorable conditions and in great pain, yet he will not give up, for he knows that his toil and his agony are a price he has to pay to see that the basic needs of his family are met. When a good son sees that his father or mother needs help, he will lend a helping hand or he will care for his siblings.

A powerful example of male caring was provided by Kramer and Weaver (2007) in which Dr. William Weaver, chief of surgery at the Morehouse School of Medicine, recalled how he measures himself as a man in relation to the model of caring provided by his father, who spent his life as a janitor and chauffer. He recalled,

> When I was in high school I was taking algebra, and I was sitting at the kitchen table trying to do my homework. I got frustrated ... and my father said, "What's the problem?" I said, "It is this algebra." He said, "Let me look at this." I said, "They didn't even have algebra in your day" (laughing). And I went to sleep, and around 4 o'clock in the morning he woke me up and said, "Come on[,] get up." He set me at the kitchen table and he taught me algebra. What he had done was sit up all night and read the algebra book and then he explained the problems to me so I could do them and understand them. And to this day I live my life trying to be half the man my father was.

Every day, in so many different ways, boys and men express caring for their fellow human beings. By acknowledging and promoting these varied forms of male caring, counselors can help boys to enjoy fulfilling lives.

Male Self-Reliance

In its most extreme form, male self-reliance keeps boys and men from seeking help when they are in serious trouble, such as when they have significant medical conditions or overwhelming psychological distress (Courtenay, 2001). In its more moderate forms, however, self-reliance is a desirable trait to have. A boy or man who is sustained by healthy doses of self-reliance has the fortitude to face the challenges the world throws his way. He can figure things out on his own and then take action to fulfill his duties as a man and solve the problems he may encounter. His self-reliance is expressed in relation to the important people in his life, and he often takes the time to be by himself to determine how he can best serve the people he cares about. Unlike a person who displays dysfunctional self-reliance characterized by a separateness that keeps him from ever getting close to others, particularly during times of crises, a boy or man who has a healthy sense of self-reliance maintains boundaries with others that are permeable yet clear: He may seek guidance from others he trusts, yet he will not allow others to force their decisions upon him, remaining "his own man" in matters that are important to him. A boy or man who can "take care of his business" in this way earns the appreciation of his family and respect in his community (Hernandez, 2002). Thus, healthy male self-reliance means that a boy or man is competent to handle difficult situations, connects with others, and is admired by people around him. Consequently, practitioners can promote the well-being of boys by recognizing, teaching, and fostering healthy male self-reliance.

The Worker–Provider Tradition

Being a worker and a provider is an important source of identity and self-esteem for men. For many men, work is so central to their identity that they "define who they are in the world through work" (Heppner & Heppner, 2001, p. 371).

There are many reasons why work is so crucial to the psychological well-being of men. There is a cultural expectation that a man will work, so engaging in work helps a man to feel that he has achieved one of society's criteria for manhood (Skovholt, 1990). Earning an income through employment allows a man to fulfill his culturally prescribed role as a provider for his loved ones. Work also provides men with a sense of purpose and meaning. Through work, men demonstrate great creativity and productivity, which can be tremendous sources of pride and accomplishment. Devotion to the duty of taking care of loved ones and meeting standards of excellence with regard to work performance motivates many men to withstand long hours of labor, often in dangerous and unhealthy work environments. So, work by men is often an act of love and achievement, producing many benefits for men, their families, and society. Just think of all that men gave of themselves when thousands of laborers and engineers constructed the Hoover Dam and the Panama Canal, when Michelangelo painted the ceiling of the Sistine Chapel, and when Jonas Salk invented the polio vaccine. Each of these achievements is a monument to the toil, perfection, and love expressed by men and their work.

Understanding the relationship between positive masculinity and work has several implications for clinical practice for boys. First, because work is a rite of passage for boys into manhood and work is central to the identity of many males, all mental health professionals must know how to assist boys with their career development and decisions (Heppner & Heppner, 2001). Second, we must teach boys about what it means to be a good worker and provider, because these are likely to become important sources of their self-esteem and potentially crucial vehicles to helping them lead a mentally healthy life. Third, during the early stages of counseling and psychotherapy, one way to establish rapport with boys is to tap the great work and task orientations of males by letting them know that engaging in counseling means that we "have a job to do" and will "dive into our work together." Finally, during any stage of counseling and psychotherapy, a therapist can help a boy to open up by talking to the client while working on a project together (Kiselica, 2001, 2006b), such as the building of a Lego castle in a school or office setting or the construction of a campfire in an adventure-based counseling environment.

Male Daring, Courage, and Risk Taking

Boys and men tend to be risk takers. Although risk taking can take the form of harmful recklessness (picture young men experimenting with dangerous drugs or Ben Rothlisberger, the current starting quarterback for the Pittsburgh Steelers, speeding on his motorcycle without a helmet, then crashing and shattering the bones in his face), it is our contention that most males demonstrate healthy levels of daring, courage, and risk taking. Throughout history, it was primarily men who explored unknown regions of the worlds, often facing great peril in the process. In times of war, heroic men have stared into the face of death, taking life-threatening risks to protect their fellow countrymen and countrywomen. Through such acts of bravery, men have made great discoveries, defined the limits of human capabilities, and preserved the lives and freedom of the people they love. But on a less grand scale, boys and men demonstrate courage and take risks every day, especially in certain careers that are male dominated. Policemen protect communities from criminals. Firefighters risk life and limb to put out fires. Utility workers dangle from high wires and work with high-voltage electrical currents that could fry them in a second. Steel erectors build skyscrapers at heights from which a fall would mean certain death. Brave boys, who know the dangers in allowing themselves to be intimidated, figure out ways to manage the threats of bullies. Little boys attempt acrobatic jumps and somersaults, and they hang from places that can make their parents' hearts stop. In short, boys and men display many forms of daring, and the courage they muster while taking worthwhile risks is admirable.

We want to be clear that we are *not* advocating for the glorification of war or the approval of foolhardiness by stating we owe boys and men our respect for their displays of *desirable* risk taking. What we *are* promoting is the notion that certain forms of male daring have merits, and boys must learn when risk taking is warranted and when it is not. Related to the task of teaching this distinction, practitioners can foster the well-being of boys by helping them to consider carefully the merits of worthwhile risk taking and the perils associated with recklessness. And, based on the recommendations of Heppner and Heppner (2001), we can enhance the effectiveness of counseling with boys if we (a) affirm with our young, male clients the courageous acts they do; and (b) help boys who are reluctant to participate in counseling and psychotherapy by expressing our respect for the courage it takes to resolve personal difficulties. Stating this last point in a different way, we can tell our boy clients, "It takes *guts* to face your problems, and I respect you as a man for your decision to do so."

The Group Orientation of Boys

Although rugged individualism is a quality often associated with traditional masculinity in American culture, it is also true that males in the United States and boys and men across cultures and throughout history have socialized and worked in groups. Research has shown that males spend more time in coordinated group activity, and females engage in longer episodes of dyadic interaction (Benenson, Apostoleris, & Parnass, 1997). Andronico (1996) cogently described the importance and function of groups for men in the following commentary:

> Men have participated in groups for centuries. They have gathered together in armies, monasteries, universities, Alcoholics Anonymous fellowships, and industrial groups. Younger men have found satisfaction in Boy Scouts, athletic teams, and fraternities. This orientation toward banding together for a common purpose and a shared group identity makes groups ideal settings in which men can explore and learn new gender roles and responsibilities. (pp. xviii–xix)

Although many discussions of boys and men in groups are focused on dysfunctional group behavior by males (e.g., gang violence and warring armies of men), Andronico's quote says it all about the positive aspects of male groups: Boys and men value groups, groups provide males with many benefits, and, consequently, group psychoeducation and group psychotherapy are potentially powerful modalities for helping men to deal with their problems and to learn new ways of behaving. A positive psychology of boys must therefore include the study of young men in groups: how boys form groups, the impact of having a group identity on the personal well-being of boys, and the utility of psychotherapeutic groups for the prevention and resolution of the problems of boys. For example, in *BAM! Boys Advocacy and Mentoring*, which is another book in the Routledge Series on Counseling and Psychotherapy With Boys and Men, Mortola, Hiton, & Grant (2008) explained how to use various forms of preventive groups to foster the emotional development and skills competencies of boys.

The Humanitarian Services of Fraternal Organizations

Seligman and Csikszentmihalyi (2000) proposed that one way to study positive psychology is by examining positive institutions. We concur with this recommendation and note that throughout history, men have formed organizations whose primary mission is to provide service to others. These organizations represent a particular category of male groups that warrant the separate discussion provided here, as well as our appreciation for their existence.

It is uplifting to discover that numerous fraternal organizations in the United States have continued the long-standing tradition of humanitarian service by men. Here are just two examples:

- The Loyal Order of the Moose was first established in the late 1800s as a purely social organization for men. In the early 20th century, however, the Moose organization changed its mission to be one of service and to work toward brightening the lives of children and the elderly in need; and in 1913, the Moose fraternity began to admit women into its ranks, although it remains a primarily male organization. Today, one of the main beneficiaries of the many fundraising activities of the Moose is Mooseheart, a 1,000-acre residential facility located near Chicago for children and teens whose families are unable to care for them. Moose International also provides worldwide disaster relief, and it operates Moosehaven, a residential care facility for the elderly in Orange Park, Florida (Moose International, 2004).
- The motto of Lions Clubs International is "We Serve." Formed by a group of businessmen in 1917, there are now 45,000 Lions Clubs in 199 countries. Lions Clubs are recognized throughout the world for their service to people who are blind or visually impaired. For example, in 1990, Lions launched its most aggressive sight preservation effort, SightFirst. This $143.5 million program strives to rid the world of preventable and reversible blindness by supporting desperately needed health care services. In addition to sight programs, Lions Clubs International is committed to providing services for youth. Lions Clubs also work to improve the environment, build homes for the disabled, support diabetes education,

conduct hearing programs, and, through their foundation, provide disaster relief around the world (International Association of Lions Clubs, 2006).

How often do we read about organizations such as the Loyal Order of the Moose or the Lions Clubs in the professional literature about boys and men? Rarely, if ever. How many mental health professionals know that the motto of the Moose is "Forward in the Good, Onward in the Right"? Most probably do not. How many practitioners actually encourage boys to join these types of organizations? Very few.

Involvement in service organizations provides opportunities and experiences for boys to develop social interest. Alfred Adler proposed that the true measure of mental health was high social interest, which can be defined as a sense of belonging and participating with others for the common good. It includes the notion of striving to make the world a better place (Carlson & Englar-Carlson, 2008). We have the potential for cooperation and social living, but the aptitude for social interest is developed into a rudimentary ability to express social interest through social cooperation in various activities like community service. We contend that promoting the involvement of boys in male-led service organizations is a powerful way to foster the psychological well-being of boys. Specifically, a boy's involvement in groups like the Moose and the Lions Clubs can promote the development of his personal and collective identity, his connection to older generations of men, his sense of social responsibility, his hopefulness about the future, and his sense that he can make a difference in society (Youniss & Yates, 1997). Because these are such desirable outcomes, we recommend that helping professionals learn more about these types of organizations and how they can help boys to become a part of them.

Boys' and Men's Use of Humor

A small number of individuals are so uncomfortable with intimacy that they use humor as a means to distance themselves emotionally from others whenever a very personal or sensitive subject is brought up. Unfortunately, many people, including far too many helping professionals, are under the mistaken impression that this method of distancing is the norm for males because they don't understand the functions of humor for boys and men. Although it is true that some boys and men use humor to *avoid* intimacy, it is also true that many boys and men use humor as a vehicle to *attain* intimacy (Kiselica, 2003b). Boys like to joke with their buddies as a means of having fun. Boys love to laugh, and sharing a good laugh is one of the tools boys use to create happy experiences with other boys. These cheerful experiences can be one of the foundations for building and supporting a friendship. Boys also use joking as a way to demonstrate that they care about others. Many boys will try to lift the spirits of a dejected friend by getting him to laugh. Furthermore, boys tell jokes as a strategy to reduce tension and manage conflicts (Kiselica, 2001). Finally, research indicates that humor can be a healing and coping tool in times of stress (Brooks & Goldstein, 2001; Wolin & Wolin, 1993). Consequently, we urge helping professionals to recognize the adaptive purposes of humor in boys and to teach boys how to use humor as a friendship-building and coping mechanism. Also, we recommend that counselors infuse humor into their work with boys. A well-timed joke or a good-natured jab by the counselor can help a boy to loosen up and share his most intimate feelings and experiences.

Male Heroism

Throughout the ages, countless boys and men have exemplified the positive qualities of traditional masculinity through their heroic lives. Some of these heroes are the great men of history, such as Abraham Lincoln. Lincoln was a devoted husband and a loving father who so cherished his children that he permitted them to sit in his lap and crawl around his office while he was conducting official duties in the White House. He was also a dedicated worker who had high standards for himself and a tremendous sense of civic responsibility. Throughout his life, Lincoln coped with the serial deaths of loved ones and the burdens of leading the nation by balancing his capacity for self-reliance with the fellowship of other men to whom he regularly turned for counsel and lighthearted camaraderie (Goodwin, 2005).

Whereas Lincoln remains a majestic national icon, many other boys and men are everyday heroes who displayed the strengths of traditional masculinity without ever being elevated to the ranks of the famous people of history. For example, in his gripping account of inner-city, Chicano, adolescent fathers, Hernandez (2002) chronicled the noble efforts of several young men who were model sons, brothers, and fathers in the face of grinding poverty, crime, and limited life options. Consider the devotion of Beto, a teen father from a poor barrio in Michigan, to his family of origin, his partner, and her pregnancy:

> By the time Beto was in the eleventh grade, he was pretty much working full time, going to school and making sure that his siblings were going to school. This is when his girlfriend became pregnant for the first time. He quit school and moved his girlfriend into his mother's house. After the baby was born he had an elaborate wedding. (Hernandez, 2002, p. 19)

Jesús, another young father from Hernandez's study (2002), expressed his passionate dedication to his partner and their children:

> I love my vieja [old lady, or girlfriend]—I'd kill for her. My children, I'd kill for them and die for them all in the same day—I'd take the food right out of my mouth so they could eat. I can't imagine it being any way else for a man. He's not like that, he doesn't take care of business—he's no man. (p. 17)

Those of us who are professional counselors can help boys to understand what responsible manhood entails by teaching them about admirable role models, like Lincoln, Beto, and Jesús, who personify all that is good about being a man. Therefore, we recommend that counselors employ bibliotherapy and videotherapy, using resources that portray famous and lesser known yet respectable heroes, as a means for helping boys to develop their conceptions of healthy masculinity. We also endorse recruiting adult male mentors who are everyday heroes to offer their wisdom and guidance to boys who are seeking the direction of a caring man to assist them with the transition to manhood.

In their description of the function that men play in the healthy development of boys, adolescent males, and other men, Horne et al. (1996) described the roles of five different forms of male teachers at different developmental stages of men's lives. The five teacher roles fulfill each of the categories of healthy development described throughout this chapter. For infant males and young boys, the importance of male *nurturing* is critical for the establishment of a strong sense of healthy masculinity. The nurturers, ideally, are fathers who are available to their infants to provide the often physical male interactions that complement the maternal support all children crave and need. For boys and young males, healthy male *role models* within the community are essential for helping boys learn the healthy patterns of being male, including providing various examples of male ways of being and doing that allow them to fill the roles described in this chapter. There are many role models available to boys in our culture; unfortunately, not all are positive examples, and it is essential that for healthy development, the role models provide positive options. The third level of teacher necessary for the healthy development of young males is that of *initiator*, a role generally filled by teachers who bestow upon young males a validation of their achieving manhood. Whereas some societies have formal initiation rites for young men, our culture does not have a single process that bestows adulthood upon men, and so a number of initiation procedures have been developed, including admission into male societies such as the Moose Club, but also through military, sports, and other affirming organizations. The fourth level of male teacher is that of *mentor*, a man who mentors young men into adulthood and into the ins and outs of professional and career development, but who also provides guidance on effective living and family responsibilities. The fifth level of teacher is that of the *elder*, a man whose role is to share wisdom and to transmit the cultural knowledge of generations on to younger men. Unlike the mentor, who is more focused on guiding the process of being successful in work and the community, the elder passes on the wisdom of caring for the greater good and maintaining the cultural heritage of being male. Each of these five teacher roles emphasizes healthy development and highlights the power and value of males helping other males to thrive in positive and nurturing ways for themselves, their families, and their communities (Horne et al., 1996).

CONCLUSION

So often, boys and male adolescents are discouraged by greater society. To many adults, young boys of all cultural backgrounds appear scary, violent, unpredictable, hyperactive, and intimidating. For young men of color, these perceptions can be all encompassing and devastating to the collective self-esteem (Franklin, 1999). Popular portrayals of boys in the media often depict them according to the stereotypes of being disruptive, dangerous, and violent (Katz, 1999). Something needs to change to allow young men the breathing room to feel better about who they are and who they could be. The time for recognizing and celebrating the many strengths of traditional men is long overdue. We have an obligation to teach the young men in our world about the qualities of good men and their great legacies in order to provide mentors and role models. If we do, we are likely to preserve and foster all that is good about being a man in our nation's sons as we lead them toward a bright future.

As we teach boys about the good men of this world and their admirable qualities, we must learn how to listen to our young male clients tell us *their own stories* of heroism as a stimulus for creating therapeutic change. Duncan, Miller, and Sparks (2007) noted that common factors in outcome research with children and youth highlight that change does not result from focusing on disorders or dysfunction, but from focusing more on resources, creativity, and building relational support networks. Specifically, it is the resources (e.g., faith, optimism, persistence, or membership in a supportive organization) that youth bring into the counseling setting that serve as the greatest contributor to outcome (Hubble, Duncan, & Miller, 1999). Duncan et al. (2007) used the phrase "uncommon heroism of youth" to speak to the process of recognizing that a client's strengths, and the ability to use them in his treatment, will often do more good than specific interventions.

Counselors can foster positive development in male youth by casting their clients as the primary agents of change and by listening for and being curious about the existing competencies in a boy's life. For boys, this would mean examining the stories of courage that reflect overcoming obstacles, highlighting how a boy and his friends have initiated some type of action, noting how a boy builds and receives social support from his peers and family, looking at his adaptive strengths associated with developing independence and self-reliance, and affirming how a boy has followed through on making positive changes as he works to achieve clinical goals. Because many young male clients appear in our offices already attached to some form of diagnostic label (depressed, suicidal, aggressive, antisocial, or violent) or baggage (juvenile offender, court mandated, or school dropout), counselors can respond with empathy to difficulties and concerns yet direct mindful attention toward resources, strengths, and resiliency. Most troubled boys already know how others easily and routinely minimize their potential and contributions to the greater good. As positive forces in our male clients' lives, we have to shine a different light on our clients. This means a counselor carefully listens to the whole story, "the confusion and the clarity, the suffering and the endurance, the pain and the coping, the desperation and the desire" (Duncan et al., 2007, p. 36).

REFERENCES

Andronico, M. (Ed.). (1996). *Men in groups: Insights, interventions, and psycho-educational work*. Washington, DC: American Psychological Association.

Aspinwall, L. G., & Staudinger, U. M. (2003). A psychology of human strengths: Some central issues of an emerging field. In L. G. Aspinwall & U. M. Staudinger (Eds.), *A psychology of human strengths: Fundamental questions and future directions for a positive psychology* (pp. 9–22). San Francisco: Berrett-Koehler.

Benenson, J. F., Apostoleris, N. H., & Parnass, J. (1997). Age and sex differences in dyadic and group interaction. *Developmental Psychology, 33*, 538–543.

Brooks, R., & Goldstein, S. (2001). *Raising resilient children*. Chicago: Contemporary Books.

Buhrmester, D. (1996). Need fulfillment, interpersonal competence and the developmental contexts of early adolescent friendship. In W. M. Bukowski, A. F. Newcomb, & W. W. Hartup (Eds.), *The company they keep: Friendship in childhood and adolescence* (pp. 158–185). New York: Cambridge University Press.

Cabrera, N. J., Tamis-LeMonda, C. S., Bradley, R. H., Hofferth, S., & Lamb, M. E. (2000). Fatherhood in the twenty-first century. *Child Development, 71*(1), 127–136.

Camarena, P. M., Sarigiani, P. A., & Petersen, A. C. (1990). Gender-specific pathways to intimacy in early adolescence. *Journal of Youth and Adolescence, 19*, 19–32.

Cancian, F. M. (1987). *Love in America: Gender and self-development*. Cambridge: Cambridge University Press.

Carlson, J. D., & Englar-Carlson, M. (2008). Adlerian therapy. In J. Frew & M. Spiegler (Eds.), *Contemporary psychotherapies for a diverse world* (pp. 93–140). Boston: Lahaska Press.

Clinchy, B., & Zimmerman, C. (1985). *Growing up intellectually: Issues for college women*. (Work In Progress, No. 19). Wellesley, MA: Wellesley College, Stone Center for Developmental Services and Studies.

Courtenay, W. H. (2001). Counseling men in medical settings: The six-point HEALTH plan. In G. R. Brooks & G. E. Good, (Eds.), *The new handbook of psychotherapy and counseling with men: A comprehensive guide to settings, problems, and treatment approaches*. Volume I (pp. 59–91). San Francisco: Jossey-Bass.

Dollahite, D. C., & Hawkins, A. J. (1998). A conceptual ethic of generative fathering. *Journal of Men's Studies, 7*, 109–132.

Duncan, B. L., Miller, S. D., & Sparks, J. (2007). Common factors and the uncommon heroism of youth. *Psychotherapy in Australia, 13*, 34–43.

Franklin, A. J. (1999). Invisibility syndrome and racial identity development in psychotherapy and counseling African American men. *The Counseling Psychologist, 27,* 761–793.

Goodwin, D. K. (2005). *Team of rivals: The political genius of Abraham Lincoln.* New York: Simon & Schuster.

Grant, S., Hiton, H., & Mortola, P. (2008). *BAM! Boys advocacy and mentoring: A guidebook for leading preventive boys groups.* New York: Routledge.

Hawkins, A. J., & Dollahite, D. C. (Eds.). (1996). *Generative fathering: Beyond deficit perspectives.* Thousand Oaks, CA: Sage.

Heppner, M. J., & Heppner, P. P. (2001). Addressing the implications of male socialization for career counseling. In G. R. Brooks & G. E. Good (Eds.), *The new handbook of psychotherapy and counseling with men* (pp. 369–386). San Francisco: Jossey-Bass.

Hernandez, R. (2002). *Fatherwork in the crossfire: Chicano teen fathers struggling to take care of business* (Report No. JSRI-WP-58). East Lansing: Michigan State University, Julian Samora Research Institute. (ERIC Document Reproduction Services No. ED 471 926)

Horne, A., Jolliff, D., & Roth, E. (1996). Men mentoring men in groups. In M. Andronico (Ed.), *Men in groups: Insights, interventions, and psycho-educational work* (pp. 97–112). Washington, DC: American Psychological Association.

Hubble, M., Duncan, B., & Miller, S. (1999). *The heart and soul of change: What works in therapy.* Washington, DC: APA Press.

International Association of Lions Clubs. (2006). *Lions Clubs International history.* Retrieved July 20, 2006, from http://www.lionsclubs.org/EN/content/lions_history.shtml

Katz, J. (1999). *Tough guise: Violence, media, and the crisis of masculinity.* Boston: Media Education Foundation.

Kiselica, M. S. (1995). *Multicultural counseling with teenage fathers: A practical guide.* Newbury Park, CA: Sage.

Kiselica, M. S. (1996). Parenting skills training with teenage fathers. In M. P. Andronico (Ed.), *Men in groups: Insights, interventions, and psychoeducational work* (pp. 283–300). Washington, DC: American Psychological Association.

Kiselica, M. S. (1999). Counseling teen fathers. In A. M. Horne & M. S. Kiselica (Eds.), *Handbook of counseling boys and adolescent males: A practitioner's guide* (pp. 179–198). Thousand Oaks, CA: Sage.

Kiselica, M. S. (2001). A male-friendly therapeutic process with school-age boys. In G. R. Brooks and G. Good (Eds.), *The handbook of counseling and psychotherapy with men: A guide to settings and approaches* (Vol. 1, pp. 43–58). San Francisco: Jossey-Bass.

Kiselica, M. S. (2003a, Autumn). Male-sensitive counseling with boys. *Counselling in Education,* 16–19.

Kiselica, M. S. (2003b). Transforming psychotherapy in order to succeed with boys: Male-friendly practices. *Journal of Clinical Psychology: In Session, 59,* 1225–1236.

Kiselica, M. S. (2006a). Helping a boy becomes a parent: Male-sensitive psychotherapy with a teenage father. In M. Englar-Carlson & M. Stevens (Eds.), *In the room with men: A casebook of therapeutic change* (pp. 225–240). Washington, DC: American Psychological Association.

Kiselica, M. S. (2006b, August). Contributions and limitations of the deficit model of men. In M. S. Kiselica (Chair), *Toward a positive psychology of boys, men, and masculinity.* Symposium presented at the annual convention of the American Psychological Association, New Orleans, LA.

Kiselica, M. S., Englar-Carlson, M., & Fisher, M. (2006, August). A positive psychology framework for building upon male strengths. In M. S. Kiselica (Chair), *Toward a positive psychology of boys, men, and masculinity.* Symposium presented at the annual convention of the American Psychological Association, New Orleans, LA.

Kiselica, M. S., & O'Brien, S. (2001, August). Are attachment disorders and alexithymia characteristic of males? In M. S. Kiselica (Chair), *Are males really emotional mummies? What do the data indicate?* Symposium conducted at the annual convention of the American Psychological Association, San Francisco.

Kiselica, M. S., Rotzien, A., & Doms, J. (1994). Preparing teenage fathers for parenthood: A group psychoeducational approach. *Journal for Specialists in Group Work, 19,* 83–94.

Kiselica, M. S., Stroud, J., Stroud, J., & Rotzien, A. (1992). Counseling the forgotten client: The teenage father. *Journal of Mental Health Counseling, 14,* 338–350.

Kramer, S. (Producer), & Weaver, W. (Presenter). (2007, April 13). *The measure of a man and his father* [Podcast radio program]. Washington, DC: National Public Radio. Retrieved April 13, 2007, from http://www.npr.org/templates/story/story.php?storyId=9546699

Lamb, M. E. (Ed.). (2003). *The father's role in child development* (4th ed.). New York: Wiley.

Levant, R. F. (1995). Toward the reconstruction of masculinity. In R. F. Levant & W. S. Pollack (Eds.), *A new psychology of men* (pp. 229–251). New York: Basic Books.

McNelles, L., & Connolly, J. (1999). Intimacy between adolescent friends: Age and gender differences in intimate affect and intimate behaviors. *Journal of Research on Adolescence, 9*(2), 143–159.

Moose International. (2004). *Moose: The family fraternity.* Retrieved July 20, 2006, from http://www.mooseheart.org/default.aspx

Mortola, P., Hiton, H., & Grant, S. (2008). *BAM! Boys advocacy and mentoring: A leader's guide to facilitating strength-based groups for boys.* New York: Routledge.

O'Neil, J. (2006). Helping Jack heal his emotional wounds: The gender role conflict diagnostic schema. In M. Englar-Carlson & M. S. Stevens (Eds.), *In the room with men: A casebook of therapeutic change* (pp. 259–284). Washington, DC: American Psychological Association.

Rohner, R. P., & Veneziano, R. A. (2001). The importance of father love: History and contemporary evidence. *Review of General Psychology, 5*(4), 382–405.

Seligman, M., & Csikszentmihalyi, M. (2000). Positive psychology: An introduction. *American Psychologist, 55*(1), 5–14.

Seligman, M., Rashid, T., & Parks, A. (2006). Positive psychotherapy. *American Psychologist, 61*(8), 774–788.

Skovholt, T. (1990). Career themes in counseling and psychotherapy with men. In D. Moore & F. Leafgren (Eds.), *Men in conflict* (pp. 39–53). Alexandria, VA: American Association for Counseling and Development.

Snyder, C. R., & Lopez, S. J. (2007). *Positive psychology: The science and practical explorations of human strengths.* Thousand Oaks, CA: Sage.

Surrey, J. L. (1985). *Self-in-relation: A theory of women's development.* [Work in progress, (13)]. Wellesley, MA: Wellesley college, store center for developmental services and studies.

Swain, S. (1989). Covert intimacy: Closeness in men's friendships. In B. J. Risman & P. Schwartz (Eds.), *Gender in intimate relationships: A microstructural approach* (pp. 71–86). Belmont, CA: Wadsworth.

Wester, S. R., Vogel, D. L., Pressly, P. K., & Heesacker, M. (2002). Sex differences in emotion: A critical review of the literature and implications for counseling psychology. *The Counseling Psychologist, 30,* 629–651.

Wolin, S. J., & Wolin, S. (1993). *The resilient self.* New York: Villard.

Youniss, J., & Yates, M. (1997). *Community, service, and social responsibility in youth.* Chicago: University of Chicago Press.

3

Establishing Rapport with Boys in Individual Counseling and Psychotherapy
A Male-Friendly Perspective

MARK S. KISELICA AND MATT ENGLAR-CARLSON

Getting boys to open up during counseling and psychotherapy can be a tough challenge for mental health professionals. Many boys are just not well suited for a traditional psychotherapy environment, and they can drive dedicated practitioners who work in these environments crazy. For example, during an initial session, a counselor may probe a troubled boy with caring open invitations to talk, such as "Tell me what happened," or with open-ended questions, such as "How did that make you feel?" to which the youngster might respond with a shrug of his shoulders and the familiar and maddening reply "I don't know." After a series of these interchanges, the counselor may get frustrated and conclude that the young man is resistant, uninterested in getting help, or flawed in fundamentally important ways, and the boy may shut down and decide that counseling is nonsense and a waste of his time. But what's really going on? Is counseling a futile effort with boys who respond in this manner? Are these boys truly averse to being helped? What can be done to get through to them?

THE MISMATCH BETWEEN THE TRADITIONAL COUNSELING ENVIRONMENT AND THE RELATIONAL STYLES OF BOYS

There is a fundamental mismatch between the way counseling and psychotherapy tend to be conducted and the relational styles of most boys, and this mismatch plays a major role in the failure of many professionals to establish rapport with boys. Nearly 30 years ago, Monroe Bruch (1978) observed that the counseling environment is a great fit for certain types of individuals but not others. Utilizing Holland's (1973) personality theory, Bruch argued that counseling and psycho-therapy are tailor-made for people who have a "social" personality type. Social types thrive in situations that provide them with the opportunity to engage others in an emotionally intimate and engaging manner. They are comfortable and skilled at talking about their feelings, and they enjoy self-reflection. Because the process of counseling and psychotherapy as it is traditionally practiced involves these types of interactions, people who are social personality types can step into the world of therapy, feel right at home, and dive into the work of exploring their concerns. However, many other individuals who have different personality types feel out of place in the traditional counseling environment. For exam-ple, individuals with a "conventional" or a "realistic" personality prefer activities that involve the manipulation and organization of data and objects, and they tend to avoid the type of less structured, interper-sonal, and exploratory activities that are employed by many counselors. So, these individuals are likely to feel ill at ease with counseling as it is customarily practiced.

Many boys and men, especially males who adhere to traditional notions of masculinity, are also out of place in the world of conventional psychotherapy. From an early age, boys tend to lag behind girls in their early brain development in ways that make it slightly more difficult for boys to acquire language, which places many boys—especially those who develop reading and language skills at a later age—at a disadvantage when it comes to being able to label things, including emotions (Gurian, 1997). Some boys are also exposed to a socialization process that discourages them from being in touch with their vulnerable emotions (Levant et al., 2006). In addition, boys tend to develop friendships through the sharing of instrumental activities with other boys, such as enjoying rough-and-tumble games, participating in sports, playing video and computer games, going fishing, hanging out, and working on projects that involve manual labor (Clinchy & Zimmerman, 1985; Kiselica, 1995, 1999, 2003a, 2003b, 2006). As a result of these varied experiences, many boys tend to be "doers" rather than highly expressive "feelers," even though they are capable of forming deep, secure bonds, and experiencing very powerful emotions, including joy, sorrow, happiness, and anger (Heesacker et al., 1999; Kiselica & O'Brien, 2001).

So, a boy who is not a social personality type or who has been socialized to have an action orientation to life may feel uncomfortable in the typical counseling climate. He is likely to have difficulty responding in a manner that the counselor prefers, which could lead to problems in forming a therapeutic bond with the counselor who misinterprets the boy's behavior as a sign of resistance, rather than recognizing that the problem is due to a lack of fit between the client and the counseling environment (Kiselica, 2003a, 2003b, 2006; Kiselica & Horne, 1999). Further, for years multicultural scholars (Parham, White, & Ajamu, 1999; Sue & Sue, 2003) have identified how both the theories of psychotherapy and the actual practice of contemporary counseling arise from a Western European context. Thus, the worldview of racial-ethnic minority groups in the United States may not be honored or clearly respected in the counseling setting. Therefore, many non-Caucasian boys and male adolescents find counseling settings to be a poor fit—one that does not seem to adapt to the fact that they are boys or to the fact that their own cultural identity and heritage are not Western European. This problem is analogous to a clothing manufacturer who insists on selling only a one-size-fits-all glove, which would actually provide a good fit for only a small percentage of customers (Kiselica, 2003b). Just as insisting on the continued sale of the single-size glove is a formula for a product that will fail in the marketplace, the rigid adherence to traditional notions of counseling and psychotherapy is a recipe for failure with boys in counseling. Male-friendly adjustments in the helping process must be made in order to correct for this mismatch between conventional counseling practices and the relational styles of boys.

MALE-FRIENDLY COUNSELING WITH BOYS

In this chapter, we describe a number of transformations in the process of counseling and psychotherapy that reflect a male-friendly perspective on engaging boys. By *male friendly*, we mean tapping into the natural ways boys relate to the world and employing a wide range of strategies and activities that appeal to male youth and have been shown through research to facilitate the establishment and maintenance of rapport with young boys and adolescent males.

Many of the rapport-building strategies described in this chapter are drawn from numerous studies that have identified effective outreach with teenage fathers (Achatz & MacAllum, 1994; Barth, Claycomb, & Loomis, 1988; Brindis, Barth, & Loomis, 1987; Brown, 1990; Hendricks, 1988; Hernandez, 2002; Huey, 1987; Klinman & Sander, 1985; Kost, 1997; Lesser et al., 2005; Mazza, 2002; Sander & Rosen, 1987; Smith, 1988). Because these investigations involved hundreds of culturally diverse teenage boys and young adult men from both rural and urban areas of the United States, their findings have strong external validity for therapeutic work with boys in general. The results of this research are useful because they have been demonstrated repeatedly across time through research that has spanned the 1980s through the 2000s. We chose the research literature on adolescent fathers because this population historically has been neglected and misunderstood by mental health practitioners, and because young fathers were once very difficult to engage in social service, psychoeducational, and mental health programs. The lessons learned from successful work with teen fathers are instructive for all professionals who want to work more effectively with boys, especially young men who are hard to reach through traditional counseling practices.

Do Boys and Adolescents Want to Come to Counseling?

This may seem like an odd question to pose, because most adults would not choose to come to a counselor. In fact, a well-established line of empirical research on men and help seeking for mental health concerns indicates that some men are generally disinclined to seek mental health services and actually seek mental health services at rates much lower than women (see Addis & Mahalik, 2003). Men with more traditional conceptions of masculinity also hold more negative attitudes toward their use of both mental health (Addis & Mahalik; Good & Wood, 1995; Robertson & Fitzgerald, 1992) and career-related services (Rochlen & O'Brien, 2002), and have lower perceptions of treatment helpfulness (Cusack, Deane, Wilson, & Ciarrochi, 2006). The picture for boys and male adolescents is not as clear. I (MEC) remember being a school counselor in a K–8 school and recording the help-seeking patterns of my students. Boys represented a majority of my clients and referrals (about 80%), yet most of these boys were not self-referred—most came to me via their classroom teacher, their parents, and the assistant principal. These boys were not exactly resistant to seeing me; it was more that given the choice, most of the boys would have initially opted out of seeing the school counselor. Though girls represented a much smaller amount of my caseload and referrals, I found it fascinating that most of my female clients either were self-referred or came to see me willingly. To them, it seemed like seeing the counselor was a natural or even fun way to solve problems, whereas for the boys it appeared to be more forced.

Yet, how do boys and adolescents envision the utility of counseling? Interestingly, Smith (2004) investigated the views of adolescent males on the use of mental health services and found that even though most of the adolescents associated mental health counseling with mental illness and pathology, the majority (69%) of the participants indicated willingness to seek future mental health assistance with life's concerns. That is a surprising but hopeful finding indicating that adolescent males can see the potential benefit of getting some assistance for their concerns. Additionally, the male adolescents indicated a preference for action-oriented services and valued the idea that a counselor would be a good listener who ensured confidentiality and was a trustworthy person. These findings present a blueprint of how to work with adolescent males.

It is worth considering how boys and adolescents find their way to the offices of mental health professionals. Equally interesting is the question of why boys and adolescents do not find ways to seek help for their concerns. To address the former question, unfortunately many boys and adolescents do not have much of a choice whether to be in counseling, as many of the significant adults in their lives (parents, guardians, school personnel, and legal authorities) have made this choice on behalf of the boy. Thus, at first, counseling can have a "mandated" feel to it, and boys can see themselves as being forced into the counselor's office. In some cases, this is compounded when boys are not even sure why they are seeing a counselor. So it is not surprising to experience some boys as resistant or uncooperative about being in counseling. On the other hand, many boys know exactly what has contributed to their visit to the counselor, and it has to do with various forms of "being in trouble." Building upon the findings of Smith (2004) from above, in both situations the immediate task for the counselor is to work on conveying good listening and trustworthiness to boys. Addressing resistance is not like flicking on a light switch; in many ways, it is akin to slowly using a dimmer to brighten a room. Engaging boys in counseling is the process of conveying an awareness of the situation from both sides, and then starting the process of brightening, or even enlightening, the boy about how counseling can assist in addressing his own concerns.

The latter question from the previous paragraph of why it is difficult for boys to seek help is one that Pollack (1998) theorized is grounded in male socialization and development. He noted that one of the four imperatives of the Boy Code is to be stoic, stable, and independent, and to essentially never show weakness. This particular code may deter boys from seeking assistance from mental health professionals. Other multicultural scholars have noted how this theme of being self-reliant and the importance of displaying a "strong" image cut cross-culturally for many boys. Arcaya (1999) wrote about the pressures Hispanic American boys and adolescents face to cultivate a strong public image of fulfilling the expectation of manhood as a way to protect one's personal and family reputation. This can be viewed when boys are encouraged to show less dependence on others in the effort to "be a man" as quickly as possible. Drawing attention to oneself and showing vulnerability or helplessness, which is often equated with mental health help seeking, would be discouraged. In that sense, Hispanic boys and adolescents may minimize difficulties or concerns as a way to keep these concerns private. Asian American boys and adolescents may experience pressures around traditional male Asian cultural expectations (avoidance of shame, emotional self-control, family recognition through achievement, and humility; Kim Atkinson, & Umemoto, 2001; Kim, Atkinson, & Yang, 1999) that influence their ability to seek and be open to counseling. Finally, Majors and Billson (1992) used their book *Cool Pose* to illustrate a ritualized form of adolescent African American masculinity encouraging youth to project the notion "that everything is cool," regardless of the situation or life circumstance. Any internal or external difficulties are then buried within a young male's psyche in order to keep the outside image of being OK.

Perhaps the most fundamental lesson from the research on teen fathers was the surprising finding that young men want help with their concerns from professional helpers. However, many of these youth are turned off by youth programs that are out of touch with the needs and psyches of boys. By comparison, effective programs have counselors who utilize numerous male-friendly strategies that foster male engagement. An overview of these strategies follows in the sections below.

Provide Counseling Services in Informal Settings

One of the common shortcomings of many services targeting boys is that they are typically offered in an office-type setting, whether in a school, agency, or private practice. Within all of these settings, it is common practice for the counselor to meet with a young man in his or her office with the door closed and the counselor and client seated face-to-face. The two remain seated while the boy is expected to spill his guts about very personal matters. Many boys who are placed in this situation feel like aliens in a strange and foreign land. The problem with this arrangement is that it is too formal and contrary to the natural way that boys are accustomed to forming intimate relationships. For example, boys typically do not sit down and jump into dramatic, heart-to-heart conversations with other boys as the starting point for forming a friendship. Instead, they tend to play some sort of game or engage in some other activity during which they talk about their interests and experiences. Over the course of time, boys form deep bonds by sharing in this manner, building friendships with other boys that are characterized by closeness, loyalty, and fun. So, for many boys, sitting still in a chair and talking to an unfamiliar adult about very private concerns in an office is an unnatural undertaking, and they are likely to experience difficulty opening up to counselors who conduct their practice in this manner, even when they want help with their problems.

Fortunately, there are several simple solutions to this problem, the first of which is to conduct initial counseling sessions in informal settings. For example, the counselor can hold the first few sessions in a gym or playground, taking turns shooting baskets with a boy while the two talk about the youngster's interests. Alternatively, they can go outside and pass a football or baseball back and forth, or just go for a walk while chatting together. Many boys find it easier to talk while eating or playing a video game or checkers. Some effective counselors have even helped boys to explore their concerns while fishing or working on a car engine together.

One of the hurdles in operating in a more flexible manner is for counselors to overcome their own clinical training, biases, and ideas of what signifies an appropriate setting for therapeutic work. A guiding question when stepping out of the counseling "box" is to ask yourself how the counseling relationship is being built and developed by operating in a more informal manner. In essence, counselors can give themselves permission to drop some of the professional pretense and mythology around the traditional counseling setting and create a more tailored setting for their young male clients.

Use Flexible Schedules and Drop-In Times

Our system of mental health delivery is dictated by the tradition of the so-called 50-minute hour—50 minutes of psychotherapy, followed by 10 minutes of recording progress notes about what just happened during a session. This is a very odd and artificial concept considering that the needs of clients and the time required to address those needs vary greatly from client to client. Some boys need their initial sessions to be very brief. They may want to merely stop in for a quick visit to check out a counselor to determine if the person is trustworthy before they can commit to longer visits. Other boys may prefer short sessions because they benefit best from a psychoeducational approach to counseling through which they briefly describe their concern to the counselor, acquire some useful reading or video from the counselor that can educate them about their problem, and then head home to absorb and reflect on the information conveyed in the psychoeducational materials. Other boys, especially those who are in an acute crisis, may need the benefit of an unrushed period of time, characterized by some action-oriented, rapport-building activity, followed by an in-depth exploration and discussion of some issue.

In light of these varied needs, it behooves counselors and psychotherapists to be flexible with their appointment schedules with boys. Appointments with boys should be provided at times that are convenient for them (Hendricks, 1988), and the length of time for sessions should be determined by a young man's needs (Kiselica, 2003b). Professionals must remember that some boys, particularly those from disorganized and emotionally disengaged families, tend to be poor time managers who have difficulty keeping appointments that are scheduled for set times. For these boys, providing drop-in periods is recommended (Kiselica, 2003b).

Help Boys and Their Families With Their Practical Needs

Another reason counselors must be prepared to work in informal settings and use flexible time schedules is that many of the boys referred for counseling need assistance with practical concerns that are significant for them and their families and that may demand the counselor to step out of the office for extended periods of time in order to be truly helpful. Unless these concerns are addressed, they could get in the way of a boy being able to avail himself of counseling either because they impede his family from taking him for sessions or because they distract the boy from focusing on his referral issues. For example, Hendricks (1988) reported that many case managers earned the confidence of teenage boys by helping them with practical matters, such as getting a driver's license or a job, which were crucial to the young men. Hernandez (2002) went to great lengths to earn and maintain the trust and respect of several of his clients and their families. For example, he accompanied one young man on a trip to visit his older brother in prison. He assisted another youth by repairing a broken water heater at the home of the boy's mother. In both cases, the young men saw these substantial investments of time and assistance as signs that Hernandez was sincere and concerned about their well-being, which led to their sharing the most intimate details of their lives with him.

Sometimes a boy's own practical need may not necessarily seem at first like a counseling goal, but counselors can be strategic in how they pursue the goals of counseling. I (MEC) can remember working with Jacob, an 11-year-old boy who was referred to me for having an "attitude" at home, for social isolation, and because he was being ignored by his peers and teased at school. After a quick assessment, it became clear that his self-esteem was not necessarily low; in fact, he felt OK about himself (he liked being different and did not want to be like the other kids) in terms of being a student and was not too upset about not having friends. What really bothered him was that he was considered "terrible at sports." Jacob considered himself a sports fanatic. What Jacob really wanted to do with his counseling time was talk about basketball and how to make layups so that he could contribute if and when he played basketball at recess and in gym class. I took this opportunity to teach Jacob how to play basketball, and we spent most of our early sessions under a basketball hoop. I taught him about legendary basketball coach John Wooden and his pyramid of success (http://www.coachwooden. com; Wooden, n.d.) as a way to develop a path for improvement and to develop focus. While shooting and talking, Jacob was calm and revealing about his inner world and his relationships with his peers. It seemed helpful for him to vent a little and also for me to know that Jacob did not considered himself as "less than," which was the way he felt his parents and teacher viewed his self-image. Jacob practiced layups on his own and showed me his progress. Over time his shooting improved, and not surprisingly, his parents noticed a change in his attitude and Jacob began to gain some positive attention from his peers.

Assure the Boy That You Will Not "Play Games With His Head"

Many boys who have a history of prior contacts with mental health professionals are concerned that every word they say will be analyzed and could be used against them somehow. This is especially true for boys who have run into trouble with the school officials or the criminal justice system. These boys tend to fear that "shrinks" will "mess with their heads." Consequently, a boy who expresses this concern needs reassurance that the counselor has no intention of playing mind games with him. In a case study involving a 16-year-old boy who was leery of psychologists due to some prior bad experiences with several therapists, I (MK) described the approach I used to allay the young man's fears about counseling:

> I explained to him that I had helped a lot of guys who were in his situation and that I was not the kind of shrink who would play games with his head. I promised him that I would tell him what I was thinking at all times so that he wouldn't have to worry about me playing any mind games with him. I assured him that all I wanted to do was to get to know him, and if he then felt I was OK, we could take it from there. (Kiselica, 2006, p. 230)

In response to these reassuring words and a number of other male-friendly responses, the teen was able to tell me about his role in an out-of-wedlock pregnancy, his feelings about being an adolescent father, and the issues he had with the mother of his child, her parents, and his own mother and father.

Develop an Understanding of the Young Man's Culture

The problems that boys experience occur within a unique cultural context that can influence how a boy views his problems and how he attempts to handle those difficulties. For example, boys who become fathers during their teenage years face a number of serious challenges, such as preparing for parenthood, negotiating changes with the immediate and extended family, and sorting out educational and career plans. These universal challenges are played out in a cultural context that promotes a culture-specific perspective about the world. For example, there is still a strong social stigma among White, non-Hispanic Americans toward adolescent, premarital childbearing, which helps to explain why White families have tended to resolve unexpected pregnancies by forcing the young couple to marry. African American families commonly have a historical mistrust of the social service and mental health systems due to the effects of institutional racism, which deters many Black teen fathers from seeking the assistance of a professional counselor, social worker, or psychologist. Hispanic teen fathers raised in a household adhering to traditional gender roles are likely to experience vexing values conflicts if their partners have been socialized to embrace the androgynous gender roles that have become more commonplace in mainstream society (Kiselica, 1995). Culture is also a major determinant in how a boy views his masculinity and a man's role in the world.

Recognizing the powerful influence of culture, it is imperative that mental health professionals educate themselves about the cultural backgrounds of the boys they counsel. Counselors must be willing to ask a boy to explain his cultural values and traditions and how those shape his identify, beliefs, and behavior. The counselor must also be ready to address any issues related to race and discrimination that might be on the mind of a boy who has experienced prejudice or racism. The willingness of a counselor to discuss these sensitive yet salient issues can go a long way to cementing trust with the youngster.

Model Self-Disclosure

Modeling self-disclosure is another practice that can strengthen the relationship between counselors and boys who have difficulty revealing personal matters. A boy who is scared or unsure about how much he should reveal about himself can find it easier to talk about his experiences when the counselor models self-disclosure for him. For example, I (MK) routinely show pictures of my family members to my young male clients, and I also tell them a little bit about where I was raised and where I now live. I have found that these disclosures help many boys to tell me about the important people in their lives and their relations with those people (Kiselica, 2003a, 2003b).

Hernandez (2002) also found that self-disclosure promoted bonding and sharing with his clients. During sessions, he "traded anecdotes and stories about barrio life that sometimes turned nostalgic" (Hernandez, 2002, p. 14). During these conversations, young men would tell Hernandez about their love for their family members and stories about substance abuse, drug trafficking, family violence, teenage parenthood, school difficulties, unemployment, and father absence. The Latino concept of *personalismo* (Paniagua, 2005), in which young male clients become more oriented toward people and warmth, seems to apply here. Many boys want to be treated as people first, and not problems to be dealt with or fixed. When a counselor shares something about whom he or she is, it can go a long way toward showing a client that he is important. Further, it can model openness and appropriate self-disclosure.

Use Timely Doses of Good-Natured Humor

Many boys and men use humor as a vehicle to attain intimacy (Kiselica, 2003b) and to reduce tension and manage conflicts (Kiselica, 2001). They appreciate people who can loosen things up with a joke (Kiselica, 2001), and they express affection through good-natured ribbing (Kiselica, Englar-Carlson, & Fisher, 2006). For example, while lifting weights together, two boys exchanged humorous accounts of the problems they were having with their respective parents, using lighthearted jibes to keep each other at ease as they told their painful stories. Consequently, counselors must be able to recognize when boys are using humor as an entrée to discussing serious topics, and they must be willing to employ some well-timed humor with boys to help facilitate client self-disclosure.

Create a Welcoming Space for Boys

All counselors have personal preferences and ideas about what an appropriate healing space looks like. Writing on understanding the practice of psychotherapy, Jerome Frank (1982) noted the importance of a healing setting to address a client's emotional and behavioral concerns. The contemporary healing setting for counselors often includes the traditional diplomas on the wall or particular décor such as two chairs, soft lighting, and pastoral or projective artwork. The central question when working with boys is whether your counseling space welcomes boys into the room. As many young male clients feel awkward or out of place coming to counseling, it is not surprising that boys would look for familiar items or images as a grounding point to gain a feeling of welcoming and a sense of comfort and control. If you are meeting the client in your office, one way to begin this process before the session is to ensure there are magazines displayed in the waiting area that teenage boys can identify with, especially sports publications. Sweet (2006) added the need to reflect on how male clients are greeted and welcomed into the office. Is this done with a smile and a handshake, or something that is a bit more standoffish? Other ways to create a boy-focused counseling space is to have small tactile balls (e.g., Koosh Balls and Nerf Balls) and small items for boys to hold during the session. Rather than being a distraction, these items can allow boys to work on some nervous energy, can keep their hands occupied during the session, or can be tossed back and forth as the client talks with you about his concerns. Consider what a boy will see when he enters your room. Will he see things that are familiar and interesting to him? I (MK) tend to have compact discs lying around, sports- and activity-based posters, a few musical instruments (guitar and small drums), and sport memorabilia (some trading cards, signed baseballs, basketballs, and footballs) in plain view as a way to create conversations about interests. Counselors may also want to have media-playing devices (e.g., DVD/VCR, CD player, and computer) available so boys can bring in and share or show the counselor what they are interested in listening to and seeing.

Other Rapport-Building Tactics

Many other tactics (see Hendricks, 1988; Kiselica, 2003b) can foster trust and promote self-disclosure with boys in counseling and psychotherapy, including the following:

- Have all calls held during the interview to show the boy that he is important during his time with you.
- Sit side by side, rather than face-to-face, in order to reduce suspiciousness and self-consciousness.

- Help the boy to relax by offering a soft drink or snack prior to the start of the session or by discussing his interests or events in the community.
- If you are wearing a long-sleeve shirt, roll up your shirtsleeves to convey to the youth your readiness to work with him.
- Be knowledgeable about the slang he may use. However, if the boy uses slang expressions you do not understand, ask him to explain the expressions to you, rather than pretend you understand him.
- Avoid using open-ended questions, such as "How are you feeling?" because they tend to be ineffective with this population. Instead, conduct content-specific discussions centered on helping the client with his most pressing concern.
- Take it slow, follow the boy's lead, and carefully monitor the client's cues regarding his comfort level with topics.
- Be prepared to do a lot of listening, and avoid asking too many questions so as to avoid being too intrusive.
- Be empathic, available, and honest.
- Explore with the boy his expectations about psychotherapy, and clear up any misconceptions he might have about you and your role.
- Respect the young man's autonomy by scheduling appointments with him, rather than through his parents, and by giving him your business card.
- Focus on concerns that are foremost on the young man's mind, and then bridge to any other topics that must be addressed, including issues that parents, school officials, or other authority figures might have with the boy.
- Keep initial interview sessions brief (a maximum of 45 minutes) unless he shows a keen interest in extending the session.

When Possible, Work With Boys in Groups

Although some boys are introverted and prefer to do things alone, many other boys enjoy spending their time with other boys in groups. Playing on athletic teams, being a member of a scout troop, and running with a gang are common experiences through which boys learn how to cooperate, relate, and bond with each other. Therefore, tapping into the group orientation of boys can be an effective way to entice many boys to enter and remain in counseling. For example, one veteran counselor reported that she successfully recruits boys for counseling by regularly forming "guys' groups" in her school over lunch periods during which the participants hang out, eat, play games, and talk together. According to Hedges-Goett and Tannenbaum (2001), significant behavioral and relational improvements can be made when adolescent boys participate in interpersonal group therapy that includes the teaching of social skills. Because many of the problems adolescent boys face are related to deficits in their acquisition of social skills, therapeutic groups can provide a safe environment for learning, testing, and refining new behaviors and coping skills.

Other professionals have run very successful holistic group programs for boys that involve weaving therapeutic services into recreational programs for boys. For instance, I and two of my colleagues (Kiselica, Rotzien, & Doms, 1994; see also Kiselica, 1996) developed after-school programs for expectant teenage fathers in which the participants introduce themselves and then play basketball for approximately a half hour. Afterwards, while having a drink or a snack, the boys watch and react to educational videos that are designed to help them clarify their attitudes about fatherhood and to express their feelings about becoming a parent. Other sessions are focused on teaching the participants important life skills, such as child care and financial and time management skills. This approach taps the instrumental, group-oriented relational style of traditional boys, while capitalizing on the support of a therapeutic group. Another type of group therapy for boys is called *boys advocacy and mentoring* (Mortola, Hiton, & Grant, 2008). This program for adolescent boys uses physical challenges and strategic storytelling to help boys connect and develop stronger relational skills.

A group approach also is an efficient means of helping because it allows practitioners to reach large numbers of boys at one time. Group therapy with boys may be particularly necessary in school settings, where there is, on average, only one counselor for every 513 students in our nation's elementary and secondary schools (Barstow, Urbaniak, & Holland, 1999).

Working With Boys and Emotionality

In order to explore the process of facilitating emotional expression in boys, one must first look at boys' emotional development. Pollack (1998) theorized that boys lose their emotional voices in early childhood. In addition, Pollack questioned the early societal push for little boys to become little men in which the expression of emotions and language usage to express emotions are often discouraged. Shepard (2005) also expressed concern regarding boys and their emotional development, conjecturing that anger is the one feeling that is acceptable for boys to express. He indicated that boys might be excused from their angry behavior on the basis of the "Boys will be boys" theory. Shepard pointed out that this type of socialization leads to boys being more comfortable with their aggressive side, and all other emotions that they experience are funneled through anger. Mercurio (2003) suggested that the media are another important societal influence on emotional expression in boys. She reported that men typically do not show fear, sadness, or empathy in the media. The only emotion that is normally shown is anger. Other research (Chaplin, Cole, & Zahn-Waxler, 2005) indicates that girls express more submissive emotions, including sadness and anxiety, than boys. Parents, particularly fathers, often responded to these emotions in gender-differentiated ways.

Although there appears to be pressure on boys to constrict their emotional expression, it must be emphasized that there is extensive empirical research demonstrating that boys and men are more like, rather than different from, girls and women in their emotional makeup. In a very careful critique of the research literature on gender difference in emotion, Wester, Vogel, Pressly, and Heesacker (2002) documented that there are major similarities between the sexes in their emotions. On the whole, both and boys and men and girls and women tend to be capable of recognizing and expressing a wide range of emotions. However, boys and men are more likely to be influenced by social contexts when it comes to emotional expression. Thus, a challenge for counselors is to understand the contexts that are conducive to emotional expression in boys and to replicate those contexts in counseling and psychotherapy (Kiselica, 2003b).

In a prior publication (Kiselica, 2003b), I (MK) proposed that it is vital to be aware of the fact that boys express their emotions differently than girls. Therefore, it is essential to adjust counseling methods so that they will be effective with adolescent boys. I suggested engaging boys through activities that match male relational styles, such as engaging boys in rough-and-tumble games, playing video and computer games, fishing, hanging out, and working on projects that involve manual labor. Within the contexts of these activities, boys will often open up about their feelings. An alternative way to help boys explore their emotional world is the use of artistic expression in therapy. These approaches include music therapy, art therapy, and drama therapy. Currie (2004) suggested that adolescent boys will show significant improvements relationally as well as behaviorally when they are taught to express their anger through the use of percussion instruments. Haen and Brannon (2002) indicated that using drama therapy helped boys to express their feelings and emotions in a nonthreatening manner. Boys may also find the use of drawing, cartooning, and storytelling as a way to express parts of their emotional world.

CONCLUSION

In this chapter, we have argued that the challenge of getting boys to open up in counseling and psychotherapy can best be achieved when mental health professionals adapt their methods to suit the relational style of boys. The research cited in our review has demonstrated that there are numerous "tried-and-true" tactics that can be used to create a male-friendly counseling environment with young men. We invite practitioners to use these strategies so that they can discover the joy and fulfillment of helping boys to reach their fullest potential.

REFERENCES

Achatz, M., & MacAllum, C. A. (1994). *Young unwed fathers: Report from the field.* Philadelphia: Public/Private Ventures.

Addis, M. E., & Mahalik, J. R. (2003). Men, masculinity, and the contexts of help seeking. *American Psychologist, 58,* 5–14.

Arcaya, J. (1999). Hispanic American boys and adolescent males. In A. M. Horne & M. S. Kiselica (Eds.), *Handbook of counseling boys and adolescent males: A practitioner's guide* (pp. 101–116). Thousand Oaks, CA: Sage.

Barstow, S., Urbaniak, J., & Holland, H. Z. (1999, June). Washington update: "100,000 new counselors" voted in. *Counseling Today, 1,* 10–11.

Barth, R. P., Claycomb, M., & Loomis, A. (1988). Services to adolescent fathers. *Health and Social Work, 13,* 277–287.

Bruch, M. A. (1978). Holland's typology applied to client-counselor interaction: Implications for counseling men. *The Counseling Psychologist, 7,* 26–32.

Brindis, C., Barth, R. P., & Loomis, A. B. (1987). Continuous counseling: Case management with teenage parents. *Social Casework, 68,* 164–172.

Brown, S. (1990). *If the shoes fit: Final report and program implementation guide of the Maine Young Fathers Project.* Portland: Human Services Development Institute, University of Southern Maine.

Chaplin, T. M., Cole, P. M., & Zahn-Waxler, C. (2005). Parental socialization of emotion expression: Gender differences and relations to child adjustment. *Emotion, 5,* 80–88.

Currie, M. (2004). Doing anger differently: A group percussion therapy for angry adolescent boys. *International Journal of Group Psychotherapy, 54,* 275–294.

Cusack, J., Deane, F. P., Wilson, C. J., & Ciarrochi, J. (2006). Emotional expression, perceptions of therapy, and help-seeking intentions in men attending therapy services. *Psychology of Men and Masculinity, 7,* 69–82.

Frank, J. D. (1982). Therapeutic components shared by all psychotherapies. In J. H. Harvey & M. M. Parks (Eds.), *Psychotherapy research and behavior change* (pp. 9–37). Washington, DC: American Psychological Association.

Good, G. E., & Wood, P. K. (1995). Male gender role conflict, depression, and help seeking: Do college men face double jeopardy? *Journal of Counseling and Development, 74,* 70–75.

Gurian, M. (1996). *The wonder of boys.* New York: Tarcher.

Haen, C., & Brannon, K. H. (2002). Superheroes, monsters, and babies: Role of strength, destruction and vulnerability for emotionally disturbed boys. *The Arts in Psychotherapy, 29,* 31–40.

Hedges-Goett, L., & Tannenbaum, M. (2001). Navigating the social landscape: A rationale and method for interpersonal group therapy with pre-adolescent boys. *Journal of Child and Adolescent Group Therapy, 11,* 135–146.

Heesacker, M., Wester, S. R., Vogel, D. L., Wentzel, J. T., Mejia-Millan, C. M., & Goodholm, C. R. (1999). Gender-based emotional stereotyping. *Journal of Counseling Psychology, 46,* 483–495.

Hendricks, L. E. (1988). Outreach with teenage fathers: A preliminary report on three ethnic groups. *Adolescence, 23,* 711–720.

Hernandez, R. (2002). *Fatherwork in the crossfire: Chicano teen fathers struggling to take care of business* (Report No. JSRI-WP-58). East Lansing: Michigan State University, Julian Samora Research Institute. (ERIC Document Reproduction Services No. ED 471 926)

Holland, J. L. (1973). *Making vocational choices: A theory of careers.* Englewood Cliffs, NJ: Prentice-Hall.

Huey, W. C. (1987). Counseling teenage fathers: The "Maximizing a Life Experience" (MALE) group. *School Counselor, 35,* 40–47.

Kim, B. S. K., Atkinson, D. R., & Umemoto, D. (2001). Asian cultural values and counseling process: Current knowledge and directions for future research. *The Counseling Psychologist, 29,* 570–603.

Kim, B. S. K., Atkinson, D. R., & Yang, P. H. (1999). The Asian Values Scale: Development, factor analysis, validation, and reliability. *Journal of Counseling Psychology, 46,* 342–352.

Kiselica, M. S. (1988). Helping an aggressive adolescent through "the before, during, and after program." *School Counselor, 4,* 299–306.

Kiselica, M. S. (1995). *Multicultural counseling with teenage fathers: A practical guide.* Thousand Oaks, CA: Sage.

Kiselica, M. S. (1996). Parenting skills training with teenage fathers. In M. P. Andronico (Ed.), *Men in groups: Insights, interventions and psychoeducational work* (pp. 283–300). Washington, DC: American Psychological Association.

Kiselica, M. S. (1999). Counseling teen fathers. In A. Horne & M. S. Kiselica (Eds.), *Handbook of counseling boys and adolescent males* (pp. 179–197). Thousand Oaks, CA: Sage.

Kiselica, M. S. (2001). A male-friendly therapeutic process with school-age boys. In G. R. Brooks & G. E. Good (Eds.), *The new handbook of psychotherapy and counseling with men* (Vol. 1., pp. 41–58). San Francisco: Jossey-Bass.

Kiselica, M. S. (2003a, Autumn). Male-sensitive counseling with boys. *Counselling in Education,* 16–19.

Kiselica, M. S. (2003b). Transforming psychotherapy in order to succeed with boys: Male-friendly practices. *Journal of Clinical Psychology: In Session, 59,* 1225–1236.

Kiselica, M. S. (2006b). Helping a boy become a parent: Male-sensitive psychotherapy with a teenage father. In M. Englar-Carlson & M. Stevens (Eds.), *In the room with men: A casebook of therapeutic change* (pp. 225–240). Washington, DC: American Psychological Association.

Kiselica, M. S., Englar-Carlson, M., & Fisher, M. (2006, August). A positive psychology framework for building upon male strengths. In M. S. Kiselica (Chair), *Toward a positive psychology of boys, men, and masculinity.* Symposium presented at the annual convention of the American Psychological Association, New Orleans, LA.

Kiselica, M. S., & Horne, A. M. (1999). For the sake of our nation's sons. In A. M. Horne & M. S. Kiselica (Eds.), *Handbook of counseling boys and adolescent males: A practitioner's guide* (pp. xv–xx). Thousand Oaks, CA: Sage.

Kiselica, M. S., & O'Brien, S. (2001, August). Are attachment disorders and alexithymia characteristic of males? In M. S. Kiselica (Chair), *Are males really emotional mummies? What do the data indicate?* Symposium conducted at the annual convention of the American Psychological Association, San Francisco.

Kiselica, M. S., Rotzien, A., & Doms, J. (1994). Preparing teenage fathers for parenthood: A group psychoeducational approach. *Journal for Specialists in Group Work, 19,* 83–94.

Klinman, D. G., & Sander, J. H. (1985). *The teen parent collaboration: Reaching and serving the teenage father.* New York: Bank Street College of Education.

Kost, K. A. (1997). The effects of support on the economic well-being of young fathers. *Families in Society, 78,* 370–382.

Lesser, J., Verdugo, R. L., Koniak-Griffin, D., Tello, J., Kappos, B., & Cumberland, W. G. (2005). Respective and protecting relationships: A community research HIV prevention program for teen fathers and mothers. *AIDS Education and Prevention, 17*(4), 347–360.

Levant, R. F., Good, G. E., Cook, S. W., O'Neil, J. M., Smalley, K. B., Owen, K., et al. (2006). The Normative Male Alexithymia Scale: Measurement of a gender-linked syndrome. *Psychology of Men and Masculinity, 7,* 212–224.

Majors, R. G., & Billson, J. M. (1992). *Cool pose: The dilemmas of Black manhood in America.* New York: Lexington.

Mazza, C. (2002). Young dads: The effects of a parenting program on urban African-American adolescent fathers. *Adolescence, 37*(148), 681–693.

Mercurio, C. M. (2003). Guiding boys in the early years to lead to healthy emotional lives. *Early Childhood Education Journal, 30,* 255–258.

Mortola, P., Hiton, H., & Grant, S. (2008). *BAM! Boys advocacy and mentoring: A leader's guide to facilitating strength-based groups for boys.* New York: Routledge.

Paniagua, F. A. (2005). *Assessing and treating culturally diverse clients: A practical guide* (2nd ed.). Thousand Oaks, CA: Sage.

Parham, T. A., White, J. L., & Ajamu, A. (1999). *The psychology of Blacks: An African centered perspective* (3rd ed.). Englewood Cliffs, NJ: Prentice-Hall.

Pollack, W. S. (1998). *Real boys: Rescuing our sons from the myths of boyhood.* New York: Henry Holt.

Robertson, J. M., & Fitzgerald, L. F. (1992). Overcoming the masculine mystique: Preferences for alternative forms of assistance among men who avoid counseling. *Journal of Counseling Psychology, 39,* 240–246.

Robinson, B. E. (1988). *Teenage fathers.* Lexington, MA: Lexington Books.

Rochlen, A. B., & O'Brien, K. M. (2002). The relation of male gender role conflict and attitudes toward career counseling to interest and preferences for different career counseling styles. *Psychology of Men and Masculinity, 3,* 9–21.

Sander, J. H., & Rosen, J. L. (1987). Teenage fathers: Working with the neglected partner in adolescent childbearing. *Family Planning Perspectives, 19,* 107–110.

Shepard, D. (2005). Male development and the journey toward disconnection. In D. Comstock (Ed.), *Diversity and development: Critical contexts that shape our lives and relationships* (pp. 133–160). Belmont, CA: Thompson Brooks/Cole.

Smith, J. M. (2004). Adolescent males' view on the use of mental health counseling services. *Adolescence, 39,* 77–82.

Smith, L. A. (1988). Black adolescent fathers: Issues for service provision. *Social Work, 33,* 269–271.

Sweet, H. (2006). Finding the person behind the persona: Engaging men as a female therapist. In M. Englar-Carlson & M. Stevens (Eds.), *In the room with men: A casebook of therapeutic change* (pp. 69–90). Washington, DC: American Psychological Association.

Sue, D. W., & Sue, D. (2003). *Counseling the culturally diverse: Theory and practice* (4th ed.). New York: Wiley.

Wester, S. R., Vogel, D. L., Pressly, P. K., & Heesacker, M. (2002). Sex differences in emotion: A critical review of the literature and implications for counseling psychology. *The Counseling Psychologist, 30,* 629–651.

Wooden, J. (N.d.). *The official site of Coach John Wooden.* Retrieved July 2, 2007, from http://www.coachwooden.com

Part 2

Helping Special Populations of Boys

CHAPTER 4

Surviving in a Sea with Few Lifeboats

Counseling Boys from Impoverished Families

JOSEPH M. CERVANTES AND
MATT ENGLAR-CARLSON

In recent years, there has been a growing societal concern about the emotional well-being of boys.* New research has demonstrated that boys face special challenges related to the male socialization process (Bradley & Corwyn, 2002; Bradley, Corwyn, McAdoo, & García Coll, 2001; Conger, Conger, & Elder, 1997; Leventhal & Brooks-Gunn, 2000, 2004) and that the developmental trajectory of a boy is greatly influenced by the cultural context in which he is raised (Kiselica & Horne, 1999). Compared to girls, boys are disproportionately responsible for problems associated with aggression due to their difficulties managing anger and the pervasive influence of violent gangs on young men (Hardy & Laszloffy, 2005). Furthermore, the high divorce rate has resulted in a loss of a stable male identification figure for boys raised in households headed by single mothers (Wallerstein & Lewis, 2004).

---

* Pseudonyms are used for all of the people described in the case studies appearing in this chapter in order to protect the anonymity of those individuals. Further, other descriptive and demographic information has been masked and altered to further protect their identities.

Although understanding these issues is central to the process of helping boys, with few exceptions (e.g., Horne & Kiselica, 1999) there are a limited number of resources that cover the unique developmental, cultural, and psychological challenges of young boys and adolescent males. There are even fewer resources on the manifestations of these issues in boys from low-income families and how to help them. In addition to the myriad of challenges faced by anyone living in a socioeconomically disadvantaged environment, boys and male adolescents face additional difficulties associated with being a member of a lower social class. The purpose of this chapter is to address this void in the professional literature by discussing the complex adjustment difficulties that are specific to low-income boys. Drawing from my (JC) extensive clinical experiences with this population and the professional literature on the subject, we chronicle the hardships, resiliency, and strengths of boys from low-income neighborhoods and the process of counseling them and their families.

As the title of this chapter suggests, life for boys residing in low-income communities is akin to surviving in a sea with few lifeboats. Many of these boys live in pseudo war zones where their families are challenged every day just to get by (Garbarino, 1995). Lacking the resources and support available to more affluent people, impoverished families must somehow cope with a variety of disruptive and destabilizing conditions, such as substandard housing, limited employment opportunities, widespread crime, and an overwhelming ethos of hopelessness and desolation. Families often have to send their school-age children to educational systems that tend to view the children and the parents they are charged with serving with mistrust while disregarding their potential (Lott, 2001). Even within social service settings, poor families often face judgmental attitudes, which blame families for substance abuse, homelessness, and economic dependence, and see families as a burden on society (Minuchin, Colapinto, & Minuchin, 1998).

A theoretical conceptualization that remains true even in the new millennium is whether one should speak about high-risk boys as opposed to high-risk families. As understood from a systemic point of view, and still consistent with my (JC) own family therapy training in the 1970s, one is interrelated with the other. Simply put, high-risk boys often live in problematic families and environmental contexts. This chapter focuses on the relational style and personality characteristics of boys, and the sociocultural factors salient for low-income boys and their families. Rather than to utilize a *DSM-IV-TR* (American Psychiatric Association, 2000) diagnostic framework to highlight specific behaviors that would identify a problem with an individual, the chapter focuses on the broader family system as it interrelates with the specific symptomology in the outcome of a given boy's behavior.

In this chapter, case examples are used to dramatize the desperate lives of boys who are raised in these stressful conditions. We offer several principles for counseling boys from lower socioeconomic backgrounds.

This chapter also examines specifics interventions that are helpful in the therapeutic process with this population. Consistent with a family systems perspective, boys experiencing difficulties are portrayed as the symptom bearers of their families, rather than as pathological individuals requiring a diagnosis (Goldenberg & Goldenberg, 2008).

MALE DEVELOPMENT IN A WORLD OF POVERTY

Over 40 years ago, Minuchin, Montalvo, Guerney, Rosman, and Schumer (1967) demonstrated in their classic publication, *Families of the Slums*, that the deplorable characteristics of low-income neighborhoods complicate personal development and family connectedness and stability for boys raised in American ghettos and barrios. This cogent observation still applies today in regard to boys from impoverished communities. Recent research has demonstrated that boys who spend a significant portion of their lives living in poverty are at risk for a host of significant psychological and interpersonal problems, including physical or sexual abuse (Wagner, 1997), problems of self-control (Bolger, Patterson, Thompson, & Kupersmidt, 1995; Campbell, Shaw, & Gilliom, 2000), antisocial behavior (Eamon & Mulder, 2005), low education outcomes (Leventhal & Brooks-Gunn, 2004), impulsiveness (Skowron, 2005), polydrug use (Black & Krishnakumar, 1998), aggression (Loeber & Farrington, 2000), and depression (Lewinsohn, Joiner, & Rohde, 2001). Boys of color are also affected by the destructive forces of oppression, prejudice, and racism (Boyd-Franklin, 1989; Boyd-Franklin, Toussaint, & Franklin, 2001; Bradley et al., 2001; Chen, Langer, Raphaelson, & Matthews, 2004; Choi, Harachi, Gillmore, & Catalano, 2006; McLoyd, 1998), and the threat of deportation looms over the lives of many boys from immigrant families, especially those who are illegal aliens (Cervantes, Guerrero, & Mejia, 2007; Suarez-Orozco, Todorova, & Louie, 2002).

Families living in low-income areas are confronted with the challenges of population density. Any discussion of counseling boys from low socioeconomic status (SES) environments must incorporate the living and social space occupied by these boys. Evans (2004) noted that poor children are consistently confronted with environmental inequalities. He noted that their air and water are more polluted, and their homes and neighborhood are more crowded, noisier, and of lower quality. Further, the schools, child care services, and municipal services are of lower quality and suffer more deterioration. The consistent exposure to poverty-stricken neighborhoods serves as a psychological pathogen. Black and Krishnakumar (1998) noted that a frequent outcome of these social dynamics for urban ethnic minority populations was an association with unemployment, low educational attainment, polydrug use, and the subsequent development of more serious mental illness. Eamon and Mulder (2005) found that Latino boys and youths who lived a higher proportion of their lives in poverty exhibited higher levels of antisocial behavior. In addition, Eamon and Mulder commented on the distinct developmental risks for this population that include birth to teenage mothers, living in single-mother and large-family households, attending low-quality educational school systems, and having limited access to resources in their respective neighborhoods.

Social class is a powerful socializing agent in that it bestows or limits power (Liu, 2001; Liu, Ali, et al., 2004). When children are raised in a poor community, they acquire skills necessary to navigate in that particular environment, yet they probably do not learn the skills necessary to advance into more economically privileged classes. Indeed, many children from lower- and working-class backgrounds do not benefit from the type of social capital that most middle-class children do—values that encourage children to pursue higher education as a means to a comfortable life (Littrell, 1999). Social capital includes wisdom about how to advance educationally or economically, social contacts that facilitate advancement, and knowledge about how to work within social systems (Bubolz, 2001).

The social class system in the United States is dominated by the belief in upward mobility, based on the notion that hard work and educational attainment allow anyone to achieve and advance (Liu, 2001). This belief has been associated with the centrality of individual achievement and the Protestant work ethic (Mirels & Garrett, 1973). In the context of a capitalist economic structure, getting ahead and acquiring possessions are seen as primary life goals. Hard work, delayed gratification, and sacrifice are all accepted means of achieving the socially constructed, highly touted American dream, and upward mobility is a strong part of the American consciousness and the notion of access to a better life (Liu, 2002). However, the existing evidence (Bullock & Lott, 2001; Lott, 2002; Shapiro, Greenstein, & Primus, 2001) contradicts the notion of upward mobility and indicates that the poor get poorer as the gulf between the poor and wealthy continues to grow. This means that most boys who grow up in poor neighborhoods will become men who live in these same poor neighborhoods. Existing evidence indicates that lower-class men are more likely to experience a host of damaging and life-threatening psychological and physical health difficulties (for more detail, see Liu, 2002).

OUR PROFESSIONAL AND THEORETICAL LENS

Although we have been influenced by several theoretical postures, a primary influence in our work with boys and their families is underscored with a family systems or multicultural perspective. This approach is invested in understanding the infrastructure of families relative to power hierarchies, relationship alliances, and boundaries between and among family members, and appreciating the overall structure as it engages and interacts outside of the familial boundaries

(Goldenberg & Goldenberg, 2008). Further, our perspective is also informed with acknowledging the context of where individuals and families are embedded relative to gender, ethnicity, sexual orientation, social class, and so forth (McGoldrick, 1998). A significant aspect of understanding context is the role that socioeconomic status plays in the formation of belief systems and access to opportunity and resources that can impact a family member's behavior and aspirations (American Psychological Association [APA] Task Force on Socioeconomic Status, 2007).

There has been increased interest in the issues of socioeconomic status reflected in a report by the APA Task Force on Socioeconomic Status (2007), which provides a current overview on some of those primary issues impacting individuals, families, and communities relative to poverty, limited resources, and subsequent psychological consequences. Further, Minuchin, Colapinto, and Minuchin (2007) articulated a renewed perspective and interest in working with families of the poor and provided important guidance relative to this specific population. Their model outlines several defining elements that include skillful practitioners of family-based services, consistent family-oriented procedures within the organization, social support for family-oriented procedures within the organization, and social support for family-oriented practice. It is our perspective that effective counseling work should include involvement at each of these levels. This focus promotes the understanding that human development is framed within the larger context of the sociocultural environment, economics, and social class (APA Task Force on Socioeconomic Status, 2007).

In our work, we see the theoretical relationship between a family systems approach (Goldenberg & Goldenberg, 2008) and a family psychology perspective (Pinsof & Lebow, 2005). This model suggests a more comprehensive approach that includes a systemic view that describes the family system and its evolution and development over time. Wachtel (2004) noted systemic concepts in terms of the role of children in families. These include the ideas that there is a structural problem in the family in which the symptomatic child is part of a dysfunctional triangle, that children are self-sacrificing in order to prevent the disintegration of the family or their parents' marriage, and that children are induced into acting out disowned aspects of the self or play the role of family members with whom there is unfinished business. This perspective allows counselors to understand a boy's problem with a wide angle of views. Consequently, we have found integrating a family psychology approach to be useful in our work with families as it provides the language, focus on specific behavioral assessment, and conceptual tools to understand the various and intricate dynamics that occur across the diverse sector of families. In particular, this perspective allows the counselor to focus on what the individual boy is bringing to the system and how he helps shape systemic interactions. Following the ideas of Wachtel (2004), this integration allows us to

> [t]hink of individual concerns and difficulties as *influencing* and being *influenced by* the system yet having a separate and distinct existence. Symptoms in both adults and children are therefore partially autonomous from the system in which they flourish and which, in fact, they may play a role in maintaining. (p. 14)

The cases described in this chapter are characteristic of the professional manner in which we understand family dynamics; attend to a variety of textual factors, particularly socioeconomic status; and utilize other therapy strategies that provide guidance and direction in our interventions with boys. Counseling with boys who are poor must be guided by several principles that reflect a sensitive understanding of the contextual, developmental, cultural, and familial issues facing this population. An overview of these principles that we have found salient in our practice follows in the next section.

RECOMMENDATIONS FOR WORKING WITH LOW SOCIOECONOMIC STATUS BOYS AND THEIR FAMILIES

Our professional careers have yielded wisdom and appreciation for the wealth of relationships that we each had growing up, which has served as an initial key toward the development of a reflective posture. Our professional counseling experiences provided each of us opportunities to learn from the boys and their families that we have seen, and widened our perspectives in regard to their histories, struggles, and achievements that have been gained at great costs. Each of these implications for counseling with boys suggests that the family plays a significant role in their development, socialization, and individualization (Skowron, 2005).

Although a practitioner can see family disorganization at all levels of SES, on the lower end of the class spectrum the issues become more complicated due to the presence of poverty, potential homelessness, and the lack of financial means to physically provide for oneself (APA Task Force on Socioeconomic Status, 2007). These issues are often complicated with an unstable residence and work assignment, and the cycle of poverty, which itself has its own dynamic and problems in contributing negatively to the well-being of others (Minuchin et al., 2007). In brief, family disorganization is an outcome of many of these factors and one that further complicates any work with boys in counseling.

As mentioned earlier, it is not surprising that the problems of boys in families (school difficulties, problems with the legal system, and/or behavioral disruptions at home) serve as the presenting problem. Yet, a family systems perspective teaches counselors to understand a boy's difficulties both as a symptom of family dysfunction and as serving a role in the family's life (Wachtel, 2004). Helping boys extricate themselves from the internalized sense of helplessness and develop some level of hope, while at the same time having boys not label themselves as incapacitated or powerless, is often the first aspect to treatment. Instillation of hope is a powerful therapeutic factor that can be the foundation of a good counseling outcome in individual and family counseling (Blow, 2001; Sprenkle, 2004; Thomas, 2006). Part of this is helping a boy develop the ability to not view himself as a "problem" child within the family or problem person in a troubled community (Freeman, Epston, & Lobovits, 1997). A further goal is helping a boy sort out his family relationships so that he can be shielded from negative life events (e.g., domestic violence, presence of gang activity, and resisting drugs). These are all important dimensions to dealing with the issues of disorganization in low-income families. Below are some of the observations and learning gained from our work with boys and the blueprint we often use when working with boys and their families that are struggling to be the best that they can be in spite of the challenges laid out before them.

Gain Perspective on the Day-to-Day Living Conditions in Low-SES Communities

Regardless of the developmental age of a boy, the contextual environment of that individual's background is important to consider. For boys with a low-SES background, issues related to poverty, violence, and residential and employment instability all are significant factors that must be weighed (Black & Krishnakumar, 1998; Evans, 2004; Garbarino, 1995; Leventhal & Brooks-Gunn, 2000). The role of violence particularly tends to be an important consideration given that the issues of safety in a boy's environment may play a role in everything from compliance with treatment to a major therapeutic issue for that client (Garbarino; Hardy & Laszloffy, 2005). Sometimes it may be important for the counselor to leave the surroundings of one's clinic or practice to make the rounds to lower-SES areas where clients reside and become more alert to the socioenvironmental and safety issues that may be evident in a boy's life (Repetti, Taylor, & Seeman, 2002). Part of this awareness allows the counselor to understand how coming to counseling might be different for low-income families and boys.

For many families and individuals from poor backgrounds, the barriers to mental health help seeking go beyond cultural and societal dictates against psychological services to include simple realities of life unique to low-income populations (Minuchin et al., 1998). Economic barriers related to mental health are real, particularly for those without health insurance and those who fear using available governmental assistance due to illegal alien status (Cervantes et al., 2007). Many boys and their families from low socioeconomic status have difficulty committing to counseling because parents are unable to leave work and there is no transportation available. Many times, just having the family arrive at the office on a timely basis is a small victory. Consequently, when providing treatment to families with limited resources, issues of economic concern, chronic transportation problems, and lessened motivation should be addressed at the start (Falicov, 1998). Sometimes, viewing one's first treatment session as if it were the last can be helpful with respect to dealing more appropriately with assumed expectations on the part of the boy and his family, and expected psychological care (Boyd-Franklin & Franklin, 1998). It is also an important dynamic when practicing with this population to provide useful assistance not knowing whether you will see a family again while at the same time trying to extend hope for the future. A realistic approach to a boy's situation or to family dysfunction is that the practitioner also maintains a balance about what is possible given the framework of a given family (McGoldrick, 1998). Without this framework, increased frustration on the part of the counselor and a sense of helplessness about a boy's situation can easily occur.

Pay Careful Attention to Under- and Overinvolvement

The challenge of working with boys, especially those coming from low socioeconomic status, tends to prompt a review of one's own personal history as a boy (Boyd-Franklin, 1989; Boyd-Franklin et al., 2001; Franklin, 2004). I (JC) learned that reconnecting with my adolescent background and the struggles that were part of that process has helped immediately in developing the needed empathy in many of my more difficult cases. I (JC) also learned that it is important to maintain a delicate balance between overinvolvement in a case while minimizing underinvolvement as well. Lott (2002) articulately chronicled ways the helping professions cognitively distances from poor and low-income clients, yet I find the opposite is often true for me. I am often drawn into the world of my client, and I struggle with the economic disparities of the young men I see. Overinvolvement tends to cause a set of problems that impact judgment and prompts a countertransference reaction to the individual. Underinvolvement tends to lead to disconnection and the development of a nontherapeutic disconnection between therapist and client that can negatively impact the counseling relationship.

A related issue to awareness of one's overinvolvement in a case is the feelings of powerlessness that many children experience coming from limited incomes with poor access to needed resources (Lott, 2001, 2003; Smith, 2005). Boyd-Franklin (1989) and Franklin (2004) each highlighted the tribulations and clinical perspectives that are important in working with low-income African American families, especially with boys. A reflective question that may arise with this population is as follows: Are understanding and empathy enough when working with low-income families? Perhaps a more appropriate question for the mental health professional to begin asking is how to balance one's therapeutic relationship with that of providing a framework for community organizations to assist families to empower themselves. Minuchin et al. (2007) noted the continuum between providing direct service and involving oneself in social advocacy. It is a relevant continuum for counselors to consider whether one is in independent practice or employed in a community mental health agency. The issue of balancing roles, responsibilities, and professional obligations is a fundamental aspect of successful practice, and important in administering to the needs of those families that are less fortunate and are frequently powerless.

Use Rituals to Honor Male Transitions

Counseling with boys has always involved some level of need for a transformative experience from nonmaturity to maturity that assists in the change process. As a result, ceremonial ritual typically plays an important role in our work with boys (Hubble, Duncan, & Miller, 1999; McGoldrick, 1998). Imber-Black, Roberts, and Whiting (2003) devoted an edited volume to the use of rituals and families in family therapy. A resource such as this can be useful in the designing of interventions that will assist boys to develop the level of consciousness that is needed beyond just a behavior change that sometimes could be only temporary and frequently undermined by negative peer influence and impaired communication with a parent. Rituals are especially salient over issues concerning transitions to manhood and to establish those necessary supports and awareness that would lead one toward a greater understanding of one's place in the collective. This transformative doorway can occur as easily as having a family of origin group celebration in a family counseling visit where a boy is recognized for having graduated from middle school with related commentary about how he has grown emotionally in preparing to step into the shoes of young manhood. Another example can involve helping a boy to label those life challenges that he might confront on a regular basis and redesigning this critical information as goals that can merit points toward being a person of integrity (i.e., movement into manhood). The designated completion of dealing appropriately with some of these life events can potentially be recognized not only in the consulting room but also perhaps with a "certificate of manhood development" that can be issued by a school counselor or a teacher who can incorporate some trusted friends (Minuchin et al., 2007). These examples of ritual and public acknowledgment can go a long way toward the incorporation of relevant meaning and the subsequent internalization of a code of ethics for boys in their later development.

Remember the Whole Family System

Being trained as a family therapist during my early career formation (JC), I have always viewed this education as an asset, which has given me an opportunity to understand systemic thinking and to broaden my focus as suggested by Minuchin et al. (1967) and others (McGoldrick, Giordano, & Garcia-Preto, 2005). It is important for counselors seeing boys not to neglect the available support system that is charged with the emotional nurturance of a boy. To neglect the immediate family system is like being blindfolded in one's professional work. When working with families, we tend to assess for those family members, both immediate and extended, who can serve appropriate role models and mentors for boys. Much has been written about the lack of male role models in many families. This is especially relevant for poor families. Estimates indicate that only 33% of poor children reside with their fathers, as opposed to 70% of nonpoor children (U.S. Department of Health and Human Services, 1999). Though biological fathers may not be in contact with their sons, attention can be given toward social fathering—the role of men such as stepfathers, uncles, maternal partners, relatives, and friends who play a father-figure role (Coley, 2001). We have learned to broaden our understanding of family to engage all of those resources that can be positive forces in a boy's life.

The Power and Influence of Peers Are Paramount

Along with expanding the family system, it is important not to neglect a boy's friendship networks (Broderick & Blewitt, 2006). Friends provide significant influence and support, both negative and positive, to a boy's personal and social development (Horne & Kiselica, 1999). As boys move through preadolescent and adolescent years, they become increasingly reliant on those peer networks that teach socialization skills, provide rituals and practices that are consistent with their particular community, and initiate a working dialogue in order to participate in one's reference group (Martin, 2003). Boys develop friendships for many reasons, and a good counselor looks to understand the attraction to both negative and positive influences.

Don't Be Afraid to Talk About How
Low-SES Boys See Class Differences

There has been increased attention regarding the gaps of income and wealth and the direct impact of the consequences for access to goods and services (APA Task Force on Socioeconomic Status, 2007). It is possible that a boy's understanding of social class can provide hope and expectation. Goodman, Adler, Kawachi, Frazier, and Huang (2001) found that most working-class youth, but especially young males, expected to become upper middle class as adults. Compared to their female counterparts, adolescent males believed they would have the personal opportunity to get ahead in the world. Those lower down on the social hierarchy expect greater social mobility. Clearly, low-SES boys see the gaps in social class standing.

These gaps can influence the perceptions of low-SES boys who get exposed to all of those things that they may not be able to have, at least immediately, because of their family's depressed social and economic status (Liu, 2002; Liu, Soleck, Hopps, Dunston, & Pickett, 2004). This can cause significant frustration and anger in their personal lives and perpetuate a level of anger that could impact their peer network and attitudes and behaviors. Some discussion with boys about their feelings relative to what they have or don't have at least materially may be relevant, especially if this is an emerging issue that has been troubling them. This mentality could cause significant frustration and potentially lead to antisocial behavior.

Working With Low-SES Boys Involves Advocacy

Several authors have commented on and provided evidence to the fact that poverty leads to sociopathology of one form or another (Aronen & Arajärvi, 2000; Black & Krishnakumar, 1998; Bradley & Corwyn, 2002; Costello, Compton, Keeler, & Angold, 2003; Evans, 2004; Gilman, Kawachi, Fitzmaurice, & Buka, 2002; Leventhal & Brooks-Gunn, 2000, 2004; Leventhal, Fauth, & Brooks-Gunn, 2005; McLoyd, 1998; Minuchin et al., 2007; Repetti et al., 2002; Smith, 2005; Wagner, 1997; Xue, Leventhal, Brooks-Gunn, & Earls, 2005). All of these writers indicated that coming from low-SES environments tends to be highly predictive of future mental health issues and the development of a continued culture of poverty. These issues begin to place an interesting advocacy role for counselors, who are trying to provide alleviation for boys' problems but at the same time trying to balance how much of that work should be crisis management, and how much should address the social system. At the very least, counseling with boys from low-SES environments suggests that interventions may include the development of some level of dual relationships that allow for peer mentoring and involvement in a boy's life that are still in balance with one's role as a counselor. Beyond the individual level, counselors can acknowledge that some level of restoration of community may also play a role (Minuchin et al., 2007; Smith, 2005). This latter aspect may mean serving on a community board, or providing face-to-face consultation with a school, a probation officer, or the church. Social advocacy extends that professional work to attention that is given to social justice issues of boys and young men (see Kiselica & Woodford, 2007, for a more detailed perspective of social justice and healthy male development). Although this chapter is not necessarily about social systems interventions, it is crucial to acknowledge there may be a degree of involvement in working with boys that may prompt a social advocacy role at some point in one's professional work.

Examine Your Own Social Class Biases

Being ignorant or intolerant, or simply avoiding issues of social class and the impact of poverty on families, is consistent with unethical practice. It is known that classism shapes values, worldviews, and behaviors of individuals (Liu, 2002; Liu, Soleck, et al., 2004). Treating poor people as other and lesser than oneself is central to the concept and practice of classism (Lott, 2002). As such, it is important to examine one's social class biases and how they may impact one's relationship to the client. Lott (2002) outlined the many ways that mental health workers do not feel comfortable with low-income clients and have difficulty empathizing with them. Low-income clients are more likely than others to receive therapy that is brief and drug centered and to be treated by students or low-status professionals. Leeder (1996) noted that mental health workers often see poor clients as "inarticulate and suspicious ... resistant, apathetic and passive" (p. 52). Multicultural competency requires the examination of cultural biases, and one's own classism is a core component to be explored. Guidelines issued by the APA on multicultural competency (2003) offer additional support and prompting regarding our responsibilities as professionals relative to social class in counseling practice.

Discuss Emerging Ideals of Manhood

In each of the three cases described later in this chapter, as well as a majority of counseling cases we have seen with boys, the role of initiating the process of manhood is pivotal (Boyd-Franklin et al., 2001; Franklin, 2004). As characteristic of the individual differences with clients, any dialogue of manhood has a unique spin that is reflective of the developmental age of the boy, maturity level, contextual background, and other nonspecific factors that influence how manhood is perceived (Boyd-Franklin & Franklin, 1998). An observed consistent theme noted throughout our work has been the therapeutic dialogue of maturity and the need for appropriate role modeling and discussion consistent with how manhood is defined and what this means for each particular boy. My experience in these cases is that the dialogue of manhood is influenced by sociocultural factors. It is not the purview of this chapter to talk extensively about this area but at least to indicate that the ethnic diversity of a boy will dictate how a narrative understanding of manhood is to proceed. Rather than assume a universal notion of manhood and masculinity, we encourage counselors to ask boys and young men about their own ideas about "what it means to be a man."

For many boys, counselors can specifically model and instruct boys on how to be a man of integrity. One of the most important levels of awareness gained through working with boys is the issue of teaching about how to be an honorable man. The combinations of a single mother raising boys, low SES, and the presence of domestic violence and/or mental illness all make for significant challenges toward this expected developmental trajectory (Garbarino, 1995; Gilman et al., 2002; Leventhal & Brooks-Gunn, 2000, 2004; Lott, 2002; Smith, 2005). Life events that are nonsupportive and sequential distractions can easily lead a boy toward self-destructive activity (Kuther & Wallace, 2003). In these instances, the issue of becoming a man often takes second place (Liu, 2002). Achieving healthy manhood is very difficult when the only role models that exist are ones that glorify violence, disrespect, abandonment, and minimal involvement in one's community (Liu, Soleck, et al., 2004). Consequently, becoming a man takes on a very different emotional and psychological platform relative to a model that may stress exploitation instead of honesty, physical toughness rather than interpersonal sensitivity, and impulsivity and short-goal realization over thoughtfulness and resilience. In brief, becoming a man has a distinct socioenvironmental and socioeconomic dimension that impacts the developmental process of defining maleness. Awareness of multicultural expectations, especially where low SES is a factor, may have a direct impact on how manhood is understood and integrated into an adolescent's sense of self.

Evaluate and Examine Spirituality With Boys

A significant influence in my (JC) own training, experience, and work as a psychotherapist has been the role of spirituality. As such, teaching boys to reconnect to a larger, more complete picture of themselves that includes their interrelationships with family and community, and their place in the larger collective, is an important evolution that affects their behavior and attitudes (Hay & Nye, 1998; Roehlkepartain, King, Wagner, & Benson, 2006). Consequently, having boys realize the interconnectedness of the web of life can assist them with taking more responsibility for themselves and their environments. Hay and Nye (1998), in their classic text on childhood spirituality, commented extensively on the need for children to develop perspective taking as a primary dimension to self-reflection and subsequent development and awareness of one's personal, familial, and social environments. This perspective taking is especially critical in clinical practice with boys from low-SES environments, where the incorporation of negative aspects of their social ecology can significantly deter the necessary stages toward self-restoration without any degree of personal realization of one's life circumstances.

A dialogue of spirituality with boys from my (JC) frame of reference tends to be described in a more generic way that is respectful of one's religious denomination or subsequent spiritual beliefs, how one connects to others, the meaning behind that connection, and the role one plays in the larger picture of who he perceives himself to be is the context in which this spirituality is played out in my work with boys.

CASE EXAMPLES OF BOYS, THEIR FAMILIES, AND RELEVANT THERAPEUTIC INTERVENTIONS

These three cases are drawn from the first author's (Joseph M. Cervantes) clinical work, and thus the voice in this section moves to the first person to reflect his own experiences. The discussion of the cases that follow is contextualized within a family systems paradigm that is integrated within the larger conceptual framework of family psychology (Pinsof & Lebow, 2005). In brief, I address the relevant emotional and psychological issues as they are framed within the family system and pay specific attention to those factors that are impacted by low SES. Each of the cases would be classified as economically impoverished families where the roles of poverty and a lack of resources were common themes interwoven into the lives of boys and their respective families. In each case discussion, the combination of boys and adolescent males presented had some expectation of hope in their life circumstances. At times, this hope was centered in their family of origin, and at other times it was directed toward an extended family, a peer group, or a larger system that would appreciate the resilience abilities of each of these boys. This section will follow with a brief outline of the family dynamics and the particular boy or adolescent male that is contextualized within this system, and his specific emotional and psychological concerns.

Keeping Afloat in a Multicrisis Poor Family: The Case of Jimmy

Jimmy Washington was a 13-year-old Caucasian male seen in family counseling with his mother, two younger sisters (ages 11 and 9), and new stepfather. His mother had been employed in a low-end, minimum-wage job until 2 years prior, when she married her current husband, Juan Gomez, who was an undocumented Mexican national. An interesting aspect of this family dynamic was that Juan spoke minimal English and Jimmy's mother spoke no Spanish. Jimmy's mother had been receiving state aid for the last several years and living in a low-income project in the inner city with her three children prior to her new marriage. Juan had not been married before and was 10 years junior to his current wife. He was making minimum wage working inconsistent hours at a local car wash and was making additional money as a dishwasher in the evening at a family restaurant.

The family's living environment did not change dramatically with the new marriage as they continued to live in low-income housing within a part of the community known for regular drug deals among many residents living in this area. The primary reason for our consultation was Jimmy's academic problems in his school and the fact that he was reacting to having a new parent directing his behavior and managing control over his home situation. This family was treated for intermittent family therapy sessions, with the base of this work over the course of 9 months focused exclusively on the emotional and psychological concerns for Jimmy.

Jimmy presented as a husky boy who was personable in his manner, somewhat oppositional, yet open to a counseling relationship. His primary complaint was that he wanted to "hang with the boys," including his new stepfather; however, this proved awkward because Juan spoke no English, making their relationship difficult. An interesting sideline to Jimmy was his actual physical appearance. Although he was a good-looking boy with a natural curiosity and mischievousness in his eyes, it was clear that he came from a household with limited financial means. His blue jeans were too small to fit his growing body, his shirts were clearly hand-me-downs or from the local Salvation Army store, he wore tennis shoes that could stand to be recycled, and he would never dress warmly other than having a thin windbreaker even on the coldest and rainiest of days. During counseling visits with Jimmy, there were frequent comments about his feeling of not fitting in and of having limited opportunities to develop relationships with other kids with whom he felt comfortable. Some of these personal reactions were described as being labeled the "dumb kid" in class because of how inadequate he felt in his academic studies. But the primary emotional issue was Jimmy reacting to being the "poor kid" who never had any money, and he was ashamed over his mother's lack of participation in his school activities. The former issue proved to be a significant theme relative to Jimmy's feeling that he had limited access to resources because he came from a low-SES environment. Consequently, he perceived fewer opportunities and more doors closed to him because of his family's economic limitations.

Family counseling with Jimmy and his mother and stepfather proved to be tedious work. This was due primarily to a lack of English-speaking ability evident with his stepfather and his apparent lack of interest in developing a more intimate and caring role as a parent toward Jimmy. Including the parents in counseling became more difficult when Jimmy showed less interest in involving his stepfather. This created some problems in maneuvering through the relational boundaries and hierarchy that had been artificially put in place by his mother's new remarriage. Lastly, Juan did little to increase the financial security or stability of this family unit, as he had minimal formal education and was employed in low-end, minimum-wage jobs that had no future tied to them.

Over time, Juan participated less frequently in family counseling sessions due to both his lack of motivation and his scheduled work hours. Consequently, Jimmy's mother became his sole vested interest in the counseling process, and this allowed for a smoother dialogue to occur and for an easier resolution of issues related to Jimmy's well-being, self-esteem, and concerns surrounding his lack of support from a caring adult male figure.

What I soon discovered in counseling was Jimmy's propensity toward being personable and likeable, in spite of his oppositional streak, and the fact that he enjoyed being the class clown. This position as a jokester apparently was a popular characteristic that many of his peers enjoyed because he was a very good stand-up comedian and could mimic other schoolmates, teachers, and television personalities. The problem with his unrecognized talent was he would often put himself in situations that would not place him in a good light (e.g., talking during class or in mimicking others in inappropriate situations or in a mean way), and consequently caused him to be seen as disrespectful and inappropriate in his commentaries about others. In addition, it was discovered that Jimmy had good coordination, was athletic, and excelled at basketball and baseball. As such, although he had shied away from engaging in team sports for the school league, counseling encouraged him to try out and be recognized for his abilities.

A third issue discussed during the several months of counseling was his relationship to me. Because Jimmy had no historical contact with his biological father, and because he felt that he could not recognize his new stepfather because of language, cultural differences, and increased interpersonal distance, he grew increasingly interested in a more personal, father–son relationship with me. This last issue became an important element with Jimmy as he began idolizing a "what if" scenario: *What if* I could serve as a sort of big brother or surrogate father for him in some capacity?

As the therapeutic relationship developed, Jimmy's oppositionalness decreased, and he became more focused in wanting to please his teachers as well as me. Consequently, Jimmy's behavior at school became more recognized for his talents, and he started to win accolades for his skills as a stand-up comedian and abilities in sports. The issue that remained unresolved as counseling came to an end was that his mother, although obviously supportive of him, chose not to participate in any school functions, as was also the case with Juan, who felt ill prepared to navigate an English-speaking school environment. In addition, Jimmy's mother felt a certain level of shame for being poor and inadvertently placed that emotional burden on Jimmy, who carried those feelings into his interactions with others outside of his home. Some of the therapeutic dialogue that was interwoven through the period of time that I saw this boy focused on themes relative to concerns about not having financial resources and about how to cope with taunting from other kids. In addition, Jimmy was learning to handle his own personal reactions with a degree of integrity and without shame or embarrassment.

After 9 months of weekly counseling with Jimmy and some interviewing visits for family counseling, our visits were abruptly ended due to the family's move out of state. Jimmy and his mother were encouraged to continue his counseling in the new area where they would be living so that he could continue building on his personal strengths and self-confidence that would assist him as he moved into high school.

Commentary

Jimmy turned out to be quite a likable young boy. His comedic manner and ability to mimic many personalities were infectious, and provided an immediate therapeutic connection by way of his natural talent and spontaneous enjoyment of living. In brief, Jimmy found himself easily reinforced by my positive energy toward him and the ensuing paternal relationship that developed. In turn, I was also engaged in his dynamic style, and I desired to be a protective parent of him.

Over the years my paternal transference reaction with Jimmy has been a common feature evident in my work with boys. Young and older adolescent males who are missing father figures or who appear vulnerable in some capacity can cause vulnerability for counselors (Hardy & Laszloffy, 2005; Martin, 2003). There is a need to balance how to give, when to give, and in what setting to allow that giving to occur when navigating one's personal reactions in counseling with boys. To remain neutral is to intentionally maintain a nonaffected stance that can be countertherapeutic and potentially harmful in a therapeutic relationship (Hubble et al., 1999). The countertransference reaction to working with adolescent boys is a common feature that a practitioner should expect (Martin, 2003). This reaction is especially evident with boys with less emotional availability and limited resources with which to navigate personal and life circumstances. Counselors can detect immediate feelings of vulnerability, and counselors may wish to provide beyond what is customary in a counseling relationship.

Navigating the Water's Edge of Immigrant, Undocumented Status: The Case of Rogelio

Rogelio Cruz was a 15-year-old boy of Salvadorian ancestry and the oldest of four other brothers and sisters. His parents, who immigrated to the United States from San Salvador, the capital city of El Salvador, approximately 3 years ago, brought Rogelio to counseling. The family's immigration was considered illegal given that this family unit migrated together by taking buses from El Salvador to the border town of Tijuana, Mexico. The family was smuggled through a secret tunnel that connected Tijuana to the adjoining border town in the United States. Following several life-threatening escapes that occurred throughout this journey, inclusive of the actual crossing into this country, the family eventually landed in southern California, where they were received by compatriots who provided food and shelter while they were able to get on their feet. This family was eventually able to rent a small converted garage where everyone lived in approximately 500 square feet. The parents, Juan and Socorro, found employment quickly, although they were paid at below minimum wage. They still felt grateful to earn a paycheck in the United States.

Rogelio's referral was due to his low school performance, the emotional adjustment with transitioning from El Salvador to a set of different realities and expectations in the United States, and his parents' nonavailability due to their work schedules. The referral for this case came from an immigration attorney with whom I had previously conducted several immigration evaluations. Although Rogelio was in a local high school, the language barrier proved to be a major issue for him, and he felt intimidated by many of the other Latino students at his school. Apparently, Rogelio was the only Salvadorian among groups of

Mexican or Mexican American students. As a result, he frequently was the object of teasing for "being too foreign" and because he was from a different sociocultural and political environment that was not Mexican descended. In addition, the fact that he did not have access to resources that many of his classmates had (i.e., available disposable funds, money for school lunch, and easy access to school materials) contributed to Rogelio feeling alone and disconnected.

Counseling was interwoven with individual and family therapy. Family therapy focused on learning to acculturate and developing the necessary tools to establish the family in a way to provide increased financial, educational, and employment security. This approach is often a primary clinical agenda in working with Latino, undocumented immigrants (Falicov, 1998; Santiago-Rivera, Arredondo, & Gallardo-Cooper, 2002). The issue of the parents' nonavailability due to work eventually changed so that there would always be a parent at home who could attend to homework, support involvement in after-school activities, and provide a consistent level of care. Individual counseling with Rogelio focused on helping him become part of a peer group that would give him support and a feeling of fitting in. The counseling process proved to be more of a series of discussions about how to acculturate into a new community as well as how to be a teenager in an environment where there was significantly more access to opportunities. The issue of acculturation proved to be a major hurdle for Rogelio given that he had come from a middle-class environment in El Salvador where his father was a high school teacher and his mother ran a small community center in San Salvador.

Family counseling was found to be well received and highly supportive by this Salvadoran family. Sessions focused primarily on helping members to learn how to fit into a social system that was different and often challenging to the social norms that they had been socialized to in their own country of origin. The parents were pronounced in their intent to be successful in the United States, as they felt they had no other alternative but to advance themselves and their children in this new country. In spite of the barriers faced with limited English-speaking ability and the economic limitations that they had anticipated, this family was found to move quickly in their success as a result of their intrinsic desire, their determination not to return to El Salvador, and firm belief in their vision for the future.

Rogelio and I focused on recognizing the unique differences and strengths of the new country that he had now moved to. As a result, the issue of limited financial means became less important, and his intent to better himself and his family proved to be the signifying motivation that assisted him. Rogelio was seen weekly over a period of 6 months due in large part to his parents' high level of motivation to ensure that their son would not fall into gang activity and that he would learn how to improve himself in his new surrounding. Consequently, the support of his parents proved to be a significant foundation toward his ability to increase his coping and improve his life circumstances. Toward the end of counseling, due to both his improved social status in his peer group and the increased stability and support of his parents, Rogelio was able to find part-time employment working for a local grocery store. Rogelio's English had improved, and he was taken in by the owner of a family supermarket who felt that because of his industrious nature, goodwill, and growing bilingual ability, this boy could be an asset to his own customers.

Commentary

Latina/oimmigrant families have several additional barriers and challenges to handle when they immigrate to the United States (Cervantes et al., 2007; Falicov, 1998). Those challenges become more complex if they are from Central America. A salient aspect of families from Guatemala, El Salvador, and Nicaragua is vivid memories of civil wars that have ravished their communities. For Rogelio's parents, they recalled the terror evident in the 1980s when the counterrevolutionary army would wage war in various communities both within and outside their country's capital, San Salvador. Although Rogelio was not yet born to experience the atrocities of civil war in his country, he nevertheless heard stories from his parents and extended family members about how things used to be and the dangers that were evident just a few years before his birth. Hearing his family's stories of past pain and suffering helped motivate Rogelio to build a better life for him in his new country.

Rogelio demonstrated a high degree of motivation and desire to be a model citizen in the United States. However, a critical distinction for Rogelio, as for many undocumented immigrants, is the fear of deportation (Suarez-Orozco et al., 2002). Rogelio and his family's fragile status in southern California found him to be alert for threats posed by immigration authorities, and the concerns about whether his parents would be discovered while they were working. Sometimes he would have nightmares about his parents being abducted by the Department of Homeland Security. Because of this realistic threat, the parents had enacted certain emergency procedures in the event that they were immediately deported and Rogelio and his younger brothers and sisters were left alone.

This last issue proved to be particularly difficult for me as the treating psychologist with Rogelio's family. I became a relevant contact person for Rogelio in the event that his parents were deported. Clearly, there was an additional personal and professional responsibility unique to clinical practice in this case (Cervantes et al., 2007). This responsibility was framed within an assumed expectation that should Rogelio's parents be deported, I would assume immediate involvement in ensuring that Rogelio and his younger brothers and sisters would be cared for and protected. The role I perceived myself to play was in ensuring that a relative would be available to assist in temporary shelter until the parents' legal situation could be addressed and handled.

Rogelio's short outpatient counseling seemed to provide the necessary foundation for him to quickly thrive given his motivation, intelligence, and desire to succeed in this country. Though Rogelio had several strong male role models in his family, I seemed to play a specific role for Rogelio in being a model of a Latino male who was successful in the United States. Several years have passed since Rogelio was seen, and there have been many "Rogelios" who I have treated professionally with various similar stories, although not always related outcomes. Rogelio went on to be successful, and his family was able to gain citizenship and prosper in this country. Other boys have not had as much good fortune because of either the subsequent deportation of the family or the threat of deportation prompting the family to move out of state.

The Calming Wave in an Unsteady Sea: The Case of Thomas

Thomas Jordan was a 10-year-old African American boy from the projects who was brought into counseling by his maternal grandmother, Ella Daniels. Thomas lived with his grandparents, mother, and three younger brothers and sisters. Mother Ella, as she chose to be called, indicated that her daughter, Thomas's mother, had a serious mental illness since the birth of her youngest child, now age 4. This condition was diagnosed as paranoid schizophrenia for which she was hospitalized on at least two occasions and was taking psychotropic medication. Mother Ella supported the family on a meager salary as a part-time housekeeper and with some aid that she received from the state due to her daughter's mental condition. She reported that the primary reason to pursue counseling for her grandson, Thomas, was due to his continuing history of nightmares, which she felt were prompted by his mother's unstable emotional behavior, her frequent aggression, and her disruptive behavior when she went off her medication.

Thomas impressed as a boy much younger than his stated age with doe-like eyes that made him appear fragile and vulnerable. Thomas reported that he had many friends at school but that he was ashamed to talk about his family because of his mother. Thomas's perceptions of his mother were that "she's crazy all the time and she acts funny and she scares us all." Thomas said all of his aunts and uncles would talk about her, and that made him feel uncomfortable because he wanted to defend her, but did not know how. This concern was one of the primary issues initially in counseling. In addition, Thomas reported having a premonition that something negative would befall his mother. Consequently, it was important that Thomas resolve this issue and feel secure about the home environment where he lived with his grandmother and extended family.

The initial focus in counseling for Thomas was related to the mental illness of his mother, what schizophrenia meant, and the medications that she was taking. In addition, a family genogram was constructed with Thomas's help that focused primarily on those family members who were most helpful and taught him about having good feelings for himself and those whom provided less assistance and were more critical of him and his mother. This dialogue permitted clarity to be reached about his family tree. Thomas became increasingly insightful about what teachings he learned from which relative, and how to access that level of support more readily. Further, this dialogue assisted Thomas to recognize his own innate talents, resources, and possible ways to be increasingly more protective of his mother. After several weeks of working with Thomas, he became more verbal in his assertions about having others not be critical, and assumed a helper role relative to her compliance with medication.

In spite of Thomas and his family's low SES, he always presented himself for counseling neatly dressed, clean, and feeling proud of his appearance. This was related to a comment that Mother Ella had noted earlier about how she felt that for him to grow up and be a "civil individual," he first needed to learn how to dress himself to feel good about his appearance. This was an important lesson gained from Mother Ella, but more importantly it provided the seeds for other therapeutic dialogue about other important lessons Thomas had learned from either immediate family or extended family, friends, or other concerned adults. Thomas and I worked together over a period of one year, as his grandmother felt counseling was providing some safety and she was seeing some positive outcomes. Mother Ella also assured me that Thomas would make all counseling visits as scheduled because keeping promises to others was a lesson Thomas was learning.

Family counseling with Thomas and his maternal grandmother was found to be didactic, where I often supported lessons provided by his grandmother. In brief, the grandmother was moderately authoritarian; however, her strong support of her grandson and the therapeutic process overshadowed any potential negative aspects of her need for control. For example, Mother Ella would frequently comment on what her grandson needed to do to better himself and to increase his success in school. These comments were often buffered with a loving presence and affection that she had for her grandson and a respectful relationship that she perceived to have with me as a counselor. It was clear during those family visits with Mother Ella that she was in charge; however, she always provided a forum for me to comment on her thoughts that would typically be in concert with how I viewed the counseling process to benefit Thomas. Recognition of the grandmother's relational style and the directives that she was trying to teach her grandson was a significant aspect that helped to foster the therapeutic exchange and the support that Mother Ella provided me as a counselor for her grandson.

Toward the latter part of our time together, Thomas's mother had to be hospitalized due to a deterioration of her psychiatric condition. This hospitalization proved difficult for Thomas to witness, as he saw her placed in five-point restraints due to aggressive and assaultive behavior toward all family members. These observations, however, were also helpful in helping him begin to appreciate his mother's fragileness and her inability to fend for herself. This last theme highlighted a discussion about being fragile and how this was inconsistent with the lessons that he was learning from Mother Ella. This therapeutic dialogue involved themes about behaviors and attitudes that are important in growing up to be a man. The discussion focused on being prepared for life's challenges, including seeing many of his peers fall by the wayside due to drug or alcohol problems, and expecting occasions where he may fall down as a result of stresses on his life. Mother Ella's dictates were in concert with our discussion about how he could pick himself up and keep on moving forward.

This dialogue of manhood was short-lived as Thomas and his family were forced to move to another part of the city due to the condemnation of their aging low-income housing. This move made it increasingly more difficult for Mother Ella to bring Thomas for counseling. However, he maintained contact with me through telephone calls over the next year and a half about how he was progressing in school.

Commentary

Thomas was a bright and engaging young boy who had a fierce determination to protect his mother and be a favorite son with his maternal grandmother. In spite of the gloomy environmental circumstances, Thomas was appreciative of all the love and attention he received from his immediate family. Thomas felt like a boy who was destined to succeed because of the strong influence of his grandmother in his life coupled with his own sense of resilience about how he wanted to be successful (Boyd-Franklin, 1989). In addition, Thomas was thoughtful of individuals other than himself, particularly regarding the fragile status of his mother.

This latter aspect, related to his protectiveness of his mother, was a theme used in counseling as part of distinguishing those immediate and extended family members who were helpful from those who were not. This intervention had a direct relationship toward learning how to seek out family resources that could provide his mother the attention and support that she needed (Pruitt, 2007). I felt that Thomas needed to learn how to solicit the support of other family members in caring for his mother. If this was not done, the task would prove to be taxing and overwhelming for this boy. Consequently, providing him the awareness and skills about how to activate levels of support from trusting family members was an effective manner to assist Thomas with this likely overwhelming agenda (Minuchin et al., 2007).

The fact that Thomas was able to maintain contact with me over the next year and a half was confirming of a positive outcome he experienced in his therapeutic relationship. In this case, Thomas already had a strong caring relationship with his maternal grandmother who was determined to see that he was going to be successful in his life. This provided me assurance that even after his premature move from counseling, Thomas would have more than a few life boats to survive as he was navigating his way through adolescence.

FROM THE MOUTHS OF BOYS TO LESSONS FOR THE COUNSELOR: SOME CLOSING COMMENTS

The practice of seeing families for many years has permitted the blending of theory and experience to understand and design unique approaches to working with difficult family systems. As professionals with some learned savvy on navigating treacherous waters in clinical practice, we have worked with children and adolescents as part of our life contribution to provide for the betterment of communities. Experience with boys has taught us many things relative to the issues of manhood, particularly on the importance of role modeling, emotional support, and helping young males develop a perspective on their own lives while taking precautions to avoid therapeutic pitfalls (Hardy & Laszloffy, 2005; Minuchin et al., 2007; Rhule, 2005; Smith, 2005).

Low-income children have an interesting perspective on life. Because of their acute awareness of having limited resources, they also develop unique levels of insightfulness regarding their current circumstances (Boyd-Franklin, 1989). This development of insight appears to be prompted by an increased energy or desire to improve oneself, by learning the language of the street, and by adapting to the more refined language and set of expectations in school. These qualities can help boys to maneuver through various difficult life situations. As such, a state of awareness and hyperalertness tends to be the natural evolution that allows for this navigation process to develop (Boyd-Franklin, 1989; Franklin, 2004). For example, Jimmy Washington's propensity toward being a jokester became an outgrowth of his awareness that this level of interaction with his peers could boost his popularity in school, and perhaps hide some of his shame regarding his impoverished income status. In a similar manner, Rogelio Cruz understood that to succeed, he needed to learn the rules consistent with the new culture of his now adopted country even better than those who were lifetime residents. Lastly, Thomas was bright and quickly able to discern his life circumstances while at the same time never losing sight of his desire to protect his mother. He was alert to what would be most helpful for him, how other relationships could encourage his positive development, and he learned to designate other caretakers for his mother. Consequently, viewing boys from a perspective of hope and competence can provide unique realizations and a gateway toward appropriate interventions that can benefit their future.

Working with boys can provide humility about their particular life circumstances and marvel about their resilience in view of the various challenges to becoming young men. Ultimately, the goal of working with boys is to teach particular developmental skills that allow them to mature, be appropriate and affirming caretakers of themselves and their families, *and provide a legacy for those after them to follow, such that a cycle of wellness becomes a significant agenda in the future of those boys who are watching the evolution of those who have gone before.* Teaching the journey of manhood is an important one for practitioners to recognize as the core of work in the counseling of boys (Hay & Nye, 1998; Roehlkepartain et al., 2006). Toward this end, we as practitioners become accountable to our clients, their respective families, our mutual communities, and the greater vision to share in a better future for everyone.

REFERENCES

American Psychological Association. (2003). Guidelines on multicultural education, training, research, practice, and organizational change for psychologists. *American Psychologist, 58,* 377–402.

American Psychological Association Task Force on Socioeconomic Status. (2007). *Report of the APA Task Force on Socioeconomic Status.* Washington, DC: American Psychological Association.

American Psychiatric Association. (2000). *Diagnostic and statistical manual of the mental disorder: Text revision* (4th ed.). Washington, DC: Author.

Aronen, E. T., & Arajärvi, T. (2000). Effects of early intervention on psychiatric symptoms of young adults in low-risk and high-risk families. *American Journal of Orthopsychiatry, 70,* 223–232.

Black, M. M., & Krishnakumar, A. (1998). Children in low-income, urban settings interventions to promote mental health and well-being. *American Psychologist, 53,* 635–646.

Blow, A. (2001). Common factors across theories of marriage and family therapy: A modified Delphi study. *Journal of Marital and Family Therapy, 27,* 385–402.

Bolger, K. E., Patterson, C. J., Thompson, W. W., & Kupersmidt, J. B. (1995). Psychosocial adjustment among children experiencing persistent and intermittent family economic hardship. *Child Development, 66,* 1107–1129.

Boyd-Franklin, N. (1989). *Black families in therapy: A multi-system approach.* New York: Guilford Press

Boyd-Franklin, N., & Franklin, A. J. (1998). African Americans couples in therapy. In M. McGoldrick (Ed.). *Re-visioning family therapy: Race, culture, and gender in clinical practice* (pp. 261–281). New York: Guilford.

Boyd-Franklin, N., Toussaint, P. A., & Franklin, A. J. (2001). *Boys into men: Raising our African American teenage sons.* New York: Dutton.

Bradley, R. H., & Corwyn, R. F. (2002). Socioeconomic status and child development. *Annual Review of Psychology, 53,* 371–399.

Bradley, R. H., Corwyn, R. F., McAdoo, H. P., & García Coll, C. (2001). Home environments of children in the United States: Part 1. Variations by age, ethnicity, and poverty status. *Child Development, 72,* 1844–1857.

Broderick, P. C., & Blewitt, P. (2006). *The life span: Human development for helping professionals.* Upper Saddle River, NJ: Pearson/Merrill Practice Hall.

Bubolz, M. M. (2001). Family as source, user, and builder of social capital. *Journal of Socio–Economics, 30,* 129–131.

Bullock, H. E., & Lott, B. (2001). Building a research and advocacy agenda on issues of social justice. *Analyses of Social Issues and Public Policy, 1,* 147–162.

Campbell, S. B., Shaw, D. S., & Gilliom, M. (2000). Early externalizing behavior problems: Toddlers and preschoolers at risk for later maladjustment. *Development and Psychopathology, 12,* 467–488.

Cervantes, J. M., Guerrero, A., & Mejia, O. (2007). The role of serial migration, psychological hardships, and psychological issues with undocumented Latino Families. Manuscript submitted for publication.

Chen, E., Langer, D. A., Raphaelson, Y. E., & Matthews, K. A. (2004). Socioeconomic status and health in adolescents: The role of stress interpretations. *Child Development, 75,* 1039–1056.

Choi, Y., Harachi, T. W., Gillmore, M. R., & Catalano, R. F. (2006). Are multiracial adolescents at greater risk? Comparisons of rates, patterns, and correlates of substance use and violence between monoracial and multiracial adolescents. *American Journal of Orthopsychiatry, 76,* 86–97.

Coley, R. L. (2001). (In)visible men: Emerging research on low-income, unmarried, and minority fathers. *American Psychologist, 56,* 743–753.

Conger, R., Conger, K., & Elder, G. (1997). Family economic hardships and adolescent development: Mediating and moderating processes. In G. Duncun & J. Brooks-Gunn (Eds.), *Consequences of growing up poor* (pp. 288–310). New York: Russell Sage Foundations.

Costello, E. J., Compton, S. N., Keeler, G., & Angold, A. (2003). Relationships between poverty and psychopathology: A natural experiment. *Journal of the American Medical Association, 290,* 2023–2029.

Eamon, M. K., & Mulder, C. (2005). Predicting antisocial behavior among Latino young adolescents: An ecological systems analysis. *American Journal of Orthopsychiatry, 75,* 117–127.

Evans, G. W. (2004). The environment of childhood poverty. *American Psychologist, 59,* 77–92.

Falicov, C. (1998). *Latino families in therapy: A guide to multicultural practice.* New York: Guildford Press.

Franklin, A. J. (2004). *From brotherhood to manhood: How Black men rescue their relationships and dreams from the Invisibility Syndrome.* New York: Wiley.

Freeman, J., Epston, D., & Lobovits, D. (1997). *Playful approaches to serious problems: Narrative therapy with children and their families.* New York: Norton.

Garbarino, J. (1995). *Raising children in a socially toxic environment.* San Francisco: Jossey-Bass.

Gilman, S. E., Kawachi, I., Fitzmaurice, G. M., & Buka, S. L. (2002). Socioeconomic status in childhood and the lifetime risk of major depression. *International Journal of Epidemiology, 31,* 359–367.

Goldenberg, H., & Goldenberg, I. (2008). *Family therapy: An overview.* Belmont, CA: Thomson Brooks/Cole.

Goodman, E., Adler, N., Kawachi, I., Frazier, A., & Huang, B. (2001). Adolescents' perception of social status: Development and evaluation of a new indicator. *Pediatrics, 108,* 1–8.

Hardy, K. V., & Laszloffy, T. A. (2005). *Teens who hurt: Clinical interventions to break the cycle of adolescent violence.* New York: Guilford Press.

Hay, D., & Nye, R. (1998). *The spirit of the child.* London: Harper Collins.

Horne, A. M., & Kiselica, M. S. (Eds.). (1999). *Handbook of counseling boys and adolescent males: A practitioner's guide.* Thousand Oaks, CA: Sage

Hubble, M. A., Duncan, B. L., & Miller, S. D. (Eds.). (1999). *The heart and soul of change: What works in therapy.* Washington, DC: American Psychological Association.

Imber-Black, E., Roberts, J., & Whiting, R. A. (Eds.). (2003). *Rituals in families and family therapy.* New York: Norton.

Kiselica, M. S., & Horne, A. M. (1999). For the sake of our nation's sons. In A. M. Horne & M. S. Kiselica (Eds.), *Handbook of counseling boys and adolescent males: A practitioner's guide* (pp. xv–xx). Thousand Oaks, CA: Sage.

Kiselica, M. S., & Woodford, M. S. (2007). Promoting healthy male development: A social justice perspective. In C. Lee (Ed.), *Counseling for social justice* (pp. 111–135). Alexandria, VA: American Counseling Association.

Kuther, T. L., & Wallace, S. A. (2003). Community violence and sociomoral development: An African American cultural perspective. *American Journal of Orthopsychiatry, 73,* 177–189.

Leeder, E. (1996). Speaking rich people's words: Implications of a feminist class analysis and psychotherapy. In M. Hill & E. Rothblum (Eds.), *Classism and feminist therapy: Counting costs* (pp. 45–57). New York: Haworth.

Leventhal, T., & Brooks-Gunn, J. (2000). The neighborhoods they live in: The effects of neighborhood residence on child and adolescent outcomes. *Psychological Bulletin, 126*(2), 309–337.

Leventhal, T., & Brooks-Gunn, J. (2004). A randomized study of neighborhood effects on low-income children's educational outcomes. *Developmental Psychology, 40,* 448–507.

Leventhal, T., Fauth, R. C., & Brooks-Gunn, J. (2005). Neighborhood poverty and public policy: A 5 year follow-up of children's educational outcomes in the New York City moving to opportunity demonstration. *Developmental Psychology, 41,* 933–952.

Lewinsohn, P. M., Joiner, T. E., & Rohde, R. (2001). Evaluation of cognitive diathesis-stress models in predicting major depressive disorder in adolescents. *Journal of Abnormal Psychology, 110,* 203–215.

Littrell, B. (1999). The liberal arts and the working class. *Peace Review, 11*(2), 267–273.

Liu, W. M. (2001). Expanding our understanding of multiculturalism: Developing a social class world view model. In D. B. Pope-Davis & H. L. K. Coleman (Eds.), *The intersection of race, class, and gender in counseling psychology* (pp. 127–170). Thousand Oaks, CA: Sage.

Liu, W. M. (2002). The social class-related experience of men: Integrating theory and practice. *Professional Psychology: Research and Practice, 33,* 355–360.

Liu, W. M., Ali, S. R., Soleck, G., Hopps, J., Dunston, K., & Pickett, T., Jr. (2004). Using social class in counseling psychology research. *Journal of Counseling Psychology, 51*(1), 3–18.

Liu, W. M., Soleck, G., Hopps, J., Dunston, K., & Pickett, T. (2004). A new framework to understand social class in counseling: The social class worldview model and modern classism theory. *Journal of Multicultural Counseling and Developmental, 32,* 95–122.

Loeber, R., & Farrington, D. P. (2000). Young children who commit crime: Epidemiology, developmental origins, risk factors, early interventions, and policy implications. *Development and Psychopathology, 12,* 737–762.

Lott, B. (2001). Low-income parents and the public schools. *Journal of Social Issues, 57*(2), 247–259.

Lott, B. (2002). Cognitive and behavioral distancing from the poor. *American Psychologist, 57,* 100–110.

Lott, B. (2003). Recognizing and welcoming the standpoint of low-income parents in the public schools. *Journal of Educational and Psychological Consultation, 14,* 91–104.

Martin, D. G. (2003). *Clinical practice with adolescents.* Belmont, CA: Brooks/Cole.

McGoldrick, M. (Ed.). (1998). *Re-visioning family therapy: Race, culture, and gender in clinical practice.* New York: Guilford Press.

McGoldrick, M., Giordano, J., & Garcia-Preto, N. (Eds.). (2005). *Ethnicity and family therapy* (3rd ed.). New York: Guilford Press.

McLoyd, V. C. (1998). Socioeconomic disadvantage and child development. *American Psychologist, 53,* 185–204.

Minuchin, P., Colapinto, J., & Minuchin, S. (1998). *Working with families of the poor.* New York: Guilford Press.

Minuchin, P., Colapinto, J., & Minuchin, S. (2007). *Working with families of color.* New York: Guilford Press.

Minuchin, S., Montalvo, B., Guerney, B. G., Rosman, B., & Schumer, F. (1967). *Families of the slums: An exploration of their structure and treatment.* New York: Basic Books.

Mirels, H. L., & Garrett, J. B. (1973). The Protestant ethic as a personality variable. *Journal of Consulting and Clinical Psychology, 36,* 40–44.

Pinsof, W. M., & Lebow, J. L. (Eds.). (2005). *Family psychology: The art of the science.* New York: Oxford Press.

Pruitt, I. (2007). Family treatment approaches for depression in adolescent males. *American Journal of Family Therapy, 35*(1), 69–81.

Repetti, R. L., Taylor, S. E., & Seeman, T. E. (2002). Risky families: Family social environments and the mental and physical health of offspring. *Psychological Bulletin, 128,* 330–366.

Rhule, D. M. (2005). Take care to do no harm: Harmful interventions for youth problem behavior. *Professional Psychology: Research and Practice, 36,* 618–625.

Roehlkepartain, E. C., King, P. E., Wagner, L., & Benson, P. L. (Eds.). (2006). *The handbook of spiritual development in childhood and adolescence.* Thousand Oaks: Sage.

Santiago-Rivera, A. L., Arredondo, P., & Gallardo-Cooper, M. (2002). *Counseling Latinos and la familia.* Thousand Oaks, CA: Sage.

Shapiro, I., Greenstein, R., & Primus, W. (2001, May 31). Pathbreaking CBO study shows dramatic increases in income disparities in 1980s and 1990s: An analysis of CBO data. Center on Budget and Policy Priorities. Retrieved December 17, 2001, from http://www.cbpp.org/5-31-01tax.htm

Skowron, E. A. (2005). Parent differentiation of self and child competence in low-income urban families. *Journal of Counseling Psychology, 52,* 337–346.

Smith, L. (2005). Psychotherapy, classism, and the poor: Conspicuous by their absence. *American Psychologist, 60,* 687–696.

Sprenkle, D. (2004). Common factors and our sacred models. *Journal of Marital and Family Therapy, 30,* 113–129.

Suarez-Orozco, C., Todorova, I. L., & Louie, J. (2002). Making up for lost time: The experience of separation and reunification among Immigrant families. *Family Press, 41,* 625–643.

Thomas, M. (2006). The contributing factors of change in a therapeutic process. *Contemporary Family Therapy: An International Journal, 28,* 201–210.

U.S. Department of Health and Human Services. (1999). *Trends in the well-being of America's children and youth: 1999.* Hyattsville, MD: Author.

Wachtel, E. (1994). *Treating troubled children and their families.* New York: Guilford Press.

Wagner, B. M. (1997). Family risk factors for child and adolescent suicidal behavior. *Psychological Bulletin, 121,* 246–298.

Wallerstein, J. S., & Lewis, J. M. (2004). The unexpected legacy of divorce: Report of a 25-year study. *Psychoanalytic Psychology, 21,* 353–370.

Xue, Y., Leventhal, T., Brooks-Gunn, J., & Earls, F. J. (2005). Neighborhood residence and mental health problems of 5- to 11-year-olds. *Archives of General Psychiatry, 62,* 554–563.

5

Promoting Strength and Recovery

Counseling Boys Who Have Been Sexually Abused

MARK S. KISELICA AND GERALD NOVACK

Over the course of the past 27 years, dozens of boys and men who have been sexually abused have made their way to me in counseling, shattered and trying to cope with nightmares that have become realities for them.* Some of them were abused by their fathers, forced to perform unspeakable acts that robbed them of their dignity. Others became the unwilling sexual partners of their mothers, violated at an early age and left with a warped sense of intimacy. Most were gradually seduced by the seemingly caring but lecherous ploys of significant adult men in their lives whom they had come to trust, whereas others experienced the sudden and shocking terror of a gang rape perpetrated by groups of violent, older boys.

Where does a boy turn when his basic sense of trust has been destroyed? What can a sexually traumatized young man do about his overpowering feelings of fear, pain, and rage? How can he ever feel whole again after his body and soul have been ravaged? These are just

---

* The first-person accounts reported in this chapter are drawn from the clinical experiences of the senior author (MK). In compliance with professional ethical standards, the details pertaining to these experiences have been reported in a way that protects the anonymity of the persons who were involved.

a handful of the central questions that haunt the psyche of boys who have been sexually maltreated, and this chapter is a description of the clinical process of helping these boys to find strength and recovery in the aftermath of child sexual abuse.

This chapter begins with a definition of child sexual abuse, statistics regarding the extent of this serious social problem, and an overview of the traumatic impact of sexual abuse on boys. The characteristics of perpetrators and the recent scandal regarding the widespread sexual abuse of boys by Catholic priests are reported. The process of establishing rapport with boys who have been sexually molested is described, and several key clinical issues pertaining to this work are explored. Throughout the chapter, important cultural factors regarding sexual abuse and boys are considered.

WHAT IS CHILD SEXUAL ABUSE?

Child sexual abuse is the use of a child by another, older individual for his or her own sexual stimulation or for the sexual gratification of others, such as the presentation of children in pornography (Farley, Hebert, & Eckhardt, 1986). According to Oz and Ogiers (2006), the sexual abuse of children takes many forms, including the following:

> Inappropriate sexual remarks made to a minor by an adult; ogling of a child or teenager by an adult; an adult's exposure of his or her sexual organs in view of a minor; peering at a child or teen who is dressing, using the toilet, in the bath, etc.; kissing; fondling; mutual masturbation; [and] penetration. (p. 4)

Although every type of child sexual abuse usually has some adverse effect on the victim, certain forms of maltreatment can be especially harmful and precipitate a psychiatric emergency. Farley and his colleagues (1986) have argued that various types of sexual assault represent the most serious forms of child sexual abuse. These include (a) the penetration of a child's body through either vaginal or anal intercourse or oral sex; and (b) incest, which involves sexual maltreatment by an immediate family member.

HOW COMMON IS THE SEXUAL ABUSE OF BOYS?

Although estimates of the sexual abuse of boys vary widely, they consistently demonstrate that the terror of sexual abuse occurs far too often among boys. According to Baker and King (2004), 16% of adult men claim that they were the victims of child sexual abuse. Other authorities on the subject of child maltreatment have reported that at least 3% and as many as 20% of all boys have been the victim of sexual exploitation (Associated Press, 1998; Holmes & Slap, 1998), and although clear data on racial and ethnic differences are lacking, the best available evidence indicates that most victims are Whites, followed by African Americans, Latinos, and then Asian Americans (Kenny & McEachern, 2000). In a Harris poll of over 3,000 adolescent boys, one in eight reported that he had been sexually abused (*New York Times*, 1998). Based on these various estimates and considering that there are over 10 million boys in the United States (Martin et al., 2005), it is clear that hundreds of thousands, if not millions, of the males who are boys today have suffered some form of sexual abuse.

WHY IS THE SCOPE OF THE PROBLEM DIFFICULT TO ESTIMATE?

Why is it so difficult to get a clear handle on the extent of this problem? One reason has to do with how *sexual abuse* is defined. For example, some officials and researchers may limit their consideration of child sexual abuse to cases involving some form of penetration of the child's body, whereas other professionals include a much broader range of abusive behaviors, including making sexually suggestive comments or fondling a child (Oz & Ogiers, 2006). Another reason the scope of this problem is uncertain has to do with the era during which the sexual abuse of boys has been studied. Decades ago, there was a widespread, mistaken assumption that only girls were victimized, so the problems of boys who were sexually traumatized went overlooked (Bolton, Morris, & MacEachron, 1989). It was also the case that many reported incidents of abuse of young boys were swept under the table by the adults who were responsible with investigating the matter, which was a common response by officials of the Catholic Church until the scandal of priests violating boys became public knowledge a few years ago (Plante, 2004). Homophobia is another factor related to underreporting; many boys who have been violated by other males fear that they will be labeled a "fag" or a "homo" if they reveal the abuse to anyone, so they keep it a secret (Cabe, 1999; Gartner, 1999). Traditional male gender role expectations might also play a role in underreporting: Because males "have been socialized not to show weakness, they are less likely to come forward with an accusation even if they know that, as children, they were smaller and less powerful than their perpetrators" (Long, Burnett, & Thomas, 2006, p. 262). Cultural factors may contribute to underreporting in some cases. For example, taboos about having open discussions about sexuality and an emphasis on emotional stoicism may deter disclosure among some Asian American populations, whereas the Latino cultural norm that children obey adults may lead Latino boys to "comply with adults' sexual advances and to maintain silence if any adult has forbidden disclosure" (Kenny & McEachern, 2000, p. 911). Underreporting is also common with boys who feel guilty about the abuse, fear retaliation from the perpetrator if the abuse is disclosed, or worry that reporting will result in the splitting up of his family, which is a likely outcome when incest has occurred (London, Bruck, Ceci, & Shuman, 2005). Because much of the problem remains hidden, an untold number of violated boys suffer in silence.

WHAT IS THE IMPACT OF SEXUAL ABUSE ON A BOY?

The sexual abuse of boys has far-ranging effects. Almost all boys who have been sexually abused experience some type of symptom. Nightmares, depression, posttraumatic stress disorder, hyperactivity, fear, anxiety, and rage are common reactions (Kempe & Kempe, 1984; Travers, 2002; Whealin, 2006). For some boys, the intense psychological distress associated with the abuse can trigger extreme forms of emotional and behavioral problems, including suicidal behavior, the abuse of drugs and alcohol, and aggressive, delinquent, or criminal transgressions (Giardino, Finkel, Giardino, Seidel, & Ludwig, 1992; Prevent Child Abuse America, 2006). Many boys develop the humiliating problem of encopiesis (involuntary defecation), whereas others lose the healthy sense of comfort that accompanies eating, becoming bulimics who purge themselves of food after binging (Prevent Child Abuse America, 2006). Violent vomiting, physical ailments, the use of laxatives, and bedwetting can also occur (Cabe, 1999; Shrier, Pierce, Emans, & DuRant, 1998). Boys who are forced to have sex against their will are at risk to develop sexually related problems, ranging from the avoidance of anything related to sexuality, the rejection of his genitals, and sexual dysfunction to excessive genital stimulation, seductiveness, hypersexuality, prostitution, not using a condom, sexually aggressive behavior, being involved in an adolescent pregnancy and confused sexual identity (Bolton et al., 1989; Cabe; Prevent Child Abuse America; Saewyc, Magee, & Pettingell, 2004; Shrier et al., 1998). In addition, they are at risk to dissociate from their feelings, repress their awareness of the abuse, and have memory difficulties (Johnson, 1998). A small percentage of boys who have been sexually abused, especially those who also have been the victims of emotional and physical abuse, become sexual offenders (Whealin). Collectively, these outcomes may lead to poor school performance, running away from home, legal trouble, and HIV infection (Prevent Child Abuse America, 2006; Whealin, 2006).

Sexual abuse can shatter a boy's spirit. His childhood is taken from him, and he can become emotionally disfigured. Victimized boys report feeling "dirty," "ugly," and "no good." Typically, they are racked with guilt and filled with a toxic dose of shame. They feel betrayed, fundamentally exploited, "jagged, awry, fractured, [and] recklessly hurt" (Gartner, 1999, p. 13). Incest is an especially damaging trauma for a boy because it

> [i]s a psychologically catastrophic form of sexual abuse. It has even more far-reaching consequences than extrafamilial sexual abuse because it

occurs, often chronically, in the context of a family system that somehow supports it. This is particularly true when the abuser is a parent, because the child grows up chronically trapped in at least one twisted primary relationship. Incest therefore constitutes betrayal at a most profound level. (Gartner, p. 15)

Not surprisingly, boys who have been sexually abused face a lifetime of difficulty with experiencing trust and intimacy. Stripped of their dignity at an early age, many grow up to be damaged men who need help to recover from the maltreatment they were subjected to by their abusers.

WHO ARE THE PERPETRATORS?

One of the shocking—and frightening—facts about the people who sexually abuse boys is that the majority of them are "not remarkably different from other troubled individuals with the exception of the perpetration of the sexual assault and in demonstrating some difficulty in establishing satisfactory emotional and sexual relationships with opposite sex peers" (Bolton et al., 1989, pp. 47–48). What do we know about these individuals?

According to Prevent Child Abuse America (2006),

Sexual abusers of boys tend to be males who are known by the victim, but unrelated to the victim. They tend to abuse the child outside of the home, repeat the abuse, and involve some form of penetration. But, females can also be the perpetrators (boys are more likely than girls to be abused by a female) and tend to use persuasion rather than force or the threat of force. Threats of physical force or actual force are more common with male perpetrators and older victims. (p. 2)

The National Center on Post Traumatic Stress Disorder (Whealin, 2006) confirmed many of these observations, reporting that men are perpetrators in about 86% of male victimization cases. In addition, contrary to the frequent assumption that only gay men would assault boys, "most male perpetrators identify themselves as heterosexuals and often have consensual sexual relationships with women" (Whealin, 2006, p. 1). It is common for the assaults to take place in isolated areas where help is not readily available. Although most perpetrators know their victim, "boys are more likely than girls to be sexually abused by strangers" (p. 1). Boys are also more likely than girls to be assaulted by "authority figures in organizations such as schools, the church, or athletics programs" (p. 1).

According to Kenny and McEachern (2000), there are a few cultural differences associated with who perpetrates the abuse. For example, African American children are most likely to be abused by a biological father, a stranger, or a parent's boyfriend or girlfriend. Mexican American children are more likely to be abused by an extended family member. Among victimized White children, the perpetrators are most often parents and baby sitters.

Bolton et al. (1989) noted that the sexual abuse of boys by family members is probably higher than official estimates would indicate, concluding that incest between both fathers and sons and mothers and sons does occur. However, the authors also hypothesized that certain forms of mother–son abuse, such as fondling, exposure, caressing in a sexualized manner, and forced sexual contact, might be masked as maternal child care and therefore go undetected. Furthermore, although the extent of sibling incest is unclear, there are many cases of incest in which an older sibling uses a younger child rather than a same-age peer as a safe mechanism to explore sex. In other cases where there is a high degree of coercive control, parent–child incest, and/or sibling rivalry in highly dysfunctional families, older siblings have perpetrated highly aggressive sexual assaults of younger siblings.

All perpetrators—whether they are adults or older children and adolescents, family members or nonfamily members, or known figures or strangers—exploit their position of power over a boy to coerce him to have sex against his will. Gartner (1999) explained,

> All sexual acts between children and the people who have power over them are sexually abusive. This is true if the power derives from the actual structure of the relationship (as in the case, for example, of a child abused by a babysitter, teacher, or parent). But it is equally true if the power is inferred by the child because of the age difference between him and the abuser (as in the case, for example, of a young boy abused by a teenager in the neighborhood who is not his caretaker). It is also true no matter how willing the child appears to be to participate in the sexual activity.... "Willing" or not, the child is abused by having the natural developmental unfolding of his sexuality violated and hurried into awareness. (pp. 14–15)

THE SEXUAL ABUSE OF BOYS BY CATHOLIC PRIESTS

Much of the current public awareness and concern about the sexual exploitation of boys was sparked by the stunning disclosure of the widespread abuse of boys by Catholic priests and the long-standing cover-up of this abuse by officials in the Catholic Church. The revelation of this scandal has produced both positive and troubling developments. On the one hand, it helped many men who had been abused by priests when they were boys to seek professional treatment and to take legal action against the perpetrators and the Catholic Church. On the other hand, it has fueled an unfortunate and destructive stereotype depicting priests as pedophiles. Because the Catholic Church and the abuse of boys are topics that are often linked together in the minds of many people, a brief discussion of this scandal, how it was uncovered, and the facts and myths it has spawned is warranted.

Although the sexual abuse of boys by Catholic priests has been a problem for more than 1,000 years (Plante, 2004), it did not become a public concern until the latter part of the 20th century. During the 1960s and 1970s, taboos about the open discussion of sexual matters were gradually lifted. Consequently, sexually related problems, such as child sexual abuse, were moved gradually into the spotlight, prompting government officials to pass mandatory child abuse reporting laws, which allowed officials to get a better understanding about the scope of the problem (Bolton et al., 1989). Initially, public concern was focused on the sexual abuse of girls. However, during the late 1980s and throughout the 1990s, advocates for boys and men began to address the hidden problem of the sexual abuse of males. For example, in 1988 a group of mental health professionals dedicated to helping adult men who had been victims of sexual abuse when they were children organized a national conference on male sexual victimization. Several of the key organizers of this conference formed the National Organization on Male Sexual Victimization (NOMSV) in 1994 (Male Survivor, 2004). NOMSV and other similar organizations, such as SNAP: The Survivors Network of Those Abused by Priests, helped many men who were survivors of child sexual abuse to find support and healing from the damage that had been inflicted upon them by their perpetrators, many of whom had been Catholic priests (SNAP, 2006). As more and more survivors filed charges against allegedly offending priests and lawsuits against various Catholic dioceses, the abuse of boys by priests became an international sensation.

When did this abuse occur, and how common was the problem? Citing the results of a study conducted by the John Jay College of Criminal Justice in New York, which surveyed all Catholic dioceses in the United States, Bono (2006) reported that "4,392 clergymen—almost all [of whom were] priests—were accused of abusing 10,667 people, with 75% of the incidents taking place between 1960 and 1984" (¶ 2). Eighty-one percent of these victims were males, and 40% of the victims were boys aged 11 to 14. Most of the accused had allegedly committed a variety of serious sexual offenses, and although the abuse occurred in many places, most incidences of abuse took place in the residence of the priest. The offending priests lured their victims into having sex through a number of ploys, such as buying the victim gifts, allowing the victim to drive a car, and taking the victim to a sporting event. Abuse occurred in 95% of the Catholic dioceses in the United States (Bono, 2006).

When alarmed parents approached Catholic officials with concerns that their children had been abused, official responses varied from diocese to diocese and included suspension, placement on administrative leave, and referral of offending priests for medical evaluation and treatment (Bono, 2006). However, in some dioceses church officials engaged in an elaborate cover-up of abuse cases and merely transferred offending priests to different parishes. One of the most shocking examples of this practice took place in the archdiocese of Boston, where church officials shuttled offending priests from parish to parish while stonewalling or paying off the victims of abuse. As a result of this practice, several priests became serial sex offenders, including John J. Geoghan, who allegedly fondled or raped over 130 children "during a three-decade spree through a half-dozen Greater Boston parishes. Almost always, his victims were grammar school boys. One was just 4 years old" (Globe Spotlight Team, 2002, ¶ 2–3).

After these disturbing practices were revealed by the media and in response to public outcry for reforms, in 2002 the United States Conference of Catholic Bishops proposed *The Charter for the Protection of Children and Young People,* a new policy for dealing with abusive priests, which called for the barring of offending priests from having any contact with parishioners (Religionlink.org, 2006, ¶ 4). In addition, the Catholic Church has issued recent policy statements proclaiming that the sexual abuse of children is a sin and that the covering up of abuse is a breach of secular law (Wikipedia, 2006, ¶ 5). Furthermore, the Catholic Church in the United States has taken many recent measures to prevent sexual abuse within the Catholic community (Thavis, 2004).

In spite of these recent actions, the Catholic Church remains under a veil of suspicion. Many victims of abuse by priests are not satisfied with the church's response to the crisis.

> Victims['] groups say the new policy does not go far enough because it does not call for the automatic defrocking of priests, nor does it assign any blame or responsibility to bishops who moved abusive priests from parish to parish. (Religionlink.org, 2006, ¶5)

The atmosphere of mistrust has been devastating for the vast majority of priests who are not child molesters. Jokes about priests being pedophiles are rampant, many Catholic parents are leery of leaving their children alone with priests, and many fine priests themselves are concerned about ministering to children in one-on-one situations (Paulson, 2002).

What does all of this mean for mental health professionals? Above all else, professional helpers must think complexly about priests and the sexual abuse of boys, understanding the scope of the problem, while countering harmful stereotypes about priests. Specifically, counselors must recognize that thousands of males have been victimized by disturbed priests. These boys and men, their families, and the parishes to which they belong need the compassionate assistance of professionals as they struggle to recover from the trauma of abuse and the impact it has had on their lives and their communities. At the same time, counselors must avoid stereotyping priests as sexual predators. The data from the John Jay study show that 96% of priests have never been charged with committing any sexual offense (Bono, 2006), which suggests that the vast majority of priests are decent men who are dedicated to their ministries. Affirming these good men and working to eradicate pejorative stereotypes about them will help the Catholic community to be a place of healing for the males who were the tragic victims of abuse by the clergy they had trusted.

PROMOTING STRENGTH AND RECOVERY WITH BOYS WHO HAVE BEEN SEXUALLY ABUSED

Counseling boys who have been sexually abused is a delicate process that varies according to when and how the abuse has been disclosed. In my experience, most boys begin psychotherapy after the abuse has been revealed, and they are brought to the counselor's office by a caring parent or a child protection worker seeking assistance for the boy in the aftermath of a sexual assault. In other instances, which tend to be less common, a boy reveals the abuse to his therapist during treatment for some other difficulty, such as counseling for anger management problems and acting-out behaviors that are affecting the boy's adjustment at home and school. Although both types of cases involve boys and families who are in a crisis, the latter cases tend to be more difficult to manage because the disclosure of the abuse during therapy triggers an intense and frightening period of mandated reporting of the abuse by the therapist, official investigations into the matter by child protection workers, and tremendous uncertainty about how the crisis will be played out. Because counselors who work with boys are likely to experience each type of situation, both are addressed here in our approach to counseling boys who have been sexually abused and their families.

As a preliminary note, we must acknowledge our discussion does not include an overview of the medical evaluation of a boy who is a suspected victim of sexual abuse, which is a very detailed assessment that should be conducted by a competent health care professional. We refer readers who want to learn more about these evaluations to excellent resources on the subject by Giardino et al. (1992), and Heger, Emans, and Muram (2000). Furthermore, we have chosen not to describe the process of family therapy that includes the participation of the perpetrator in cases involving incest because this approach to treatment is highly controversial and complicated. Victim advocacy groups argue that therapy with incest victims should emphasize protection of the child, removal of the offending family member from the home, and punishment of the perpetrator. Some family systems professionals, however, prefer to work with all family members, including perpetrators, to address the conditions of betrayal, secrecy, boundary violations, denial, sexual dynamics, and coalitions that foster the incestuous abuse of a child. This controversy and the family systems approach to the treatment of incest that includes the perpetrator are complex subjects that cannot be covered adequately in a single chapter. Therefore, readers are directed to Friedrich (1990) for his overview of this controversy and to Faller (1988) and Friedrich for in-depth descriptions of the challenging clinical process of addressing incest with the entire family system. All of our suggestions about family counseling in this chapter do not involve the presence of the perpetrator in family sessions.

WHAT TO DO WHEN A BOY REPORTS DURING
COUNSELING OR PSYCHOTHERAPY THAT
HE HAS BEEN SEXUALLY ABUSED

Keeping the secret of sexual abuse from others is a terrible burden for a terrified, wounded boy to bear. Nevertheless, fear can cause a boy to lock the truth about his horrific experience inside of him. He may hide his abuse for weeks, months, or even years, while the weight of his private ordeal drags him down, affects his well-being, and lands him in the office of a counselor for help with some "other problem," such as depression, suicidal ideation, drug abuse, running away from home, or fighting. During the process of addressing these sorts of problems under the compassionate guidance of a caring counselor, a damaged and frightened boy can learn that it is possible to trust his counselor with *anything—even the unmentionable*. It is then that he will risk telling his counselor about his living nightmare.

Imagine what this moment must be like for the boy in this situation. He is racked with fear. He is confused. He is angry. He is in pain. And he is unsure about what lies ahead. *What he needs most of all at this moment is an anchor*—someone to steady him and keep him from being engulfed by the stormy seas that are threatening to sweep over him. He needs his counselor to remain calm. He needs his counselor to give him direction. *And he needs his counselor to believe him.*

Travers (2002) urged counselors to avoid overreacting to a child who has just disclosed that he has been sexually abused. Overreacting can fuel the child's fear. By comparison, remaining concerned but calm gives the worried boy a message that the counselor is in command and knows how to handle the situation. Initially, the counselor should refrain from asking too many questions and allow the boy to tell his story at his own pace (Travers, 2002). We suggest that the counselor carefully follow the boy's cues, and once it is clear that the boy has shared all that he had to say on his own, the counselor should inquire further about what happened to the boy and begin forecasting for him what will take place now that the abuse has been disclosed.

What information should this forecast include, and how should it be delivered? We urge counselors to remember that the purposes of information giving during counseling or psychotherapy are to help a client cope with difficult situations, gain new perspectives about his or her problems, and anticipate and understand difficult situations. Furthermore, information giving must be provided in simple, clear terms and in doses that the client can absorb. In addition, the counselor must help the client to process the impact of the information and assist the client to handle any "disequilibrium that comes with the news" (Egan, 2002, p. 206). Applying these considerations in therapy with a sexually traumatized boy, the counselor's job is to weave information about sexual abuse into a therapeutic process whereby the counselor helps the boy to understand and adjust to the information. We offer the following recommendations pertaining to these tasks, which we based on our clinical experiences with boys and several other sources (Ludwig, 1995; Travers, 2002; Vancouver Incest and Sexual Abuse Center, 1991a, 1991b):

- Praise the boy for his courage in telling you about the abuse. Empathize with how difficult it must have been for him to carry his secret and to risk sharing it with you.
- Report to the boy that research shows that most sexually victimized boys and men feel relief after revealing the abuse to someone. At the same time, tell him that it is natural to be afraid about what might happen next and that you will support him during this period of uncertainty.
- Tell the boy that you must ask him a few questions to clarify what happened to him, and then find out where, when, and for how long the abuse occurred; the nature of the abuse; and who the perpetrator was.
- Take your time while acquiring this information from him, and use more than one session if necessary. Also, comfort the boy by offering him a drink or candy to consume or, with a young boy, toys to play with or a teddy bear to hold while he tells you his story. (It would be prudent not to use these means, however, if they were used as part of the abuser's repertoire to abuse the boy.)
- Explain to the boy that you have a legal obligation to report the allegation of abuse to child protection authorities. Let him know that these individuals will investigate the situation, interview him, protect him from additional abuse, and potentially take action against the perpetrator.
- Prepare him for the possibility that he might have to undergo a medical examination, the police might get involved, and, if there is enough evidence to prosecute the perpetrator, court proceedings might take place. Forewarn him that he might have to testify before the court and his abuser, but that he will be protected from any harm if that situation arises.
- Explore the possible outcomes of a court case with him. If the abuser is found guilty, he or she will receive a sentence and some type of punishment, which could include imprisonment. If the abuser is found innocent, he or she will be set free.
- Let the boy know that you can help him to tell his parents and investigating officials about his abuse if he wants your assistance in doing so.
- Predict that he will likely need to participate in counseling for some time to help him understand and cope with everything that he has been through and with any difficulties that might arise in the future. Reassure him that counseling can help him to feel better about himself and his world around him.

- Process the boy's reactions and answer his questions pertaining to each of these pieces of information. Assure him that you will be by his side throughout the investigation and prosecution phases of his experience.
- Carefully document the information the boy has disclosed to you so that you can provide an accurate report to the appropriate child protective agency in your state.

AFTER THE ABUSE HAS BEEN DISCLOSED: ESTABLISHING TRUST AND RAPPORT WITH A BOY WHO HAS BEEN SEXUALLY ABUSED

Cabe (1999) noted that most people have difficulty talking about sex with a stranger. So, Cabe continued, imagine how uncomfortable it must be for a boy in acute psychic pain and filled with shame to describe to a counselor the details of his experiences of being sexually abused. With such a boy,

> Rapport is, at its most basic level, a willingness by the therapist to endure the suffering of the child with an accurate and child-focused empathy. If we recoil at his disclosures, no matter how horrific, he will not disclose. If we do not feel his pain, he will endure it alone. If we cannot be truly present with him and allow him to be fully present with us and then allow ourselves to enter his pain, he will not heal. (Cabe, 1999, p. 205)

A boy who has been sexually abused needs to know what to expect in his interactions with a counselor, because entering ambiguous situations in the aftermath of abuse can be extremely frightening. Bolton et al. (1989) recommended explaining to the boy that the purpose of counseling is to help him learn how to discuss the details of his abuse in a safe place, to express and accept his feelings about the abuse, to understand that he is not responsible for the assault he suffered, and to feel better again. Both Cabe (1999) and Camino (2000) underscored the importance of assuring the boy that everything he tells the counselor will be held in the strictest confidence except in cases where there is clear duty to break confidentiality. In these special cases, referred to in the professional literature as *duty-to-warn obligations*, the counselor must help the boy to understand that it may be necessary to warn his parents or some outside authorities if further abuse is revealed or if the client becomes a risk to hurt himself or someone else. Camino added that whenever a professional complies with duty-to-warn requirements, the counselor must apprise the client that he or she is doing so, whereas Cabe (1999) urged counselors to inform the boy that other individuals, including parents and foster parents, will be invited into sessions only with the child's permission.

The process of helping a sexually traumatized young man to tell his story cannot be rushed. The counselor must wait the boy out, while trying to get to know the boy. Kiselica (1999, 2006) recommended that counselors employ several male-friendly tactics that can help a troubled boy feel at ease. For example, the counselor can play board and electronic games, toss a ball, share a snack and a drink, go for side-by-side walks in places where a boy feels safe, talk about sports and music, tell a timely joke, and employ self-disclosure to help a boy become comfortable (Kiselica, 1999, 2006). Counselors can help a younger boy to relax by playing with him, using toys, dolls, and puppets (Bolton et al., 1989). Kiselica (1999, 2006) noted that boys often share bits of personal information about themselves, including significant clinical material about their sexual lives and traumatic events, over an extended period of time while participating in these types of activities. Thus, the counselor must be patient with the boy and may have to piece his story together after it has been disclosed in a sometimes haphazard and interrupted manner.

Cabe (1999) also accentuated the necessity of taking things slowly with a boy who has been sexually abused, noting that he may be so damaged that simply trying to exist can be an emotionally exhausting experience for him. In addition, Cabe urged counselors to be extremely cautious about touching the boy at any time without his permission, because he may view any physical contact as a potential attempt to hurt him. These measures create healthy and safe boundaries within which the boy can begin the process of addressing the difficult issues that affect him.

LONG-TERM COUNSELING WITH BOYS
WHO HAVE BEEN SEXUALLY ABUSED

Once the therapist senses that he or she has earned the trust of the boy, the process of conducting long-term therapy can begin. But how should this therapy be structured? One approach, proposed by Bolton et al. (1989), is to systematically address (a) distorted beliefs and attitudes, (b) affective reactions, and (c) dysfunctional behavioral responses to the abuse. For example, the belief that the world is a reasonably safe place is shattered for a boy who has been sexually abused. He may blame himself for the abuse and, because he is a male, may conclude that he should have been tough and smart enough to protect himself from the perpetrator. He may see all adult men as potential abusers if the perpetrator was an adult male, see all older teenager boys as dangerous if he was assaulted by an older boy, and be sexually attracted to only older women if he was exploited by an adult woman. If his abuser was a male, the boy may fear that he is bound to become a homosexual. No matter who his abuser was, he might be filled with rage and a desire to seek revenge, sometimes displacing his anger onto other innocent victims through physical or sexual aggression. To counter these maladaptive beliefs, feelings, and behaviors, Bolton et al. recommended the following:

- Explain to him that some adults (or older, more powerful children) want to have sex with children even when they know they shouldn't. These adults (or older children) have a problem and exploit their position of power, and the abuse is their responsibility, not the boy's.
- Point out to him that *some* but not *all* adults (or older children) are interested in sexual activity with children. Discuss with the boy the people in his world who have related to him in a respectful and protective manner so that he has a better sense of the people in his life whom he can trust.
- Help him to assert his power and social competency by teaching him to tell others when he feels afraid or to learn how to avoid potential abusers and dangerous situations.
- Assure him that the abuse had nothing to do with his sexuality and that he will not necessarily become a homosexual because his perpetrator was male. Explain to him that sexual identity is the result of a complex interplay of factors, not sexual abuse. Affirm him, and address any signs of internalized homophobia if he appears to have a homosexual identity.
- Desensitize his fear of certain situations by gradually exposing him to those situations while armed with coping skills, such as relaxation responses and positive self-statements.
- Acknowledge that it is normal to feel angry at his abuser, and help him to find appropriate means of expressing that anger (e.g., talking about his anger or producing stories with angry feelings).
- Teach him that being angry doesn't mean that it is OK to hurt someone else or to behave in a sexually reckless manner. Discourage aggressive and sexually inappropriate behavior, and provide instruction and reinforcement of anger control and sexually healthy behavior.

Camino (2000) emphasized addressing power issues with abused boys. When a perpetrator forces him or herself on an innocent boy, the boy is overpowered and helpless. Unless he resolves his feelings of powerlessness, Camino added, he is at risk to continue to see himself as a helpless victim or he might try to regain power by dominating others through aggressive and abusive behaviors. Consequently, a foundation for shepherding a boy toward a healthy recovery is to help him address his feelings of powerlessness and to differentiate between negative and positive uses of power: "During therapy boys are taught that exerting power and control over one's own behavior is positive and desirable, whereas exerting power and control over another person is not" (Camino, 2000, p. 8). Specifically, during counseling, the therapist must help the boy to see the power he has over the behaviors he engages in and to take full responsibilities for his actions. With the help of the therapist, he must learn how to evaluate the effectiveness of every decision he makes, to learn from his mistakes, and to replace problematic behavior patterns with effective ones. Furthermore,

> Authority tends to be threatening for a sexually abused boy, so you need to remember that part of your responsibility is to correct his image of authority figures. You can provide a positive image by giving support, setting limits firmly and gently, demonstrating respect for the boy's personal boundaries, and showing that you believe in what he tells you. (Camino, p. 9)

One of the concerns an abused boy may have about his own sense of power is his fear that he might become an abuser himself. In response to this concern, Camino (2000) recommended empathizing with this concern while explaining to the youngster that the majority of children who have been sexually abused do not become sexual offenders. Also, directly talk with the boy about these fears, and help him to learn the distinction between being powerful and controlling others.

Another approach to fostering a healthy sense of power is to teach a wounded boy about sex. Lamb (2006) suggested that therapists do sex education, particularly emphasizing positive sexual relations, with boys who have been sexually abused to help address the questions they have about sex. Discussions about sex with a caring therapist within the safe confines of the therapeutic relationship can help an abused boy to sort through the confusion he has about sex, intimacy, trust, and power.

A boy who has been sexually abused has a variety of needs that must be addressed if he is to feel whole again. First and foremost, he must feel safe. In cases where incest has occurred, the boy may have to be removed from his home in order to assure his safety (Cabe, 1999). Regardless of whom the perpetrator was, the counselor must work with the authorities to ensure that the boy is never left alone with his perpetrator (Bean & Bennett, 1997). Encouraging him to join team sports and school clubs can foster his sense of belonging, which can be crucial for his recovery (Cabe, 1999). As he strives to develop a trusted support network, it can help to share with him these words of advice from Bean and Bennett (1997):

> It is important to set up a system of safe, protective, and caring people who will give you support when you have difficulties dealing with your abuse issues. These are people who respect you physically and emotionally. They listen to you and demonstrate that they heard and understood you. They don't touch you when you don't want to be touched, and they don't force you to talk when you don't want to. They respect your boundaries.
>
> When considering who are safe people for you, determine whether they care about you and your welfare even when you make mistakes, rather than turn away from you....We have different friends for different reasons. It is the same with safe people. You may feel comfortable talking with your best friend about your anger at your parent(s) but not about your other feelings. You might prefer telling an older cousin or a counselor about those other feelings.
>
> Both adults and other kids can be safe people. They may be family members, friends, therapists, school personnel, or clergy. Often school

counselors and clergy will make time to talk with you even if they don't already know you. They can be a good beginning in developing a safety network. (p. 3)

Although the creation of a support network can help a boy who has been sexually abused to feel safer, he may still feel permanently damaged and require special interventions designed to eliminate his sense of being "damaged goods":

> In some cases, especially those involving force, physical injury may have occurred. In most of the cases I have seen, the boy will feel as if others can somehow tell what was done to him, and he feels as if others view him as damaged. A simple mirror in the therapy room may help to alleviate the second of those concerns, and a good examination can alleviate the first, assuming that the physical damage is repaired. Self-portraits, photos of the child before and after the assault, full-body drawings for younger boys, and the positive, understanding, nonjudgmental regard of the therapist and significant others in the child's life will all help heal his sense of damage. (Cabe, 1999, p. 208)

These latter strategies illustrate that therapists may have to use many creative approaches with boys who have been sexually abused, which vary according to a child's age. For example, play therapy and art therapy are excellent modalities for counseling younger boys who have been sexually abused because these approaches to therapy do not require participants to put their experiences into words, which can be a very difficult task for a traumatized young boy to do. Cabe (1997) recommended Grounded Play Therapy, which is the use of various forms of media to help boys who have been sexually abused to express and come to terms with their traumatic experiences. Toys, artwork, kinesthetic activities, self-portraits, and games (e.g., *The Talking, Feeling, Doing Game* by Gardner, 1973) are used in developmentally appropriate ways to help victimized boys release pent-up emotions and to address issues of powerlessness within the sanctuary of play. For example, a therapist and a boy pound pillows, or a youngster can draw and shred drawings of monsters or pop balloons with nasty faces on them, all as a means to express anger (Cabe, 1999). Dozens of play therapy techniques have been developed, and they are described in detail in several fine resources on the subject (Ater, 2001; Cabe, 1997; Homeyer, 2001; Kaduson & Schaefer, 1997; Lamb, 2006).

Waller (2001) has observed that art therapy is a particularly effective creative approach to helping sexually abused children achieve recovery:

> Engaging in art therapy may give an opportunity to open a window onto the child's world and their experience of internal damage, and enable them to form a relationship with someone who will be able to cope with their communication, however painful and messy without retaliation. (p. xv)

According to Murphy (2001b), art therapy offers a child a transitional space that is safer and less intense than verbal therapy. The use of art materials with traumatized children provides "a means of expressing, holding and recognising the feelings resulting from traumatic experience and so the beginning of separating from it" (Murphy, 2001b, pp. 3–4). For example, sculpting with clay and finger painting can help a boy who dissociates from his feelings to reawaken his emotions and release them in a safe and acceptable manner. Horrible assaults can be "described" and chronicled symbolically through drawings until the boy is able to put his trauma behind him (Murphy, 2001b). For a more extensive description of art therapy with sexually abused children, please refer to Brooke (1997), Gil (2003), Klorer (2003), and Murphy (2001a).

Although art therapy can be used with boys of all ages, some older boys prefer concrete, direct activities that help them address specific issues and challenges related to their abuse, such as understanding their symptoms, how and when to share the story of their abuse with others, and whether or not they should confront the offender. For these boys, we recommend reading the superb self-help book, *The Me Nobody Knows: A Guidebook for Teen Survivors* (Bean & Bennett, 1997), which is written specifically for teenagers who have been sexually abused and includes exercises addressing numerous, common concerns of abuse survivors. We also recommend *Treatment Strategies for Abused Adolescents: From Victim to Survivor* (Karp, Butler, & Bergstrom, 1998), which contains 61 activities that are designed to help sexually abused teenagers move through four stages of the recovery process: (a) developing a therapeutic relationship with the therapist, (b) processing the abuse, (c) repairing the sense of self, and (d) becoming more future oriented. A similar body of activities that is designed for use in group work with sexually abused youth is described in *Group Work With Sexually Abused Children: A Practitioner's Guide* (Grotsky, Camerer, & Damiano, 2000).

FAMILY COUNSELING

The sexual assault of a boy can plunge his entire family into a crisis. Loving parents can feel their son's pain, as can his siblings, even when they have not been told about their brother's abuse. The family system can be thrown out of kilter, as family members, especially parents, try to cope with their own feelings about the ominous shadow that has been cast over their family:

> They feel threatened. They feel shame and guilt. Their personal self-esteem is lowered. They are anxious and fearful about what will be said about their family and their ability to protect. In the worst case, the parent who does not know how to help becomes frustrated and angry at the child victim: angry for "getting yourself into a situation in which such a thing could happen!".... The minimal treatment[,] then, is to provide an atmosphere in which the whole family can come to understand why sexual assault sometimes occurs and how it can be prevented from happening again. (Bolton et al., 1989, pp. 125–126)

Faller (1988) suggested that there are several crucial treatment issues that must be addressed with families, including the following: helping family members to process their feelings about the abuse, shifting responsibility for the sexual abuse away from the family or the victimized boy to the perpetrator, resolving any disputes in the family that may be related to the abuse or had existed prior to the onset of the abuse, and managing child management problems the parents might be having with the abused child or his siblings.

Therapists must be sensitive to address the needs of a boy's parents as they work with the therapist to help their son recover from his traumatic experiences. As a starting point, Camino (2000) suggested educating the parents about sexual abuse and its ramifications. We agree with this recommendation, but we forewarn counselors that receiving this information can intensify the feelings of guilt some parents may have about not protecting their son, their anger at the perpetrator, and, in rare cases, even their anger at their own son for "allowing this to happen." Consequently, the counselor may have to spend time responding to these reactions, genuinely empathizing with the parents' experiences during this troubling time. At the same time, the therapist must delicately redirect the parents away from any counterproductive thoughts, feelings, and behaviors, to the conviction that recovery for their son is not only possible but also likely if the parents follow the counselor's advice about how to help him. For example, as Camino (2000) noted, the parents may believe that their son should have known how to stop the abuse, or they may fear that being molested will make their son less of a man. In response, the therapist must assure the parents that any child can be sexually victimized by a more powerful, cunning perpetrator and that an abused boy can grow up to be a vibrant, strong, and self-reliant man if he is nurtured and reassured by his parents during this difficult chapter in his life. Specifically, Camino recommended that parents can guide their son to recovery by doing the following:

- Helping to restore his sense of personal power
- Protecting him from further harm
- Validating his feelings
- Enhancing his self-esteem
- Encouraging him to safely manage his anger
- Enforcing privacy and boundaries in the home
- Providing sex education for him

CASE STUDY: HELPING ED TO FEEL WHOLE AGAIN

Ed was a 15-year-old African American boy who had been referred for counseling by his grandmother, Mrs. T., Ed's legal guardian. Mrs. T. was deeply worried about Ed, who had started running away from home about 5 years before the start of psychotherapy. For the past 2 years, Ed had run away for long periods, ranging from several days to months at a time, and he would get arrested on vagrancy and drug possession charges while he was on the run. Mrs. T. was concerned that Ed would never catch up in school and would end up in jail, so she initiated counseling with the hope that a trained professional could help Ed "to turn his life around."

Mrs. T. and Ed attended the initial session with the senior author (MK). During this session, the therapist warmly greeted Mrs. T. and Ed; informed them about the confidential nature of counseling, including circumstances that might warrant a duty to break confidentiality; and asked them to tell him about their concerns. Throughout most of the first session, Mrs. T. reported the history of problems with Ed, who was mainly silent though respectful toward his grandmother. After getting a good sense of Mrs. T.'s concerns, the therapist asked Mrs. T. for her permission to talk with Ed alone and explained to her that the therapist's approach to counseling involved a balancing of individual and family sessions. Mrs. T. approved of this plan, and said that she sensed the therapist cared for her and her family. Because that was the case, she was fine with Ed talking privately with the therapist, adding that she wanted Ed to find someone he could trust "to take care of whatever is troubling him."

When Mrs. T. left the room, the therapist explained to Ed that he sensed Ed was reluctant to talk at this time. He assured Ed that it was OK to take his time and that it might help Ed to know the therapist's approach to counseling. He explained that he would not play any head games with Ed and that he would use their first couple of sessions to get to know each other. They could have their sessions with his grandmother or alone, whichever Ed preferred, and gradually they would discuss the issues that were triggering Ed's running away from home.

Much to the therapist's pleasant surprise, Ed responded by saying how badly he felt for having hurt his grandmother. He was grateful for his grandmother's love and considered her the last person in the world he would ever want to hurt. But, he said, "I am f—ked-up in the head," and it seems "I always manage to hurt somebody. A lot of wild shit has happened, and if I don't tell somebody about it soon, I may end up killing myself."

In response to this last statement, the therapist did an extensive suicide assessment with Ed, and determined he had suicidal thoughts and periodic impulses to overdose on drugs, but had never actually tried to kill himself. Although he knew how to get access to "any type of drug," he currently had only a couple of joints of marijuana hidden away at home. His love for his grandmother was keeping him alive, but he still felt very depressed and confused about "a lot of things." The therapist empathized with Ed's depression and confusion, and determined that Ed was not quite ready to talk about those "things," but got assurances from Ed that he would not attempt to hurt himself before their next session.

The therapist gave Ed his card and also the phone numbers of a suicide crisis line and a teen runaway center, getting Ed to promise that he would turn to these contacts should he experience a crisis in the next 24 hours. In addition, he expressed his concern for Ed, and offered to squeeze Ed in for another session the next day if Ed was OK with that. Ed accepted this offer, and, after Mrs. T. approved the follow-up appointment, Ed returned to see the therapist the next day.

Ed began the next session with a bright affect and an air of excitement in his voice, while Mrs. T. waited for Ed in the lobby. Ed related to the therapist as though he had found a new friend, eager to talk and connect. Ed jumped from one subject to the next, telling the therapist about the music he loved, the drugs he had done, and some of his adventures while he "was on the road"—meaning when he had run away. Gradually, he became more serious and subdued as he talked about these experiences, and rather quickly admitted that he had turned to prostitution to support himself during some of his more desperate moments on the run when he was living on the streets. Specifically, he had sold his body for sex with adult men, and he was deeply ashamed and in a state of disbelief that he had actually engaged in such behavior.

The admission of his acts of prostitution prompted the therapist to question Ed in a gentle manner about his sexual experiences and why he had run away from home in the first place. It was then that Ed admitted he had been sexually abused for the first time at the age of 7 by an uncle who had lived with him and his grandmother for several years. The uncle had been a transvestite and a drug abuser, who was in and out of jail for drug offenses until he died of a heroin overdose when Ed was 13 years old. Prior to his death, the uncle had forced Ed to engage in oral sex repeatedly, and he had sodomized Ed many times. He also had forced Ed to dress up in women's clothing and, in an almost affectionate way, taught Ed "how to become a woman." The abuse always occurred when his grandmother was out at the two jobs she held to support her, Ed, and her son, who was Ed's uncle.

These experiences created tremendous turmoil for Ed. He started abusing drugs at age 9 and running away from home "by age 10 or 11" when he felt the need to escape from his uncle. Over time, his abuse of drugs became more intense, including the use of pot, uppers, and downers, and his runs from home became more frequent, longer in duration, and more daring. It was during his long-term runs of a month or more that he had turned to prostitution to survive. Through prostitution he was abused by many men, all strangers who took advantage of Ed even though he was a minor. One had beaten him with hangers during sex, and others had him get high with them during their encounters.

In response to this startling information, the therapist developed a therapeutic plan that included two stages. In the first stage, the therapist would report the many acts of abuse Ed had suffered to a state child protection agency charged with handling child abuse matters, and he would support Ed during the associated investigatory process that would follow. Although the therapist was unsure if the state would take any action because one of the perpetrators was dead and the others were strangers, he decided that it would be prudent to have the abuse on record and to try and get the state to offer support for Ed, Mrs. T., and their family. In the second stage, the therapist would assist Ed with the many long-term issues stemming from the abuse.

Stage 1 posed many challenges to the therapeutic relationship. Ed was terribly troubled that reporting the abuse would get his grandmother in trouble, and he didn't want that to happen. The therapist realized that Ed might try to protect his grandmother by running away from home again before a caseworker could become involved with him. So, the therapist decided to take action right away to minimize the chances that Ed would flee the area. The therapist talked with Ed about his fears and empathically predicted for Ed that he would have the urge to run now that he had revealed his history to someone. The therapist urged Ed to consider telling his grandmother about the abuse immediately rather than running away, and proposed that he ask his grandmother to join them in the session and ask her help reporting the abuse to the authorities. Although Ed was on the verge of panic, the therapist comforted him, telling him it was normal to experience panic now that his secrets had been revealed. Ed was also concerned about how his grandmother would take the news. He feared that she would reject him because she was a devout Christian, and he wondered if he was gay, which she might view as a sin. The therapist responded by accentuating the concern the grandmother had shown for Ed by taking him in for counseling, and he promised to help both of them as they reacted to the news that was about to be revealed. Although Ed had his doubts, he trusted the therapist, and agreed to go ahead with the plan. The therapist rehearsed with Ed how he would tell his grandmother—telling her generally what had happened by stating that he had been "molested" but not going into extensive details.

Fortunately, Mrs. T. could not have been more supportive when Ed finally broke the news to her. She cried and stated, "I can't believe this has happened to my baby!" Nevertheless, her only impulse at this moment was to protect her grandson, and she reached out and held onto Ed as she sobbed for him. Ed took great comfort in his grandmother's arms, and it appeared that both of them experienced some relief now that the root issue associated with his running away was in the open. Following the guidelines that were described earlier in this chapter, the therapist explained to them what would happen once the abuse was reported to the authorities, and that a likely outcome would be the provision of supportive services, given that the authorities would be unlikely to find any of the perpetrators. And that is exactly what happened a few days later after Ed, Mrs. T., and the therapist reported the abuse to a caseworker, who investigated the matter, which eventually culminated in the provision of state-funded service for the both of them.

The second stage of therapy lasted for several years. One of the first things the therapist did during the second stage of therapy was to arrange for Ed to enter a therapeutic group program for teens with substance abuse issues. In addition, he continued to have both individual sessions with Ed and family sessions with Ed and Mrs. T. During individual therapy, the therapist and Ed addressed his feelings about the abuse using the book *The Me Nobody Knows* (Bean & Bennett, 1997) as a stimulus for discussions between them. At times, the therapist helped Ed to vent his anger in creative ways. For example, they once went to a junkyard, lined up a row of old bottles, and Ed smashed them with rocks, finding relief in watching the glass shatter. On several occasions, the therapist employed the empty chair technique as another vehicle for unloading and understanding the mixed feelings he had toward his uncle. The therapist also helped Ed to see the link between his abuse and his habit of running away. The therapist explained to Ed that running away from home was a way to exert power to escape from an intolerable situation, but that running would no longer help him. They discussed alternate ways that Ed could exert power, such as being cautious around more powerful people who might be in a position to exploit him, and talking to his therapist, crisis phone workers, or his peers in the addictions treatment group when he felt overwhelmed. The therapist also engaged Ed in career counseling, helping him to identify the graphic arts as a direction he might like to pursue, which inspired him to invest himself more eagerly in his education.

All of these interventions helped Ed to become more stable. However, he continued to struggle with other issues that were much more difficult to rectify. For example, an extensive amount of time was devoted to helping Ed clarify his sexual identity. At the start of therapy, Ed was unsure if he was gay, a transvestite, or possibly a transsexual. He reported that he had had sex with girls to prove that he was not gay "like them"—his perpetrators. However, he gradually admitted that he was never attracted to girls and had always felt a strong pull toward boys, even before the abuse had occurred. He explored websites, such as freetobeme.com (n.d.) and http://www.outproud.com (1995/2007) where he was able to investigate his questions about his sexuality in a safe manner and then discuss his reactions to these websites in therapy. The therapist helped him to understand the difference between pedophiles, who sexually prey on children, and gay men, who have a homosexual identity. By the time he terminated counseling, he was still a bit confused about his sexual identify, but he recognized that most gay men were decent people whom he had no reason to fear. He became more accepting of his growing gay awareness, and he made plans to join a support group for gay, lesbian, bisexual, and transgendered youth at a community college, where he intended to enroll in courses after completing high school.

A related issue for Ed was trying to like himself and to fit in. Initially, he felt like a freak and hated himself for having been a prostitute. His self-hatred was also related to internalized homophobia. His education about homosexuality and the acceptance of the therapist helped him to realize that the prostitution had been a dangerous but transient survival strategy and that there was nothing wrong with being gay. On the contrary, the therapist taught Ed about gay pride, but Ed was still confused enough about his sexual identity that he was not ready to come out about his sexuality. Nevertheless, he was heading in that direction at termination, and he felt much better about himself as a person. His feelings of self-acceptance were bolstered by his acceptance by other students who shared his interest in art. He joined an art club, and enjoyed hanging out with other teenagers who were handy with generating art on the computer.

Ed and Mrs. T. did tremendous work during their family sessions. Initially, the focus of these sessions was focused on Mrs. T.'s guilt for the presence of her son in their home and the abuse he had inflicted on Ed. Ed was very kind to his grandmother whenever this issue came up, assuring her that she was not to blame for his abuse. On the contrary, he told her that she was "his heart" and that she had been the one who had adopted him when his own mother had proved to be unfit due to her addiction to drugs. Recognizing the importance of extended kin in African American families (see Boyd-Franklin, 2003), the therapist discussed with Ed and Mrs. T. the idea of inviting extended family members to sessions to help Ed deal with his loneliness and depression. Together, Ed and Mrs. T. determined that one of Ed's older cousins, Donnie, was a trustworthy relative who could mentor the boy. So, Donnie attended a couple of sessions and identified activities the two could do together, such as going to movies and concerts. Donnie's mentorship and the caring stance of the therapist helped Ed to learn to trust men again, which was a crucial development in his gradual recovery from the abuse.

CONCLUSION

In this chapter, we have provided an overview of the sexual abuse of boys, the common adjustment difficulties these boys experience, and the process of helping them. Through our discussion of the case pertaining to Ed and his family, we illustrated the challenges associated with earning the trust of a boy who has been sexually abused, reporting abuse to authorities, addressing the long-term issues of a boy who is a survivor, considering culture-specific strategies that are required for an effective intervention, and juggling individual and family sessions.

Although the problem of the sexual abuse of boys has gained increased attention over the past few years, which has resulted in a growing literature on how to serve this population, we remain concerned that there is not enough instruction in graduate programs in psychology, counseling, social work, and marriage and family therapy about working with boys in general and boys who have been sexually abused in particular. Consequently, we recommend that academicians develop more specialized courses on counseling boys and men and that those courses include sections on helping boys and men to recover from the horror of childhood sexual abuse. In addition, we observe that there is very little empirical research evaluating the effectiveness of therapy with this population. The literature cited in this chapter is drawn from the anecdotal reports of veteran counselors and psychotherapists who have reported on the methods they use to successfully treat boys who have been sexually abused and their families. We encourage therapists who work with boys who have been sexually abused in individual therapy to employ single-case research designs as a preliminary way to more clearly identify effective strategies with this population. In addition, we urge clinicians who facilitate therapeutic groups with boys who have been sexually abused to use comparison-group designs to evaluate the relative efficacy of different approaches to treatment. Collectively, these strategies will help us to learn more about better serving boys as they move from being wounded victims to thriving survivors.

REFERENCES

Associated Press. (1998, December 2). Boys don't report sex abuse. *Bucks County (Pa.) Courier Times*, p. A1.

Ater, M. K. (2001). Play therapy behaviors of sexually abused children. In G. L. Landreth (Ed.), *Innovations in play therapy: Issues, process, and special populations* (pp. 119–130). Philadelphia: Brunner-Routledge.

Baker, D., & King, S. E. (2004). Child sexual abuse and incest. In R. T. Francoeur & R. J. Noonan (Eds.), *International encyclopedia of sexuality* (pp. 1233–1237). New York: Continuum.

Bean, B., & Bennett, S. (1997). *The me nobody knows: A guidebook for teen survivors*. San Francisco: Jossey-Bass.

Bolton, R. G., Morris, L. A., & MacEachron, A. E. (1989). *Males at risk: The other side of child sexual abuse*. Thousand Oaks, CA: Sage.

Bono, A. (2006). *John Jay study reveals extent of abuse problem*. Retrieved April 14, 2006, from http://www.americancatholic.org/News/ClergySexAbuse

Boyd-Franklin, N. (2003). *Black families in therapy: Understanding the African American experience* (2nd ed.). New York: Guilford.

Brooke, S. L. (1997). *Art therapy with sexual abuse survivors*. Springfield, IL: Charles C. Thomas.

Bryant-Davis, T. (2005). *Thriving in the wake of trauma: A multicultural guide*. Westport, CT: Greenwood.

Cabe, N. (1997). Conduct disorders: Grounded play therapy. In H. G. Kaduson, D. Cangelosi, & C. Schaefer (Eds.), *The playing cure* (pp. 229–253). Northvale, NJ: Jason Aronson.

Cabe, N. (1999). Abused boys and adolescents: Out of the shadows. In A. M. Horne & M. S. Kiselica (Eds.), *Handbook of counseling boys and adolescent males: A practitioner's guide* (pp. 199–218). Thousand Oaks, CA: Sage.

Camino, L. (2000). *Treating sexually abused boys: A practical guide for therapists & counselors.* San Francisco: Jossey-Bass.

Egan, G. (2002). *The skilled helper: A problem-management and opportunity-development approach to helping* (7th ed.). Pacific Grove, CA: Brooks/Cole.

Faller, K. C. (1988). *Child sexual abuse: An interdisciplinary manual for diagnosis, case management, and treatment.* New York: Columbia University Press.

Farley, G. K., Hebert, F. B., & Eckhardt, L. O. (1986). *Handbook of child and adolescent psychiatric emergencies.* New York: Elsevier Science.

Freetobeme.com. (N.d.). *Free to be me: Becoming the person I want to be.* Retrieved July 2, 2007, from http://www.freetobeme.com

Friedrich, W. N. (1990). *Psychotherapy of sexually abused children and their families.* New York: Norton.

Gardner, R. (1973). *The talking, feeling, doing game.* Creskill, NJ: Creative Therapeutics.

Gartner, R. B. (1999). *Betrayed as boys: Psychodynamic treatment of sexually abused men.* New York: Guilford.

Giardino, A. P., Finkel, M. A., Giardino, E. R., Seidl, T., & Ludwig, S. (1992). *A practical guide to the evaluation of sexual abuse in the prepubertal child.* Newbury Park, CA: Sage.

Gil, E. (2003). Art and play therapy with sexually abused children. In C. A. Malchiodi (Ed.), *Handbook of art therapy* (pp. 152–166). New York: Guilford.

Globe Spotlight Team. (2002). *Church allowed abuse by priests for years.* Retrieved August 21, 2006, from http://www.boston.com/globe/spotlight/abuse/stories/010602_geoghan.htm

Grotsky, L., Camerer, C., & Damiano, L. (2000). *Group work with sexually abused children: A practitioner's guide.* Thousand Oaks, CA: Sage.

Heger, A., Emans, S. J., & Muram, D. (Eds.). (2000). *Evaluation of the sexually abused child* (2nd ed.). Oxford: Oxford University Press.

Holmes, W. C., & Slap, G. B. (1998). Sexual abuse of boys: Definition, prevalence, correlates, sequelae, and management. *JAMA, 280,* 1855–1862.

Homeyer, L. E. (2001). Identifying sexually abused children in play therapy. In G. L. Landreth (Ed.), *Innovations in play therapy: Issues, process, and special populations* (pp. 131–154). Philadelphia: Brunner-Routledge.

Johnson, K. (1998). *Trauma in the lives of children: Crisis and stress management techniques for counselors, teachers, and other professionals.* Alameda, CA: Hunter House.

Kaduson, H., & Schaefer, C. (Eds.). (1997). *101 favorite play therapy techniques.* Northvale, NJ: Jason Aronson.

Karp, C. L., Butler, T. L., & Bergstrom, S. C. (1998). *Treatment strategies for abused adolescents: From victim to survivor.* Thousand Oaks, CA: Sage.

Kempe, R. S., & Kempe, C. H. (1984). *The common secret: Sexual abuse of children and adolescents.* New York: Freeman.

Kenny, M. C., & McEachern, A. G. (2000). Racial, ethnic, and cultural factors of childhood sexual abuse: A selected review of the literature. *Clinical Psychology Review, 20,* 905–922.

Kiselica, M. S. (1999). Counseling teen fathers. In A. M. Horne & M. S. Kiselica (Eds.), *Handbook of counseling boys and adolescent males: A practitioner's guide* (pp. 179–198). Thousand Oaks, CA: Sage.

Kiselica, M. S. (2006). Helping a boy become a parent: Male-sensitive psychotherapy with a teenage father. In M. Englar-Carlson & M. Stevens (Eds.), *In the room with men: A casebook of therapeutic change* (pp. 225–240). Washington, DC: American Psychological Association.

Klorer, P. G. (2003). Sexually abused children: Group approaches. In C. A. Malchiodi (Ed.), *Handbook of art therapy* (pp. 339–350). New York: Guilford.

Lamb, S. (2006). *Sex, therapy, and kids: Addressing their concerns through talk and play.* New York: Norton.

Lewin, T. (1998, June 26). One in eight boys of high-school age has been abused, survey shows. *New York Times*, p. A11.

London, K., Bruck, M., Ceci, S. J., & Shuman, D. W. (2005). Disclosure of child sexual abuse: What does the research tell us about the ways that children tell? *Psychology, Public Policy, and Law, 11,* 194–226.

Long, L. L., Burnett, J. A., & Thomas, V. (2006). *Sexuality counseling: An integrative approach.* Upper Saddle River, NJ: Pearson/Merrill/Prentice/Hall.

Ludwig, S. E. (1995). *After you tell.* East York, Ontario: The Sex Information and Education Council of Canada. Retrieved September 22, 2006, from http://www.phac-aspc.gc.ca/ncfv-cnivf/familyviolence/html/nfntsxarevel_e.html

Male Survivor. (2004). *Our history.* Retrieved August 21, 2006, from http://www.malesurvivor.org/About%20Us/index.htm

Martin, J. A., Hamilton, B .E., Sutton, P. D., Ventura, S. J., Menacker, F., & Munson, M. L. (2005). Births: Final data for 2003. *National Vital Statistics Reports, 54*(2). Hyattsville, MD: National Center for Health Statistics.

Murphy, J. (Ed.). (2001a). *Art therapy with young survivors of sexual abuse: Lost for words.* Philadelphia: Brunner-Routledge.

Murphy, J. (2001b). Introduction. In M. Murphy (Ed.), *Art therapy with young survivors of sexual abuse: Lost for words* (pp. 1–15). Philadelphia: Brunner-Routledge.

New York Times, June 26, 1998, p. A11.

Outproud.org (1995/2007). *Outproud: Be yourself.* Retrieved July 2, 2007 from http://www.outproud.org

Oz, S., & Ogiers, S. (2006). *The wall of fear: Recovery from childhood sexual abuse.* New York: Haworth Maltreatment and Trauma Press.

Paulson, M. (2002). *After sex abuse scandals, many priests tread warily.* Retrieved September 15, 2006, from http://www.boston.com/globe/spotlight/abuse/stories/011302_wary.htm

Plante, T. G. (Ed.). (2004). *Sin against the innocents: Sexual abuse by priests and the role of the Catholic Church.* Westport, CT: Greenwood.

Prevent Child Abuse America. (2006). *Fact sheet: Sexual abuse of boys.* Retrieved August 21, 2006, from http://member.preventchildabuse.org/site/PageServer?pagename=research_fact_sheets

Religionlink.org. (2006). *Sexual abuse and Catholic Church's civil liability.* Religion Newswriters Foundation. Retrieved September 15, 2006, from http://www.religionlink.org/tip_020624c.php

Saewyc, E. M., Magee, L.L., & Pettingell, S. E. (2004). Teenage pregnancy and associated risk behaviors among sexually abused adolescents. *Perspectives on Sexual and Reproductive Health, 36,* 98–105.

Shrier, L. A., Pierce, J. D., Emans, J., & DuRant, R. H. (1998). Gender differences in risk behaviors associated with forced or pressured sex. *Archives of Pediatric Adolescent Medicine, 152,* 57–63.

SNAP. (2006). *SNAP mission statement.* Retrieved August 21, 2006, from http://www.snapnetwork.org/links_homepage/mission_statement.htm

Thavis, J. (2004, February 18). *Vatican: Church must work with scientific experts to prevent abuse.* Washington, DC: Catholic News Service/U.S. Conference of Catholic Bishops. Retrieved September 16, 2006, from http://www.catholicnews.com/data/stories/cns/20040218.htm

Travers, P. (2002). *The counselor's helpdesk.* Pacific Grove, CA: Brooks/Cole.

Vancouver Incest and Sexual Abuse Center. (1991a). *When boys have been sexually abused: A guide for young boys.* Retrieved September 22, 2006, from http://www.phac-aspc.gc.ca/ncfv-cnivf/familyviolence/nfntsabus_e.html

Vancouver Incest and Sexual Abuse Center. (1991b). *When teenage boys have been sexually abused: A guide for teenage boys.* Retrieved September 22, 2006, from http://www.phac-aspc.gc.ca/ncfv-cnivf/familyviolence/nfntsabus_e.html

Waller, D. (2001). Foreword. In M. Murphy (Ed.), *Art therapy with young survivors of sexual abuse: Lost for words* (pp. xv–xvi). Philadelphia: Brunner-Routledge.

Whealin, J. M. (2006). *Men and sexual trauma.* Washington, DC: National Center for PTSD. Retrieved August 21, 2006, from http://www.ncptsd.va.gov/facts/specific/fs_male_sexual_assault.html

Wikipedia. (2006). *Roman Catholic sex abuse cases.* Retrieved September 16, 2006, from http://en.wikipedia.org/wiki/Roman_Catholic_Church_sex_abuse_scandal.

6

Examining Depression and Suicidality in Boys and Male Adolescents

An Overview and Clinical Considerations

MARK C. FLEMING AND MATT ENGLAR-CARLSON

For years, adolescence was depicted as a time of "emotional turmoil" as characterized by G. Stanley Hall's phrase of "storm and stress" and highlighted by supposed shifts in personality and conflicts with parents. The contemporary awareness of adolescence now recognizes this period as a significant transitional phase of life distinct from childhood and adulthood marked by psychosocial transformations that include pubertal growth, identity formation, individuation from parents, and the establishment of intimate relationships (Gerard & Buehler, 2004). Although this transition period has never been easy, adolescence is a powerful period of self-discovery and emerging independence. At the same time, there are specific vulnerabilities associated with adolescence linked to developmental changes and certain risky behaviors (Irwin, Burg, & Cart, 2002). The onset of adolescence for many adolescents is often associated with more frequent negative affect (Larson & Lampman-Petraitis, 1989), more negative life events (Larson & Ham, 1993), and increased rates of behavioral and psychological problems (Petersen & Hamburg, 1986). For some, transition and change during this time of life are greatly influenced by experiencing depression. Adolescent depression is widely recognized as being severely debilitating (Lewinsohn, Rohde, & Seeley, 1998) and associated with numerous negative events, including suicide (Beautrais, Joyce, & Mulder, 1996) and future adult psychopathology (Lewinsohn et al., 1998), with prevalence rates similar to those seen in adults (Schraedley, Gotlib, & Hayward, 1999). Of particular concern is evidence indicating that depression may have a more negative impact on adolescents than on adults (Gotlib, Lewinsohn, & Seeley, 1995; Rohde, Lewinsohn, & Seeley, 1994).

For males, there are special considerations in adolescence that can contribute to an array of complicated feelings, emotions, and thoughts that contribute to adolescent depression and suicidality. Though many boys and male adolescents experience normal adolescent development without any major psychological or emotional problems, some may react to this time of life by developing various forms of melancholy, including depressed mood, depressive syndrome, clinical depression, and suicidal ideation (Culp, Clyman, & Culp, 1995). Compared to girls, boys tend to experience higher rates of chronic stress (Shih, Eberhart, Hammen, & Brennan, 2006) related to noninterpersonal stressors (e.g., academic; Sund, Larsson, & Wichstrom, 2003). For boys, there may also be questions and conflicts associated with navigating the masculine socialization process. Pollack (1998) outlined the difficulties associated for boys in attempting to live up to traditional conceptions of masculinity that may be in conflict with a boy's own emotions, thoughts, and lived experiences.

The clinical issues of assessing and treating adolescent depression and suicidality are of importance for all counselors who treat boys and male adolescents. There is a recent emphasis on understanding the unique manner in which depression manifests in males that is not represented by typical categorical notions of depression (e.g., the *Diagnostic and Statistical Manual*, or *DSM*; for the *DSM-IV-TR*, see American Psychiatric Association, 2000). Although primarily focused on adult men, the concept of male depression assumes that the well-known depressive symptoms in males are compensated for or masked by external behavioral patterns, which are atypical for depression and therefore not included in conventional depression inventories (Cochran & Rabinowitz, 2003). Many young male clients will not freely admit or reveal the depths of their depression or suicidal thoughts. In terms of depression, adolescents are less likely to accurately assess symptoms of depression in boys, and when they do, girls are more successful in labeling depression than boys (Burns & Rapee, 2006). For counselors, one of the difficulties in assessing and understanding boys and depression can be assessing between normative adolescent behavior, normative male adolescent behavior, and adolescent depression. This chapter explores adolescent depression and suicide in boys and male adolescents, strategies for establishing rapport, and interventions for working with depressed and suicidal boys. A case study illustrating the clinical process of working with a depressed boy is provided.

ADOLESCENT DEPRESSION

It has been only in the last 30 years that mental health professionals operated with the understanding that adolescents could experience depression. Depression was traditionally assumed to be an "adult disease," thus the mental health profession's knowledge about adolescent depression is still limited, yet growing at a fast pace. It is now clear that adolescent depression is a common, chronic, and serious illness (Evans et al., 2005; Haavisto et al., 2004). Separate diagnostic categories for mood disorders in children or adolescents are not found in the *DSM-IV* (American Psychiatric Association, 2000). The symptoms required to be diagnosed with a major depressive disorder are the same for children, adolescents, and adults except for one variation. For children and adolescents, irritable mood can be substituted for a depressed mood. Major depression is often first experienced in adolescence and young adulthood, with prepubertal onset being less common (Evans et al.). Although boys present a similar or even slightly higher rate of depressive symptoms than girls prior to adolescence, girls become more depressive than boys during their teenage years (Marcotte, Fortin, Potvin, & Papillon, 2002). However, it is possible that many cases of depressed among teenage boys may go undiagnosed because they might be masked by substance abuse and acting-out behaviors (seekwellness. com, 2005).

Depression among teenagers has emerged as a major mental health problem. Between 20% and 35% of boys and 25% to 40% of girls have been identified as having experienced a depressed mood (Petersen et al., 1993). The Youth Risk Behavior Surveillance data for 2005 (Centers for Disease Control and Prevention [CDC], 2007) indicated that 28.5% of youth (36.7% female and 20.4% male) felt so sad or hopeless almost every day for 2 weeks or more in a row that they stopped doing some usual activities during the past 12 months. Prevalence rates for adolescent depression tend to be similar to those for adult populations. Leadbeater, Blatt, and Quinlan (1995) reviewed multiple studies on prevalence and found that 13.5% to 34% of adolescents reported moderate levels of depression, whereas 5% to 8.6% of adolescents reported more severe levels of depressive symptoms. Other evidence indicates that adolescent depression is likely underdiagnosed. Roberts, Lewinsohn, and Seeley (1995) examined depressive symptoms with 1,710 adolescents and found that 30% of the adolescents reported at least one current symptom of major depression, but only 2.6% had received a diagnosis. Lewinsohn et al. (1998) estimated that approximately 28% of adolescents will have an experience of major depression disorder by the time they are 19. The finding that adolescent girls experience higher rates of depression compared with boys is robust and has been consistent over time, with most studies reporting a typical ratio of 2:1 (Evans et al., 2005; Leadbeater et al., 1995; Lewinsohn et al., 1998). This is similar to the ratio of adult depression between male and female adults. Even though girls do report higher rates of depressive disorders, the rate of male depressive symptoms is serious and warrants much closer attention than has been previously available.

Adolescent depression can manifest in a number of ways including feeling sad, lonely, unloved, and worthless, and through feelings of helplessness, hopelessness, inferiority, inadequacy, and perceiving a failure to meet the internalized needs of others (Culp et al., 1995; Dixon, 1987). Depression in adolescents may also manifest in the form of impairments and hardships, such as psychosocial dysfunction, psychiatric comorbidity, withdrawal from social activities, academic failure, substance use, and suicidal behavior (Haavisto et al., 2004). Specifically, boys are likely to endorse depressive symptoms that express antagonism, aggression, and an inability to work (Leadbeater et al., 1995). The consequences of a depressive episode during adolescence are serious, the most dramatic being the risk of school dropout and suicidal behavior (Lewinsohn, Gotlib, & Seeley, 1995). Puig-Antich et al. (1993) found that adolescents with depression have shorter friendships and are less popular among their peers in school. Moreover, the probability of experiencing a second depressive episode during adolescence or early adulthood constitutes a major risk (Kandel & Davies, 1986).

Although the difficulties associated with depression may first arise during adolescence, they have been shown to predict future problems, such as dropping out of school, becoming unemployed, abusing alcohol and drugs, engaging in illegal activities, and having an increased risk of depression in adulthood (Haavisto et al., 2004; Kandel & Davies, 1986). About two thirds of adolescents who experience depression between the ages of 14 and 16 will experience another episode of depression before the age of 21 (Fergusson & Woodward, 2002).

How Is Depression Different Between Boys and Girls?

Though there are similarities in the experience of depression, there are also noted differences between boys and girls. For girls, early changes associated with puberty have been associated with depression, yet in contrast, many of the changes associated with puberty for boys (e.g., increased height and weight) are associated with higher status. However, the timing of pubertal changes (e.g., girls with early pubertal changes and boys with later pubertal changes), relative to one's peers, has been related to depressed mood among both boys and girls (Siegel, Aneshensel, Taub, Cantwell, & Driscoll, 1998). Some studies have strongly linked physical and sexual abuse to depression in boys (Schraedley et al., 1999). A few studies have specifically found that adolescent girls tend to experience more interpersonal stress, whereas boys report more school-related or noninterpersonal stress (Larson & Ham, 1993; Rudolph & Hammen, 1999). Adolescent boys' depressive symptoms are more strongly correlated with noninterpersonal stressors. Specifically, boys are more reactive to school-related stress, suggesting that this may be a domain that boys value more (Sund et al., 2003). Bennett, Ambrosini, Kudes, Metz, and Rabinovich (2005) found that depressed girls and boys had similar symptom prevalence and severity ratings for most depressive symptoms on the Beck Depression Inventory, but boys had higher clinician ratings of anhedonia, depressed morning mood, and morning fatigue. In a 10-year follow-up study of adolescent boys, Haavisto et al. (2004) found that at age 18, the male participants who were depressed had poor adaptive functions with family and school, had somatic health complaints, and used illicit drugs. Self-reported depressive symptoms at age 8 predicted increased numbers of symptoms at age 18. This suggested that child-hood depression in boys may be overlooked and thus go untreated. These same boys were at risk for dropping out from meaningful life goals and becoming marginalized in society. An interesting finding from this study was the association between depressive symptoms and having fewer than two friends. This tends to question the idea that boys are not vulnerable to depression as a function of their interpersonal relation-ships. Pollack (1998) noted the understanding that strong relationships for boys can serve a preventative function and keep depression at bay.

As with adults, comorbidity with other disorders is often the rule rather than the exception for adolescent depression (Angold, Costello, & Erkanli, 1999). Adolescent boys tend to experience more externalizing problem behaviors (e.g., oppositional disorders, delinquency, and school problems; Leadbeater et al., 1995). There are particular concerns with depression and conduct problems in boys because studies of the co-occurrence between depression and conduct or oppositional disorders suggest an elevated risk for the other (Angold & Costello, 1993). One of the questions in term of adolescent depression in boys is whether depression contributes to comorbid problems or whether other dis-orders or problems lead to adolescent depression. Beyers and Loeber (2003) found that depressed mood tended to predict a variety of delin-quent acts in a sample of male adolescents. Specifically, depressed mood in their sample significantly predicted a more positive rate of change in delinquency.

There are specific considerations in regard to diverse groups of boys and depression. Social class and race or ethnicity have been identified as correlates of adolescent depressive symptoms (Siegel et al., 1998). Being of lower social class is associated with higher emotional distress among adolescents (Kaplan, Hong, & Weinhold, 1984). This effect may be associated with the greater number of undesirable life events that poor youth experience (Gore, Aseltine, & Colton, 1992). Furthermore, long-term poverty has a more detrimental effect on children's mental health than transient poverty (McLeod & Shanahan, 1996).

Rates of adolescent depression may be higher among adolescents in some ethnic groups or their subgroups (Rushton, Forcier, & Schectman, 2002). However, it is difficult to determine the exact differences because racial and ethnic disparities on depressive symptoms are not consistent in the literature. For example, in a study of multiethnic adolescents, Siegel et al. (1998) found that compared to Whites, African Americans, or Asian Americans, Latinos reported more symptoms of depressed mood. In terms of gender, Latino boys reported the highest level of depressive symptomology, whereas White boys reported the lowest levels (Siegel et al., 1998). Gore and Aseltine (2003) also reported that Latino American adolescents had higher levels of depression than other ethnic groups. Further, African American adolescents had higher levels of depression than either Whites or Asian Americans. In a review of community studies of adolescent depression, Fleming and Offord (1990) reported that African American adolescents had higher rates of depressed mood than Whites.

There are special issues regarding the relationship between academic success, the academic environment, and the mental health of ethnic or racial minority boys. Research shows that among some minority boys and girls, scholastic activity threatens peer acceptance (Gerard & Buehler, 2004). In their study on school environment and maladjustment, Gerard and Buehler (2004) found that scholastic ability heightened the risk for depressed mood among at-risk African American and Hispanic boys and girls. In my (MF) clinical work, I have worked with many African American adolescent boys who were depressed and, at times, suicidal. For some of these boys, their depression was directly related to scholastic issues. One young man was depressed because he was the only African American in his classes. He was in the honors program in his school and was often teased by his African American peers for being too White and for being smart. He was constantly told and reminded by his African American and Caucasian peers that African American boys who were that smart were either gay or wanted to be White. He struggled immensely as he tried to navigate his parents' high academic expectations and his need for acceptance amongst his peer group.

The conflict created by trying to meet opposing values of one's peer group and society can lead to emotional distress, particularly when boys deal with various types of pressure to conform to group standards (Luther & McMahon, 1996). Specifically, Osborne (1999) reviewed the literature surrounding identification and achievement in African American boys. His review of the literature showed that African American boys are often faced with the dilemma of attaining academic success while simultaneously attempting to identify with their nonsuccessful academic peers. Fordham and Ogbu (1986) noted that academic success in the African American male peer group is often neither rewarded nor accepted, and it can be detrimental to one's social identity. As a result, African American boys are forced to cope with membership in a stigmatized group that espouses opposition to academic success. Helping African American boys to sort through these perceptions and pressures might play a key in preventing depression among some members of this population.

Why Is Depression Different in Boys?

One explanation to explain gender differences regarding depression during adolescence is Hill and Lynch's (1983) gender intensification hypothesis. This model hypothesized that body changes related to puberty heighten teenagers' attention to the significance of their gender. Because adolescents are still navigating and exploring their gender role identification, they may tend to rely more on gender stereotypes as models. In accordance with that perspective, Alfieri, Ruble, and Higgins (1996) observed an increased adherence to feminine stereotypes in girls with age as well as an increased identification with masculine stereotypes in boys. Thus, the socialization of girls and boys is related to differences found in the expression of psychological distress, with girls showing more internalizing patterns of symptom expression and boys showing more externalizing patterns (Leadbeater et al., 1995).

Other ideas as to why adolescence girls experience higher rates of depression than boys include notions that girls have a greater exposure and reactivity to stressors; specifically, girls tend to put more importance on interpersonal relationships, they generate more interpersonal stress than boys (Rudolph, 2002), and thus they experience more interpersonal stress than boys (Shih et al., 2006). Girls may also experience more stressors related to their social networks (e.g., friends and family), whereas boys tend to experience stress that directly affect themselves, rather than family and friends (Gore, Aseltine, & Colton, 1993). Further, exposure to stressful life events tends to be more predictive of depression in girls than in boys (Marcotte et al., 2002; Schraedley et al., 1999). Interestingly, girls tend to experience more episodic stress, whereas boys report higher levels of chronic stress (Shih et al., 2006). In terms of experiencing depression, it seems that boys express their difficulties through externalizing problem behaviors (e.g., oppositional disorders, delinquency, and school problems).

Other attempts to understand depression and boys are based on developmental and gender socialization theories and are generated from notions about the experience of adult men and depression. In this regard, there has been an emphasis on understanding adult male depression in response to research indicating that men are diagnosed with depression less frequently than women yet complete suicides two to four times more often (Cochran, 2001; Cochran & Rabinowitz, 2000; Möller-Leimkuehler, 2003). Depression in men is likely to be underdiagnosed due to the expression of symptoms that differ from the *DSM-IV-TR* criteria (American Psychiatric Association, 2000; Real, 1997). Cochran and Rabinowitz (2003) noted the influence of male gender role socialization, which encourages stoicism and suppression of emotion, as one of the several factors that obscures the expression of depressed mood in many men. Masculine prohibitions placed on men against the experience of mood states of depression (e.g., sadness) and the behavioral expression of these mood states (e.g., crying) make clear and simple descriptions of male depression difficult (Cochran & Rabinowitz, 2000). In this regard, though men show lower rates of depression, it is posited this is due to underdiagnosis because men tend to "mask" their symptoms and thus are not diagnosed or referred for counseling.

Male socialization has been described as promoting the avoidance of emotional expression, the absence of weaknesses or vulnerabilities, and the need to solve problems without the help of others, all factors potentially inhibiting males from showing vulnerabilities (e.g., depression) and asking for assistance (Mahalik, Good, & Englar-Carlson, 2003). Of course, most males are socialized in these tenets in boyhood and adolescence (Pollack, 1998). In terms of counseling boys and male adolescents, Pollack (2006) emphasized the importance of recognizing that depression in boys may go dangerously unnoticed due to boys' attempts to mask and cover up feelings of pain and susceptibility. He noted that presenting the outward impression that "everything's just fine" while remaining emotionally stoic, despite internal feelings and life events that suggest otherwise, was part of typical boyhood social-ization. The implication for depression is that boys may learn to hide their feelings to conform to social pressures, and this tendency becomes the template for addressing feelings of depression from childhood into adulthood. A significant concern is that boys mask feelings of sadness, hopelessness, and depression to the point where it becomes severely debilitating, and potentially fatal in the case of contributing to suicidal thoughts, feelings, and behavior.

UNDERSTANDING SUICIDALITY IN MALE ADOLESCENTS

Suicide is the third leading cause of death among adolescent males aged 15 to 24, and shows a steady age-related increase in rates from the ages of 11 to 21 (Conner & Goldston, 2007). For this group, only accidents and homicide claim more lives (McIntosh, 2000). In 2001, 3,971 suicides were reported in this group. Of the total number of suicides among adolescents aged 15 to 24 in 2001, an alarmingly 86% (n = 3,409) were male and 14% (n = 562) were female (Anderson & Smith, 2003). The most current Youth Risk Behavior Surveillance (YRBS) data for 2005 (CDC, 2007) indicated that 8.4% (10% of females and 6% of males) of U.S. high school youth made one or more suicide attempt. Of those suicide attempts, 2.9% (2.3% female and 1.8% male) required medical attention. Further, 16.9% (21.8% female and 12% male) of high school youth seriously considered attempting suicide, and 13% (16.2% female and 9.9 % male) went so far as to create a suicide plan. Because the YRBS data are high school based, the actual statistics related to youth suicide are likely greater because youth not attending high school are at even higher risk for suicide (Hendin et al., 2005).

Clearly, there are distinct differences in the rates and lethality of suicide attempts between adolescent boys and adolescent girls (CDC, 2007; McWhirter, McWhirter, McWhirter, & McWhirter, 2004). Girls attempt suicide at a rate two times more than boys, but males between the ages of 15 and 19 are seven times more likely to complete suicide than females in the same age group (CDC). One of the primary reasons for this sex difference in suicide is that boys use more lethal means, such as firearms, to attempt suicide than do girls, who are more likely to use less harmful methods, such as swallowing pills or superficially cutting themselves (McWhirter et al., 2004). In 2001, firearms were used in 54% of youth suicides (Anderson & Smith, 2003). The violent means used by boys reinforce the traditional masculine notion that boys should "give 'em hell" and act out with bravado, aggression, and violence (Pollack, 1998).

The suicide rate among youth has risen since the 1950s, and it has been suggested that this has paralleled the rise in the rate of depression (Hendin et al., 2005). Suicide before the age of 12 is rare, but suicide rates increase with every year past puberty (CDC, 2007). According to the U.S. Office of the Surgeon General (2006), the incidence of suicide attempts reaches a peak during the midadolescent years, and mortality from suicide steadily increases through the teen years. Some hypothesize one of the main reasons for this trend is because adolescents have more of a tendency to catastrophize what adults would consider a minor event (Emslie & Weinberg, 1994). Specifically, adolescents have yet to develop the ability to contemplate certain issues outside of the context of polarized thinking. In line with this, adolescents who have symptoms of depression and who believe they must take care of problems by themselves are overrepresented among teenagers who think of attempting suicide (Culp et al., 1995). Adding to this phenomenon is the fact that teenagers are inundated with new stimuli and choices that can be overwhelming (Caldwell, 1999).

Studies have consistently found previous suicidal behavior to be the most important risk factor associated with suicidal risk (Hawton & Sinclair, 2003), with repetition of suicide attempts increasing the risk of completion (Gould & Kramer, 2001). This is particularly the case with youth experiencing mood disorders (Brent, Baugher, Bridge, Chen, & Chiappetta, 1999). Specifically for boys, a previous suicide attempt is the most potent predictor of a completed suicide, increasing the rate over thirtyfold. It is followed by depression (increasing the rate by about 12 times), disruptive behavior (increasing the rate two times), and substance abuse (increasing the rate just under two times; Shaffer et al., 1996). Conduct disorder is also prevalent in male adolescents with suicidal behavior, as are substance use disorders, anxiety, and depression (Gould et al., 1998). Suicidal behavior in boys has been linked to social connections. Rohde, Seeley, and Mace (1997) found that boys were more likely to think about suicide if they were suffering from stressful life events and if they lacked social supports in situations where they had few family members or felt lonely.

Boys who are suicidal and depressed often have not developed the tools and the range of coping skills that well-adjusted boys use to deal with everyday life events or experiences that might be perceived as traumatic. Randell, Eggert, and Pike (2001) stated that adolescents at risk for suicide possess fewer positive coping strategies and often do not seek assistance for their problems. Whereas emotionally healthy adolescent males deal with pitfalls and other negative feelings and circumstances in life-enhancing ways, boys who are suicidal see suicide as the only way of handling traumatic events. Often, the boy who considers suicide feels hopeless and is unaware of other options available to him. In our clinical experiences, these boys typically do not want to die, but they have a hard time seeing how life can continue.

For many adolescents, suicides (Brent et al., 1999) and near suicides (Simon et al., 2001) are impulsive acts. Simon et al. (2001) found in a study that 24% of suicide attempts were preceded by 5 minutes or less of planning. Though suicides are often precipitated by acute stressful events, it is important to understand how suicides may also represent a chain of developmental nonsuccess for boys (Conner & Goldston, 2007). Boys who attempt suicide may build up to the actual suicidal event over time as they experience developmental problems. In that regard, the recurrent experience of suicidal ideation is likely to occur. Over time, suicidal ideation may lower the threshold for eventual acts of suicide (Joiner, 2005). Thus, for boys, a chain of negative events (e.g., fights with peers and parents, relationship breakups, and trouble with the law or school system) may lower the threshold for what appears to be an impulsive suicide following an acute stressful event (Conner & Goldston).

Depressed and suicidal boys also tend to engage in faulty thinking patterns (Metalsky, Joiner, Hardin, & Abramson, 1993), including cognitive constriction, cognitive rigidity, and cognitive distortion (McWhirter et al., 2004). *Cognitive constriction* is an inability to see more than two options for situations. *Cognitive rigidity* is a way of interacting in the world that restricts a boy's ability to cope and form alternatives. *Cognitive distortion* is magnifying a problem and often generalizing the problem to a variety of situations.

Differences between healthy and depressed boys in coping with adverse life events were illustrated by two different 15-year-old males whom I (MF) was counseling during the same time period. Both boys were dealing with issues of coming out and embracing their sexual identity. One of the boys came from a supportive family and felt connected to his faith and peers. The other boy came from a family whom he perceived to persecute people who identified as gay and who adhered to religious beliefs that condemned gay people to hell. The first boy developed a healthy network of friends and support systems in his life that helped him in the process of coming out. The second boy felt that he could not go on with his life after he came out. He tried to end his life because he felt he had no other option for dealing with his shame and mixed emotions. He felt he would never fit into his family again. In our work together, we were able to get him to a place of having more hope and connections with other family members, peers, and support networks that were able to help him embrace his emerging identity. The crux of the work with this boy was helping him consider other options besides suicide, and then we built the coping tools to realize these options. These examples highlight how much boys need acceptance and support from their families. Further, adolescent boys who feel connected to their families are much less likely to engage in suicidal behavior (Kilmartin, 2007).

Suicide and Diversity Among Boys

Patterns of suicidal behavior vary widely among diverse groups of boys. Though once thought to be primarily an issue among European American boys, some studies show that Latino boys have a higher rate of suicide than European American boys (CDC, 2007; Queralt, 1993). The 2005 Youth Risk Behavior Surveillance data (CDC) indicated the percentage of boys by race that made a suicide attempt in the past year. Hispanic boys (7.8%) showed the highest percentage, whereas African American (5.2%) and White boys (5.2%) had the same percentages. The suicide rate among White adolescent males reached a peak in the late 1980s (18.0 per 100,000 in 1986) and has since declined somewhat (13.57 per 100,000 in 2004; National Center for Injury Prevention and Control [NCIPC], 2004), whereas among African American male adolescents, the rate increased substantially in the same period (from 7.1 per 100,000 in 1986 to 11.4 per 100,000 in 1997; CDC, 1998). Native American boys have the highest rate of suicide among all ethnic groups in the United States (Gould & Kramer, 2001). The elevated rate of suicide among Native Americans of all ages (12.3 per 100,000 in 2004) is substantially accounted for by the particularly high suicide rate of young Native American males. American Indian and Alaskan Natives have the highest rate of suicide in the 15 to 24 age group (CDC, NCIPC, 2004). Across all ethnic groups, the suicide rate among gay boys is extremely high, possibly accounting for 30% of all adolescent suicides (Borowsky, Ireland, & Resnick, 2001). Gay adolescents have shown twofold to seven-fold increased risk for suicidal behavior (American Academy of Child and Adolescent Psychiatry and the American Psychiatric Association, 2004).

What can account for the different suicide rates among these diverse groups? Hendin et al. (2005) noted that the reasons underlying the differential distribution of suicide rates are still unclear, yet some theories do exist. The rise in suicide among African Americans has been focused in the black middle class. It has been hypothesized that African American boys entering the middle class find themselves faced with new levels of stressors not previously seen in the community. These stressors include performing well academically while navigating a community that does not value academic success, perceptions from peers that intelligence is weak or acting White, and potential sexual identity concerns (Fordham & Ogbu, 1986; Osborn, 1999). According to the U.S. surgeon general (U.S. Public Health Service, 1999), from 1980 to 1996, the suicide rate for African American males aged 15–19 has increased 105%. Some research has pointed to increased access to firearms in African American communities. The only consistent research findings, however, point to very similar risk factors for young African Americans as those for White youth, including long-term depression and substance abuse. More research is needed to determine what, if any, other risk factors are attributable to the rise in African American youth suicide. For Native American adolescent males, suicide attempts have been associated with friends or family members attempting or completing suicide, alcohol and drug use, and the availability of firearms. Protective factors against suicide attempts in this population include discussing problems with friends or family, emotional health, and connectedness to family (Borowsky, Resnick, Ireland, & Blum, 1999). May and Van Winkle (1994) suggested that the high adolescent suicide rates among some tribes were linked to a loosening of social integration as tribal members become increasing acculturated in the larger society.

For gay and lesbian youth, isolation, rejection from family and peers, emotional confusion, and religious anxieties contribute to the higher number of suicide attempts and completions (Borowsky et al., 2001). Gay adolescents carry a number of risk factors for suicidal behavior, including high rates of drug and alcohol use. Further, gay adolescents are at significant risk for suicide due to chronic bullying and victimization at school (American Academy of Child and Adolescent Psychiatry and the American Psychiatric Association, 2004).

Distinguishing Between Self-Injury and Suicide

Before going further, it is important to briefly differentiate between self-injury and suicide. Self-injury is not the same as a suicide attempt and therefore ought to be understood and treated differently (Zila & Kiselica, 2001). Some have assumed that because the observable behaviors of self-injury (e.g., cutting, burning, and smashing body parts) and parasuicide exhibit a similar manifestation, the two behaviors are similar. However, the underlying reasons for the behaviors are understood as different. Self-injury is the deliberate, direct destruction or alteration of body tissue without conscious suicidal intent, but resulting in injury severe enough for tissue damage to occur (Gratz, Conrad, & Roemer, 2002). It is intentional, self-effected, low-lethality bodily harm of a socially unacceptable nature, performed to reduce psychological distress (Walsh, 2006). Self-injury is often a means for the individual to cope and continue living with pain, whereas suicide is a means to end life in order to no longer experience the pain (Favazza, 1998).

It is estimated that between 2 and 4 million people deliberately injure themselves each year. That is nearly 30 times the rate of suicide attempts and 140 times the rate of completed suicides (Strong, 1998). Adolescence is the age group with the highest prevalence of self-injury, where the estimates range from 14% to 39% in community samples and 40% to 60% in psychiatric samples (Nock & Prinstein, 2005). Until recently, self-injury was considered to largely be restricted to adolescent girls and women; however, recent evidence has indicated comparable rates of self-injury among female and male college students (Gratz et al., 2002) and adolescents (Muehlenkamp & Gutierrez, 2004; Zoroglu et al., 2003).

Self-injury is currently understood as a coping mechanism that serves multiple functions for the individual, including regulating intense overwhelming emotions, decreasing tension, and providing a means to end or induce states of dissociation, a method of self-punishment, a way of regaining a sense of control, and a means of communication and boundary definition (Favazza, 1998; Nock & Prinstein, 2005; Strong, 1998; Walsh, 2006).

This chapter deals mostly with suicide, but there is research that shows boys often engage in other types of self-harming behaviors, such as violently punching a wall, scratching the surface of the skin, or burning holes into one's forearm with a lit cigarette (Selekman, 2005). The principal factors associated with increased risk of self-harm among children and adolescents are mental health or behavioral issues (e.g., depression, severe anxiety, and impulsivity), a history of self-harm, experience of an abusive home life, poor communication with parents, and living in care or in secure institutions (Social Care Institute for Excellence, 2005). Unique environmental risk factors for males include caregiver separation (Gratz et al., 2002) and childhood physical abuse and emotional dysregulation (Gratz & Chapman, 2007). Self-harm can often lead to suicidal behaviors, but it is imperative to remember that both forms of self-destruction have similar triggers, such as family conflict, rejection, and the death of a loved one or close friend.

Suicide, Shame, and Guilt

Some suicidal boys will use suicide as a form of self-punishment to deal with guilt or shame (McWhirter et al., 2004). Pollack (1998) noted the traditional masculine notion of being the "big wheel" (e.g., demanding respect), in which boys are taught to avoid shame at all costs. For example, I (MF) worked with a 15-year-old male who felt suicidal because he was beginning to connect with his feelings of sexual attraction toward other boys. He knew that his father loathed homosexuals, and he felt his only option was to kill himself and not deal with the pain of embarrassing his family or alienating himself from his father. This example highlights the conflicts that many boys who are gay or questioning their sexual orientation face. Masculinity and heterosexuality are intertwined. One of the core components of traditional masculinity is the avoidance of characteristics associated with femininity and homosexuality (O'Neil, 1982; Smiler, 2004), and it is not uncommon for boys and adolescents to experience a type of gender role conflict around questions of sexual orientation and attraction (Pleck, 1995). In fact, gay adolescents can be viewed as an at-risk population due to marginalization and discrimination. Some estimate that between 25% and 30% of gay adolescents have made at least one suicide attempt (Hetrick & Martin, 1988).

But shame and guilt are not limited to conflicts associated with homosexuality. A boy may feel that he has not lived up to rigid expectations of what it means to be a man. Traditional masculinity has several connections to suicidal behavior (Kilmartin, 2007). If he is not tough enough, not smart enough, or not successful enough, or if in any way he shows himself to be a "sissy," a boy may be racked with shame for not living up to his perceptions of what others expect him to be and of what he expects for himself. And those feelings of shame can be the source of his desire to punish himself. Whereas girls and women often learn to express their pain, take care of themselves, and reach out to others for social support, men are traditionally socialized at a young age to act on problems, be independent, and disdain emotional pain. In this regard, males are often alone with their pain, and feel they cannot express it or ask for help. In these circumstances, suicide can be viewed as one of few options (Kilmartin).

Suicide and Absolution

Boys who are suicidal may also see suicide as a way to provide absolution for past behaviors (McWhirter et al., 2004). I (MF) worked with Samuel, a 17-year-old male who was failing out of college after his first semester. He had come to school at an earlier age than his peers and did not have the coping skills to truly be on his own in the college environment. He desperately wanted to fit in, and thus Samuel spent his entire first semester socializing, partying, drinking, and avoiding his academics. He quickly fell behind to the point where he could no longer see any way out. Samuel felt he was letting his family down, and had come to the conclusion that there was nothing else awaiting him in the future once he failed out of school. His solution for dealing with this problem was suicide. In his mind, he would be absolved of neglecting his studies and partying by committing suicide.

Suicide as Revenge

McWhirter et al. (2004) noted that boys who are depressed may attempt suicide for perverted revenge. *Perverted revenge* is a twisted means of getting back at someone. I (MF) worked with Albert, a 14-year-old boy who was physically abused by his father for most of his childhood. Albert's mother was out of the picture, driven away by his alcoholic father. Now Albert's father was completing a rehabilitation program and was attempting to start a new relationship with Albert, but Albert did not want any part of it. Albert had seethed for years, blaming his father for all of the abuse and for driving away his mother, and now his father was trying to pull him back in to him. A teacher had noticed some angry and violent imagery in some of Albert's writing and artistic work and had expressed concern. After some time in counseling, Albert informed me of his idea of killing himself at his father's workplace in front of his coworkers. Albert wanted to get back at his father for the years of abuse and emotional pain. He felt he was not big enough to beat up his father, so he wanted to find another way of hurting him. In Albert's mind, his father was on the road to recovery, and what better way to get revenge on him than to kill himself so his father will live the rest of his life feeling guilty for his death? This case example highlights the masculine norm of independence. Albert felt that he was alone, his pain was intractable, and his problem seemed unsolvable. Suicide was seen as an option. What I (MF) ascertained was that for Albert, his suicidal ideas were a way of reaching out to me and telling me about his pain. He was giving me a message and asking for me to provide support and validation that bad things had happened to him by the hand of his father.

Suicide and Gaining Control

Boys who are suicidal also might be motivated by a fantasy of omnipotent domain or the vision of having complete control over oneself and others (McWhirter et al., 2004). Pollack (1998) noted that the gender differences between adolescent suicide rates may be related to families' demands for hyperindependence in boys. Boys are often taught the traditional masculine notion of being the "big wheel" and acting like everything is under control, even when it is not. Some depressed and suicidal boys feel they live in a world where they have no power or control. In their mind, one way to have absolute control is to determine when, where, and how they are going to die. Gaining control also reinforces the traditional masculine norm of the "sturdy oak" by valuing independence and keeping concerns to oneself. As a result, boys not only have power over their own physical life, but also have power over the emotions of others who will mourn their death.

Suicide and Academic Achievement

For most boys, it is crucial to consider the influence that school and academics have on a boy's life. Boys can have a difficult time adjusting to school environments. Pollack (1998) stated that too many boys are misunderstood by educational professionals. School environments as a whole are often not set up to accommodate the high energy levels of young boys. As a result, boys are often punished for engaging in behaviors that are natural for them. As a result of feeling misunderstood or confused about how to successfully navigate an environment that forces them to deny some of their natural needs, some boys may act out by skipping school, not completing homework assignments, disrespecting the teacher, and showing no interest in the educational process. They also can begin to believe that their failure indicates that they are a failure as a person. For boys, these behaviors and beliefs can be signs of anxiety and depression. It is important to help depressed boys who have school adjustment difficulties to navigate and adjust to the academic environment so that feelings of depression do not deteriorate into thoughts of suicide.

IMPLICATIONS FOR COUNSELING
DEPRESSED AND SUICIDAL BOYS

Depressed and suicidal boys often have a more difficult time adjusting to the typical challenges of adolescence than do their emotionally healthy peers. Blending an understanding of male socialization with the unique features of each client can lead to effectively tailored and well-considered intervention efforts. The helping process must begin with an understanding of what it takes to establish rapport with a boy who feels forlorn, helpless, and suicidal. Equally important is helping the client to quickly develop effective coping strategies to address emotional pain. This is especially critical when boys are actively considering suicide.

There is mounting evidence that depression in boys is undertreated due to not only a lack of help seeking (Möller-Leimkuehler, 2002; Sen, 2004) but also a problem of detecting depression in boys (Gasquet, Chavance, Ledoux, & Choque, 1997; Möller-Leimkuehler, Heller, & Paulus, 2007). The concept of *masked depression* deserves some attention by counselors working with boys and male adolescents. Although the primary symptoms and eventual course of depression are similar in adult men and women (Simpson, Nee, & Endicott, 1997; Young, Scheftner, Fawcett, & Klerman, 1990), some masculine-specific modes of experiencing and expressing depression have been identified. From these modes, parallels can be drawn to how boys may experience and express depression. Some men mask depressive symptoms through alcohol and drug abuse or other abusive equivalents (Hanna & Grant, 1997). It is not too much of a stretch to think that this phenomenon could also occur in adolescent males. There is a tendency for depressed men to show increased interpersonal conflict (Williamson, 1987). For boys, this may be expressed by getting in more fights and showing difficulties with peers and other adults. Depressed men tend to experience problems at work (Vredenburg, Krames, & Flett, 1986); thus, boys may show problems at school or at a job. Of course, counselors can help parents look for signs of depression. If parents are unaware that a melancholy mood, irritability, early morning fatigue, and substance abuse could be signs of depression, an adolescent boy who exhibits these symptoms might be perceived as defiant, lazy, and unmotivated for school, rather than suffering from a potentially serious mental health problem. As a result, practitioners must be able to recognize various manifestations of depression in boys in an effort to offer treatment, educate parents and clients, and prevent the onset of major depression and suicide.

STRATEGIES FOR ESTABLISHING RAPPORT

Establishing rapport with depressed and suicidal boys can be complicated. Often boys are brought into the therapeutic situation by a parent or guardian who may be unaware of why the child is misbehaving or acting out. In our clinical experience, it is rare that an adolescent boy will come into counseling and report he is feeling depressed. More often, it is an external problem (e.g., anger, academic trouble, cursing, fighting, and disobedience) that precipitates a referral. So even though the underlying problem may be depression, the boy and his parents may believe it is behavioral problems that need to be addressed in counseling. Boys often externalize difficulties and act out as a way to mask the difficulties experienced in their inner world. If the boy is at a place emotionally where he does not understand or recognize his feelings of depression, he may connect to feelings of anger and attempt to bring those into the room through silence, rudeness, or extreme agitation or frustration. Counselors must not get turned off or snowed over by a boy's expression of anger. Instead, remember that many boys are socialized to believe that anger is the only acceptable emotion to express. Although boys may be scolded by teachers and parents for expressing angry emotions, they are not shamed as being "sissies." Boys may be excused for angry behavior on the basis of the "Boys will be boys" theory, but humiliated for displays of more vulnerable emotions. Eventually, anger may become a funnel emotion; that is, feelings like grief, fear, shame, and sadness may all be converted to and expressed as anger (Shepard, 2005). So, knowing that in most cases the angry boy, the acting-out boy, and the aggressive boy may actually be experiencing some depression and difficulties coping may help the relationship grow deeper and at a quicker rate. By being aware that presenting problems may actually be masking deeper or more critical problems, a counselor will be less likely to miss what is really happening in the boy's life. We have noticed how many boys express relief when someone is able to help them understand at a deeper level what is really happening for them.

For many boys, counseling may be viewed as a punishment, the final straw in a long line of threats, or some cruel attempt by his parents to get back at him. In our clinical work, we have had parents bribe their sons to come to counseling with food, money, or other gifts. I (MF) have actually walked out to the car of the boy in an effort to meet him on his grounds first. In light of these considerations, counselors must also consider the context where the therapeutic relationship is beginning.

Though some boys who are depressed and suicidal come into the counseling situation looking for help, our experience shows that many feel resentful and ready to do battle. The counselor must be prepared for this type of encounter and empathize with the boy's point of view as a way to defuse the situation and win the boy's trust.

It is advisable to avoid using words like *depressed* and *suicidal* over and over again because the boy may not connect to these words or be ready to discuss them. Terms like *depression* and *suicide* are used differently across cultures, and the ways in which these are manifested can vary, too.

Racism is a salient issue for many depressed boys. White counselors may have trouble connecting with African American or Hispanic adolescent males who are not sure they can trust White individuals due to the history of racism in this country (Sen, 2004). Lindsey et al. (2006) found that the African American boys often stated that they doubted White professionals could understand where they were coming from. Rather than become defensive in response to the boy's mistrust, the counselor can try to understand how the boy's perspective was shaped by the context of growing up in a minority status within the United States. Communicating to the boy your understanding of racism, prejudice, and other such issues can help boys feel safer and more comfortable opening up in an honest way. Equally important is for minority counselors to be aware of their own "isms" when working with Caucasian boys who might have their own issues pertaining to race and prejudice. Again, it is possible to work through these issues and still develop a therapeutic relationship. As an African American counselor, I (MF) have worked with many young men who have told me they were racist or heard racist language in their house growing up. Allowing the client the opportunity to express this in a safe zone, while simultaneously allowing him to know me as a person and not only as a Black person, helped in the development of the relationship.

INTERVENTIONS

In the following section, we describe some of the ways counselors can intervene with adolescent boys dealing with depression and suicide. The first part of the section focuses on various assessment techniques. The remainder of the section explores treatment options from both a psychological and psychopharmacological perspective.

Assessment Techniques

Several instruments for identifying depression in children and adolescents are available. The Reynolds Adolescent Depression Scale (RADS) is the only assessment tool of depression developed specifically for use with adolescents (Ramsey, 1994). It is a short, easily administered, self-report instrument that is helpful in determining depressive symptomatology and takes only 5 to 10 minutes to take. The Reynolds Child Depression Scale (RCDS) was developed for kids in grades 3 through 6 (Ramsey). The Children's Depression Inventory (CDI) is a 27-item forced-choice assessment tool that measures depressive symptomatology (Reynolds, 1990). The Children's Depression Rating Scale—Revised (CDRS-R) takes about 20 to 30 minutes to administer and is used for adolescents between the ages of 13 and 19 (Reynolds). The Hamilton Depression Rating Scale (HDRS) measures the level of depressive symptoms through the medium of a clinical interview (Reynolds). Lastly, the SAD PERSONS Scale assesses the probability that someone will actually attempt and succeed at suicide (Ramsey). The acronym SAD PERSONS was created by using the first letters of 10 suicide risk factors: **S**ex, **A**ge, **D**epression, **P**revious attempt, **E**thanol abuse, **R**ational thought loss, **S**ocial supports lacking, **O**rganized plan, **N**o spouse, **S**ickness.

One final assessment tool is the clinical interview. Cochran's (2005) suggestions for using clinical interviews to assess for depression in men can be applied in counseling with boys. Cochran proposed that there are four intersecting dimensions of male psychological conflict that should be assessed. The first dimension pertains to the male client's relational experiences. The second area covers how the male client learns to manage feelings of sadness, grief, and loss. The third dimension includes the male client's insight into behaviors and values around masculine role behaviors. The final dimension is measuring the male client's balance between doing and being in his life. Males are often socialized to overvalue doing at the expense of the capacity for being with oneself and others. This assessment can look at how the client is able to balance these dimensions, often with an emphasis on helping the client develop more capacity to "be" more with himself. In general, the less satisfied the boy is in his relationships, the less he allows himself to express sadness and other vulnerable emotions, the less he understands the impact of traditional masculinity ideology on his functioning, and the less balance he has in his life, the more likely the boy will be depressed. Other areas for assessment during the clinical interview include exploring masculine gender role socialization (Mahalik, 2001) and alexithymia (e.g., difficulties with identifying and verbalizing feelings and emotions; Levant, 1998).

Another step in assessing depression and suicidality in adolescent boys is being aware of the behavioral ways in which depression may manifest. As mentioned earlier, many boys will not come into the counseling situation and report feeling depressed or suicidal. For example, one of the first key signs of a deeper depression in adolescent boys is risky behavior. Other signs include hopelessness, sadness, social isolation, low self-esteem, difficulty with concentration, poor academic performance, irritability and hostility and aggression toward authority figures (Hallfors, 2005), and fatigue (Wolbeek, van Doornen, Kavelaars, & Heijnen, 2006).

Clearly, counselors working with depressed boys and adolescents must assess for suicidality on a continual basis. All threats of suicide ideation must be taken seriously. Though it may seem like asking about suicidal thoughts and intention has the potential for being harmful, the contrary is often true. Most people benefit and express relief from talking openly about suicidal thoughts and plans. It is as if one is finally free to share a dark and shameful secret. During this dialogue, be careful to do a thorough assessment and evaluation of suicidal ideation, suicidal fantasy, suicidal plans, and access to the means to carry out the plan.

TREATMENT OPTIONS

There are limited evidence-based treatment options for treating male adolescent depression. Reviews of the clinical treatment literature (Michael & Crowley, 2002; Milin, Walker, & Chow, 2003) have identified that, generally, psychosocial treatment options (e.g., cognitive-behavioral therapy and interpersonal therapy) are clinically meaningful for affected youth and adolescents. At this time, however, there are no clinical treatments specifically validated for working with boys and male adolescents. In fact, in a meta-analytic review of treatments for child and adolescent depression, Michael and Crowley (2002) found that girls tended to fare better than boys in treatment. Yet they cautioned that many of the treatments tended to focus on emotional awareness and expressiveness, which parallel traditional expectations of girls and women; thus, boys may initially be at a disadvantage. To address this concern and provide a more appropriate clinical experience, counselors can be mindful of ways to tailor intervention efforts to take into account the gender socialization of boys. The section below examines the use of evidence-based therapies for treating adolescent depression. Others have outlined how other clinical approaches, including family therapy (Pruitt, 2007) and group therapy (Rice & Meyer, 1994; Stark, Swearer, & Sommer, 1998), can be helpful for boys and adolescents.

Cognitive-Behavioral Therapy

Cognitive-behavioral therapy (CBT) focused on treating adolescent depression has been shown to be efficacious in reducing symptoms of depression (Lewinsohn & Clarke, 1999; Reinecke, Ryan, & DuBois, 1998; Weisz, McCarty, & Valeri, 2006). CBT traditionally has heavily emphasized approaches that stress altering unrealistic negative cognitions (e.g., cognitive-restructuring treatments) and negative thought patterns, and improving disturbed behavioral self- and social regulation skills thought to underlie adolescent depression (Evans et al., 2005). Yet other evidence supports the use of noncognitive behavioral-activation strategies, suggesting that beneficial treatment for youth depression may not require altering cognitions as much as changing behavior (Weisz et al., 2006). Generally, CBT treatment for adolescent depression includes techniques such as (a) mood monitoring; (b) cognitive restructuring; (c) behavioral activation, pleasant activity scheduling, and goal-setting strategies; (d) relaxation and stress management; (e) social skills and conflict resolution training; and (f) general problem-solving training (Kazdin & Weisz, 1998).

Social skills training has been shown to be effective in addressing adolescent depression (Chambless & Hollon, 1998). Social skills training specifically looks at skills training to enhance social interactions (e.g., how to start a conversation or make a friend), enhance social problem solving (e.g., how to resolve conflict without alienating others), reduce anxiety in social settings, and other competencies relevant to self-esteem (e.g., setting performance goals and reaching them). Goals are to provide real-world skills that can be used immediately and the ability to cognitively select situations that will increase positive reinforcement.

Though there are not CBT treatment models specifically developed for boys, counselors can tailor interventions to address many of the difficult situations and cognitive distortions experienced by boys. Though primarily focused on adult men, Mahalik's (2001) book chapter on cognitive therapy with men lists masculine gender-related cognitive distortions such as "If you walk away, you are a coward"; "If I share my feelings with others, people will think I am a sissy"; and "Asking for help is a sign of failure." He further listed rational responses to address these distortions. These ideas may be helpful for cognitive work with boys and male adolescents because most masculine norms and injunctions are honed and reinforced during childhood and adolescence. Therefore, these same masculine distortions from adulthood are equally powerful at a younger age.

Interpersonal Therapy for Adolescents

Interpersonal therapy (IPT) is a time-limited form of counseling focusing on the relationship between interpersonal interactions and one's psychiatric symptoms. As a descendant of psychodynamic therapy, IPT emphasizes the ways in which a person's current relationships and social context cause or maintain symptoms rather than exploring the deep-seated sources of the symptoms. Its goals are rapid symptom reduction and improved social adjustment. One of the reasons IPT may be effective is that individuals with depression are often interpersonally difficult, which results in a greater disruption in their social networks (Evans et al., 2005).

Though IPT was developed for use with adults diagnosed with major depression, IPT has been modified for use with adolescents diagnosed with depression (IPT-A). No specific studies have solely explored its use with male adolescents. In IPT-A, a counselor and the client explore developmental issues such as separation from parents, the client's authority in the relationship with his parents, the development of interpersonal relationships, concerns and experiences around the death of a relative or friend, peer pressure, and family dynamics. The course of counseling is typically 12 weeks, with once-weekly additional phone contact during the first 4 weeks of treatment. Parents are included in the initial session to get a solid client history, and to educate both the parents and the male client about depression and possible treatments. The counselor primarily uses supportive listening in IPT-A. IPT-A has been effective in treating moderately to severely depressed adolescents and with adolescents who have been experiencing depression lasting several months (Mellin, 2001; Santor & Kusumakar, 2001). A completed efficacy trial of IPT-A indicated that clients reported a significant decrease in depressive symptoms and improvement in functioning (Mufson, Dorta, Moreau, & Weissman, 2005).

Psychopharmacology

Historically, tricyclics have been the medications of choice for treating depression in children and adolescents (Reynolds, 1990; U.S. Office of the Surgeon General, 2006). Michael and Crowley (2002) reported that most pharmacological interventions were not necessarily effective in treating depressed children and adolescents, yet they noted evidence that selective serotonin reuptake inhibitors (SSRIs) were more effective and showed greater promise. According to the U.S. Office of the Surgeon General (2006), SSRIs have become more popular with regard to treating depression in adolescents, and SSRIs have shown good results (Treatment for Adolescents With Depression Study Team, 2004). Recently, there has been some concern that SSRI antidepressants may induce suicidal thoughts and attempts in some adolescents (Vitiello & Swedo, 2004), leading regulatory agencies to issue safety warnings for pediatric use (U.S. Food and Drug Administration, 2004). Simon (2006) tried to clarify this controversy, noting that the confusing research results might be more evidence that adolescent depression does not have just one biological underpinning, meaning that antidepressant medications will help some and possibly hurt others. He noted there is a small risk of suicide for some adolescents taking antidepressant medication, yet this should be balanced by the possible benefits. In terms of actual medication, only fluoxetine (Prozac) has been clinically proven to be effective with adolescents. Considering the potential benefits of certain medications in treating depression in adolescents, it is important for counselors to consistently work with psychiatrists and primary care physicians to ensure that the adolescent is receiving a well-rounded treatment regime.

THE CASE OF BAXTER

The following case example from Mark Fleming looks at how issues of cultural identity, masculinity, and depression can present in counseling. I (MF) am one of the few African American male psychologists in my area, and I have found over the years that my private practice increasingly is filled with African American boys and men. As a psychodynamic counselor,

I tend to work with depressed and suicidal boys from a dynamic per-spective, blending aspects from other theoretical techniques. I attempt to understand a boy in the context of his family. Furthermore, I explore patterns of behaviors, patterns in relationships, and patterns of thoughts and beliefs that have helped create and form the person in my office. I often use cognitive restructuring to examine and refute cognitive dis-tortions that might be contributing to a client's depressed mood. Some of the more common cognitive distortions I come across from boys include, "I made a bad grade, so I must be a bad student"; "I don't have a girlfriend, so no one must like me"; and "If people knew how I really felt, I would never be accepted." Finally, I utilize coping skills training as a way to help boys develop positive coping strategies, seek emotional support from others, and accept positive affirmations from others.

Baxter was a 15-year-old, biracial boy of European American and African American descent. His introduction to me was rather memorable as he shook my hand and said, "I really don't mind that my parents made me come here, but it will really be a big waste of time." I said, "Let's see what we can do. My name is Mark. Grab a seat." I normally allow my adolescent male clients to call me by my first name in order to alleviate some of the power differential in the room. I asked Baxter why he came to see me, and he responded, "My mom has a problem with me. She gets on my case and bugs me, and now I yell back. Actually, the rest of my family seems to have a problem with me. They all are pissing me off!"

Background Information

Baxter was the eldest of four children who were all adopted by White European American parents. All of his siblings were White and European American. His younger sister was 13, his younger brother was 10, and his youngest brother was 6 months old. None of the children were bio-logically related. His dad was a top executive in a major corporation, and his mom was a stay-at-home mother who was responsible for the day-to-day operations of the household. The family lived in a predominately White neighborhood in the suburbs of a small city.

Baxter had little interaction with other African Americans. He and his school-age siblings all attended the top private schools in the city. There were few African American students in his school, and Baxter felt that made him stand out. His parents seemed aware of this, and tried to provide opportunities for Baxter to meet other African Americans. They went to a predominately African American church, but even though Baxter attempted to made social connections, they were rather rare. His father also took him to an African American barber in a predominately African American community. Although Baxter could appreciate these efforts, they seemed to discourage him. Baxter felt that "real Black people" did not consider him Black. He felt culturally White and that he "could not hang in the hood with the Black guys from New York or the hood."

Baxter was an intelligent and articulate young man. He was on the honor roll in a school that was academically competitive. He did not play sports but was in the band and chorus, and participated in various plays and other stage productions. Baxter described himself as artistic with a wonderful singing voice. During one of our early sessions, he sang the national anthem to give me a sense of his talents. Baxter wanted to be a Broadway singer and actor. He was dating a young African American girl who attended the same private school his sister attended. The two had been dating for a little over a year. Baxter reported that there was no sexual activity in the relationship and that he felt he was not ready to go down that road. He felt some pressure from her, but stated he had his beliefs and values.

Presenting Problem

Baxter was referred to counseling by his parents for issues of anger, anxiety, and behavioral outbursts. His mother noted Baxter had become increasingly irritable and hostile toward his parents and siblings. He was never aggressive physically, but was verbally abusive toward his parents and often cursed at them. He was disrespectful and often acted as if he did not like them. Following these outbursts, he would withdraw to his room. Baxter maintained a Web page where he would often write derogatory blogs about his family. His parents had reached their limit with regard to his behavior at home. To complicate matters, Baxter had recently failed his math course and needed to make it up or repeat the eighth grade. He seemed to act like school was fine, but his parents noticed that he was spending less time with peers and more time at home in his room. The final straw was an argument from the prior week when Baxter got angry with his family for planning to come to a scheduled vocal performance. Though he was angry with the whole family, he seemed particularly angry at his mother, and through both anger and tears, Baxter told her to "never come to one of my fucking performances again."

Baxter reported having had a good relationship with his mother when he was younger, but that changed as he got older and recognized "just how annoying she is." He stated his father was mean, absent, and hyper-critical, and often engaged in behaviors he punished Baxter for engaging in himself. Baxter said, "Dad yells at me for not picking up my shoes and my stuff, but his stuff is all over the house!" Baxter added that he hated school most of the time and was sick of going. He felt he did not have any close friends because he was just known as "the Black guy." Further, being involved in singing and drama had led his peers to tease him about being gay since before he could remember. He was never beat up, but he was constantly teased and taunted at school, and this past year had been particularly bad.

Case Formulation

Though Baxter seemed forthcoming during our first meeting, I could sense sadness behind his bravado. Between his complaints about his parents, there were extended pauses and a weariness as if he had to gather his strength to engage with me. Some of Baxter's anger was related to perceptions he had of his parents. Baxter did not play sports, but his sister and brother did. He felt his father resented him for not playing sports, and Baxter's response to this was to withdraw from his father. Some of what Baxter was experiencing was normal developmental issues between teenagers and their parents, but there was more happening with him that indicated some deeper concerns and potential depression.

As Baxter was getting older, he was becoming more aware of how he differed culturally from other African Americans he encountered. His failed attempts to connect with other African Americans, coupled with constant reminders from White peers that he was Black, created a cultural identity conflict. He also was teased at school for breaking some of the basic tenets of the Boy Code, and this also seemed to intersect with being African American. Baxter was smart, did well in school, and liked music and drama. In a sense, it seemed that the constant teasing from other males his age, and maybe even from his dad, all seemed like attempts to get Baxter to be aware that he was behaving in nontraditional masculine ways (e.g., being a sissy). I had a feeling that part of his anger toward his parents stemmed from his father mirroring what his male peers at school did (e.g., sending the message that he needed to be more masculine to be accepted), yet his anger toward his mother might be connected to him feeling like she was the cause of him not being "more manlike and doing more manly things" because she encouraged and valued his vocal and dramatic talents.

The combination of all of these stressors seemed to be wearing Baxter down. It seemed that Baxter was experiencing depression, and I was worried about what would happen to him if he did not get some help. The anger, academic trouble, and peer teasing in school all seemed related to his search for his identity as an African American male in a hostile environment. I also wondered if he might have some sexual identity concerns that he was denying. He was not sharing his identity confusion or the extent of his inner turmoil with anyone else, and at this point he seemed to be getting more and more down. He was masking his depression with his anger, which felt like his way of asking for some attention to his problems. I felt empathy for Baxter not only as his counselor but also as a fellow African American male. He was smart and gifted, and it seemed like he was being punished for that. I decided not only to validate his anger but also inquire about his energy level and how "good" he felt. Baxter confirmed that he was feeling low energy and irritable, and he was not spending time with his peers. He noted that he felt "bad" most of the time, and that it had gotten worse in the past

2 months. I asked him if he ever thought about harming himself, and he quickly said, "No," but as I inquired further he admitted to dreaming sometimes that all his "stuff" would go away if he were dead. As we talked more it seemed these were fantasies Baxter had, and then he clearly stated that he would never "whack himself." I told him it was important to talk about these fantasies when they came up, especially if they were more serious, and he felt that was fine.

Our Clinical Work Together

During our first session I met with Baxter and his parents in the beginning of the session and then Baxter alone. While his parents were in the room, we discussed their concerns, their goals for counseling for Baxter, and their desire to have peace in the house. Baxter was given a chance to respond. Baxter haughtily replied that he did not want them in the room, and then proceeded to interrupt and curse at his parents. Before the parents left the room, we discussed confidentiality and what would be shared from Baxter's sessions.

Having worked with many boys of this age, I am familiar with the culture of the current generation around music, movies, and rhetoric. As a result, I engaged Baxter on his pop culture interests. He immediately began discussing his interest in music and singing. We spent the first session getting to know each other better, and I asked Baxter to help me understand what was happening in his life. I self-disclosed about some of my own experiences (e.g., some of my own struggles in regard to being African American, male, smart, and academically motivated) in an effort to gain his trust and to help him feel more comfortable in the room, and it seemed to bring us closer together. We talked about the strangeness of counseling, and at the end I mentioned to him that I was concerned that he might be experiencing depression. I normalized this with Baxter, and said that this happens to many kids. Baxter had more of a nonresponse by shrugging his shoulders, and I spoke with Baxter about sharing my clinical observation with his parents. With Baxter's parents in the room, I offered some brief ideas about the potential course of our work and shared my impression about Baxter's depressed mood. At the end of our time together, Baxter and his parents showed some relief on their faces. As Baxter was leaving, he turned back to me and said, "Hey Mark, that was not bad and I will see you next week."

Baxter and I met for a total of 21 individual sessions. We maintained a good therapeutic relationship, and I think he really appreciated that he was accepted by a fellow African American male, because he struggled with this in his life. Baxter cried in front of me, and he allowed himself to be challenged and to challenge some of his old notions. I worked from a psychodynamic perspective with regard to helping Baxter become more insightful and self-aware about the inner conflict associated with his growing identity as an African American adolescent male and his relationship to his European American parents. In that regard, we talked about the creation of defense mechanisms and how they were both normative and protective, yet in times of overwhelming stress and tension, they often break down. He gained insight into how he struggled against the Boy Code (Pollack, 1998) and felt persecuted when other males teased and punished him for transgressions.

We discussed a variety of issues that helped him understand his world better and how he navigated in that world. We spoke about race, depression, sexuality, sex, anger, depression, being teased, his relationship with his parents, and his fears about not passing his math course in the summer. We explored some of the inner conflict Baxter had about being adopted, and how his growing independence and identity were challenging his acceptance as a family member, as a man, and as an African American. I shared with Baxter ideas about multiple identities and notions about Black Male Authenticity (Ellis & Dermer, 2007) that helped Baxter understand the notion of masculinities (e.g., there is not one way of being masculine, but instead multiple ways that vary with cultural orientation). He resonated with this notion, and felt drawn to Black Male Authenticity because it posited an identity of knowing and being true to the sociopolitical history of African Americans that required Black men to be smart, successful, and proud. Baxter felt this was closer to who he was compared to some of the other popular perceptions of African American men (e.g., athletes and rap stars) that he could not attain.

In terms of his depression, early on I felt that his parents and Baxter might want a referral to a psychiatrist for an evaluation to consider whether or not Baxter might need medication to treat his mood swings. The psychiatrist prescribed Prozac for Baxter, and this ended up being helpful to him. We also explored some of the core beliefs and discouraging self-talk that seemed to get Baxter down. Over the course of 2 weeks, Baxter kept a thought and mood diary to get an idea of his intermediate and core beliefs. Not surprisingly, Baxter had many rigid beliefs about what it meant to be an African American male (e.g., men don't ask for help, and men act like everything is cool and deal with their own problems), but most damaging were cognitions about being tough and not being a "wussy." Baxter loved singing and acting, but increasingly he was conflicted about showing these interests to others because they drew the ire of his peers and often led to Baxter's own negative self-talk in regard to being "man enough." Also, Baxter admitted that he really did not like his girlfriend all that much, but that he dated her because "that's what guys do." In a sense, dating a girl gave Baxter some masculine credibility, but it also provided internal conflict.

To address these cognitions, Baxter began to broaden his understanding about "what it means to be a man," and he developed thought-stopping skills to catch himself when he was too self-critical. We also began to broaden Baxter's social skills to help him identify male peers who might be more kind and accepting of Baxter. Like other boys who are teased and persecuted for not being "manly enough," Baxter had developed an idea that the way to be accepted was to gain the approval of both the bullies and the boys who seemed most masculine. Baxter tried this to no avail at school and at church. As we deconstructed this in session, Baxter actually felt it was funny that he would do this because it seemed so illogical that he could ever win their approval. Instead, Baxter began to identify young males who shared similar interests and seemed open and accepting, and Baxter began to reach out to them. After a couple of attempts, Baxter began to find some guys at his church who seemed to accept him.

Outcome and Prognosis

Baxter and his father were able to reconcile their differences about sports. Baxter's father realized he was not upset that Baxter was not in sports, but also that he did not have a lot of interest in Baxter's singing and acting. He wanted to support Baxter, but felt no strong attachment to these activities. Most importantly, however, was that his father unequivocally made it clear that he loved and supported Baxter regardless of what he did. Further, his father made efforts to consistently show that acceptance to Baxter. This shift really made an impact on Baxter, and he was able to accept that his father was not as interested in his activities, but that his love and acceptance were not tied to what he did, but to who he was.

We also determined that being teased at school, and the way this activated Baxter's negative self-talk, was the root of Baxter's depression. His anger was a manifestation of that depression and was an immature attempt to gain some control. Baxter acted out on his parents what he felt he could not do in school for fear of getting beat up or teased more. Baxter also began to open the door of sexual identity concerns, yet he was clear that he was not sure if he was gay or straight at this point and did not want to have to choose right now. He was able to tell his parents, who completely supported this decision. He also was able to tell his mother that he felt she was, in part, the reason why he was "so effeminate," but as Baxter was beginning to own and value these parts of him, he noticed his aggravation toward her declining.

As we ended our work together, Baxter seemed to be happier and more accepting of the man he was becoming. Not everything was perfect, but he was able to create some new support networks with his parents and peers that did not exist before. Most importantly, Baxter felt validated and accepted by many of the people around him. This allowed Baxter to outwardly show some of his internal pride for being intelligent and artistically gifted. He still had to take the math class during the summer, but Baxter was developing a new African American male identity that valued academic success and being responsible. Overall, my work with Baxter was successful, and I was really impressed by the young man Baxter was becoming. He sent me an e-mail about 6 months after our work together, informing me that everything was going well, that he and his parents were getting along much better, and that he felt happier.

CONCLUDING THOUGHTS

Working with depressed and suicidal boys does not have to be a daunting task. Boys and male adolescents are often discouraged and down, and counseling can be unfamiliar and scary. By understanding how depression may manifest in boys and remaining patient throughout the therapeutic process, counselors can provide new options to boys that both value and validate who they are. We believe that boys and male adolescents desperately want help, but sometimes it is hard to find the right person who will listen. Take young male clients seriously, assess for depression and suicidality, and learn who these young men are and who they want to become—following these notions will help pave the way to therapeutic success. Finally, be aware of the importance of understanding adolescent males from a cultural lens. Masculinity is not a unitary construct, but one that varies with each person. Listening without judging will help both the client and the counselor grasp the client's concerns in a contextual framework that includes the client and society as a whole.

REFERENCES

Alfieri, T. J., Ruble, D. N., & Higgins, E. T. (1996). Gender stereotypes during adolescence: Developmental changes and the transition to junior high school. *Developmental Psychology, 32,* 1129–1137.

American Academy of Child and Adolescent Psychiatry and the American Psychiatric Association. (2004). *Joint statement from the American Academy of Child and Adolescent Psychiatry and the American Psychiatric Association for the Senate Substance Abuse and Mental Health Services Subcommittee of the Health, Education, Labor and Pensions Committee Hearing on Suicide Prevention and Youth: Saving lives.* Retrieved April 4, 2007, from www.aacap.org/galleries/LegislativeAction/SuicideH.pdf

American Psychiatric Association. (2000). *Diagnostic and statistical manual of the mental disorder: Text revision* (4th ed.). Washington, DC: Author.

Anderson, R. N., & Smith B. L. (2003). Deaths: Leading causes for 2001. *National Vital Statistics Report, 52,* 1–86.

Angold, A., & Costello, E. L. (1993). Depressive comorbidity in children and adolescents: Empirical, theoretical, and methodological issues. *American Journal of Psychiatry, 150,* 1779–1791.

Angold, A., Costello, E. L., & Erkanli, A. (1999). Comorbidity. *Journal of Child Psychology and Psychiatry, 40,* 57–87.

Beautrais, A., Joyce, P., & Mulder, R. T. (1996). Risk factors for serious suicide attempts among youths aged 13 through 24 years. *Journal of the American Academy of Child and Adolescent Psychiatry, 35,* 1174–1182.

Bennett, D. S., Ambrosini, P. J., Kudes, D., Metz, C., & Rabinovich, H. (2005). Gender differences in adolescent depression: Do symptoms differ for boys and girls? *Journal of Affective Disorders, 89,* 35–44.

Beyers, J., & Loeber, R. (2003). Untangling developmental relations between depressed mood and delinquency in male adolescents. *Journal of Abnormal Child Psychology, 31*(3), 247–266.

Borowsky, I. W., Ireland, M., & Resnick, M. D. (2001). Adolescent suicide attempts: Risks and protectors. *Pediatrics, 107,* 485–493.

Borowsky, I. W., Resnick, M. D., Ireland, M., & Blum, R. W. (1999). Suicide attempts among American Indian and Alaska Native Youth: Risk and protective factors. *Archives of Pediatric Adolescent Medicine, 153,* 573–580.

Brent, D. A., Baugher, M., Bridge, J., Chen, T., & Chiappetta, L. (1999). Age- and sex-related risk factors for adolescent suicide. *Journal of the American Academy of Child and Adolescent Psychiatry, 38,* 1497–1505.

Burns, J., & Rapee, R. (2006). Adolescent mental health literacy: Young people's knowledge of depression and help seeking. *Journal of Adolescence, 29*(2), 225–239.

Caldwell, C. (1999). Counseling depressed boys. In A. M. Horne & M. S. Kiselica (Eds.), *Handbook of counseling boys and adolescent males* (pp. 279–292). Thousand Oaks, CA: Sage.

Centers for Disease Control and Prevention. (1998, August 14). *Youth risk behavior surveillance—United States, 1997. Morbidity and Mortality Weekly Report (MMWR), 47*(No. SS-3). Retrieved July 2, 2007, from http://www.cdc.gov/mmwr/PDF/SS/SS4703.pdf

Centers for Disease Control and Prevention. (2007). *Youth risk behavior surveillance system.* Retrieved April 2, 2007, from http://www.cdc.gov/healthyyouth/yrbs/index.htm

Centers for Disease Control and Prevention, National Center for Injury Prevention and Control (Producer). (2004). *Web-based injury statistics query and reporting system.* Retrieved April 2, 2007, from http://www.cdc.gov/ncipc/wisqars/default.htm

Chambless, D. L., & Hollon, S. D. (1998). Defining empirically supported therapies. *Journal of Consulting and Clinical Psychology, 66,* 7–18.

Cochran, S. V. (2001). Assessing and treating depression in men. In G. R. Brooks & G. E. Good (Eds.), *The new handbook of psychotherapy and counseling with men: A comprehensive guide to settings, problems, and treatment approaches* (pp. 444–463). San Francisco: Jossey-Bass/Pfeiffer.

Cochran, S. V. (2005). Evidence-based assessment with men. *Journal of Clinical Psychology, 61,* 649–660.

Cochran, S. V., & Rabinowitz, F. E. (2000). *Men and depression: Clinical and empirical perspectives.* San Diego, CA: Academic Press.

Cochran, S. V., & Rabinowitz, F. E. (2003). Gender-sensitive recommendations for assessment and treatment of depression in men. *Professional Psychology: Research and Practice, 34,* 132–140.

Conner, K., & Goldston, D. (2007). Rates of suicide among males increase steadily from age 11 to 21: Developmental framework and outline for prevention. *Aggression and Violent Behavior, 12,* 193–207.

Culp, A. M., Clyman, M. M., & Culp, R. E. (1995). Adolescent depressed mood, reports of suicide attempts, and asking for help. *Adolescence, 30,* 827–837.

Dixon, S. L. (1987). *Working with people in crisis* (2nd ed.). Columbus, OH: Merrill.

Ellis, C. M. (Presenter), & Dermer, S. (Ed.). (2007, February 8). *Black male authenticity* [Podcast]. Kent, OH: Counseloraudiosource.net. Retrieved March 14, 2007, from http://www.podcastdirectory.com/podshows/1143407

Emslie, G. J., & Weinberg, W. A. (1994). Diagnosis and assessment of depression in adolescents. In T. C. R. Wilkes, G. Belsher, A. J. Rush, & E. Frank (Eds.), *Cognitive therapy for depressed adolescents* (pp. 45–68). New York: Guilford.

Evans, D. L. (Chair), Beardslee, W., Biederman, J., Brent, D., Charney, D., Coyle, J., et al. (Eds.). (2005). Defining depression and bipolar disorder. In D. Evans, E. B. Foa, R. E. Gur, H. Hendin, C. P. O'Brien, M. E. P. Seligman, & B. T. Walsh (Eds.), *Treating and preventing adolescent mental health disorders* (pp. 3–27). Oxford: Oxford University Press.

Favazza, A. (1998). The coming of age of self-mutilation. *Journal of Nervous and Mental Disease, 186,* 259–268.

Fergusson, D. M., & Woodward, L. J. (2002). Mental health, educational, and social role outcomes of adolescents with depression. *Archives of General Psychiatry, 58,* 225–231.

Fleming, J., & Offord, D. (1990). Epidemiology of childhood depressive disorders: A critical review. *Journal of the American Academy of Child & Adolescent Psychiatry, 29*(4), 571–580.

Fordham, S., & Ogbu, J. (1986). African American students' school success: Coping with the burden of "acting white." *Urban Review, 18,* 176–206.

Gasquet, I., Chavance, M., Ledoux, S., & Choque, M. (1997). Psychosocial factors associated with help-seeking behavior among depressive adolescents. *European Child Adolescent Psychiatry, 6,* 151–159.

Gerard, J. M., & Buehler, C. (2004). Cumulative environmental risk and youth maladjustment: The role of youth attributes. *Child Development, 75,* 1832–1849.

Gore, S., & Aseltine, R. H., Jr. (2003). Race and ethnic differences in depressed mood following the transition from high school. *Journal of Health and Social Behavior, 44,* 370–389.

Gore, S., Aseltine, R. H., Jr., & Colton, M. E. (1992). Social structure, life stress and depressive symptoms in a high school-aged population. *Journal of Health and Social Behavior, 33,* 97–113.

Gore, S., Aseltine, R. H., Jr., & Colton, M. E. (1993). Gender, social-relational involvement, and depression. *Journal of Research on Adolescence, 3,* 101–125.

Gotlib, I. H., Lewinsohn, P. M., & Seeley, J. R. (1995). Symptoms versus a diagnosis of depression: Differences in psychosocial functioning. *Journal of Consulting and Clinical Psychology, 63,* 90–100.

Gould, M. S., King, R., Greenwald, S., Fisher, P., Schwab-Stone, M. D., Kramer, R., et al. (1998). Psychopathology associated with suicidal ideation and attempts among children and adolescents. *Journal of the American Academy of Child and Adolescent Psychiatry, 37,* 915–923.

Gould, M. S., & Kramer, R. A. (2001). Youth suicide prevention. *Suicide and Life Threatening Behavior, 31,* 6–31.

Gratz, K., & Chapman, A. L. (2007). The role of emotional responding and childhood maltreatment in the development and maintenance of deliberate self-harm among male undergraduates. *Psychology of Men and Masculinity, 8,* 1–14.

Gratz, K., Conrad, S., & Roemer, L. (2002). Risk factors for deliberate self-harm among college students. *Journal of Orthopsychiatry, 72*(1), 128–140.

Haavisto, A., Sourander, A., Multimski, P., Parkkola, K., Santalahti, P., Helenius, H., et al. (2004). Factors associated with depressive symptoms among 18-year-old boys: A prospective 10-year follow-up study. *Journal of Affective Disorders, 83*(2/3), 143–154.

Hallfors, D. (2005). Which comes first in adolescence—sex and drugs or depression? *American Journal of Preventive Medicine, 29,* 163–170.

Hanna, E., & Grant, B. (1997). Gender differences in DSM-IV alcohol use disorders and major depression as distributed in the general population: Clinical implications. *Comprehensive Psychiatry, 38,* 202–212.

Hawton, K., & Sinclair, J. (2003). The challenge of evaluating the effectiveness of treatments for deliberate self-harm. *Psychological Medicine, 33,* 955–958.

Hendin, H., Brent, D. A., Cornelius, J. R.., Coyne-Beasley, T., Greenberg, T., Gould, M., et al. (2005). Defining youth suicide. In D. Evans, E. B. Foa, R. E. Gur, H. Hendin, C. P. O'Brien, M. E. P. Seligman, & B. T. Walsh (Eds.), *Treating and preventing adolescent mental health disorders* (pp. 434–443). Oxford: Oxford University Press.

Hetrick, E. S., & Martin, A. D. (1988). The stigmatization of the gay and lesbian adolescent. *Journal of Homosexuality, 51,* 163–312.

Hill, J. P., & Lynch, M. E. (1983). The intensification of gender-related role expectations during early adolescence. In J. Brooks-Gunn & A. Petersen (Eds.), *Girls at puberty: Biological and psychosocial perspectives* (pp. 201–208). Hillsdale, NJ: Erlbaum.

Irwin, C., Burg, S. J., & Cart, C. U. (2002). America's adolescents: Where have we been, where are we going? *Journal of Adolescent Health, 31,* 91–121.

Joiner, T. (2005). *Why people die by suicide.* Cambridge, MA: Harvard University Press.

Kandel, D. B., & Davies, M. (1986). Adult sequela of adolescent depressive symptoms. *Archives of General Psychiatry, 43,* 255–262.

Kaplan, S. L., Hong, G. K., & Weinhold, C. (1984). Epidemiology of depressive symptomatology in adolescents. *Journal of the American Academy of Child and Adolescent Psychiatry, 23,* 91–98.

Kazdin, A. E., & Weisz, J. R. (1998). Identifying and developing empirically supported child and adolescent treatments. *Journal of Consulting and Clinical Psychology, 66,* 19–36.

Kilmartin, C. T. (2007). *The masculine self* (3rd ed.). Cornwall-on-Hudson, NY: Sloan.

Larson, R., & Ham, M. (1993). Stress and "storm and stress" in early adolescence: The relationship of negative events with dysphoric affect. *Developmental Psychology, 29,* 130–140.

Larson, R., & Lampman-Petraitis, C. (1989). Daily emotional stress as reported by children and adolescents. *Child Development, 60,* 1250–1260.

Leadbeater, B., Blatt, S. J., & Quinlan, D. M. (1995). Gender-linked vulnerabilities to depressive symptoms, stress, and problem behaviors in adolescence. *Journal of Research on Adolescence, 5,* 1–29.

Levant, R. F. (1998). Desperately seeking language: Understanding, assessing, and treating normative male alexithymia. In W. S. Pollack & R. F. Levant (Eds.), *New psychotherapy for men* (pp. 35–56). New York: Wiley.

Lewinsohn, P. M., & Clarke, G. N. (1999). Psychosocial treatments for adolescent depression. *Clinical Psychology Review, 19,* 329–342.

Lewinsohn, P. M., Gotlib, I. H., & Seeley, J. R. (1995). Adolescent psycho-pathology: IV. Specificity of psychosocial risk factors for depression and substance abuse in older adolescents. *Journal of the American Academy of Child and Adolescent Psychiatry, 34*, 1221–1229.

Lewinsohn, P. M., Rohde, P., & Seeley, J. R. (1998). Major depressive disorder in older adolescents: Prevalence, risk factors, and clinical implications. *Clinical Psychology Review, 18*, 765–794.

Lindsey, M. A., Korr, W. S., Broitman, M., Bone, L., Green, A., & Leaf, P. J. (2006). Help-seeking behaviors and depression among African American adolescent boys. *Social Work, 51*, 49–59.

Luther, S. S., & McMahon, T. (1996). Peer reputation among inner city adoles-cents: Structure and correlations. *Journal of Child Psychology and Psychiatry, 34*, 441–453.

Mahalik, J. R. (2001). Cognitive therapy for men. In G. Brooks & G. Good (Eds.), *The new handbook of psychotherapy and counseling with men* (pp. 565–581). San Francisco: Jossey-Bass.

Mahalik, J. R., Good, G. E., & Englar-Carlson, M. (2003). Masculinity scripts, presenting concerns, and help seeking: Implications for practice and training. *Professional Psychology: Research and Practice, 34*, 123–131.

Marcotte, D., Fortin, L., Potvin, P., & Papillon, M. (2002). Gender differences in depressive symptoms during adolescence: Role of gender-typed charac-teristics, self-esteem, body image, stressful life events, and pubertal status. *Journal of Emotional and Behavioral Disorders, 10*, 29–42.

May, P. A., & Van Winkle, N. (1994). Indian adolescent suicide: The epide-miologic picture in New Mexico. In C. W. Duclos & M. Manson (Eds.), *Calling from the rim: Suicide behavior among American Indian and Alaska Native adolescents* (pp. 2–23). Boulder: University of Colorado Press.

McIntosh, J. L. (2000). Epidemiology of adolescent suicide in the United States. In R. W. Maris, S. S. Canetto, J. L. McIntosh, & M. M. Silverman (Eds.), *Review of Suicidology, 2000* (pp. 3–33). New York: Guilford.

McLeod, J. D., & Shanahan, M. J. (1996). Trajectories of poverty and children's mental health. *Journal of Health and Social Behavior, 37*, 207–220.

McWhirter, J. J., McWhirter, B. T., McWhirter, E. H., & McWhirter, R. J. (2004). *At-risk youth: A comprehensive response* (3rd ed.). Belmont, CA: Brooks/Cole.

Mellin, E. A. (2001). Interpersonal theory and depressed adolescents: An overview of method and outcome (ERIC Document Reproduction Ser-vice No. ED451458). East Lansing, MI: National Center for Research on Teacher Learning.

Metalsky, G. I., Joiner, T. E., Hardin, T. S., & Abramson, L. Y. (1993). Depressive reactions to failure in a naturalistic setting: A test of the hopelessness and self-esteem theories of depression. *Journal of Abnormal Psychology, 102*, 101–109.

Michael, K., & Crowley, S. L. (2002). How effective are treatments for child and adolescent depression? A meta-analytic review. *Clinical Psychology Review, 22*, 247–269.

Milin, R., Walker, S., & Chow, J. (2003). Major depressive disorder in adoles-cence: A brief review of the recent treatment literature. *Canadian Journal of Psychiatry, 48*(9), 600–606.

Möller-Leimkuehler, A. (2002). Barriers to help-seeking in men. A review of the socio-cultural and clinical literature with particular reference to depression. *Journal of Affective Disorders, 71,* 1–9.

Möller-Leimkuehler, A. M. (2003). The gender gap in suicide and premature death or: Why are men so vulnerable? *European Archives of Psychiatry & Clinical Neuroscience, 253,* 1–8.

Möller-Leimkuehler, A., Heller, J., & Paulus, N. (2007). Subjective well-being and "male depression" in male adolescents. *Journal of Affective Disorders, 98,* 65–72.

Muehlenkamp, J. J., & Gutierrez, P. M. (2004). An investigation of differences between self-injurious behavior and suicide attempts in a sample of adolescents. *Suicide and Life-Threatening Behavior, 34,* 12–23.

Mufson, L., Dorta, K., Moreau, D., & Weissman, M. (2005). Efficacy to effectiveness: Adaptations of interpersonal psychotherapy for adolescent depression. In E. D. Hibbs & P. S. Jenson (Eds.), *Psychosocial treatments for child and adolescent disorders: Empirically based strategies for clinical practice* (2nd ed., pp. 165–186). Washington, DC: American Psychological Association.

Nock, M., & Prinstein, M. (2005). Contextual features and behavioral functions of self-mutilation among adolescents. *Journal of Abnormal Psychology, 114*(1), 140–146.

O'Neil, J. M. (1982). Gender role conflict and strain in men's lives: Implications for psychiatrists, psychologists, and other human service providers. In K. Solomon & N. B. Levy (Eds.), *Men in transition: Changing male roles, theory, and therapy* (pp. 5–44). New York: Plenum.

Osborne, J. W. (1999). Unraveling underachievement among African American boys from an identification with academics perspective. *Journal of Negro Education, 68,* 555–564.

Petersen, A. C., Compas, B. E., Brooks-Gunn, J., Stemmler, M., Ey, S., & Grant, K. E. (1993). Depression in adolescence. *American Psychologist, 48,* 155–168.

Petersen, A. C., & Hamburg, B. (1986). Adolescence: A developmental approach to problems and psychopathology. *Behavior Therapy, 13,* 480–499.

Pleck, J. H. (1995). The gender role strain paradigm: An update. In R. F. Levant & W. S. Pollack (Eds.), *The new psychology of men* (pp. 11–32). New York: Basic.

Pollack, W. S. (1998). *Real boys: Rescuing our sons from the myths of boyhood.* New York: Random House.

Pollack, W. S. (2006). The war for boys: Hearing real boys voices, healing their pain. *Professional Psychology: Research and Practice, 37,* 190–195.

Pruitt, I. (2007). Family treatment approaches for depression in adolescent males. *American Journal of Family Therapy, 35*(1), 69–81.

Puig-Antich, J., Kaufman, J., Ryan, N. D., Williamson, D. E., Dahl, R. E., Lukens, E., et al. (1993). The psychosocial functioning and family environment of depressed adolescents. *Journal of American Academy of Child and Adolescent Psychiatry, 32,* 244–253.

Queralt, M. (1993). Risk factors associated with completed suicide in Latino adolescents. *Adolescence, 28,* 831–850.

Ramsey, M. (1994). Student depression: General treatment dynamics and symptom specific interventions. *School Counselor, 41,* 256–262.

Randell, B., Eggert, L. L., & Pike, K. (2001). Immediate post intervention effects of two brief youth suicide prevention interventions. *Suicide and Life Threatening Behavior, 31,* 41–61.

Real, T. (1997). *I don't want to talk about it: Overcoming the secret legacy of male depression.* New York: Fireside.

Reinecke, M. A., Ryan, N. E., & DuBois, D. L. (1998). Cognitive-behavioral therapy of depression and depressive symptoms during adolescence: A review and meta-analysis. *Journal of the American Academy of Child & Adolescent Psychiatry, 37,* 26–34.

Reynolds, W. M. (1990). Depression in children and adolescents: Nature, diagnosis, assessment, and treatment. *School Psychology Review, 19,* 158–173.

Rice, K., & Meyer, A. (1994). Preventing depression among young adolescents: Preliminary process results of a psycho-educational intervention program. *Journal of Counseling & Development, 73*(2), 145–152.

Roberts, R. E., Lewinsohn, P. M., & Seeley, J. R. (1995). Symptoms of DSM-II-R major depression in adolescence: Evidence from an epidemiological survey. *Journal of the American Academy of Child and Adolescent Psychiatry, 34,* 1608–1617.

Rohde, P., Lewinsohn, P. M., & Seeley, J. R. (1994). Are adolescents changed by an episode of major depression? *Journal of the American Academy of Child and Adolescent Psychiatry, 33,* 1289–1298.

Rohde, P., Seeley, J. R., & Mace, D. E. (1997). Correlates of suicidal behavior in a juvenile detention population. *Suicide and Life-Threatening Behaviors, 27,* 164–175.

Rudolph, K. D. (2002). Gender differences in emotional responses to interpersonal stress during adolescence. *Journal of Adolescent Health, 30,* 3–13.

Rudolph, K. D., & Hammen, C. (1999). Age and gender as determinants of stress exposure, generation, and reactions in youngsters: A transactional perspective. *Child Development, 70,* 660–677.

Rushton, J. L., Forcier, M., & Schectman, R. M. (2002). Epidemiology of depressive symptoms in the National Longitudinal Study of Adolescent Health. *Journal of the American Academy of Child and Adolescent, 41,* 199–205.

Santor, D., & Kusumakar, V. (2001). Open trial of interpersonal therapy in adolescents with moderate to severe major depression: Effectiveness of novice IPT therapists. *Journal of the American Academy of Child & Adolescent Psychiatry, 40*(2), 236–240.

Schraedley, P., Gotlib, I. H., & Hayward, C. (1999). Gender differences in correlates of depressive symptoms in adolescents. *Journal of Adolescent Health, 25,* 98–108.

Seekwellness.com. (2005). *Men's depression.* Retrieved April 15, 2007, from http://www.seekwellness.com/conditions/mental/mens_depression.htm

Selekman, M. (2005). *Pathways to change: Brief therapy with difficult adolescents.* New York: Guilford Press.

Sen, B. (2004). Adolescent propensity for depressed mood and help seeking: Race and gender differences. *Journal of Mental Health Policy and Economics, 7*(3), 133–145.

Shaffer, D., Gould, M. S., Fisher, P., Trautment, P., Moreau, D., Kleinman, M., et al. (1996). Psychiatric diagnosis in child and adolescent suicide. *Archives of General Psychiatry, 53,* 339–348.

Shepard, D. S. (2005). Male development and the journey toward disconnection. In D. Comstock (Ed.), *Diversity and development: Critical contexts that shape our lives and relationships* (pp. 133–160). Belmont, CA: Brooks-Cole.

Shih, J., Eberhart, N., Hammen, C., & Brennan, P. (2006). Differential exposure and reactivity to interpersonal stress predict sex differences in adolescent depression. *Journal of Clinical Child and Adolescent Psychology, 35*(1), 103–115.

Siegel, J., Aneshensel, C. S., Taub, B., Cantwell, D. P., & Driscoll, A. K. (1998). Adolescent depressed mood in a multiethnic sample. *Journal of Youth and Adolescence, 27,* 413–427.

Simon, G. E. (2006). The antidepressant quandary: Considering suicide risk when treating adolescent depression. *New England Journal of Medicine, 355,* 2722–2723.

Simon, T. R., Swann, A. C., Powell, K. E., Potter, L. B., Kresnow, M., & O'Carroll, P. W. (2001). Characteristics of impulsive suicide attempts and attempters, *Suicide and Life-Threatening Behavior, 32,* 49–59.

Simpson, H., Nee, J., & Endicott, J. (1997). First-episode major depression: Few sex differences in course. *Archives of General Psychiatry, 54,* 633–639.

Smiler, A. P. (2004). Thirty years after the discovery of gender: Psychological concepts and measures of masculinity. *Sex Roles, 50,* 15–26.

Social Care Institute for Excellence. (2005). *Deliberate self-harm (DSH) among children and adolescents: Who is at risk and how is it recognized?* Retrieved April 3, 2007, from http://www.scie.org.uk/publications/briefings/briefing16/index.asp

Stark, K. D., Swearer, S., & Sommer, D. (1998). School-based group treatment for depressive disorders in children. In K. C. Stoiber & T. Kratochwill (Eds.), *Handbook of group intervention for children and families* (pp. 68–99). Boston: Allyn & Bacon.

Strong, M. (1998). *A bright red scream: Self -mutilation and the language of pain.* New York: Penguin.

Sund, A. M., Larsson, B., & Wichstrom, L. (2003). Psychosocial correlates of depressive symptoms among 12–14-year-old Norwegian adolescents. *Journal of Child Psychology and Psychiatry, 44,* 588–597.

Treatment for Adolescents With Depression Study Team. (2004). Fluoxetine, cognitive-behavioral therapy, and their combination for adolescents with depression. *Journal of the American Medical Association, 292,* 807–820.

U.S. Food and Drug Administration. (2004). *Worsening depression and suicidality in patients treated with antidepressant medications.* Retrieved April 4, 2007, from http://www.fda.gov/cder/drug/antidepressants/default.html

U.S. Office of the Surgeon General. (2006). Depression and suicide in children and adolescents. Retrieved April 1, 2007, from http://www.surgeongeneral.gov/library/mentalhealth/chapter3/sec5.html

U.S. Public Health Service. (1999). *The surgeon general's call to action to prevent suicide.* Washington, DC: Author.

Vitiello, B., & Swedo, S. (2004). Antidepressant medications in children. *New England Journal of Medicine, 350,* 1489–1491.

Vredenburg, K., Krames, L., & Flett, G. (1986). Sex differences in the clinical expression of depression. *Sex Roles, 14,* 37–48.

Walsh, B. W. (2006). *Treating self-injury: A practical guide.* New York: Guilford Press.

Weisz, J. R., McCarty, C. A., & Valeri, S. M. (2006). Effects of psychotherapy for depression in children and adolescents: A meta-analysis. *Psychological Bulletin, 132,* 132–149.

Williamson, M. (1987). Sex differences in depression symptoms among adult family medicine patients. *Journal of Family Practice, 25,* 591–594.

Wolbeek, M., van Doornen, J. P., Kavelaars, A., & Heijnen, C. J. (2006). Severe fatigue in adolescents: A common phenomenon. *Pediatrics, 117,* 1078–1086.

Young, M., Scheftner, W., Fawcett, J., & Klerman, G. (1990). Gender differences in the clinical features of unipolar major depressive disorder. *Journal of Nervous and Mental Disease, 178,* 200–203.

Zila, L. M., & Kiselica, M. S. (2001). Understanding and counseling self-mutilation in female adolescents and young adults. *Journal of Counseling and Development, 79,* 46–53.

Zoroglu, S. S., Tuzun, U., Sar, V., Tutkun, H., Savas, H. A., Ozturk, M., et al. (2003). Suicide attempt and self-mutilation among Turkish high school students in relation with abuse, neglect and dissociation. *Psychiatry and Clinical Neurosciences, 57,* 119–126.

7

Improving Self-Control

Counseling Boys with Attention Deficit Hyperactivity Disorder

GEORGE M. KAPALKA

Attention deficit hyperactivity disorder (ADHD) is one of the most frequently diagnosed psychological disorders in the pediatric population. Four to 6% of school-age children, or about one in 17, are diagnosed with ADHD (Barkley, 2006). Children with ADHD constitute a large portion of the population of children and adolescents who are brought for outpatient mental health treatment at public or private mental health facilities. The symptoms of this disorder usually affect the child's functioning at home, in school, and with peers. Consequently, mental health professionals who work with children and adolescents need to be familiar with this disorder and the most effective ways to treat those children who present with it.

ADHD is more common in boys. The ratio of boys to girls with ADHD has been reported to be between 3:1 and 10:1, and most clinicians agree that boys with ADHD outnumber girls at least 4:1 or 5:1 (Bird, 2002). In addition, boys with ADHD are more likely to present with defiance, anger, and other behaviors that are difficult for parents and teachers to manage (Barkley, 2006). Thus, clinicians who treat boys with ADHD must be particularly prepared to address the behavior management problems that boys with ADHD commonly exhibit.

In this chapter, various treatment approaches are explored. The chapter is not intended to provide detailed descriptions of all the treatment strategies. Rather, it is an overview meant to introduce the reader to the types of treatment that have been found to be effective. For each, the principles of the approach are outlined, and sources are provided for those professionals who desire to learn more about each type of treatment.

DESCRIPTION OF SYMPTOMS

Children with ADHD commonly exhibit a variety of problems across different settings. Some of these are core symptoms of the disorder, and some are secondary symptoms that develop as a boy with ADHD interacts with his family, peers, and teachers, and experiences the negative effects of displaying the symptoms of ADHD.

Core Symptoms of ADHD

The *Diagnostic and Statistical Manual of Mental Disorders* (*DSM-IV-TR*; American Psychiatric Association, 2000) identifies two dimensions of symptoms that individuals with ADHD exhibit: These are impulsivity and hyperactivity, and distractibility and disorganization.

Impulsivity and Hyperactivity

Many boys with ADHD exhibit impulsivity, but sometimes these symptoms may, at first glance, be overlooked. Boys with ADHD often act with little forethought, exhibiting a seemingly knee-jerk reactivity to environmental events. For many boys with ADHD, controlling their urges to say and do things is a major struggle. This is evident in the decisions they make—for example, chasing the ball into the street without looking whether a car is coming, not accepting that it is time to stop watching television because they have to start getting ready for bed, and not turning off the computer when it is time for homework. When they accompany parents during shopping trips (for example, in the supermarket), boys with ADHD are easily affected by what they see on the shelves, and they commonly place items into the shopping basket that catch their interest regardless of whether or not parents allowed them to do so. Consequently, boys with ADHD frequently argue with their parents.

Impulsivity and hyperactivity are closely related, and many boys who are impulsive are also hyperactive. Those boys exhibit a "driven by a motor" quality, a restlessness, and a need to constantly move about. They have difficulties sitting still when they should (for example, during meals), remaining quiet when they need to (for example, in class), and winding down after a vigorous activity (for example, after playing sports or running around). In stores, hyperactive boys wander (or run) away from their parents and require effort (and, sometimes, a chase) to bring them under control. Parents find these behaviors very frustrating, and therefore boys with ADHD frequently get reprimanded, scolded, or punished.

In school, boys with ADHD have difficulties remaining still during lectures and tend to be disruptive in class. At times, they may leave their desks and interfere with other students' ability to pay attention in class. Young boys with ADHD (i.e., those who are in kindergarten, first grade, and second grade) are also known to call out an answer to a teacher's question without raising their hand. During lunch, on the playground, in gym class, or during music and art classes, boys with ADHD easily become overstimulated, and their ability to exercise self-control is further reduced. As a result, boys with ADHD frequently get reprimanded and scolded by their teachers.

Impulsive children have difficulties sharing their toys and frequently get into arguments with other peers. During play activities, boys with ADHD often like to remain in charge and have difficulties accepting that rules must be arrived at by consensus. When seeing a group of friends talking or playing, a boy with ADHD is likely to "barge in" and try to take over the activity of the group. Consequently, peers often exclude boys with ADHD from games, sports activities, and other social interactions, and boys with ADHD usually have few friends.

Distractibility and Disorganization

Some boys with ADHD present with difficulties sustaining attention and filtering out distractions. They lose focus during class and miss much of the content of the class lectures. They may daydream and require a significant amount of redirection to remain on task. When it is time to write down their homework assignments, boys with ADHD often miss what is being assigned, and forget to bring home necessary books, handouts, and notebooks. As a result, boys with ADHD often earn poor grades and fall behind academically.

Usually, boys who are distractible are also disorganized. They have difficulties keeping track of their things and frequently lose toys, homework assignments, books, and so on. Because they easily get distracted or sidetracked, they need a lot of supervision to complete their routines and assigned tasks. They often do not exhibit the level of independence that parents expect, and therefore parents likewise find these boys frustrating to manage.

Secondary Symptoms

Boys with ADHD frequently experience conflicts and failure. They have limited frustration tolerance and often become angry and argumentative. Boys with ADHD who are impulsive are usually also defiant, because they find it difficult to suppress the impulse to protest every time they do not get their own way. Consequently, children with ADHD tend to get into conflicts with figures of authority and frequently experience getting yelled at and punished. Boys with ADHD are frequently described as "angry children," but this is a misnomer. They are not quintessentially "angry." Rather, they are "reactive," in that they have difficulties suppressing their initial urge to react and externalize whatever they feel inside.

Whether or not they are impulsive, boys with ADHD usually experience academic difficulties (Hinshaw, 2002). Whereas some of these difficulties are related to a significant overlap between ADHD and learning disorders, other factors are also notable. Those boys with ADHD who exhibit disruptive behaviors frequently get reprimanded by teachers. Those who are distractible and disorganized are often off task and exhibit difficulties keeping track of, and completing, their homework. Over time, the repeated experience of academic problems often becomes internalized, and many boys with ADHD conclude that they are not as smart as their peers. Consequently, they do not expect to succeed academically, and therefore they are not motivated to try hard and do their homework and study.

DIFFERENTIAL DIAGNOSIS

Before a treatment strategy can be selected, a differential diagnosis must be performed to determine whether or not the symptoms are caused by ADHD or another disorder. Some disorders are especially known to present symptoms that may resemble those of ADHD. Depressed boys often exhibit difficulties following directions and sustaining attention, and present with low motivation. A boy with documented depression should be diagnosed with comorbid ADHD only if there is a history of ADHD symptoms prior to the onset of depression, or if the symptoms of ADHD are severe enough (and the depression mild enough) that mood symptoms cannot account for the ADHD symptoms.

Symptoms of mania and/or agitation also resemble symptoms of ADHD, and boys with bipolar disorder usually are very impulsive. Clinical literature reveals that children with bipolar disorder often get initially diagnosed with ADHD, and only become rediagnosed with bipolar disorder after initial attempts to utilize treatments commonly useful for ADHD prove ineffective (Geller et al., 1998). Differentiating children with ADHD from children with bipolar disorder is difficult, but some guidelines do exist. For example, a child who presents with significant mood disturbance, grandiosity, impulsivity, very violent outbursts, and sleep difficulties is more likely to present with symptoms of bipolar disorder than ADHD. Of course, when any doubt remains in a clinician's mind about the accuracy of a diagnosis, a second opinion should be sought from another mental health professional. In cases where a clinician is interested in differentiating symptoms of ADHD from those of bipolar disorder, a psychiatric evaluation may prove especially useful.

Finally, environmental factors should always be considered as a potential primary source of the disturbance. Children who were exposed to trauma often exhibit a variety of emotional and behavioral difficulties that include difficulties paying attention, academic problems, low motivation, poor self-control, and acting out. Although these symptoms may appear to be characteristic of ADHD, a careful review of environmental factors may reveal that the symptoms started only after the child was exposed to a stressor (for example, parental discord, divorce, family problems, or the death of a relative). In order to rule out the contribution of such environmental factors, a careful review of personal and family history is necessary.

TREATMENT SELECTION

Treatment selection must reflect the etiology of the symptoms of ADHD. Consequently, a brief discussion of etiological factors should be helpful to guide a clinician in selecting an appropriate treatment strategy.

Etiology of ADHD

Although symptoms of ADHD have been recognized since the mid-1800s, it is only recently that a formulation of ADHD that accounts for the full breadth of the etiological factors involved in producing the symptoms of this disorder has been developed (Barkley, 2006).

Biological Factors

Individuals with ADHD exhibit differences in brain function. Brain scans reveal that individuals with ADHD exhibit lower levels of brain activation and blood flow in regions primarily regulated by dopamine—the frontal cortex and the basal ganglia. Individuals with ADHD have been noted to have smaller frontal lobes, basal ganglia, cerebellum, and corpus callosum. Usually, the difference is about 10% from non-ADHD controls (Swanson & Castellanos, 2002). Specific deficits in dopamine transporter genes have also been identified (Barkley, 2006). Although the exact nature of the contribution of these biological factors is not known, most clinicians today agree that children with ADHD are born with a genetic predisposition that decreases the activity of dopaminergic brain systems and results in brain underactivation that is partly responsible for the difficulties in self-control, impulse control, and sustained attention that children with ADHD exhibit.

Psychological Factors

Biological factors only partially explain the symptoms of ADHD, and psychological factors also play an important role. Because boys with ADHD are likely to present with significant argumentativeness and behavioral problems, parents easily become frustrated and often do not utilize consistent, appropriate parenting interventions (Donenberg & Baker, 1994). At times, they overreact, and at other times they give up in frustration and do not follow through on threatened consequences. As a result, boys with ADHD commonly experience secondary gain—the more they act out, the more they get their way. In addition, a negative pattern of interaction that exists between a boy with ADHD and his parents results in few opportunities to experience rewards and positive consequences (Barkley, 2006). Thus, the child rarely experiences situations where positive behavior and utilization of appropriate self-control result in a positive consequence.

Cognitive factors also contribute to these problems. Self-control is, in large part, a cognitive function. Impulsive children do not sufficiently utilize cognitive structures conducive to the delay of gratification and processing of expected consequences. Children with ADHD have difficulties utilizing the principle of "Think before you act" and tend to produce behaviors reactively, with little forethought. Thus, today's formulations of the etiology of ADHD focus on the interplay of biological, behavioral, and cognitive factors. Consequently, treatment approaches should include the utilization of interventions aimed at each of these components.

Unproven Treatment Approaches

As the recognition of the high prevalence of ADHD increased in the general population, parents began to search for alternatives to the most commonly recommended treatments, counseling, and medications. The market has responded with many potential choices. Unfortunately, most of these alternative approaches are unproven, and some of these approaches can actually be harmful. Mental health professionals need to be informed about these treatment approaches in order to properly guide their patients and clients.

Biofeedback professionals have reported promising results with interventions aimed at reprogramming brain waves and claim that the results produce positive behavioral changes. Unfortunately, the treatment usually lasts several months, it is not covered by most insurance plans, and the results are far from guaranteed (Loo, 2003). Many chiropractors profess proficiency with treating ADHD symptoms, and claim that adjusting the neck and/or back vertebrae improves neuronal communication. However, there is no reasonably plausible mechanism by which adjusting the neck or back will alter the functioning of the frontal lobes, the basal ganglia, or any other part of the brain. Indeed, research support for the usefulness of chiropractic adjustments to reduce symptoms of ADHD is virtually nonexistent.

Dietary changes have also been attempted, with poor results. Reducing intake of sugar has not been shown to be effective, and other dietary changes also have not shown efficacy. Although there are a few children who exhibit bona fide food hypersensitivities and/or allergies, those children are very rare. Professionals who wish to guide a patient or parent toward a source that comprehensively addresses the effect of foods on behavior should consult Conners's (2001) excellent book, *Feeding the Brain.*

Other treatments can actually be harmful. Chelation therapy has been developed to detoxify a child who has been exposed to lead or mercury, but the treatment has never been shown to be effective in scientifically controlled studies, and chelation treatment sometimes produces problems with kidneys, disturbance in blood clotting, cardiac arrhythmias, and other medical problems. In short, this is a treatment that is not only ineffective but also probably harmful (Arnold, 2002).

Many herbal and nutritional supplements have claimed success in reducing symptoms of ADHD. Some products, like the widely advertised Focus Factor, contain a mix of vitamins that sometimes also includes the Omega-3 fatty acid, but ingestion of any of these components has not been shown to reduce the symptoms of ADHD. Other supplements, like candida yeast and anti-motion-sickness compounds, have also failed to show efficacy in the treatment of ADHD (Arnold, 2002).

Some supplements can be downright harmful. Products that contain ephedra do, indeed, promote wakefulness and may improve attention, but ephedra (and its Chinese version, ma huang) has been shown to adversely affect cardiac functioning, even leading to heart attacks in some cases (U.S. Food & Drug Administration, 2004). Parents considering the use of any product that contains ephedra should carefully weigh the risks and potential benefits.

Some "natural" compounds have actually been shown to exacerbate symptoms of ADHD (for example, inositol), and some can be dangerous, especially to children (for example, gingko biloba) (Bezchlibnyk-Butler & Jeffries, 2006). Clinicians should generally caution parents against the use of most herbal and nutritional supplements with children.

The treatments reviewed in this section are meant to provide an introduction to the types of alternative treatments that mental health practitioners and parents encounter. Because the treatment of ADHD has become such a popular topic, new claims of discovering yet another alternative treatment that will reduce ADHD symptoms abound. Parents and clinicians need to be very skeptical about these claims, and should seek evidence from well-designed (preferably, those that utilize true experimental designs) scientific studies before accepting any of these claims.

Effective Treatment Approaches

Treatment approaches that have shown to be effective are based, at least in part, on understanding the etiology of ADHD and targeting specific interventions at the various mechanisms that are responsible for the symptoms of ADHD. Effective treatment of ADHD is multimodal, because each approach addresses a specific set of symptoms and/or specific settings where problems are present. The next several sections of this chapter review the treatments of ADHD that have been shown to be effective in research literature. Clinicians are encouraged to design and implement a comprehensive treatment plan that includes as many of the strategies discussed below as are necessary in order to bring the symptoms under control and improve the boy's ability to function with parents, teachers, siblings, and peers.

MEDICATIONS

The first question that parents and mental health professionals usually ask is "Should medication treatment be considered?" Although the answer depends largely on personal choice and general attitude toward medications, clinicians should remain objective about the potential benefits of medications, and when appropriate should make such a recommendation to the boy's parents.

When to Consider Medications

Whether or not to use medications is, first and foremost, dependent upon the level of severity of the symptoms. Children who present with mild impairment may not need to be medicated, and utilizing other approaches before trying medications is a sensible choice. However, children with more significant impairment may exhibit little progress without medications. The more severe the symptoms, the more important it becomes to use medication in conjunction with other treatments.

When broaching this subject with parents, clinicians often search for examples to help parents become more receptive. It helps to conceptualize ADHD as a disorder with both biological and behavioral components, similar to hypertension. When someone has hypertension, the management of the disorder depends on the level of severity. Mild cases are usually handled by behavioral changes—better diet, more exercise, keeping weight under control, and the like. The more the blood pressure exceeds the cutoffs, however, the more important it becomes to utilize medications in addition to these lifestyle changes, because the behavioral approach alone will not be sufficient and because even with proper diet, exercise, and weight within normal limits, some people still continue to have dangerously high blood pressure.

ADHD symptoms can be presented as analogous to hypertension. The more severe the symptoms, the more likely they are caused, at least in part, by significant deviations in the functioning of important brain areas (a "chemical imbalance," to borrow an overused but somewhat accurate vernacular phrase). Behavioral and cognitive techniques need to be utilized as well, but without medications, they will be as ineffective as lifestyle changes alone are to lower the blood pressure of someone with severe hypertension.

If the decision was made to implement a trial of medications, the next question usually asked is "What kind?" and "What are the benefits and drawbacks of various medication categories that can be utilized to manage ADHD symptoms?"

Stimulants

Psychostimulants continue to be the most effective medication treatments available (Greenhill, 2002). In addition, although Ritalin and other stimulants have sometimes been portrayed in the media as dangerous, the reality is that they are a category of medications that, among all psychotropics, has the *least* likelihood of side effects, and the side effects are the *least* dangerous (readers may consult Bezchlibnyk-Butler & Jeffries, 2006, for a comprehensive review of side effects of various categories of psychotropic medications). Various preparations have been developed primarily to address how long the medication will remain in the system. Ideally, a stimulant will work quickly enough to be given in the morning and produce an improvement by the time the boy begins the school day, and last long enough to continue to show clinical effects through homework time, but not long enough to interfere with dinner or bedtime. Additionally, once-per-day dosing is preferred, because it eliminates the need for the boy to have to be given a dose of medications during school hours (which is cumbersome and can be embarrassing for the boy, as he may need to explain the need to do so to his peers).

As is the case with all medications, the use of stimulants has benefits and drawbacks. On the positive side, psychostimulants can generally be given only during school days, and many parents utilize "weekend drug holidays" and do not give their son medications on the weekend unless a special circumstance warrants it (for example, an event is planned during which their son is likely to have significant difficulties exerting appropriate self-control). Psychostimulants generally have a quick onset of clinical effects, and, in most cases, their duration of effect can be dosed to last through homework, but terminate by dinnertime. Most children tolerate these medications very well, with few side effects. Contrary to some fears among parents, the use of stimulants does not produce psychological or physiological dependence, and does not predispose the recipient to future drug use (Barkley, 2006).

Psychostimulants, however, do produce some side effects. They can interfere with sleep, and so the dosing must be such that the clinical effect is terminated long before bed time. They suppress appetite, and must be dosed so that they do not interfere with the boy's appetite during dinner; otherwise, stunted growth may be a long-term risk.

Other Medications

Sometimes, stimulants are not the best choice. For example, when a trial of a stimulant produces significant side effects (severe loss of appetite, agitation, lethargy, tics, etc.), another category of medications should be considered.

Atomoxetine has been shown to be effective and does not cause difficulties with appetite. Because its action resembles that of an antidepressant, it is a good choice for children who present with more agitation and some mood disturbance. On the negative side, however, atomoxetine usually does not produce results that are as dramatic, and the onset of effect is much slower (generally, at least 2 weeks). Although stimulants can be given on some days and not others, atomoxetine must be given every day. In addition, some cardiac problems with this medication have been reported, and there is also a small, but dangerous, risk of liver problems.

Buproprion (Wellbutrin) is effective in the management of ADHD, but its effects are not as dramatic as seen with stimulants, and buproprion must be given every day. Its effects generally take about as long as those of atomoxetine. However, bupropion may address some symptoms of ADHD (for example, distractibility) better than atomoxetine. It is also a good choice to consider when a child is presenting with comorbid agitation and depression.

Clonidine (Catapress), guanfacine (Tenex), and other drugs are rarely used as first-line treatments for ADHD, and usually their side effects outweigh potential benefits. On occasion, nutritional and herbal supplements are also used. S-Adenosyl-l-Methionine (SAM-e) may improve vigilance, but its side effect profile is not known, and individual reaction varies widely. It is also expensive—more expensive than most ADHD medications. Caffeine has also been used in the management of symptoms of ADHD. Although it is widely available and inexpensive, and does not require a doctor's prescription, its benefit is less pronounced, and, because caffeine affects a broad range of chemicals within the brain, it has a greater potential for dependence than prescription stimulants. In addition, no long-acting preparation is available, and so most children will need to take caffeine at least two to three times per day in order to reduce ADHD symptoms through the school day and while doing homework.

PARENT TRAINING

The results of many research studies strongly suggest that parent training is the most effective psychological intervention to help reduce the symptoms of ADHD (Pelham, Wheeler, & Chronis, 1998). Many parent training programs have been developed and researched. Most of these utilize a short-term, structured approach where each session is designed to teach parents a specific technique aimed at addressing a specific misbehavior. The treatment is generally administered over six to 12 sessions.

Kapalka (2007) developed a parent training program that synthesized the components of many parent training programs, and restructured the sequencing of the steps to improve the cumulative effectiveness. Each step, in sequence, has been researched to investigate its contribution to the overall program. The remainder of this section will summarize that program and each of its steps.

Command Giving

Boys with ADHD exhibit significant problems with following commands. These problems are due to difficulties attending to and fully processing the command, impulsivity, and poor self-control.

In order to help improve the boy's ability to process the command, it is necessary to gain his full attention. Obtaining eye contact prior to issuing the command is crucial to improve the boy's ability to process and attend to the command, and also to interrupt an activity in which the boy may be involved long enough for him to process what was said. This is usually accomplished by calling the boy's name and/or asking him to look at the parent.

If, after parents obtain his eye contact, he ignores the command, delays performing the response, or openly refuses to obey the command, parents must control their feelings of frustration and anger, and avoid yelling and threatening, so that escalation of conflict does not take place. Instead of arguing or confronting the boy, it is best for a parent to say nothing, and just stand and look at the boy for an additional 15 to 20 seconds. This allows the boy to reprocess the situation. In many instances, this helps the boy choose to perform the stated command.

Warnings

If the above procedure does not produce compliance, it is necessary to issue a warning. It is important to avoid repetition loops during which parents repeat the command over and over, and the boy continues to ignore or refuse to obey, because this escalates conflict and often causes parents to issue threats of consequences they are not willing to administer. Instead, parents should issue a command once (as outlined in the previous step), repeat it only once, and if this single repetition did not produce compliance, issue one (and only one) warning of a realistic consequence that parents are able to implement as quickly as possible (preferably, immediately). After the warning, the parent should give it another 15–20 seconds, and implement the stated consequence if the warning was not effective. Consistency is very important. Over time, this approach helps the boy learn that when he is noncompliant, parents will implement the stated consequence. This will help him learn to process the consequences of situations before he responds, thus allowing him to begin to diminish his impulsivity.

Time Out

Impulsive boys find it difficult to contain their emotional reactions and sometimes lose control when they feel frustrated or angry. Parents need to implement a technique that helps their son calm down by being in a place that is devoid of stimulation, while also being removed from activities that he likes to perform. In these situations, time out has been found to be effective.

The time-out spot should be a place that is quiet and devoid of stimulation, near enough for parents to monitor their son, but not in the same room, because this seems to further escalate the conflict. Placement of the boy in a chair in the dining room, facing the wall (but not near enough to it so that the boy can reach it and kick it), while no one is in the room and the television, radio, and so on are not on, has been found to be effective. The length of the "minimum sentence" depends on the age of the child. Most parenting programs recommend a one-minute-per-year-of-age rule for more minor infractions, and doubling the time for more major problems.

If the boy refuses to remain in the chair and/or becomes violent, a restraint procedure should be implemented. An effective hold involves placing the child in a dining-room-style chair, preferably with no arm rests, bending the child's arms and wrists behind the backrest of the chair, and holding the child by the wrists from behind.

Behavioral Contract

Establishing a behavioral contract has been shown to be effective in reducing problems with daily routines. An exchange program is implemented wherein children earn tokens (stickers or chips) for performing routine responsibilities, and are then able to exchange these tokens for privileges and rewards. Because the parents begin to restrict certain privileges and allow their son to earn them back only after certain responsibilities were performed, parents increase their leverage and are able to utilize withdrawal of privileges effectively as a consequence. The responsibilities should primarily include daily tasks that are discrete, detailed, and easily monitored. Complex tasks (such as cleaning his room) need to be broken down into discrete components, and each has to be clearly stated in a manner that leaves little to interpretation (for example, "No clothing laying on the floor," "No garbage in the room except in the trash basket," and "No dishes or cups in the room"). Each task is assigned a chip value, and the chips are immediately dispensed after the boy completes the stated responsibility.

The list of rewards and privileges should include, first and foremost, daily privileges (watching television, playing with video games and the computer, and so on). These should be earned in time increments—one chip per each half hour of television, one chip per each 15 minutes of video game use, and the like. Parents must make sure that all privileges on the list are permitted only when the chips have previously been earned, and when the chips are exchanged right then and there to earn the privilege. Additional prizes, for greater chip amounts, are also useful, and these allow the boy to save chips over a longer period to earn an item of some monetary value (for example, a toy or a video game cartridge). It is helpful to implement the contract in stages—beginning with the most rudimentary tasks situations, and gradually expanding it as both parents and their son become used to the technique.

The boy can also lose a specified amount of tokens as punishment for a specific misbehavior. For example, raising his voice in anger (yelling at parents), using foul language, hitting, and so on all can have a specified token cost value to be taken away when these behaviors are present. It is important to use this component advisedly. Only one to two behaviors should be focused on at any one time to take chips away, and each should be specified to the boy beforehand (not "out of the blue," in the midst of a confrontation when the parent does not know what else to do).

Behavioral contract is a flexible intervention that allows both parents and the boy to be creative and design ways to earn and spend the tokens. Along the way, the boy learns valuable lessons. Tokens are earned only for positive behaviors (and may be lost for negative behaviors), and so the contract allows the parents to frequently administer consequences. These consequences teach the boy to begin to anticipate the results of his behaviors, and think through situations as they occur. In the process, impulse control and self-control gradually improve.

Homework

Boys with ADHD often resent homework and present management difficulties when asked to complete it. It is helpful to extend the behavioral contract to include the completion of homework. Parents can implement a house rule where a privilege (for example, watching television or playing with video games) is restricted until after homework is completed. In addition, homework should be performed as soon as possible after school. The longer the delay, the more tired the boy will be, thus further diminishing his capacity to pay attention and exercise self-control.

It is sensible to arrange the homework spot in a place that is quiet but close enough for the parent to monitor. Parents should not remain in the room with the boy while he completes homework, but should check in frequently to monitor his progress. When asked to help, parents should be careful not to do the work for their son. Instead, they should guide him to try to come up with the right answer, and apply the same principle to complete the other items.

Establishing effective home–school communication is a crucial component of success with homework. It is necessary to implement an effective homework journal where the boy must write his assignments while he is in school, and before he departs the teacher must check the journal for completeness and accuracy. Consistent implementation of a constructive homework procedure and effective homework journal (with collaboration from the boy's teacher) is the most effective way of improving homework problems.

Additional Situations

Boys with ADHD frequently act out while in stores, restaurants, houses of worship, and so on. They commonly interrupt adults on the telephone or during other conversations. When boys with ADHD need to switch from one activity (for example, watching television) to another (for example, coming to the dinner table), problems frequently ensue. Once an effective behavioral contract has been implemented, it can gradually be extended to include these additional problems.

For each situation, it is necessary to set one or two simple rules (for example, "Do not interrupt while I am on the telephone," or "Stay by my side while we are in the store") and establish a chip reward for successfully following these rules (for example, "You will earn five chips when we get home"). Sometimes, it can also be effective to set a token cost if the rules are not followed (for example, "If you break the rules, you will lose five chips when we get home"). The target situation should then be implemented, and the appropriate consequence should be administered immediately afterward. It is important that parents focus on only a few rules at a time. Parents must start small and expect a gradual, not instant, improvement.

INDIVIDUAL COUNSELING

Different forms of individual counseling have been attempted with boys with ADHD, including play therapy, art therapy, and various other approaches (Adlerian counseling, etc.). Unfortunately, all of these have scarce or nonexistent support and generally are not considered treatments of choice for boys with ADHD. Instead, individual counseling from the cognitive-behavioral perspective has the greatest likelihood of being effective in addressing the core and secondary symptoms of ADHD.

Core Symptoms

Boys with ADHD are often impulsive, and impulsivity affects much of their functioning at home, in school, and with peers. Whereas they usually "act before they think," it is necessary to reverse this sequence and teach boys with ADHD to "think before they act." The impulsive behavior must be deconstructed to reveal its components, and their underlying progression, in order to help the child begin to address this problem. The sequence begins with the internal reaction. Boys with ADHD are most likely to behave impulsively when emotions are aroused, and both positive and negative emotions are likely to produce impulsive behaviors. The treatment must begin with helping the boy identify what situations make him happy, curious, frustrated, angry, fearful, and so on. It is helpful for the boy to spend some time identifying those situations. As he becomes more aware when he is likely to perform behaviors that may result in troubling consequences, he will begin to prepare himself to be "on watch" for those kinds of situations.

Once the situations are identified, it is helpful to guide the boy to recognize the bodily reactions that he experiences when these situations occur. How does he know he is happy? Angry? Fearful? What is his heart doing? What about his breathing? Are his fists clenched? The more of these bodily reactions that can be identified, the more that will become available as potential signals for the boy to communicate to him that an emotional reaction has been awakened.

Along with bodily reactions, it is helpful to identify the thoughts that accompany those feelings. What is the boy saying to himself when he is angry? When he is afraid of getting punished by his parents? When his curiosity is awakened and he can't wait to see what a group of friends happens to be doing at the moment? In accordance with tenets of cognitive-behavioral counseling, thoughts precipitate behaviors, and therefore helping the boy become aware of what he is thinking before he acts is potentially very helpful. This may be a challenge. The more impulsive the boy, the less cognitive processing will occur. However, at least some cognitive processing occurs every time, however brief it may be. Children are often unaware of what they are thinking and how these thoughts affect their reactions and behaviors. Helping them become aware of this sequence and what thoughts they actually experience is a crucial step in treatment.

Once these thoughts are identified, development of a proactive self-dialogue can begin. Boys can be taught to extend the processing time to include thoughts that are more conducive to productive behavior. One approach that is helpful is to teach the boy certain slogans that he may repeat to himself in situations that evoke emotions. One slogan can be suggested for each common emotion—fear, anger, and so on. These slogans are best presented to children as "pep talks," similar to those that coaches usually give members of their teams. Boys are especially receptive to this idea—many boys are sports fans and have participated in at least some team sports, and so introducing this concept will help them recognize that they are being asked to do for themselves what the coaches have been doing for them all along. This step will likely take much practice, and will require much role play during therapy sessions. However, utilizing these pep talks will help the boy significantly increase processing time that occurs after he has been exposed to emotion-provoking situations.

Once the "pep talks" are utilized to prevent initial overreaction, more rational processing can take place. The boy needs to be taught to think about the various options for behavioral responses—different things he may do and say in the situation that just occurred. Each one needs to be followed with a brief assessment of what is going to happen if this behavior is chosen. This approach must be tailored to the boy's age. Young boys, for example, need suggestions of what they should think or say in various situations, and recognize that other things they may do or say will result in negative consequences (for example, being punished). Grounding these suggestions in examples of real situations that happened recently will make this approach more personal and effective. Older boys should be coached to develop this thought process more independently, prompting them to replay examples of recent episodes and behaviors.

The final step involves the selection of the most appropriate action. Once again, it is necessary to continue to stress to the boy that the consequences of any given behavior must always be considered and must be the primary guide that helps the boy decide what to do in any given situation. The more this approach can be utilized, the more the action–reaction sequence can be slowed down and more effective processing can be utilized, thus reducing problems with impulsivity.

Problems with distractibility affect the boy with ADHD in many ways. In school, he often daydreams and finds it difficult to pay attention during lectures and activities. At home, he spends a long time completing homework and becomes sidetracked while performing tasks that he was asked to do by his parents and caretakers. A procedure called *self-monitoring* has been shown to be effective in helping to reduce these problems.

The key to self-monitoring is teaching the boy to begin to ask himself a series of questions. During times when he knows that he must focus, he should periodically ask himself, "What am I doing?" The answer to this question should be detailed. It should include awareness of what he is looking at, what his hands are doing, what he is thinking about, and so on. However, breaking a spell of daydreaming to perform such an attention check is very difficult.

To assist with this task, it is helpful to ask the boy to identify what he usually does when he is in the midst of a task that requires sustained attention. For example, when he is at his desk and his teacher is talking, where does he usually look? Is it out the window? Or at the clock in the room? At home, during homework, where does he usually look? Identifying one or two specific items that seem to draw him when his attention is drifting is very important.

Once these items have been identified, it is necessary to teach the boy to associate seeing these items with asking himself the above question. For example, whenever he is in the classroom, he can train himself to think, "What am I doing?" whenever he catches himself looking out the window, or looking at the clock in the room.

Once the self-monitoring question is asked, the follow-up question must follow, and the boy must say to himself, "What am I supposed to be doing?" or "What is everyone else in class doing?" This will help him refocus onto the task at hand. This procedure takes some time to implement, and depending on his age and level of motivation, the boy will need a lot of practice to successfully utilize this approach. However, it has been shown to increase time on task for children with ADHD.

Homework assignments present a particularly difficult challenge. It is necessary to teach the boy to utilize a homework journal, as previously discussed in the section on parenting strategies. This should be presented to the boy in a way that portrays the journal as a tool that most everyone uses, his version of a calendar. The counselor, as well as his parents, should show the boy the way they use their calendars to schedule their tasks, events, work that is due, and so on. If he is able to make the connection that he is asked to do things that most all individuals do, he will have an easier time accepting it as a normal tool that people use to keep track of their busy lives. Through modeling and monitoring assistance, he needs to be taught to write both daily and longer-duration assignments (for example, class projects) on the day that they are due, and needs to be taught to check each day's assignments (and a check of several days ahead) at homework time.

Enlisting the parents and teachers to implement this approach is necessary. In school, the teacher must ensure that the homework journal is utilized and that all assignments are accurately written where they belong. Assistance needs to be given to help him correct any errors and omissions, and to make sure that the homework journal is placed in his bookbag.

At home, parents must ask for the homework journal at the beginning of every homework session and assist the boy in planning his study activities. For example, it is helpful to group assignments on the table or desk where the homework is being done and guide the boy to perform one assignment at a time, then show it to his parents, place it in the bookbag when it is complete, and move on to the next assignment. To assist with motivation, a privilege should be restricted until after homework is completed and should be available to him only as a reward for successful completion of homework and study assignments. When the journal was forgotten, he should be required to complete whatever he brought home, and the homework-contingent privilege should be suspended for that day.

To help him organize his bookbag, parents should ask the boy to empty all contents on the bed once per week (for example, Sunday evening, in preparation for the forthcoming week). Each item on the bed must then be examined by the child (with oversight by the parent, but the parent should not do it instead of the child), and he must explain what each item is and where it belongs. The parent then asks the child to place it where it belongs, and move on to the next item.

To organize school items, many parents find it very helpful to use trappers. Trappers should be color-coded per subject, and it may be helpful to have two sets of trappers—one in the boy's desk where all assignments and tests already marked and returned to him will be kept (as an archive), and another set that stays in the bookbag and is used to hold all homework assignments on their way to and from school. Although tedious, the use of such a procedure will, in time, help him internalize the skills necessary to keep track of his assignments and possessions.

Secondary Symptoms

Boys with ADHD often experience conflict and failure. Over time, boys with ADHD often develop negative self-image. It is necessary to address this in counseling. In order to do so, counselors should focus on the boy's strengths. Although boys with ADHD often exhibit an academic weakness (for example, difficulties with written language), they may also exhibit a strength (for example, being good in math). The counselor can help the boy become aware of his pattern of strengths and weaknesses, and help him recognize that most children have a similar pattern. This can normalize his school experience and help him recognize that he is just like any other boy his age.

Recognition of strengths should extend beyond academics. Most boys will have at least one interest or skill where they are more accomplished. It may be a sport, or an ability to play a musical instrument, or a knowledge of cars or dinosaurs that is more extensive than most of his peers'. Helping him recognize what those skills are, and how accomplished he is in those areas, can help his self-esteem. During sessions, it is helpful to structure activities in such a way that the boy shows the therapist (and the parents) how good he is at doing something—for example, constructing a nice building with Lego blocks, winning in a game of checkers, and so on. Utilizing these activities while talking with the child in counseling is often very helpful—it assists in rapport building, and provides an opportunity for the boy to receive recognition for something he did. The therapist can even place an "art gallery" of drawings, or an "exhibition" of building block constructions, in the office and place the boy's item there to help him experience a feeling of accomplishment.

The cognitive approach to the treatment of low self-esteem is based on the recognition that negative self-statements result in negative feelings. Whereas very young boys (under age 5) may have difficulties recognizing self-dialogue, boys who are at least school age or older can begin to identify the perception they have of themselves and their self-statements. Beck and Young (1985) identified the cognitive triad that underlies the feelings of depression: a negative view of the world, the future, and oneself. Identifying these negative assumptions and replacing them with more appropriate alternatives comprise an important component of helping a boy with ADHD develop better self-esteem. Again, activities during sessions can act as triggers to identify the boy's thought patterns and replace negative self-statements with positive ones.

GROUP COUNSELING

Group counseling for boys with ADHD is often effective as an adjunct to other treatment approaches (Pelham & Hoza, 1996). Boys with ADHD commonly exhibit difficulties getting along with peers. Because they are impulsive, they find it difficult to think about the most effective strategies to join a peer group, and often attempt to "take over" when they join a group of friends who are already talking or playing together. In addition, when things do not go their way, boys with ADHD have difficulties containing their frustration and often become involved in arguments and other conflicts.

Group counseling sessions for boys with ADHD are generally skill oriented and time limited. The therapist utilizes structured exercises to create a play situation during which the children acquire and practice a given skill. The groups generally include four to eight children. Smaller and larger groups can be difficult to work with, and boys in those groups are likely to derive less benefit. The groups should be homogeneous with regard to age and sex. A boys-only group will eliminate some of the gender dynamics that are present when children of both sexes interact with each other. Although those dynamics may be helpful to observe and address, they generally interfere with the specific goals of the group. In addition, boys of varying ages generally have different play patterns and interests, and, consequently, limiting the age variation between the boys to no more than 2 years' difference is usually necessary.

Groups are usually implemented in 12–16-session, closed-ended cycles, maintaining the group membership constant and not allowing boys to join midway. Afterward, the cycle can be repeated after the addition or departure of group members. Each cycle is usually divided into modules of 3 to 4 weeks in length. One model of such an approach is summarized below.

Social Entry Skills

The first few sessions in the life of a group allow an opportunity to observe how the boys play together, and teach them how to join play activities in a constructive and respectful way. In the first two groups, therapists can allow children to play with some toys that are given to the group by the therapist—building blocks, toy cars, and so on. Invariably, small groups will develop when two or three boys are playing together with a set of toys. Along the way, some boys will quickly change groups and "barge in" on another group playing with other toys. This gives the therapist an opportunity to stop the play, ask the boys how they felt about being interrupted, and instruct the boys on how to join an existing group in a respectful manner. The boys then take turns practicing this scenario—one by one, each one has the opportunity to join the other boys while they play with a toy, and must do so in a manner that is collaborative and respectful.

As the sessions continue, boys will begin to spontaneously utilize this new skill. As they do so, the therapist utilizes a "caught you being good" technique by pointing out each instance when social entry was performed proactively. To further increase encouragement, it is helpful to implement a behavioral program in group, and every time a boy is observed to enter a peer group appropriately, he is given a "good behavior slip" (or another form of a token) that can then be exchanged for a small prize.

Listening Skills

The next phase of the group teaches the boys to play cooperatively while they are already a part of the group. This set of interventions is aimed at increasing the attention span of the children, and helping them suppress the impulse to interrupt and take over an activity or a conversation. It is helpful for the therapist to utilize some play activities or games where the boys must take turns and respond to each other's input. Various board games can be used where each boy, as he lands on a square, asks a question that the other boys must answer but only by first raising their hand (to teach impulse control). Those who did not "call out" and had the right answer (meaning, they listened) receive a token, and the boy with the highest number of tokens at the end of the session receives a prize.

A similar activity involves a game where the boys play-act a television interview. One boy is designated as the interviewer, and another as the interviewee; the rest are the audience. The interviewer asks the boy questions about what he likes, what he does in school, whether he recently got a new toy or game, and the like, and the audience must listen. After the interview is over, the therapist asks the boys to write some answers about questions the therapists poses to the audience. Boys in the audience receive a token for each correct response. The activity is brief, and is repeated during the session enough times so that each boy is a member of the audience for the same number of times. At the end of the session, the boy with the most tokens receives a prize.

Problem-Solving Skills

Boys with ADHD find it difficult to utilize the steps involved in effective problem solving. It is necessary to teach them to state a problem, define it accurately, brainstorm possible alternatives, evaluate each activity that was identified with respect to the consequence of each one, and select the alternative that is most likely to be effective in solving the initial problem. Various activities and board games can be effective in focusing the activity of the problem-solving sequence.

As an example, two games, the Classroom Behavior Game and the Getting Along Game, can be very helpful. Both are board games where children take turns throwing dice and move the specified number of spaces on the board. As they go along, they encounter squares that ask them to turn over various cards, arranged in piles, and each card presents a common vignette that requires a solution. The boy can read the card, or if it is too difficult, the therapist can read the card instead. The boy that turned the card must then follow the above procedure to define the problem, come up with alternatives, evaluate each one, and select the best one for implementation. If he is able to successfully do so, he receives five tokens. However, if he becomes "stuck" along the way, others can help and will receive one token for each helpful suggestion, so long as they were first asked to contribute it (to reduce "calling out" and help them control impulsive reactions). The board is circular, and the game continues until the therapist indicates the last go-around. At the end of the game, the boy with the most tokens receives a prize.

Anger Management

Anger management is arguably the most important of the modules, and sometimes it is effective to extend the group cycle a week or two if this component requires additional work. As with problem-solving skills, it is necessary to identify and teach an effective sequence of steps, and practice opportunities must be given to help each boy internalize these skills. Again, board games and group activities can be very helpful.

The Anger Control Game is similar to the games described above. As the children roll the dice and travel around the board, they turn over cards that ask them questions about events that happened that evoked a variety of feelings. For each feeling, they describe the precipitating event, how the event made them feel, and what bodily sensations and thoughts went along with each feeling. Other boys are also asked to think of (and share) examples of similar situations.

Identifying the bodily sensations is particularly important. Impulsive children react so quickly that catching themselves being frustrated or angry is very difficult. Becoming more aware of their bodies and how their bodies signal feelings to them can be helpful to slow down the speed of the initial reaction. Children can be taught to quickly go through a body checklist—"What are my arms or hands doing?" ("Am I clenching my fists?"), "Do I feel really warm?" "Do my legs feel like I want to kick?" and so on.

The cognitive component is equally important. Each time an event awakens feelings, the boy is taught to recognize not just how he feels, but also what he thinks about the event. Following the tenets of cognitive-behavioral approaches, it is the thought after the event, the perception and interpretation of the event, that determines the feeling, and teaching the boy to recognize how he thinks about events that happen is important.

While playing, the boys identify the bodily sensations, thoughts, and resulting feelings. As each situation is portrayed, the boys in the group are asked for alternative thoughts and perceptions that would result in feelings other than anger. As each child provides such examples, he is given a token. The game is played through the session until everyone has had a chance to make several contributions, and at the end of the session, the boy with the most tokens receives a prize.

In a manner that resembles inoculation training, it is helpful to create opportunities for boys to practice the new anger management skills. It may be helpful to extend the module for a session or two to allow play activities when the boys have the opportunity to experience frustration—for example, two boys have to learn to share the same toy they wish to play with, or the boys must jointly decide on a play activity and the one whose idea was not chosen has to deal with it constructively. Along the way, the boys are reminded of the lessons they learned while playing the anger game, and are asked to talk about their body sensations, thoughts, and feelings. When they become frustrated but react in a positive, constructive way, they are rewarded with a token that is then exchanged for a prize.

EDUCATIONAL INTERVENTIONS

Boys with ADHD commonly exhibit problems in school that often are even more severe than the problems they exhibit with parents, in out-of-home settings, or with peers. School problems can have serious consequences, including poor academic performance, failure to learn necessary academic skills, and management difficulties that often include school detentions and suspensions, and may lead to school expulsion. Consequently, it is crucial that mental health professionals devote at least as much attention to school problems as to the problems that boys with ADHD exhibit in other settings.

Problems in school must be addressed in a broad manner, because these commonly include distractibility and disorganization, as well as disruptiveness. Consequently, educators need to structure the classroom environment to help the boy learn, adjust instructional methods to improve learning and skill retention, develop interventions to reduce disorganization and distractibility, and implement a comprehensive behavior management program.

Preparation of Classroom Environment

The classroom should be prepared for teaching a child who is easily distractible. Unnecessary wall décor should be eliminated, especially avoiding posters and pictures with multiple, bright colors. The busier and brighter the postings on the wall, the more easily they will distract a boy with ADHD away from the class activities.

The seating must also be arranged accordingly. Boys with ADHD should be at least 4 to 6 feet away from other desks, all around. The traditional desk arrangement in a grid of columns and rows, all facing in the same direction (toward the teacher), is most effective. Desk arrangements in groups (for example, four desks together facing each other) invite trouble. In such a setup, the boy with ADHD will be significantly distracted by the desks of his neighbors and what the neighbors are doing at any given moment.

Class structure must also be increased. Unstructured group activities should be minimized in favor of structured activities where children follow a clearly defined set of steps and produce concrete, tangible outcomes. Group work that is most effective involves only pairs of students, and it is helpful to pair the boy with ADHD with a highly achieving, well-behaved student who is known to appropriately follow the class routine. In such an arrangement, the other student will become a de facto coach for the boy with ADHD (although this does not have to be defined overtly), and both students will derive significant benefit: The boy with ADHD will be assisted in staying on task, and the coach will experience the positive effects of being a helpful peer.

Class rules and regulations must be clearly posted, including both positive and negative consequences. It is very important to orient the rules primarily toward winning rewards, rather than avoiding punishments. In other words, the demerit-based system that many classrooms follow is likely to be ineffective. Instead, a system primarily based on earning privileges and rewards for following class rules will be more effective.

Consistent scheduling of activities will also help the boy with ADHD internalize the sequencing of academic tasks. If a particular order of tasks can be followed most days, boys with ADHD will learn to expect natural transitions and recognize cues that signal task switching. This will significantly minimize difficulties during those transitions.

Adjustments to Instructional Methods

Teachers must take the time to discover their students' pattern of academic strengths and weaknesses, and use this knowledge to plan academic assignments. Teaching a new skill should never be aimed at the boy's weakest academic modality. For example, when a boy exhibits difficulties with handwriting and written language, new academic skills should not be taught through this modality. Instead, other modalities should be used to teach new academic skills (for example, vocabulary), and the weakest modality should be utilized only to reinforce a skill that has already been learned. In general, it is helpful to teach new academic skills through a variety of modalities (reading, writing, listening, storytelling, games, hands-on projects, etc). In this way, students are able to utilize a mix of modalities (including the one that is easiest for them) to learn new academic skills.

Boys with ADHD respond especially well to stimuli that involve color, movement, sound, and touch. Teachers should utilize handouts that include a lot of color and should ask students to complete assignments, when necessary, with colored pencils, markers, or crayons. Movement also stimulates the brain to increase attention. Utilizing video clips and physical activities will help the boy remain involved in the academic activity. Computer games that teach academic skills can be especially beneficial, because they simultaneously involved numerous modalities—visual (color and movement), auditory (sounds), and tactile (manual manipulation of input devices or game controllers).

When teaching boys with ADHD, teachers must remember that boys with ADHD fatigue easily, especially with repetitive tasks. It is important to utilize novelty and variety as much as possible in order to maintain student involvement. Games and projects can especially be helpful, because they allow the students to tailor assignments to their individual preferences and interests, thus maximizing student curiosity and participation, increasing time on task, and improving the effort devoted to academic skill acquisition.

Managing Distractibility

Teachers should utilize a variety of signals, cues, and attention getters. When it is time for students to stop an activity and attend to the teacher's directions, it is helpful to teach the class to recognize a specific cue, like flicking the lights or clapping hands. It is also helpful to get all students involved in the cue—for example, asking all students at the end of an activity to clap, thus involving every student, even the one who may have missed the initial cue, in the transition.

Effective cues can be developed individually with a specific student. When the teacher wants to help a boy with ADHD refocus, he or she can approach the student's proximity without calling the student's name. Just walking over in the direction of his desk, while continuing to lecture to the class, will signal to the boy with ADHD that he needs to pay attention to the teacher. Additional cues can be arranged beforehand, one-on-one with the student. For example, the teacher can help the boy with ADHD learn to listen for a certain phrase that the teacher may say out loud that sounds innocuous to other students, but sends a signal to the boy with ADHD that he needs to look at his teacher. It is important to avoid redirecting the student by calling his name or using another technique that will clearly single him out. This will make the student uncomfortable and will point out to his peers that he is being reprimanded. Instead, private cues, although initially more difficult to implement and more time-consuming to utilize, allow the student to avoid unnecessary embarrassment while helping him to refocus.

Two additional interventions discussed in previous sections are also helpful to use with boys with ADHD. Self-monitoring (discussed in the section on individual counseling) was specifically developed to address distractibility within the classroom. Teachers can implement this technique with a student and help him select appropriate stimuli within the classroom to trigger his check of attention. Teachers can also help the student determine in which portion of his day he is most vulnerable to distractibility, allowing him to focus his efforts specifically on that time period.

A homework journal, discussed in the section on parent interventions (above), will also help the boy with ADHD improve his completion of homework assignments. Most teachers find that parents are eager to help and will monitor homework completion at home. Working jointly, parents and teacher of a boy with ADHD will help him improve his academic success.

Managing Behaviors

Boys with ADHD exhibit similar problems in the classroom that they exhibit within the home—difficulties following directions, argumentativeness, outbursts, noncompliance with academic tasks, difficulties with transitions, interruptions, and acting out in low-structure settings (on the playground, in the lunchroom, etc.).

To address these problems, it is helpful to develop a comprehensive behavior management system. The program discussed in the section on parent training (Kapalka, 2007) has also been found to be effective with teachers. Command giving and the use of warnings can be used with teachers with no major modifications and will effectively address problems with listening, arguing, or defying. Temper tantrums can be addressed with the use of time outs, although the time-out setting will likely need to be modified in order to meet the legal and practical restrictions of academic settings (for example, most teachers in regular education classrooms will not be able to isolate the boy during time out or restrain him in a chair if he refuses to remain in the time-out spot). Teachers and mental health professionals should work with school administrators to determine the most appropriate way to use time out within each school.

The establishment of a behavioral contract is likely to be the centerpiece of an effective school behavior management program. Teachers should construct a list of classroom expectations that the boy with ADHD has to follow, and assign token values to each item. These tokens can be exchanged for privileges (for example, extra time on the computer) or small prizes. When severe difficulties are present, it is helpful to focus on one behavior at a time and utilize time segments that are appropriate to the boy's age and the magnitude of the problem.

Once the contract is established, it can become a vehicle for addressing additional problems, for example difficulties with interruptions or transitions, in accordance with suggestions discussed in the section on parent training.

A CASE STUDY

The following case study exemplifies the principles outlined in this chapter.

Michael was a 7-year-old boy who presented with a long history of hyperactivity, poor self-control, distractibility, and disorganization. At home, he frequently argued with his parents, especially about household chores and homework, and establishing daily routines with him had been very difficult. Homework was a constant struggle—to his parents, he claimed that he did not have anything assigned, whereas his teacher complained that he often did not turn in his homework assignments and usually said he forgot them. In school, he appeared very active and disruptive, and he often left his desk and wandered to his peers to see what they were doing. When he did remain at his desk, he was frequently off-task, and his teacher often caught him daydreaming. With peers, Michael was described as bossy and demanding, and he found it difficult to accept when his friends did not want to do what he wanted. When frustrated, he often started to tantrum.

In order to clarify the diagnosis, Michael and his parents were interviewed, and his parents and teacher completed developmental and behavioral inventories. The information obtained from the review of history, interviews, and inventories suggested that Michael met the diagnostic criteria for attention deficit hyperactivity disorder, combined type. His parents chose to try counseling interventions first and indicated they would consider medications only if those interventions did not sufficiently reduce Michael's difficulties.

Michael and his parents started a course of counseling. Each one-hour session was divided into two portions to work with Michael and his parents. His parents completed a parent training program (Kapalka, 2007) aimed at improving their ability to remain calm, give directions, and utilize immediate consequences for positive and negative behaviors. Simultaneously, cognitive-behavioral counseling was utilized with Michael to help him develop better self-control. This phase of treatment lasted for approximately 12 sessions, and significant improvement in Michael's behavior was observed within the home.

Simultaneously, the counselor also consulted with Michael's teacher. Appropriate interventions were implemented to improve Michael's ability to remain in his seat, stay on task, and keep track of his homework. Moderate improvement was observed. However, at the beginning of the next academic year, the increased workload taxed Michael's abilities more significantly, and the problems reemerged. At that point, his parents agreed to a trial of stimulant medications. Michael was placed on a sustained-release medication in order to help him through his complete school day. The selection of the specific compound and dosage needed adjustment in order for the medication to work through the school day and long enough after school to help Michael complete homework, while at the same time allowing the medication to get out of his system in time for dinner so that his appetite was not suppressed. After three adjustments, an appropriate dose was selected, and Michael tolerated it very well with no side effects. His school performance and homework compliance improved dramatically.

After the home and school problems were resolved, his parents requested further work to help Michael improve his ability to get along with his peers. Michael was placed into a group that focused on improving his social skills, impulse control, problem solving, and anger management. Each closed-ended group cycle lasted for 12 weeks, and Michael needed two cycles before significant improvement was noted. Afterwards, Michael exhibited much improved abilities to get along with his peers, and his parents reported that Michael's ability to participate in play activities and other social settings (for example, team sports) was significantly improved. Michael's treatment lasted for about 1 year, after which his symptoms significantly improved and his parents terminated treatment (although he remained on medications).

In many cases, significant improvement can be seen in 3 to 6 months. In Michael's case, significant improvement was seen after 3 months, but nearly complete resolution of the symptoms was attained only after one year of treatment. Parents of children with ADHD need to be prepared to accept that the treatment of a child with ADHD will require commitments of time and effort. With perseverance, a multimodal approach is likely to result in a significant improvement in the symptoms across all settings.

CONCLUSIONS

Boys with ADHD present with a large number of problems in various settings, including the home, school, and peer group. Because the etiology of these problems includes multiple mechanisms that involve biological, psychological, and social factors, a multisystemic approach is most effective. This chapter reviewed various treatment approaches, including the use of medications, individual counseling, parent training, group counseling, and educational interventions. Professionals are encouraged to utilize as many of these techniques as are necessary to address each patient's or client's profile of symptoms. The more of these techniques that are utilized, the greater the likelihood will be that the symptoms will diminish and the boy's functioning at home, in school, and with peers will significantly improve. Over time, maintaining such a regimen will likely improve the long-term outcome and reduce the risk of further problems as the boy with ADHD becomes a teenager and a young adult.

REFERENCES

American Psychiatric Association. (2000). *Diagnostic and statistical manual of the mental disorder: Text revision* (4th ed.). Washington, DC: Author.

Arnold, E. A. (2002). Treatment alternatives for attention deficit hyperactivity disorder. In P. S. Jensen & J. R. Cooper (Eds.), *Attention deficit hyperactivity disorder: State of the science, best practices* (pp. 13-1–13-29). Kingston, NJ: Civic Research Institute.

Barkley, R. A. (2006). *Attention-deficit hyperactivity disorder: A handbook for diagnosis and treatment* (3rd ed.). New York: Guilford Press.

Beck, A. T., & Young, J. E. (1985). Depression. In D. H. Barlow (Ed.), *Clinical handbook of psychological disorders* (pp. 206–244). New York: Guilford.

Bezchlibnyk-Butler, K. Z., & Jeffries, J. J. (2006). *Clinical handbook of psychotropic drugs* (16th ed.). Ashland, OH: Hogrefe & Huber.

Bird, H. R. (2002). The diagnostic classification, epidemiology, and cross-cultural validity of ADHD. In P. S. Jensen & J. R. Cooper (Eds.), *Attention deficit hyperactivity disorder: State of the science, best practices* (pp. 2-1–2-16). Kingston, NJ: Civic Research Institute.

Conners, C. K. (2001). *Feeding the brain: How foods affect children.* New York: Perseus.

Donenberg, G., & Baker, B. L. (1994). The impact of young children with externalizing behaviors on their families. *Journal of Abnormal Child Psychology, 21*, 179–198.

Geller, B., Williams, M., Zimerman, B., Frazier, J., Beringer, L., & Warner, K. (1998). Prepubertal and early adolescent bipolarity differentiate from ADHD by manic symptoms, grandiose delusions, ultra-rapid or ultradian cycling. *Journal of Affective Disorders, 51*, 81–91.

Greenhill, L. L. (2002). Stimulant medication treatment of children with attention deficit hyperactivity disorder. In P. S. Jensen & J. R. Cooper (Eds.), *Attention deficit hyperactivity disorder: State of the science, best practices* (pp. 9-1–9-27). Kingston, NJ: Civic Research Institute.

Hinshaw, S. P. (2002). Is ADHD an impairing condition in childhood and adolescence? In P. S. Jensen & J. R. Cooper (Eds.), *Attention deficit hyperactivity disorder: State of the science, best practices* (pp. 5-1–5-21). Kingston, NJ: Civic Research Institute.

Kapalka, G. M. (2007). *Parenting your out-of-control child: An effective, easy-to-use program for teaching self-control.* Oakland, CA: New Harbinger.

Loo, S. K. (2003). EEG and Neurofeedback findings in ADHD. *ADHD Report, 11*(3), 1–9.

Pelham, W. E., & Hoza, B. (1996). Intensive treatment: A summer treatment program for children with ADHD. In M. Roberts & A. LaGreca (Eds.), *Model programs for service delivery for child and family mental health* (pp. 193–212). Hillsdale, NJ: Erlbaum.

Pelham, W. E., Wheeler, T., & Chronis, A. (1998). Empirically supported psychosocial treatments for attention deficit hyperactivity disorder. *Journal of Clinical Child Psychology, 27*, 190–205.

Swanson, J. M., & Castellanos, F. X. (2002). Biological bases of ADHD: Neuroanatomy, genetics and pathophysiology. In P. S. Jensen & J. R. Cooper (Eds.), *Attention deficit hyperactivity disorder: State of the science, best practices* (pp. 7-1–7-20). Kingston, NJ: Civic Research Institute.

U.S. Food and Drug Administration. (2004). *Dietary supplements containing ephedrine alkaloids: Final rule summary.* Retrieved March 17, 2006, from http://www.fda.gov

8

Counseling Aggressive Boys and Adolescent Males

LE'ROY E. REESE, ARTHUR M. HORNE,
CHRISTOPHER D. BELL, AND JOHN
HARVEY WINGFIELD

Aggression unopposed becomes a contagious disease.

Jimmy Carter

The topic of youth aggression and violence is one that has dominated the attention and work of school officials, prevention scientists and practitioners, parents, and young people for decades. Recent tragedies such as those at Columbine High School in Colorado and Heritage High School in Georgia, for example, and the spiraling rates of youth violence and homicide, only serve to accentuate the concerns of those who work to insure the safety of young people in our schools and communities. Events such as these have led to a heightened concern about the necessity—the obligation—to address youth aggression and violence with the goal of preventing the problem from occurring. Presently, there is an increased concern with the treatment of youth aggression and violence, which in turn has prompted a significant increase in the focus on violence prevention or early intervention efforts.

WHAT ARE MALE YOUTH VIOLENCE
AND AGGRESSION?

Although the terms *violence, aggression,* and *bullying* are frequently used interchangeably or as synonyms, there are some clear distinctions. These terms may be thought of as representing a continuum of intensity and intention, with one end of the continuum consisting of the rough-and-tumble play usually found among boys and adolescent males, whereas violence is on the other extreme of the continuum. Rough-and-tumble play includes such activities as joking, sports activities, or playful teasing, and is a normal and even expected aspect of boys' and adolescent males' development. Aggression, bullying, and violence, on the other hand, are not universal developmental characteristics, and they need to be prevented.

When behavior passes beyond the normal rough-and-tumble and becomes violent, what are the characteristics of this phenomenon? The World Health Organization (WHO; Krug, Mercy, Dahlberg, & Zwi, 2002) defined *violence* as follows:

> The intentional use of physical force or power, threatened or actual, against oneself, another person, or against a group or community, that either results in or has a high likelihood of resulting in injury, death, psychological harm, maldevelopment or deprivation. (p. 5)

The WHO report goes on to classify violence as interpersonal, intrapersonal, or collective. Interpersonal violence occurs when one individual acts against another, who may be a stranger, acquaintance, family member, or even friend, and can include extreme behaviors such as homicide, rape, and aggravated assault. Intrapersonal violence occurs when one commits violence against oneself, such as suicide and suicide attempts. Collective violence refers to violence committed by groups of people and includes gang violence, group bullying, and intentional acts committed by several people against others, as in mobbing.

Aggression, compared to violence, does not preclude physical acts of hostility, but generally refers to less extreme intentional behaviors that may cause psychological or physical harm to others. Although aggression can be dangerous, its effects are generally milder than those associated with hostile physical violence. Hitting, pushing, isolating a peer on purpose, and name-calling all constitute examples of aggressive behaviors.

Bullying is a subset of aggression. Bullying has several components, sometimes referred to as *Double I R* (imbalance of power, intentional acts, and *r*epeated over time). The bully is more powerful than the victim (imbalance) and commits aggressive behaviors intentionally (intentionality) and repetitively over time (repeatedly) (Newman, Horne, & Bartolomucci, 2000).

Types of aggression and bullying may be further delineated. For example, there is physical aggression, in which there is a purposeful use of physical force, such as fighting with weapons, hitting, biting, choking, and damaging property. For example, this may occur when a male child randomly hits another child despite it being clear that such behavior is unwelcome. Then there is verbal aggression in which words are used intentionally to cause harm, such as threats, yelling, coercing, blackmailing, name-calling, and teasing. Examples of verbal aggression might include locker room behavior in which a boy or boys might call another boy a *fag* or *bitch*, names used in a homophobic and sexist way to somehow marginalize the victim. A third type, relational aggression, is less common among boys but can still occur. This includes using behaviors that harm others through peer interactions, such as spreading rumors, gossiping, purposefully excluding a person, or sharing personal information about a person with others in order to hurt him or her. This form of aggression is, as mentioned previously, less common among boys but can still occur through "locker room" lies such as those that might be made up about a perceived sexual inadequacy or athletic incompetence. A fourth form is sexual aggression and includes rape, forced kissing or touching, and any unsolicited sexual advantages and comments. Sexual aggression among male adolescents might include touching a female peer inappropriately on the buttocks or communicating a sexual desire verbally.

For many, including educators, school psychologists, and counselors working with boys and adolescent males, precise distinctions of the terms *violence, aggression,* and *bullying* may not be important. What is important is that all intentional acts that may hurt others should be prevented if possible or stopped when they occur. Although some boys will claim they are only playing around, which is an expected way of learning and interacting, it is important to differentiate playing from aggression. This includes stopping interactions when they are no longer fun or when one boy hurts another: "If it hurts, it must stop." Also, it is important to examine whether the roles are interchangeable: In rough-and-tumble play, boys exchange roles, whereas in bullying one boy always aggresses against the other. Finally, although some boys, and parents for that matter, will claim that rough-and-tumble play or other forms of mild aggression are OK, if it is disruptive or bothersome to others, such as peers or teachers, it is aggression against the group, and must stop.

In understanding aggression in boys, it is crucial to appreciate the impact of the intentionality, the imbalance of power, and the repetitive components of bullying. All people experience some level of aggression in their lives, such as occurs when a student bumps into another student in the hallway or a driver cuts off another driver on a street. These examples of aggression are inappropriate and should be stopped, but they are isolated incidents. The intentionality and repetitiveness of bullying create an anticipatory fear of pain and humiliation caused by the repeated aggression for the victim. The repeated acts of aggression—one of the major distinctions between aggression and bullying—generate a deeper level of fear and intimidation than an isolated event. If a boy is hit and gets hurt as a consequence of rough-and-tumble play, in which there was no intention to hurt him, that act is not considered an act of aggression. Such injuries could just as easily occur during "pick-up" athletic games, competitive sports, or playground activities. On the other hand, if a boy intentionally throws a ball at the face of another boy but misses, it is an act of aggression even if it did not have any immediate consequences. Rough-and-tumble play frequently escalates from playing to aggression, and the point at which this transition occurs is not always clear. Indeed, the turning point from rough play to aggression may not even be the same for each child involved.

HOW COMMON IS YOUNG MALE AGGRESSION?

The current epidemiological data identify youth aggression and violence as a serious public health problem. For example, in 2004 there were 9,554 homicide arrests in the United States; 48% (4,619) of those arrested were younger than 25 years of age, and 92% of those arrested were male (Federal Bureau of Investigation, 2005). In addition, young people under age 25 accounted for 44% of all arrests for violent offenses (i.e., homicide, forcible rape, robbery, and aggravated assault). Given the perpetration of such offenses by young people, they are also disproportionately the victims of violent acts. According to the National Crime Victimization Survey, teens have the highest rates of violent crime victimization (Bureau of Justice Statistics, 2006). As further evidence, data from the Centers for Disease Control and Prevention (CDC, 2007) reveal that in 2005, over 888,000 young people between the ages of 10 and 24 were treated in emergency departments for injuries resulting from violence. Of this number, over 527,000, or approximately 60%, of those treated were males.

Gender, Ethnicity, and Youth Violence

Young men and boys are disproportionately the victims and perpetrators of youth aggression and violence as reflected in current surveillance data. For example, the Youth Risk Behavior Survey (YRBS) reflects that in 2005, 29.8% of males compared to 7.1% of female respondents reported carrying a weapon to school during the past 12 months (CDC, 2006). The YRBS also reveals that 43% of males reported being in a physical fight during the preceding 12 months compared to 30% of females. Similarly, arrest data for 2004 reveal that approximately 81% of arrests for violent crimes were for males and that 37% were for males under the age of 25 (Federal Bureau of Investigation, 2005). Data such as these only accentuate the differences between males and females in their experiences with aggression and violence. Moreover, these data strongly suggest that understanding male aggression is critical to the broader effort to prevent youth aggression and violence.

Understanding the scope and impact of male youth aggression takes on even more significance when ethnicity is entered into the equation. Specifically, African American youth, especially males, are disproportionately both the victims and perpetrators of violence (Reese, Crosby, Willis, & Hasbrouck, 2004). For the last decade, homicide has been the leading cause of death among African American youth between the ages of 10 and 24 and the second leading cause of death for their Hispanic peers (CDC, 2007). To illustrate the impact of violence on Black males in this age group, for 2004 Black males accounted for 54% of the total of 5,372 deaths caused by homicide and legal intervention (CDC), although they only represent 6% of the U.S. population. In addition, the rates of nonfatal violent injury among African American male youth outpace injury rates proportionately among other ethnic groups in this age range. For example, in 2005 Black male youth accounted for 26%, or 135,608, of the 527,163 nonfatal violent injuries among males between 10 and 24.

RISK AND PROTECTIVE FACTORS

A common inquiry is "Why do aggressive boys and adolescent males act as they do?" An answer is "Why wouldn't they? They have learned that the behavior generally pays off." Aggressive behavior is learned and is influenced by many contributing factors. There is now a large and instructive literature on a number of risk factors for youth—and specifically male—aggression and violence, and although a full review of this literature is beyond the scope of this chapter, it informs much of the preventive efforts to stop and reduce male youth aggression (see Dahlberg & Simon [2006] and Orpinas & Horne [2006] for a detailed discussion of risk and protective factors and youth aggression). A risk factor does not cause aggression in boys and male teens, but is related to the development of problems. The greater the number of risk factors male youth experience, the higher the probability of developing aggressive behavior. Risk factors can be identified in several categories based on an ecological model of aggression as indicated in Figure 8.1. There is also an emerging literature on protective factors that can help insulate young people from participating in aggressive and violent behavior that can be understood from the same ecological framework as risk factors (U.S. Department of Health and Human Services [DHHS], 2001b).

PERSONAL CHARACTERISTICS OF
A BOY OR MALE ADOLESCENT

At the core of the ecological model is the male child, who has a number of personal characteristics that may either increase or decrease his risk of behaving aggressively. First are biological characteristics, such as temperament. Temperament is influenced by the genetic makeup of the individual and can be evidenced by impulsivity, emotional intensity, activity level, adaptability to social circumstances, an approach or withdrawal tendency to new social situations, persistence at a task, and mood (Lipsey & Derzon, 1998; Martin, 1988). Behavior reflective of

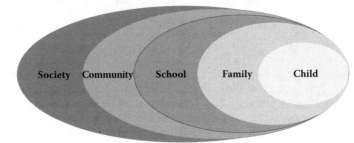

	Risk Factors	Protective Factors
Child	Norms, attitudes, & beliefs supporting aggression - High learning problems - Negative goals & strategies in interpersonal relationships - Depression, withdrawal, anxiety	Norms, attitudes, & beliefs supporting peaceful solutions to conflict - High academic performance, study skills & value on achievement - Positive goals & strategies in interpersonal relationships - Self-efficacy to use positive relationship skills - Life satisfaction - Leadership & social skills - Religiosity & spirituality
Family	Parental support for fighting - Deviant beliefs about the family - High family emotional reactivity	Parental support for peaceful solutions - Positive parental monitoring - Family connectedness - Positive relationship with parents - High parental problem-solving ability; High positive parenting; Strong family structure and cohesion ; Positive beliefs about the family; High parental involvement in school
School, Community	Student perception of: -School norms for aggression - School safety concerns	School norms for peaceful solutions - Teacher-student positive relationships - Student-student positive relationships - Sense of safety in the school, home, and community - School connectedness

Figure 8.1 An Ecological Model of Risk and Protective Factors
Source: Adapted from Orpinas and Horne (2006).

temperament may be positive, as in smiles and playful interactions, or it may be aversive, as with cries and tantrums. Young boys who are difficult to parent often experience coercive interactions with family members, resulting in parent–child relationships that are marked by anger and poor relations between the parent and the child (Patterson, Reid, & Dishion, 1992). Further, children who are more moody and who are less open to new social stimuli experience a greater level of emotional intensity and, thus, may have greater risk of developing aggressive behavior. In addition, low verbal intelligence, learning disabilities, poor motor skill development, minor physical anomalies, and head injuries have been associated with an increased risk for aggressive and violent behavior (Buka & Earls, 1993).

Another risk factor for children is the development of ineffective or poor social information–processing skills. Dodge and his colleagues (Crick & Dodge, 1994; Dodge & Coie, 1987) have developed a model for understanding children's social adjustment based on a behavioral interaction model of personal capabilities, past experiences, and methods used for processing social cues. Below are the steps of the model as explicated by Crick and Dodge (1994, p. 76): (a) encoding of external and internal cues, (b) interpretation and mental representation of those cues, (c) clarification or selection of a goal, (d) response access or construction, (e) response decision, and (f) behavioral enactment. Thus, male youth observe or experience situations, make interpretations of those situations, decide how to respond, and then take action. If male youth misinterpret the situation by interpreting the situation in a hostile manner, if their past experience has been to address similar situations in an aggressive manner, or if they lack the behavioral repertoire to respond in an effective nonaggressive manner, they are likely to engage in hostile behavior.

As described above, if aggressive boys and male adolescents lack the ability to solve problems in a peaceful manner, they resort to what they know—aggression. The attributional bias that some boys and adolescent males bring to their encounters with other children is a belief that the other child intended or meant to be hostile, and so the aggressive boy responds to, or even initiates, interactions that promote confrontation and conflict. Many aggressive male youth hold the belief that there is a threat or danger where none is intended or exists (negative attributional bias), but they respond to other children as though their perceptions are accurate, often creating a self-fulfilling prophecy of hostility.

Other personal risk factors that some children and male youth experience are emotional instability, including depression, and sometimes access to drugs and alcohol. Low academic achievement is also often associated with children at risk for violence.

FAMILY

A number of family risk factors have been identified, and these include families in which there is a lack of supervision, the parent–child relationship is marked by coercion or indifference, discipline is either very lax or very harsh, and parents support violence to resolve conflict (Farrington, 2003). Orpinas and colleagues (1999) found that children who reported a negative relationship with their parents also reported higher levels of aggression on an aggression scale, more fights at school, and a higher frequency of carrying guns and other weapons. Similarly, as parental supervision of the child's time and whereabouts decreased and parental support for fighting increased, the children's aggression scores and the frequency of fights and of weapon carrying increased (Orpinas, Murray, & Kelder, 1999).

SCHOOL

The risk factors for violence that schools may have are similar to the ones in families. For example, lower levels of supervision of students and higher rates of aggression in schools contribute to aggressive and violent behavior. Also, the poorer the relationship teachers have with students, the higher the likelihood that the students will act out or become disruptive. As with families, overly lax or harsh discipline also serves as a risk factor of children developing behavioral problems. Discipline that is too lax may encourage students to push the limits of behavior, whereas discipline that is too harsh may prompt students to rebel and act out. Schools that "look the other way" or do not attend to aggression in the school inadvertently endorse aggression as an acceptable behavior. Although few teachers would openly approve of aggression in school, a number of teachers do ignore the name-calling, teasing, and even overt behavior problems of students, thereby passively condoning it. Finally, schools that lack alternatives to violence, such as teaching effective problem-solving skills, anger management, conflict resolution, and rela-tionship development, fail to assist students in learning more effective mechanisms for managing aggression (Orpinas & Horne, 2006).

SOCIETY AND COMMUNITY

Risk factors in society at large comprise a number of characteristics, including growing up in a culture that supports violence, especially violence as it relates to males, both young and old. In fact, growing up male in a society with an emphasis on machismo, aggression, and competition may itself be a risk factor. When violence frequently occurs in the community in which the boy or male teen is living, it may be observed and experienced as normal or "just what happens." Violence on television, in music, and in films is depicted as a normal experience, and in the process desensitizes the young male to the pain and sorrow of violence. Hearing violent themes in music, presented as the norm, habituates boys to the belief that aggression is acceptable. Similarly, living in an impoverished community—where there is often more theft, violence, drugs, and unstable home environments—exposes boys to numerous models of violence. Another community risk factor involves being in a neighborhood or community in which friends, peers, and associates support violence, as occurs in neighborhoods with a heavy gang influence, or in which access to weapons is easy. As evidence of excessive violence in the community, Orpinas and colleagues (2000) found in a survey of almost 9,000 urban middle school students that, during the year prior to the survey, 30% of the children had observed a shooting in their community, 33% had seen a gun pulled out, 43% reported having a gun in the home, 50% witnessed drug deals in the community, 66% reported gangs in the community, and 79% had observed some-one being beaten. Peer factors like gang involvement (Howell, 1998), as well as the absence of health-promoting community resources (e.g., undisciplined classrooms and high crime rates) and societal messages (e.g., McLoyd, 1998; Morenoff, Sampson, & Raudenbush, 2001; Wilson, 1996), all contribute to the risk factors of young men.

Being exposed to these risk factors in society and the community does not cause boys and male teens to be violent, but these risk factors can lead to a desensitization of male youth to the dangers of violence, and they do provide role models for aggressive ways of managing conflict, with few alternatives for healthy problem solving.

PATHWAYS TO AGGRESSIVE BEHAVIOR

Two tracks for the development of aggressive behavior have been identified: early starters and later starters (DHHS, 2001b). Early starters begin disruptive and aggressive behavior early in childhood and are often identified for their aggressive behavior even before entering school. Their behavior is often difficult to treat, and they have a high potential for criminal behavior in adulthood. Early intervention with early starters is recommended, and treatment services beyond normal school offerings are usually required.

The second and largest category of aggressive children is the late starters, those whose aggressive behavior develops in early adolescence. Late starters are not always easily identifiable, any more than other non-behavior-problem boys, as having behavior problems in early childhood. Late starters are more amenable than early starters to treatment for their conduct problems, and have a lower likelihood of adult criminality. For late starters, aggressive behavior increases in both intensity and frequency in the later elementary school years, and the peak age of onset of the first serious violent act is by age 16 (DHHS, 2001b). The use of appropriate early intervention and prevention steps, relevant to the needs of the child and the resources available, should be used to help children move from an aggressive and violent developmental trajectory to one in which more effective interpersonal life skills are developed.

It is critical that counselors and other helping professionals understand and take into account the complexities of risk and protective factors in their efforts to prevent male youth aggression, and they should provide effective counsel to male youth identified as aggressive. We also think it important to understand the developmental nature of many risk factors. Specifically, some risk factors have a greater impact on youth earlier in life (i.e., early involvement in aggression), whereas others have a more pronounced effect later during adolescence (i.e., delinquent peers), and still others have an influence across the life span (i.e., parental criminality and poor supervision).

Protective Factors

The literature on protective factors to prevent male aggression is still emerging in that there isn't the level of empirical support for protective factors that exists for risk factors. However, there have been a number of factors proposed that appear to buffer boys and male adolescents against involvement in aggression and violence. For example, at the individual level prosocial socialization and religiosity are believed to serve a prophylactic function, and positive parental involvement in academic and social activities is believed to buffer against aggressive and violent behavior (Resnick, Ireland, & Borowsky, 2004). School factors include commitments by schools to the social and academic development and success of students. Positive peer factors include not associating with peers who are involved in delinquency (e.g., gangs) or who support aggressive and violent behavior (see DHHS, 2001b).

Although not exhaustive, consideration of the above factors is an important first step for professionals working with aggressive boys and male adolescents as they seek to understand what factors may be operating in their lives that either influence the aggressive behavior or may be available to stem the occurrence of such behavior. Given that we advocate a strengths-based approach, we feel it critical to identify those factors that may be available to enhance the well-being of the client and/or client system.

Finally, understanding the role of risk and protective factors is important in view of the developmental nature of aggressive behavior (in Dahlberg & Simon, 2006). Specifically, many of the developmental antecedents for the various forms of adult violence (e.g., intimate partner violence, and child abuse and neglect) begin during childhood and adolescence (Edleson, 1999; Menard, 2001). The extant literature on prevention supports the importance of early intervention for boys and young men who are identified as aggressive as a means of minimizing these behaviors in the lives of these youngsters as they mature.

A major caveat of the literature on risk and protective factors, however, is the admonition about assuming a myopic view on the causal influences for youth aggression. The danger of such views is that they tend to focus solely on the role of the individual male youth, his family, or his school; such a view is misguided. In fact, as the ecological model discussed earlier points out, it is often the case that a multitude of individual, familial, community, and societal factors conspire to put certain boys and adolescent males at heightened risk for aggression by their reciprocal influence.

The Importance of Focusing on Prevention

Much of the attention directed at the prevention of youth violence and aggression in boys and adolescent males has been school based, with fewer resources directed at the prevention of community-based aggression and violence. This observation has important implications when considering the epidemiology of male youth aggression and violence and the context (i.e., the community) in which those behaviors predominantly occur (see Anderson et al., 2001). Often, however, referrals for counseling or interventions for aggressive boys and male adolescents come via school sources, and although this source of referral addresses the needs of boys and adolescent males still within the schools, many of the young males in need of our attention may not receive it because they are likely to be out of school.

Another avenue for referral for services for many males is through their involvement in the juvenile justice system. Young men engaged in the court system are often referred for counseling and other types of psychological intervention. Often males referred from the court system have more pronounced psychological needs, may have been involved in aggressive behavior longer, and carry a much greater risk of continued delinquency and aggression. Regardless of the avenue of referral for help for boys and young men, there is a need to be more proactive in our work in helping them develop prosocial competencies such that aggressive behavior may not develop in the first place.

In recent years the focus on the prevention of youth aggression and violence has witnessed the development of a variety of prevention interventions, a number of which have proven effective, with many others showing promise in terms of demonstrating empirical effectiveness (see Orpinas & Horne, 2006; Wilson, Gottfredson, & Najaka, 2001; Wilson, Lipsey, & Derzon, 2003). An additional outcome of this work is that a number of schools have taken steps to promote school safety and nonviolent conflict resolution among their student ranks. For example, the U.S. Department of Education directed school districts around the country to adopt violence prevention programs that have demonstrated empirical effectiveness, a rare and important instance of science informing policy (http://www.ed.gov/about/offices/list/osdfs/index. html). As previously mentioned, community-based interventions for boys and adolescent males have not received the level of research support that school-based interventions have, thus there is unevenness in the empirical literature on what works at the community level in preventing youth aggression and violence.

HELPING AGGRESSIVE BOYS AND ADOLESCENTS

One of the more significant challenges faced by counseling professionals in working with aggressive youth is one of having a clear understanding of what constitutes aggressive or violent behavior, meaning that aggression can and often does mean something different in different contexts and communities. Clarity on the meaning of aggression and violence is critical for those counseling and helping professionals committed to the meaningful operationalization of social justice such that certain groups (e.g., ethnic minority male youth) aren't marginalized in a manner that suggests inherent deficits or a predisposition toward violence. Earlier in this chapter, we defined *violence, aggression, bullying,* and *rough-and-tumble play* for young males; these definitions should be helpful in guiding the understanding and work of helping professionals dealing with aggressive males across the span from boyhood to late adolescence.

A second challenge is to understand what function aggressive behavior serves for boys and adolescent males. We assert this is critical for working with males, as all behavior serves some function regardless of its appropriateness or lack thereof, and this is also true for aggressive males. As a practical matter, understanding the role and function of aggressive behavior is important to the growth and change of the client because the aggressive behavior will have to be ultimately replaced with more prosocial and conventionally acceptable behaviors. As a practical matter, this means that we have to be sure to address the function of the aggressive behavior with a more socially desirable behavior.

Several scholars (e.g., Cassidy & Stevenson, 2005; Garbarino, 1999; Horne & Kiselica, 1999; Pollack, 1999) as well as other contributions in this volume (e.g., chapters 1 and 2) provide important guidance about understanding the socialization of males in U.S. society and the unique role that aggression plays in that socialization. Moreover, this literature describes how in understanding the "positives" and "negatives" of the current socialization of males, a unique opportunity exists in the counseling process to deconstruct some of the negative and unhealthy socialization processes. Foundational to such efforts, however, is understanding what aggressive behavior represents, which most often is an effort by the young person to communicate something, often with little appreciation for the consequences for the particular communication method (i.e., aggression).

Confounding the discussion is that most boys and teens in the United States get clear messages about the appropriateness of aggression to resolve conflict, communicate concerns and problems, relate to male and female peers, and generally get what they want regardless of the sanctions for such behaviors (see Garbarino, 1999). There are multiple examples highlighting how male aggressive behavior is endorsed. Further, young males often receive conflicting messages when they physically push or roughhouse, such as alternately hearing, "Don't be so rough—play nicely," to "They're just being boys, and they will work out their difficulties." These messages can extend into adolescence around dating behavior, when males often don't understand or accept "no" to be no or that paying for a date doesn't equate to a "free pass" for unwelcome sexual behavior (Koss, 2005). These messages about what being *male* and *masculine* are about are often observed into late adolescence and young adulthood regarding what being male, masculine, and a man means (e.g., *male* means being tough; see Katz, Earp, & Jhally [1999] for an excellent video, *Tough Guise*, on the development of male aggression). The messages are easily internalized, where they can become the source of motivation of many destructive behaviors throughout adolescence and well into young adulthood.

A recent excerpt from the television program *Baghdad ER* illustrates this point. This program gives battlefield accounts about injured U.S. soldiers from the Iraqi war as they enter military hospitals and mobile hospitals for treatment. In one episode, a soldier who appears to be about 20 years of age has been wounded by enemy fire and comments when talking to the physician, "Yeah, I was just laying there like a little bitch instead of getting up." In this example, a young man injured by bullets and shrapnel is more concerned with getting back into the fight (i.e., being a man) than about his health. In light of such examples, what should the posture of helping and counseling professionals be in engaging these boys and young men about their behavior and its functionality?

The intervention approach that we offer below is based on our combined clinical experience over many years of working with boys and male adolescents in a variety of contexts (e.g., community and school settings, and group and individual counseling). Our recommendations are offered as instructional guidance or augment to the already substantive literature about what works and doesn't work in counseling young males (e.g., Horne & Kiselica, 1999). We begin with a focus on general systemic concerns about the importance of developing supportive, inviting, and encouraging environments for young men.

ACCEPTANCE AND VALIDATION

As an initial step, we believe it necessary that boys and male adolescents experience acceptance, not negative critical judgment, from the professionals who seek to help them. Why? Most often the boy or teen referred for counseling is already confused about why what he did was wrong, given the way in which he has probably been socialized. Exacerbating this confusion is the fact that the boy or male teen is now being asked to engage in a behavior often foreign to him (e.g., talking about his feelings and behavior). The experience of being judged compounds this confusion and likely leads to feelings of defensiveness, which arrest the counseling process. As counseling professionals, we must stay vigilant about the perceived contradictions of "hypermasculinity" most males come to the counseling process with and the "hypervulnerability" they assume is required in counseling (Cassidy & Stevenson, 2005). Although many of the aggressive young males we work with are mandated to counseling because of their behavior, one of our goals must be to connect with aggressive boys in genuine and meaningful ways. Because many young males feel powerless in this situation and respond with considerable defiance, resistance, or withdrawal, an objective should be to create a relationship in which it is possible to mutually define goals and expectations that can be objectively assessed and that are agreeable to both the professional and the boy or male adolescent.

We submit that acceptance by itself is inadequate in the effort to establish a meaningful therapeutic relationship, but is a lynchpin of effective helping. We believe it equally important that boys and male teens have the experience of feeling validated in terms of their self-worth as important members of their schools, families, communities, and society. Often, much of the confusion and frustration these young people experience not only are the result of their behavior but also are compounded by messages they receive about their self-worth. Messages about personal worth have relevance in terms of a boy's willingness to be open and motivated to grow and change, important factors in successful counseling. For example, it is a different experience to hear, "You bring a lot to the table and are important to this school, and your family and I really want to understand with you some of the choices you've made," versus "This is unacceptable, and you either shape up or ship out" or "You're just like those other boys—a troublemaker who's going to end up in jail." To be clear, we don't support approaches where personal accountability isn't a part of the work; our experience, however, is that we usually increase our chances for positive outcomes when we endorse that our goal is to understand and help the boy or male teen rather than judge and invalidate him. In other words, we want to empower him rather than invalidate him. For many boys and young men, rejection or not being understood has been an all too frequent part of their life experience.

Advocacy

There is an important role for advocacy and education by helping professionals who work with boys who are aggressive and/or have been labeled as aggressive. As discussed above, boys and adolescent males' experiences of being misunderstood are common and may manifest in a variety of contexts, including school, the family, and the community. At times, caregivers and peers in these different contexts will be confused and upset by the behavior of these youngsters and sometimes respond in ways that exacerbate the problem behavior or isolate the offending youth. For example, one of the authors has consulted in a number of schools where, when a male student becomes disruptive in class, that student is often isolated and labeled a troublemaker, or it may be the case in the era of zero tolerance that a male youngster may be expelled or placed in an alternative school, which in some instances is tantamount to warehousing. Our experience is that these boys and teens are typically dealing with other life issues and have no intention of being purposively or maliciously disruptive. For example, the student may be struggling academically, not knowing how to ask for help, or may be dealing with problems at home. Therefore, helping a teacher, administrator, or other caregiver develop a level of understanding or empathy for a boy or teen can relieve tensions for not only the child but others impacted by the child's behavior. This does not mean giving the boy a "free pass" for inappropriate behavior, but it does mean understanding that he is likely doing the best he can under the circumstances he has; our job is to help him with the circumstances and teach new skills for managing conflict more effectively, not reject him.

The work of deconstructing aggressive behavior and the societal norms that support its existence is not specific to only the boys and male adolescents we counsel; rather, we must address family, school, community, and societal issues exacerbating the problems of the boy. As discussed earlier, male youth don't become aggressive or violent in isolation of multiple messages and reinforcements that support that behavior. Thus, to maximize the effectiveness of our work, it is important that we avoid the problem that those, for example, in drug treatment often experience, which is that they go for treatment, get "clean," and then go back into the "dirty" environment that originally supported the behavior, thereby increasing the likelihood they will begin to use again. There is growing theoretical and empirical support that suggests that the way for boys and male adolescents not to be violent is for them to exist in nonviolent environments (Henry et al., 2000). We must remember in our work that these boys are imminently capable of positive growth and change and that their individual behavior as youth has multiple ramifications for who they will become as fathers, husbands and partners, community members, and workers as adults. Thus, to optimally help young people, our work must extend beyond our offices, our classrooms, or the athletic field. Finally, on this point, we must remember we cannot do this work of stopping male aggression on our own; we need to identify and develop allies outside our offices. As social justice advocates point out, our work must manifest in ways that are meaningful to our clients and client systems if we are to advance the well-being of our clients and the communities in which they exist (see Vera & Speight, 2003).

Counseling Modalities

Given the above, we must also consider the role of individual counseling versus, or in addition to, other forms of helping behavior. For example, we are all clear about the greater influence that the peer group assumes during adolescence or the role of the family during early and middle childhood (Maguire & Pastore, 1998). As a result, we need to take these influences into consideration during our treatment planning. For example, is it reasonable that a boy referred for individual counseling at school who is witnessing domestic violence at home is really going to improve, if the desired outcome is for him to stop repeating the behavior he witnesses at home? Or that an adolescent involved in disruptive behavior at a community center is going to relinquish that behavior when it is constantly reinforced by his peer group, a group that has more social capital and influence on the adolescent? Examples like these should influence the treatment modalities we employ in working with aggressive boys and male teens. In the first example, although there may be a real need for the young boy to receive some individual counseling, a counselor will likely have more of an impact on that individual boy's aggressive behavior by working with the family. Or, in the second example, it may be more beneficial to work with that young man in a group setting in order to leverage the influence of his peers in promoting growth and change. A helpful position to assume in working with young boys and adolescent males is that all males can learn (i.e., don't write them off, and learn to teach them); all people (boys as well as counselors and teachers) deserve to be treated with respect and dignity; and there is no room for violence in our schools and communities. These beliefs lead to counseling that emphasizes positive change, is focused on solutions rather than blaming, and declares that it is possible for change to occur.

Role Models and "Healthy" Aggression

Some might contend that there is no role at all for aggression in a healthy society, so that the pairing of *aggression* with *healthy* is a contradiction in terms. Ideas like these make for healthy debate, although for the foreseeable future, aggression is likely to continue to play a central role in U.S. society and for boys and male teens. Given this assertion, are there places where it is more acceptable for boys and teens to be aggressive? Historically, young males have been given a pass to be aggressive, even violent, on athletic fields, in military-like activities such as ROTC, and in some forms of interpersonal play such as rough-and-tumble interactions. They are also expected to learn to defend themselves, their families, and their communities; this level of aggression is seen as acceptable, even if the actions result in aggressive behavior. It is important that our society identify and provide support for the appropriate and accepted actions of aggression.

Counseling professionals, parents, and other caregivers need to be sensitive to the situations in which boys are exposed to sanctioned aggression in unhealthy ways, for it is here where the seeds of aggressive and violent behavior are often sown. For example, we have to be attentive to what these boys and adolescent males are being taught through their participation in sports. A mind-set sometimes evident in football that says, "Take their [insert expletive] head off," is troublesome. Thus, although accepted and sanctioned competitive sports can be supported, these sports must also be examined, and the violent attitudes and behaviors must be purged from these activities.

In addition, caregivers need to be attentive of what boys and male adolescents learn from adults and their caretakers regarding aggression in sports, relationships, and elsewhere. In a recent sporting event, one of the authors botched a play, and expressed his frustration through the use of an expletive. A wiser teammate pointed out that the author's then 6-year-old son had witnessed his tirade. Adults, especially men, play an important role in modeling the behaviors adopted by our sons, clients, students, and brothers, and need to be constantly aware of the impact they are having on those observing adult behavior.

Recognizing the necessity of clinical boundaries, one of the practical things that professionals can do, as appropriate, is share their experiences and struggles in managing their own behavior and growing to a place minimizing the role that aggression has in how they communicate, relate, and problem-solve. Likewise, it's important for counseling professionals to model the desired behaviors, understanding that mistakes and poor choices have been part of the learning process for all of us committed to nonviolence. It is here that we have to challenge ourselves in finding the balance regarding personal disclosure, empathy, compassion, support, and accountability. Three of the authors for this chapter are the father to at least one son, and each is aware of his occasional poor choices in terms of how he has managed himself in relation to his son or sons, but overall we reflect on and share our own process, and believe conscious awareness and intent can be important parts of the learning and modeling process.

In the experience of one of the authors (LER), who has worked extensively with boys and male teens in the child welfare system from low-income families and inner-city communities, often the male therapist may be the only positive and consistent adult male in the young male's life (Caldwell & Reese, 2005). For a number of these males, an influence on their aggressive behavior may be the lack of a role model with whom the young man can identify and who models appropriate prosocial behaviors. Conversely, many young boys and male adolescents in these circumstances are frustrated by the experience of being abandoned and rejected by their birth fathers, experiences known to influence inappropriate externalizing behaviors in male youth. Given the absence of positive male role models in the lives of many of the young boys and men we work with, it is important to understand and provide an opportunity for the male child to work through some of his transference issues in therapy. The following example helps to illustrate the impact that the absence of a positive role model can have on the development of a young boy:

The first author of this chapter (LER) was conducting a violence prevention project in an inner-city school in a large Midwestern city. During the course of this intervention, he became familiar with a number of youth in the program and one 9-year-old boy in particular. This youngster came to my attention because he was constantly being dismissed from class for creating disruptions, name-calling, and generally being uncooperative. During one of our sidebar conversations, I inquired about why he seemed to be struggling in class so often, did he have thoughts about what he wanted to do with his life, and so on. His response was instructive. This young boy told me he wanted to be an aeronautical engineer, to which I responded, "Great—what do you need to do to achieve that goal?" He proceeded to tell me all the educational and experiential requirements, as well as how he became interested in this field. Impressed with the breadth and completeness of his response, I expressed my confusion about his behavioral choices in school. He responded that being an engineer was what he wanted to be, but what he was going to be was a "drunk" like his uncle; his whole family had told him so.

This experience illustrates two things that are true for many boys. One, he identified more with his uncle and the uncle's behavior because this is the adult male behavior he saw daily; this was his role model, and his role model had a clear influence on his behavior. Two, this young boy had been told in a variety of ways that this (being a drunk) was to be his lot in life; at 9, he had been written off. Thus his behavior, though problematic, made sense, as did the life trajectory he was on without intervention. Finally, it struck me (LER) that the conversations we were having were his "therapy" and that he had limited experience with an adult male expressing a genuine interest in him, an experience that many boys and male teens have been deprived of. Counseling provides an opportunity to create these experiences for young males.

Likewise, our female colleagues have an important role to play in helping boys understand their behavior by giving them feedback on how their behavior may be received by female members of the community who are our teachers, parents, and peers. Aggressive behavior by boys and male adolescents cannot be viewed through a lens where it's viewed as a "guy thing"; instead, it must be seen as an *us* (e.g., family, community, and societal) thing as the prevention and reduction of aggression will be achieved only through a collective response, meaning that there is a role to play for all members (e.g., parents, teachers, coaches, and counselors) involved in a young male's life in ameliorating aggressive behavior.

Resource Development

As the previous recommendations suggest, aggressive behavior should not be seen and thus "treated" in isolation of the multiple contexts in which it exists. A recent newspaper example helps illustrate this point. A rapidly growing county in the southeastern United States reported that over 90% of the referrals in the county school system for disruptive behavior were for African American boys. This county is largely middle class, and there were growing numbers of middle- and upper-middle-class Blacks moving into the county, which prior to that had been overwhelmingly White. A major reason for the influx of many of the Black families was that the school system was viewed as one of the better ones in the state. So what was really going on in this situation? No reasonable person believes that African American boys constitute over 90% of the behavioral problems in this county absent biased reporting and inappropriate attributions made about these boys' and male adolescents' behavior. Left unexamined and unchecked, events such as this serve to create deep divisions within families, schools, and communities. Thus, there is a need to develop the capacity of caregivers and communities to understand and receive young people in ways that are affirming and supportive, with appropriate consequences for inappropriate behavior based upon agreed-to norms. Although there was no follow-up report on how the school board, parents, and community responded to this situation, what it represents is an opportunity for counseling professionals to have intervened at multiple levels in a effort to bridge differences, assist in the development of shared community norms, and clarify the "real" versus "perceived" problem and what to do about it.

A significant element of capacity building resides in the ability of communities to have meaningful dialogue about the needs, concerns, and solutions to the problems facing its members and, in this case, boys and adolescents. This is a role that counseling professionals interested in helping boys and male teens can facilitate and are often uniquely positioned to fulfill. Very often, young males identified as aggressive are discarded to classrooms for behaviorally disordered students, to detention, or to the juvenile justice system where it's commonly accepted these young people don't receive the services they or their families need. The manner in which these young people are received and responded to can be changed if we successfully engage those caregivers responsible for these boys and adolescents in ways that promote positive behavior and growth.

Role of Cultural Factors

The final recommendation we offer here concerns the role of culture in counseling aggressive youth. Counseling and other forms of mental health service delivery are important to efforts to improve the lives of young boys by offering assistance in managing some of the challenges they face. However, a recent *Report of the Surgeon General* on mental health (DHHS, 2001b) points out the following regarding the experience of ethnic minorities and the provision of mental health services:

1. Ethnic and racial minorities have less access in general to mental health services
2. Ethnic and racial minorities are less likely to receive needed mental health services even when access exists.
3. Ethnic and racial minorities receiving treatment often receive a poorer quality of mental health care than their White counterparts.

Earlier in this chapter, we discussed the disproportionate impact of violence on ethnic minority youth and especially African American and Hispanic male youth. We contend that issues of cultural competence and cultural relevance are central to effective helping, and although it is beyond the scope of what can be offered here, there is instructive guidance elsewhere on this topic (see Reese, Vera, & Caldwell, 2006).

A challenge that counseling professionals must balance in their work with ethnic minority male youth as well as those male youth whose life experiences (i.e., poor male youth) haven't been defined by a middle-class Western experience in the United States is the realization that much of the theory and technique in the counseling literature is founded upon a worldview often at odds with the experiences of ethnic minority boys and adolescent males (Reese et al., 2006). Likewise, issues of racial socialization for ethnic minority boys and male teens have a significant influence on the life experiences of ethnic minority male youth and have to be considered in counseling these male youth (Hughes et al., 2006). Culturally responsive counseling must not be an afterthought; it must be intentionally considered and employed for those serious about helping boys and young men struggling with aggressive and violent behavior. The results of a recent meta-analysis illustrate this point. Wilson, Lipsey, and Soydan (2003) found positive effects for interventions for delinquent youth across different ethnic groups; what they noted, however, was that for minority youth there were statistical differences in the satisfaction with, participation in, and acceptance of the interventions. These authors recommended that by tailoring programs to be optimally responsive to the needs of diverse groups, differences in participation, satisfaction, and acceptance may be reduced or ameliorated.

The recommendations that are offered here should be seen as augments to the already impressive empirical literature on counseling interventions with boys (e.g., Garbarino, 1999; Horne & Kiselica, 1999). The empirical investigations of the efficacy of behavioral, cognitive-behavioral, and social-cognitive interventions at the individual, peer group, and family levels are broad; thus, there is no need to repeat that literature here as there are comprehensive reviews and meta-analyses on these approaches elsewhere (e.g., Forehand & Long, 1988; Reid, Webster-Stratton, & Baydar,

2004). Instead, we want to focus on the continuing challenges faced by male youth involved in aggressive behavior and the parents and helping professionals who work with them. Hence, these recommendations are not offered to replace what we already know but instead to build upon that literature to offer meaningful relief to these youth and guidance for the helping professionals who work with them.

CASE STUDY: HELPING RAUL CONTROL HIS ANGER

Raul was a 13-year-old Puerto Rican boy who had been placed in a partial hospitalization program (PHP) due to his frequent aggressive outbursts at his former school. The student-clients of this program were typically on-site from 7:30 a.m. to 5:30 p.m. Over the course of the day, the student-clients would receive 6 hours of classroom academics (which were monitored by a teacher, a teacher's aide, and a behavioral specialist in a self-contained on-site classroom), 2 hours of group therapy, and 2 hours of heavily structured "free time" (including lunch); student-clients also received 1 hour of individual therapy a week. Much of the case material is drawn from group and individual therapy sessions. Family therapy was offered, though not mandated, as part of the PHP's service delivery package; however, in Raul's particular case, his family did not attend.

The reason for Raul's placement at the PHP was that he had developed several aggressive behavioral tendencies at his previous school, and following multiple in- and out-of-school suspensions, the school counselors and administrators believed that he was unable to have his educational needs met there. Most of his behaviors could be described as either aggressive bullying and/or passive bullying. He would typically identify several students who he "didn't like" and relentlessly tease them with pejorative statements, or push and smack them. Raul was taller than most of his peers, and was considerably overweight as well. Though he enjoyed the advantages of his size for the purposes of the physical bullying and fighting that he engaged in, he often wore overly baggy clothing to deemphasize his heaviness, and in our later work together he indicated that it was a source of poor self-esteem.

Following his expulsion from school and subsequent adjudication through the juvenile courts, Raul came to our facility as most do: anxious and scared, depressed, and frustrated with themselves, others, and the "system." As can be expected for an aggressive male adolescent, Raul quickly began taunting the other clients in attempts to, in his words, "size everyone up" and communicate in no uncertain terms that there would be consequences if "anyone f—ked with me." Because of Raul's difficulties with adjustment to his new environment, he had his "free time" privileges significantly restricted and was placed on a "constant watch" list, ensuring that he would never be with other student-clients without the presence of a PHP staff.

Similar to his classroom and "free time" experiences, during his group therapy sessions, he was frequently escorted from the room, as his taunts and insults to the other student-clients quickly disrupted the process. As such, Raul's only outlet for the possibility of a meaningful therapeutic or otherwise corrective relationship came during his once-weekly scheduled appointment with the PHP counselor.

Typical for rapport building in the first few weeks, the counselor escorted Raul to the playground and began to play "horse" on the basketball court. As Raul became comfortable and talkative about superficial subjects such as TV shows and movies while shooting hoops, the counselor began prolonging the time they spent in the office. This was done by the counselor casually talking with Raul while feigning a need to attend to paperwork, e-mail, and the like for increasingly longer periods of time at the start of each session. Once Raul had become accustomed to talking both on the basketball court and in the office, a deal was struck to spend half of the session in each environment, alternating which environment they would first spend time in.

The relationship between Raul and the counselor began to unfold once a feeling of mutual respect became established. This was done by cultivating an appreciation for Raul's situation (home life; struggles at school—peer related and academically related; difficulties with the courts; etc.), and dialoguing with him frequently about it.

Additionally, the use of games became central to the therapeutic relationship. As indicated above, casual games of basketball were used initially to establish rapport; however, games also provide insight into how people (and especially boys) organize their proximate experience of the world. For example, Raul frequently engaged in automatic thoughts of defeat when anticipating his free throws, self-deprecating language, and occasional outbursts of frustration when he missed the shots. This became therapeutically usable material as the counselor became increasingly direct in pointing out these tendencies to Raul.

Similarly, the utilization of board games provided insight into how Raul organized the more distal experience of the world. For example, when playing games requiring strategy (in Raul's case, chess; checkers, Pente, or Connect Four are excellent as well), he frequently made moves impulsively and without an ability to see the consequences of his move beyond that moment in time. Again, the counselor began pointing out these tendencies and encouraged Raul to explore and develop new kinds of thinking that involved seeing beyond the immediate move and, rather, viewing the game as a process of many related moves, some requiring sacrifice in the immediate term for a greater gain in the future.

In basketball, as Raul developed his ability to recognize and regulate his frustration and subsequent emotional outbursts, he was praised heavily. The praise for his emotional regulation was more emphasized than his good plays, as he was not in training to become a successful athlete, but a successful young man. Likewise, in chess he was praised for his efforts in his strategy development, planning, sacrifice, and follow-through.

It should be noted also that the counselor always played to the best of his ability in all games. This was done in order to model not only investment in outcome, but also humility in success and failure, and good sportsmanship as well. Often, counselors or other adults will intentionally lose a game to artificially prop up a young male's self-esteem. This counselor (CB) cautions against using this "technique" indiscriminately, as life is full of both success and failure, and a healthy and adaptive male needs to be able to experience each of these with grace. Additionally, most young males are smarter than they are often given credit for, and therefore can easily see though this tacit agreement, which subtly communicates an ardent belief in the inefficacy of their ability to succeed without constant assistance.

Once Raul began to modify his cognitions, emotions, and behaviors during play, he was guided by the counselor as they worked toward generalizing these lessons to the rest of his life experience. It was exciting for both Raul and the counselor to see how the lessons of the games could be applied to his particular life circumstances. As connections were explored, refined, and strengthened, it was suggested that Raul begin developing life strategies. Thus, his relationships and situations became his new games that he and the counselor bonded over. Raul and the counselor would develop strategies together, anticipate challenges of "making the moves" and anticipate the possible outcomes. They would share in the thrill of the successes and the agonies of the defeats.

In time, Raul grew in his ability to become more mindful of his internal experience as a response to his external situation, more deliberate and measured in his behaviors, and a little less dependent on the appraisal of others for his understanding of who he was and who he wanted to become.

As a result of these developments, the frequency and intensity of his outbursts decreased, and Raul eventually left the PHP, reintegrating into the more traditional public school system. He still received emotional support resources during certain periods of his day and had occasional difficulties with his peers, teachers, and family. However, it was clear that Raul had learned some very valuable lessons as a boy that would help him considerably in his journey toward becoming a man.

CONCLUSION

It is a seductive idea that in any manuscript or volume such as this, all the answers for how to work with aggressive boys and male teens might be found. Yet, as we all know, such notions are naïve at best and can be dangerous. That is why what we attempted to do is offer guidance, our best thinking based on our years as practicing psychologists, counselors, and prevention scientists.

Even in the case study, for instance, the work of the counselor "deviated" somewhat from the focus of this chapter. The majority of the work performed with Raul involved individual counseling, not the more broad approaches employed in family therapy, or in school or community interventions. This was done because Raul's family was not available for therapy, and Raul had already been placed in a partial hospitalization program, which limited his access to these larger systems. Therefore, the treatment choices were made with what was available, namely, the individual. Despite this, however, the counselor did work in a manner consistent with the core of the ecological model, working to identify the personal characteristics and risk factors that were facing Raul (e.g., emotional intensity and reduced adaptability to social situations, and ineffective or poor social processing skills), as well as developing an understanding of Raul's resiliency factors so that he could learn to rely on these strengths. This was done in the hopes that by reducing the risk factors and increasing the resiliency factors, Raul would be afforded more of an opportunity to interact more effectively with his family and these larger systems. Ideally, a counselor would strive to work in more than one modality; however, practical constraints all too often (and unfortunately) complicate this approach.

Our hope is that what we have offered will be useful in the work that counselors and other helping professionals engage in with male youth involved in aggressive behavior. As best as we could, we have tried to be clear that "counseling" has to manifest in multiple venues and with various caregivers to these youth, as often these boys and young men are only the "symptom bearers" of familial, community, and societal problems of violence. As such, those committed to reducing male youth aggression and violence will have to wear multiple hats and develop skills and resources that extend beyond the counseling room. If we allow ourselves to be limited to the counseling room, the effect of our work is limited to helping these boys and teens manage their own behaviors in a world that continues to espouse violence in a multitude of ways. We continue to believe, however, that counseling and the counseling relationship represent an important conduit in the prevention of male aggression and violence. In order to maximize the impact of our efforts, however, we will need to be strategic and critical in our efforts, recognizing that the needs of some boys and adolescents will be greater than what we alone can offer. In the face of these realities, we continue to believe in the positive possibilities for nonviolence in the lives of male youth because we have done this work and experienced the changes that committed work results in.

REFERENCES

Anderson, M. A., Kaufman, J., Simon, T. R., Barrios, L., Paulozzi, L., Ryan, G., et al. (2001). School-associated violent deaths in the United States, 1994–1999. *Journal of the American Medical Association, 286,* 2695–2702.

Buka, S., & Earls, F. (1993). Early determinants of delinquency and violence. *Health Affairs, 12,* 46–64.

Bureau of Justice Statistics. (2006). *National crime victimization survey.* Washington, DC: U.S. Department of Justice. Retrieved July 24, 2006, from http://www.ojp.usdoj.gov/bjs/cvict.htm

Caldwell, L. D., & Reese, L. E. (2005). The fatherless father. In M. Conners, L. D. Caldwell, & J. L. White (Eds.), *African American fathers: The invisible father* (pp. 169–187). New York: Erlbaum.

Cassidy, E. F., & Stevenson, H. C. (2005). They wear the mask: Hypermasculinity and hypervulnerability among African American males in an urban remedial disciplinary school context. *Journal of Aggression, Maltreatment and Trauma, 11*(4), 55–74.

Centers for Disease Control and Prevention. (2006). *Youth risk behavior surveillance: United States, 2005. Morbidity and Mortality Weekly Report (MMWR),* 55(No. SS-5): 1–108. Retrieved July 2, 2007, from http://www.cdc.gov/mmwr/preview/mmwrhtml/ss5505a1.htm

Centers for Disease Control and Prevention. (2007). *National Center for Injury Prevention and Control: Web-Based Injury Statistics Query and Reporting System (WISQARS).* Retrieved July 24, 2006, from http://www.cdc.gov/ncipc/wisqars

Crick, N. R., & Dodge, K. A. (1994). A review and reformulation of social information-processing mechanisms in children's social adjustment. *Psychological Bulletin, 115,* 74–101.

Dahlberg, L. L., & Simon, T. R. (2006). Predicting and preventing youth violence: Developmental pathways and risk. In J. Lutker (Ed.), *Violence prevention* (pp. 97–124). Washington, DC: American Psychological Association.

Dodge, K. A., & Coie, J. D. (1987). Social information processing factors in reactive and proactive aggression in children's peer groups. *Journal of Personality and Social Psychology, 53,* 1146–1158.

Edleson, J. L. (1999). The overlap between child maltreatment and woman battering. *Violence Against Woman, 5*(2), 134–154.

Farrington, D. P. (2003). Conduct disorder, aggression, and delinquency. In R. M. Lerner and L. Steinberg (Eds.), *Handbook of adolescent psychology* (pp. 627–664). New York: Wiley.

Federal Bureau of Investigation. (2005). *Uniform crime reports for the United States: Crime in the United States.* Washington, DC: Government Printing Office.

Forehand, R., & Long, N. (1988). Outpatient treatment of the acting out child: Procedures, long-term follow-up data, and clinical problems. *Advances in Behaviour Research and Therapy, 10,* 129–177.

Garbarino, J. (1999). *Lost boys: Why our sons turn violent and how we can save them.* New York: Free Press.

Henry, D., Guerra, N., Huesmann, R., Tolan, P., VanAcker, R., & Eron, L. (2000). Normative influences on aggression in urban elementary school classrooms. *American Journal of Community Psychology, 28,* 59–81

Horne, A., & Kiselica, M. (Eds.). (1999). *Handbook of counseling boys and adolescent males.* Thousand Oaks, CA: Sage.

Howell, J. C. (1998). Promising programs for youth gang violence prevention and intervention. In R. Loeber and D. P. Farrington (Eds.), *Serious and violent juvenile offenders: Risk factors and successful interventions* (pp. 284–312). Thousand Oaks, CA: Sage.

Hughes, D., Rodriguez, J., Smith, E. P., Johnson, D., & Stevenson, H. C. (2006) Parents' ethnic/racial socialization practices: A review of research and directions for future study. *Developmental Psychology, 42*(5), 747–770.

Katz, J., Earp, J. (Writers), & Jhally, S (Producer & Director). (1999). *Tough guise: Violence, media and the crisis in masculinity.* Northampton, MA: Media Education Foundations.

Koss, M. P. (2005). Empirically enhanced reflections on 20 years of rape research. *Journal of Interpersonal Violence, 20*, 100–107.

Krug, E. G., Mercy, J. A., Dahlberg, L. L., & Zwi, A. B. (2002). The world report on violence and health. *Lancet, 360*, 1083–1088

Lipsey, M. W., & Derzon, J. H. (1998). Predictors of violent or serious delinquency in adolescence and early adulthood: A synthesis of longitudinal research. In R. Loeber, & D. P. Farrington (Eds.), *Serious and violent juvenile offenders: Risk factors and successful interventions* (pp. 86–105). Thousand Oaks, CA: Sage.

Maguire, K., & Pastore, A. L. (1998). *Sourcebook of criminal justice statistics 1997.* Washington, DC: U.S. Department of Justice, Bureau of Justice Statistics.

Martin, R. P. (1988). *Assessment of personality and behavior problems.* New York: Guilford.

McLoyd, V. C. (1998). Socioeconomic disadvantage and child development. *American Psychologist, 53*, 185–204

Menard, S. (2001). *Short and long term consequences of violent victimization.* Boulder, CO: Center for the Study of the Prevention of Violence of the Institute for Behavioral Sciences.

Morenoff, J. D., Sampson, R. J., & Raudenbush, S. W. (2001). Neighborhood inequality, collective efficacy, and the spatial dynamics of urban violence. *Criminology, 39*, 517–558.

Newman, D. A., Horne, A. M., & Bartolomucci, C. L. (2000). *Bully busters: A teacher's manual for helping bullies, victims, and bystanders.* Champaign, IL: Research Press.

Orpinas, P., & Horne, A. (2006). *Bullying prevention: Creating a positive school climate and developing social competence.* Washington, DC: American Psychological Association.

Orpinas, P., Kelder, S., Frankowski, R., Murray, N., Zhang, Q., & McAlister, A. (2000). Outcome evaluation of a multi-component violence-prevention program for middle schools: The students for peace project. *Health Education Research, 15*, 45–58.

Orpinas, P., Murray, N., & Kelder, S. (1999). Parental influences on students' aggressive behaviors and weapon carrying. *Health Education and Behavior, 26*, 774–787.

Patterson, G. R., Reid, J., & Dishion, T. (1992). *Antisocial boys: A social interactional approach.* Eugene, OR: Castalia.

Pollack, W. (1999). *Real boys: Rescuing our sons from the myths of boyhood.* New York: Henry Holt.

Reese, L. E., Crosby, A. E., Willis, L., & Hasbrouck, L. (2004). Forms of violence. In I. L. Livingston (Ed.), *Handbook of African American health* (pp. 291–316). Westport, CT: Praeger.

Reese, L. E., Vera, E. M., & Caldwell, L. (2006). The role of culture in violence prevention practice and science: Issues for consideration. In J. K. Lutker (Ed.), *Violence prevention* (pp. 259–278) Washington, DC: American Psychological Association.

Reid, M. J., Webster-Stratton, C., & Baydar, N. (2004). Halting the development of externalizing behaviors in Head Start children: The effects of parenting training. *Journal of Clinical Child and Adolescent Psychology*, *33*, 279–291.

Resnick, M. D., Ireland, M., & Borowsky, I. (2004). Youth violence perpetration: What protects? What predicts? Findings from the national longitudinal study of adolescent health. *Journal of Adolescent Health*, *35*, 424e1–424e10.

U.S. Department of Health and Human Services. (2001a). *Mental health: Culture, race and ethnicity*. Rockville, MD: Author.

U.S. Department of Health and Human Services. (2001b). *Youth violence: A report of the surgeon general*. Rockville, MD: Author.

Vera, E. M., & Speight, S. L. (2003). Multicultural competence, social justice, and counseling psychology: Expanding our roles. *The Counseling Psychologist*, *31*, 253–272.

Wilson, D. B., Gottfredson, D. C., & Najaka, S. S. (2001). School-based prevention of problem behaviors: A meta-analysis. *Journal for Quantitative Criminology*, *17*(3), 247–272.

Wilson, S. J., Lipsey, M. W., & Derzon, J. H. (2003). The effects of school-based intervention programs on aggressive behavior: A meta-analysis. *Journal of Consulting and Clinical Psychology*, *71*(1), 136–149.

Wilson, S. J., Lipsey, M. W., & Soydan, H. (2003). Are mainstream programs for juvenile delinquency less effective with minority youth than majority youth? A meta-analysis of outcomes research. *Research on Social Work Practice*, *13*(1), 3–26.

Wilson, W. J. (1996). *The truly disadvantaged*. Chicago: University of Chicago Press.

9

Moving Beyond "Drinking Like a Man"

Tailoring Substance Abuse Counseling Strategies to Meet the Needs of Boys

MARK S. WOODFORD

The Monitoring the Future (MTF) study, a national survey conducted annually of secondary school students, recently reported that among the adolescent population in the United States, adolescent males tend to abuse substances at a higher rate and with greater consequences than adolescent females, particularly in terms of the cost to themselves and to society (Johnston, O'Malley, Bachman, & Schulenberg, 2006). Specifically, according to the MTF study, adolescent males were more likely than females to drink large quantities of alcohol in a single sitting, were more involved with illicit drug use than adolescent females, and reported higher rates of frequent use than females (Johnston et al., 2006).

Similar findings in terms of male and female substance abuse patterns can be found in data gathered by the Substance Abuse and Mental Health Services Administration (SAMHSA) regarding adolescent admissions rates for substance abuse treatment services. SAMHSA's Treatment Episode Data Set (TEDS) indicated that 70% of adolescent admissions, aged 12 to 17, were males (Office of Applied Studies, 2005a). This percentage was largely accounted for by admissions due to marijuana use (76%), with more than half of the admissions coming from refer-rals made through the Juvenile Justice System (53%). In terms of race and ethnicity, the TEDS reported that 58.4% of adolescent admis-sions (male and female combined) were *White (non-Hispanic)*, whereas 19.4% were *Black (non-Hispanic)*, and 16.1% were *Hispanic origin* (with *Mexican* having the highest rates in the Hispanic subgroup at 9.6%). Lastly, in terms of the types of drugs (including alcohol) abused by adolescents, the highest percentage reported in 2003 was for *both alcohol and marijuana* use at 46.0%, followed by *primary marijuana, no alcohol* at 30.3%, and *other drugs and drug combinations* at 10.2%. Interestingly, *primary alcohol, no marijuana* use was reported at 7.4% in 2003, which is a major shift from 10 years prior (24.4%; Office of Applied Studies).

These statistics outline a picture of the current "typical" adolescent male who is admitted for substance abuse treatment in the United States; in that, there is a high likelihood that he will be White, have used and/or abused marijuana, and will be drinking alcohol in a pattern that can be characterized as *binge drinking*, most often defined in the literature for males as having five or more drinks in a row, or "in a sitting" (for females, it is defined as four or more drinks in a row; Dowdall & Wechsler, 2002). Also with this composite profile, there will be about a 50% chance that he will be on probation or parole for criminal behav-ior that occurred while he was under the influence of alcohol or other drugs. And lastly, based on the TEDS data (Office of Applied Studies, 2005a), he is most likely to be 16 or 17 years of age.

If we begin with the notion that these boys tend to present in tradi-tional counseling settings with an "apparent self-sufficiency and emotional disengagement" (Levant, 2001a, p. 365), at least on the surface, and add extensive evidence that there is a strong relationship between ado-lescent substance abuse and antisocial behavior and criminal activity (Sheidow & Henggeler, in press), then we may end up with a perception that these clients will be "difficult" or "treatment resistant." As a result, we may choose to pass on an opportunity to work with an adolescent male who fits this profile.

Brooks and Good (2001) stated, "If therapists are familiar with the most salient values and meanings in their clients' lives, they will have many avenues of entry into their clients' worlds and will have far greater capacity for therapeutic empathy" (p. 16). Developing therapeutic empathy and building rapport with this population can be a challenging task, particularly if one is inexperienced with, or uninformed about, substance-abusing boys. Therefore, this chapter provides an overview of basic adjustment issues with this population and explores the "most salient values and meanings" underlying their substance-abusing behaviors with the specific aim of creating greater therapeutic empathy. Greater empathy will, in turn, facilitate rapport building and an atmosphere of trust, as well as aid in creating collaborative and effective interventions that will have meaning (saliency) for this population of boys.

ADJUSTMENT ISSUES

From a biological standpoint, adolescence is certainly a vulnerable period for both girls and boys in terms of substance use and brain development. Childress (2006) has described adolescence as a "period of developmental imbalance in the brain's 'Go!' and 'Stop!' circuitry" (p. 49). The "Go!" brain circuitry is involved in every individual's desires and motivation for the natural rewards in our environment that have kept us alive and thriving as a species for ages. For example, the drives for food and sex are part of the "Go!" neurological circuitry and are involved with stimulating our basic survival behaviors. In contrast, the "Stop!" brain circuitry is involved in inhibiting or "putting on the brakes" in order for the individual to make appropriate decisions about when to pursue a reward (Childress, 2006).

In normal adolescent development, the "Go!" system develops relatively quickly as hormones change the structure of the body (and the brain) to ensure that we are physically ready to reproduce. This "Go!" system change is much faster relative to the "Stop!" system changes, which causes an "asymmetry—a fully developed 'Go!' system and a vulnerable, not fully developed 'Stop!' system" (Childress, 2006, p. 49). Interestingly, "Go!" circuitry is located primarily in a much "older" (evolutionarily speaking) section of the brain, specifically in the mesolimbic system (which is an area of the brain that is heavily involved in the development and maintenance of addictive behaviors), whereas the "Stop!" circuitry is located in the frontal lobes, an area that does not fully mature until well into the 20s. Childress (2006) was quick to point out that even though adolescence represents a critical period of vulnerability to drugs of abuse, most adolescents who choose to drink or smoke do not become addicted. Instead, Childress referred to the imbalance of the "Go!" and "Stop!" circuitry as "a sensitive biological backdrop against which even small additional alterations in the system— by virtue of heredity, environment (including drug exposure), or their interaction—may 'tilt the scales' toward addiction" (p. 49).

Notably, Childress (2006) did not mention *sex-specific* vulnerabilities when discussing the "Go!" and "Stop!" framework for understanding adolescent brain development and substance abuse. Does this mean that, biologically, males and females might be at equal risk for developing substance abuse problems in adolescence?

In response to this question, the substance abuse literature makes several important points. First, there is no genetic explanation for the predominance of males in the prevalence of alcohol and drug disorders. Hasin, Hatzenbuehler, and Waxman (2006) stated, "A review of family and twin studies found that there are no gender differences in the genetic influence on alcoholism" (p. 70); comparable studies looking at the genetic determinants for other drugs are not available to date. Secondly, research indicates that substance abuse problems are a result of a mixture of genes and environment, with approximately 50% being genetically determined (e.g., family history of alcohol dependence and genetically influenced temperaments) and 50% being psychosocially determined (e.g., peer relations and cognitive factors) (Hesselbrock & Hesselbrock, 2006). Lastly, and most importantly in regard to adolescent substance abuse, "[E]nvironmental factors may play a larger role in *initiation* and *continuation of use past an experimental level*, while genetic factors take precedence among individuals who move from use to dependence" (Hasin et al., 2006, p. 70; emphasis added).

The abstract notion of "environmental factors" influencing adolescent substance abuse (i.e., the social context of substance use initiation, experimentation, and continuation into abuse) happens concretely through relationships with family members, peers, school systems, and surrounding communities. For example, within family environments, the level of parental modeling of appropriate substance use and the parental monitoring of the adolescent's whereabouts are two examples of environmental factors that reduce the likelihood of the development of substance abuse (Moos, 2006).

Peer relationships also have a major influence on adolescent decision making. Developmentally, adolescents tend to value their affiliations with peer groups. In the best-case scenario, they will feel a high level of fidelity to their prosocial peers (i.e., peers who are engaged in healthy behaviors and are not abusing substances), and they will have the normative perception that most youth who are their age do not abuse substances. In the worst-case scenario, an adolescent will be affiliated on a regular basis with substance-abusing peers. This affiliation may initially be attractive because of feelings of alienation from others, particularly if the adolescent lacks the social skills to establish healthy relationships without using substances. The initiation of the substance-abusing behaviors in this environment can be rationalized by thinking that one is setting oneself apart by "getting high," having the normative perception that "everybody who's cool gets high." In this latter scenario, one finds that the bonding happens through the substance-abusing and social-isolating behaviors. In each of these scenarios, there is the underlying adolescent developmental issue (for males *and* females) of finding one's identity through affiliating with various peer groups that can be found in their schools and communities, whether they are healthy or not.

To speak specifically about adolescent male development, boys are influenced by a male socialization process that is also mediated through their relationships with family members, peers, school systems, and popular culture. Images of virile males drinking alcohol ("partying hard"), often associated with sports or enhancing sexual experiences (two areas of interest that loom large in the psyche of developing boys), are an accepted phenomenon in the media (TV, movies, music videos, etc). Messages about masculinity (implicit or explicit) are often reinforced through peer and family interactions, encouraging adolescent males to "drink like a man" or to "hold your liquor (like a man)." Isenhart (2001) stated that "traditional masculine role expectations promote alcohol use as a way for a man to better fit in to the masculine role and also as a way to manage stress associated with not fitting into the role" (p. 249). Hesselbeck and Hesselbeck (2006) emphasized the importance of positive alcohol expectancies in decision making about alcohol use. Examples of positive alcohol expectancies include "social facilitation, enhanced sexual performance and pleasure, increased personal power and aggression, social assertiveness, relaxation and tension reduction, as well as a general positive outcome that may result from drinking" (Hesselbeck & Hesselbeck, 2006, p. 101). These alcohol expectancies in combination with traditional male role expectations may contribute to abusive drinking patterns. This is not to say that there is a causal relationship between these male gender role expectations and alcohol or drug abuse, but rather that there may be an association between the two. That is, alcohol expectancies that are transmitted through the male socialization process for boys could make excessive drinking behaviors more attractive and *meaningful* for them. One could test out this hypothesis in counseling by exploring how a boy's expectancies related to alcohol and drug use might be interwoven with his expectations about masculinity or "being a man" that come from the male socialization process.

Earlier in the chapter, the following question was posed: "Does this mean that, biologically, males and females might be at equal risk for developing substance abuse problems in adolescence?" The preliminary answer to that question was that it was 50% genetics and 50% environment. In this section, the emphasis has been placed on understanding the environmentally based adjustment issues that can contribute to the development of substance abuse problems among adolescent males. Although providing knowledge about genetic risk factors is important for clients and their families, addressing the environmental risk factors contributing to substance-abusing behaviors is something that can be accomplished concretely through counseling interventions. How counselors can do this in a gender-specific way will be illustrated in the case study that follows.

CASE STUDY

The following case narrative includes information that covers all of the core content areas for an appropriate adolescent substance abuse assessment as suggested by Meyers et al. (1999). This framework will highlight many of the adjustment issues that were previously discussed and lay the groundwork for demonstrating gender-specific rapport-building and intervention strategies. The client in this case study, "Jay," is fictional and will have the "typical" demographic profile based on the statistics highlighted in the introduction section at the beginning of this chapter.

Any similarities to clients who I have worked with are purely coincidental. The case background, rapport-building, and intervention sections are written in the present tense in order for readers to get a sense that they are being presented with a case for consultation (i.e., as one might be presented with a case in a clinical team staff meeting) in order to demonstrate how gender-sensitive strategies might be employed with Jay and his family.

Case Background

Jay is a 17-year-old, single, White male (approximately 6'0" and 170 lbs.) who is currently on probation for possession of marijuana. He has been referred for substance abuse and family counseling by his probation officer. Jay is usually casually (but not sloppily) dressed in a hooded sweatshirt, jeans, and work boots. He also is generally wearing a stocking cap and a heavy coat when it is appropriate. He has long black hair that he is growing into dreadlocks, brown eyes, a pale complexion, and an occasional large smile that appears to be genuine and warm.

Jay has lived with his mother and his younger brother (age 15) in their current home for the past 8 years in a predominately White, middle-class, suburban neighborhood. There are distinct areas, local to their residence, where socioeconomic disparities are evident, as the neighborhoods change from poverty-level public assistance housing to middle-class to upper-middle-class housing in a matter of a few miles.

According to Jay's mother, the extended family and the church community play an important role in their family life, particularly because of the influence of Jay's maternal grandmother. Jay does attend church occasionally because "it's real important to my grandma, and she is always asking me to help her get to church." He reports that he does believe in God, but that "the church isn't for me." There is one minister who has been involved with the family to some extent and is considered a family and community support person.

Developmentally, both Jay and his mother reported that he had no problems with meeting normal milestones (no problems walking, toilet training, reading, writing, etc.). Jay's mother describes him as having been "boisterous" in elementary school and middle school. Apparently, he was an average student in terms of reading and writing, excelled in math, and showed great potential with artistic endeavors, although he did not respond well to the art educator in his high school. During this time, Jay enjoyed sports and other physical activities. There were periods of time when Jay was an A and B student in middle school, although his mother says that he was often involved in fights (usually with groups of boys, not in one-on-one confrontations). In high school, according to Jay's mother, his grades declined sharply, as did his participation in athletics and other prosocial peer activities.

Jay's initiation with substance use in middle school and his subsequent substance abuse history moving into high school mirror his decline in school performance and prosocial activities. This pattern of behavior, correlating substance abuse, academic decline, and social and coping skills deficits in the adolescent years, is described in the literature (Henggeler, Schoenwald, Borduin, Rowland, & Cunningham, 2002). In this case, Jay started to drink alcohol at age 12 (he currently drinks 2–3 beers at a time "on average," and 6–8 beers on the weekends, reporting last drinking alcohol 2 days prior to the initial assessment). Jay also described his marijuana use as starting at age 14 (he now averages using a "few hits," with the most at any given time being "a joint" by himself; typical frequency of marijuana use is 4–5 days per week; and last use of marijuana was reportedly 2 weeks prior to the initial assessment). Additionally, Jay started smoking cigarettes at age 12 and currently averages smoking 6–10 cigarettes per day. Jay has mild asthma (related to his substance use), which appears to be the only medical complication with this case.

An important period of Jay's life from ages 12 to 16 involved increased activities with negative peer influences. Antisocial peer association (which in Jay's case certainly included peers who use drugs and alcohol) is the strongest and most direct predictor of adolescent substance use. In fact, associating with peers who abuse substances is considered the final common pathway for many indirect factors correlated with substance use in adolescents (such as social and coping skills deficits, family conflict, parental substance abuse, criminal behavior, community risk factors, academic difficulties, and comorbid disorders; Henggeler, Schoenwald, Borduin, Rowland, & Cunningham, 1998; Henggeler et al., 2002). Many of these factors were found in Jay's assessment.

Jay is currently in the 12th grade and enrolled in an alternative school due to the combination of being involved in several fights in high school and being currently on probation through the local juvenile court system. He needs to attend school only during the current spring semester in order to graduate; however, he is dangerously close to failing because of excessive absences. His teacher reports that he "does well when he attends school." He is currently taking only core courses in order to fulfill requirements for graduation. He stated on a number of occasions that he is "not worried," saying, "I can always get my GED."

Because Jay will be turning 18 in several months, his probation officer is concerned that if he is not compliant with the terms of probation by his birthday, then he will be in danger of being transferred to the adult system by the juvenile court judge overseeing his case. He has tested positive once for marijuana since his probation status began. Additionally, he has not followed through with several requirements of probation: (a) He must obtain and sustain part-time employment (meaning 10–15 hours per week), (b) he must attend outpatient alcohol and drug counseling and remain alcohol and drug free, and (c) he must maintain regular attendance at school.

Jay is not currently working, although he did start working at a local delicatessen for minimum wage upon his release from juvenile jail.

This job lasted only 4 weeks. He has applied for other jobs but has not been successful at establishing regular employment. He is fully dependent on his mother for financial support and receives an allowance for his household chores (when they are completed). Related to finances, Jay denied any involvement in gambling; however, his mother believed that he had once "gambled away his paycheck" when he was employed part-time. Jay denies this; however, there was a noticeable change in his nonverbal behavior and demeanor when responding to questions about gambling. This is one area of the assessment where Jay seemed to be more of a questionable informant. Further assessment would be warranted, including gathering collateral data wherever possible.

Importantly in terms of negative peer association, Jay's probation officer (P.O.) is concerned that he has "started running with the old crowd" and is "not serious about dealing with his drinking and drugging issues." The P.O. expressed a desire to help Jay "keep from being swallowed up by the system for good," but if counseling is not successful at helping Jay meet the terms of his probation (i.e., if another violation of probation occurs), then he will be referred to the adult probation system. The probation officer believes that Jay's mother is not aware of the seriousness of his problems with substance abuse. Meyers et al. (1999) stated that it is often typical that parents show little knowledge of the extent of their child's substance abuse history, that they are often unreliable reporters of historical events, and that they are often unaware of the effect of stressful events on their children. This is a dangerous combination of factors for Jay.

The most significant stressful events in Jay's life occurred in early adolescence. His family history includes a turbulent relationship between his parents. His father (age 44) is a successful salesperson who is currently in recovery from cocaine and alcohol dependence. Notably, Jay's father left home when Jay was 12 years old. His father did not return to participate in Jay's life until the year prior to this assessment when Jay was in juvenile jail. His relationship with his father at present is volatile. Jay's mother has always tried to "make peace" in the family (as has his paternal grandmother); however, to date, there has been little progress in this endeavor. There have been periods of occasional domestic disputes with much verbal abuse (no physical abuse reported). Despite this, according to Jay's mother, his younger brother remains open to having a relationship with their father; however, Jay does not want his father to be present at family counseling sessions.

Jay's mother has a stable, middle-income governmental job. Because his father has struggled with addiction issues and has been an inconsistent part of Jay's life, his mother has been the primary caregiver and sole source of economic and emotional support for Jay and his younger brother for most of their lives. Jay also has a good relationship with his younger brother, and will go to social activities with him from time to time.

Jay reported that he is heterosexual, that he had his first sexual encounter (intercourse) when he was 16 years old, and that he is currently sexually active with one girlfriend. He reports with bravado that there are "no problems in this area." He is, however, inconsistent in using prophylactics (reporting, "That's something that chicks need to take care of"). Jay is not opposed to testing for sexually transmitted diseases, which can be part of the treatment planning. Jay summed up his relationships with adolescent females by saying that he is "not a player like most guys" and that he usually "sticks with one girl, most of the time." Lastly, Jay reported no history of sexual abuse.

In terms of relationships with other adolescent males, Jay was more guarded. The referring probation officer believes that Jay has been involved in some gang-related activities (at least, he has been seen with gang-involved youth). Jay stated that he has several "boys" who he "runs with," but denied any gang involvement. He reports that several friends have been involved in criminal activity; during these activities, substance use was involved—primarily alcohol (beer) and marijuana ("blunts"). As will be shown, this will be an area of greater focus as it is important for Jay to develop prosocial peer supports.

In terms of strengths, Jay's family members are very supportive of his treatment and are willing to attend family counseling sessions as needed. Additionally, although Jay is very quiet and somewhat isolated at times, he appears to be a thoughtful individual, and will articulate his thoughts when approached in a respectful manner. Despite Jay's troubles with the juvenile courts, the probation officer, and school administrators, he presents as a very likable person. Lastly, he is intrinsically motivated and has expressed the desire to "get out of the system" (meaning the probation and court system) and to "have my own business someday" (possibly a screen-printing or apparel company).

Jay has sketchbooks with many drawings that he would like to turn into clothing apparel, such as T-shirts for family and friends. Interestingly, his peers will often "razz" him about his interest in drawing, and when he was younger his father has called this "an enormous waste of time." Other leisure activities for Jay include listening to music and "watching TV with my friends." Clearly, there is a need to develop leisure and recreational activities based on his interests that are not centered on the use of substances.

This is Jay's first reported substance abuse treatment attempt, although he has met with school psychologists for testing and with school counselors concerning the altercations with peers. He has never received any mental health or substance abuse counseling on a regular basis until now.

Lastly, Jay's mental status examination was normal, including no suicidal ideation or signs and symptoms of co-occurring disorders. In terms of insight, Jay possessed an understanding of his legal situation and appeared to be open to professional assistance at this time; however, during the initial assessment, he did not appear to be fully committed to treatment in order to successfully complete probation. That is to say, he appeared to be vacillating between the precontemplation stage of change in some areas (e.g., reevaluating his choices concerning environmental and peer influences) and the contemplation stage of change in other areas (e.g., abstaining from alcohol and marijuana use despite very real consequences, including jail time and loss of contact with family) (stages of change will be explained further in the next section).

Jay does meet the criteria for a diagnosis of Alcohol Abuse, Cannabis Abuse, and Nicotine Dependence (see *DSM-IV-TR*; American Psychiatric Association, 2000). Further assessment would help to rule out dependence to alcohol and marijuana; however, he denied ever having blackouts, signs of tremors, tolerance, seizures, or other problems that would indicate severe problems from his substance use.

STRATEGIES FOR ESTABLISHING RAPPORT

Before getting into specifics, two caveats are offered about the overall framework used here to present rapport-building strategies with adolescent substance-abusing boys. First, because readers will hail from various disciplinary and clinical backgrounds, the strategies will be presented in a way that will be adaptable to clinical work in a variety of settings with adolescent, substance-abusing males, whether in an outpatient office-based setting, in a community- or home-based therapeutic milieu, or in a residential treatment facility or therapeutic community. Secondly, the underlying, fundamental approach for both establishing rapport and facilitating counseling interventions presented is based on two models that were developed in the substance abuse and addiction research arena. They are (a) the stages of change model (Prochaska, DiClemente, & Norcross, 1992), and (b) the motivational interviewing approach (Miller & Rollnick, 1991, 2002). When discussing the relevance of these models to Jay's case, rather than using repeated in-text citations, I have chosen to acknowledge these as the primary sources for this section from the outset. For example, if a stage of change is mentioned, then one can assume that the respective source for this stage is Prochaska et al. (1992). Similarly, if motivational interviewing is mentioned, then Miller and Rollnick (1991, 2002) are the sources.

The Stages of Change and Motivational Interviewing

Despite his mandated-client status, Jay was a relatively reliable informant. One might say, "How fortunate for the counselor that this was one of Jay's inherent traits." But a more accurate description, which fits with the stages of change and motivational interviewing approaches, would be to say that Jay's willingness to participate in counseling (and be a "reliable informant") was a result of the dynamics of the therapeutic relationship that were mediated by the counselor through using these approaches. "Resistance" from Jay would have been seen as feedback about how the counselor is doing in terms of understanding Jay's viewpoint, values, and motivation for change.

Even though motivational interviewing (MI) is considered a client-centered style of counseling, at its core is the very directive goal to elicit behavior change through exploring and resolving ambivalence. Of great importance to the MI approach is the notion of actively listening and reflecting the client's intrinsic values and goals. If the focus of counseling is not in line with what the client values, then rapport building and, ultimately, behavior change are less likely.

A key emphasis of both the MI approach and the stages of change model is to reduce resistance by meeting the client where they are in terms of their readiness to change for each area that is to be addressed through the counseling process. For example, in the initial assessment phase, Jay can be seen as being in the "precontemplation stage of change" in regard to addressing his troubled relationship with his father. The precontemplation stage is characterized by the client's unawareness that there is even the potential for a problem. In Jay's case, he has not even considered rebuilding a relationship with his father, and he probably sees no connection between this relationship and his primary goal to be reached through counseling, succinctly articulated by Jay as "I need to get off probation before I turn 18." Even if a counselor sees the long-term therapeutic importance of Jay's addressing these specific issues with his father (e.g., anger, resentment, and abandonment issues), it would not facilitate building rapport with Jay to go in this direction in the initial phase of counseling because he is clearly not motivated to do so in the precontemplation stage of change. Jay has indicated this by sharing that he does not want his father involved in family counseling, despite the fact that Jay's father has come forward with the offer "to make amends" to his son and speak honestly with him about his recovery process from addiction.

In contrast to his precontemplative stance regarding his relationship with his father, Jay is in the "contemplation stage of change" in regard to his alcohol abuse. A key feature of this stage of change (and the addictive process in general) is that people are ambivalent about making changes in their behavior. Part of them wants to make the change, and an equally influential part of them wants things to stay the same. It is important to emphasize that this is a normal part of the change process. Jay is stuck in this ambivalence ("I want to change, but I don't want to change"), because as an adolescent male, he is unable to see a future (and, perhaps more importantly, his present) where he would not be able to "have a couple of beers" with his friends. At the same time, he knows that if he continues to drink alcohol, then he will very likely get caught in violation of his probation (due to random home visits from his P.O.) and, because he is turning 18, he will be transferred into the adult criminal justice system. Despite these dire consequences, Jay is ambivalent about making changes to his drinking. This speaks to the power and pull of peer influences on adolescents. Therefore, a counselor emphasizing the potential risk involved in Jay's continued alcohol use (which would make intuitive sense and fit with the probation officer's goals) could trigger a reaction from that side of Jay that may or may not be saying out loud, "Yeah, but what are my friends going to think? That I'm a wimp 'cause I can't have a couple of beers?"

On the surface, this kind of response could be easily interpreted as "this kid is resistant to counseling." But we know that he was motivated by one thing to show up for counseling, which is summed up in the brief, emphatic statement "I need to get off probation before I turn 18." The MI approach tries to elicit intrinsically motivated statements such as this that have meaning for Jay. Rather than trying to coerce, or persuade, or actively point out the threat of adult probation, the counselor can use the general principles of motivational interviewing (expressing empathy, developing discrepancy, avoiding argumentation, rolling with resistance, and supporting self-efficacy) to facilitate the change process. For example, let's assume that as the counselor, one hears from Jay two presumably "resistant" words: "Yeah, but ..." To help facilitate rapport building in that moment, one can stop and ask oneself, "Is Jay being resistant right now? Or am I assuming that he is at a greater stage of readiness to change his alcohol use patterns than he actually is?" His response of "Yeah, but ..." is a clue that one needs to modify one's strategies.

Let's take two of the principles of MI cited above (expressing empathy and developing discrepancy) and apply them to Jay's obvious ambivalence about not drinking alcohol with his friends. First, expressing empathy about how difficult it must be to have friends making jokes about his not being able to drink, calling him a "wimp" (essentially questioning his "manhood"), and so on can go a long way in building rapport with Jay. After his experiences with probation officers and school administrators, Jay will probably be surprised at this type of empathic response. Secondly, there is an apparent discrepancy between his choices and his motivation to be free from "the system." While emphasizing his freedom to make choices, one can also develop his awareness of this discrepancy by pointing out the irony of how his freedom has been taken away by "the system," and even though he wants freedom in the short and long term, he currently seems to be choosing to put his freedom in jeopardy by drinking alcohol while he his on probation. Admittedly, this is a delicate area for discussion; however, we know that Jay is intrinsically motivated to get his freedom back, and therefore he is more likely to be open to thinking about how his choices might affect his freedom in the short and long term.

Also of importance in the MI approach is to emphasize with clients that you want to work with them in a partnership to help them to achieve their goals. For Jay, you can emphasize that you are not part of the probation system and that you believe that by working together, you can pool your resources to help him to "get off probation." Talking about how ambivalence about changing is normal when you are faced with making tough choices, instilling hope, and supporting self-efficacy (e.g., praising Jay for showing up and talking about the tough issues) can go a long way to building rapport and a therapeutic partnership in this very crucial contemplation stage of change.

Unlike his alcohol abuse, Jay is ready to address his marijuana abuse. He is in *the preparation stage of change* in this regard. What this means is that Jay has weighed his options (knowing that drug testing will surely show any marijuana use), and, therefore, he is intrinsically motivated not to smoke marijuana—and as a result, he is "not smoking pot right now" (confirmed by random tests). The difference here in terms of the meaning of Jay's use of these two substances (at the initial phase of counseling) is related to the random drug testing that would be occurring through the probation system. Because Jay knows that traces of alcohol leave the body relatively quickly compared with marijuana, he also knows that he is very likely to get caught if he smokes pot, but only somewhat likely to get caught if he drinks alcohol. In the MI approach, this is called using a *decisional balance*, or a *cost–benefit analysis*, of making a change versus staying the course. He has done this as a part of a natural change process with the marijuana use. Subsequently, one can use the same process to help him to weigh out the consequences of his continued alcohol use while on probation.

How might gender-specific issues play into the use of the stages of change and MI approach? As was mentioned, peers (other males) are highly influential in Jay's thinking and behavior, specifically in his decision making. One cannot underestimate the importance of Jay's peers belittling him when he does not "party with them." In that moment, the expectations of male peers are a powerful influence on Jay's decision making. Therefore, from the standpoint of building rapport in the initial stages, the counselor should avoid argumentation and support the intrinsically motivated statements that Jay is making in regard to not smoking marijuana at this time (preparation stage) and express empathy and understanding about the importance of his peer relationships to him (contemplation stage), *even if* the counselor is convinced (and common sense might back this thinking) that Jay is better off not associating with his substance-abusing peers. In the rapport-building phase, to focus on emphasizing in a pointed manner that Jay needs to change his peer group would most likely stifle the development of rapport and trust. Holding this position as a substance abuse counselor can feel unnatural, especially if one has been trained to challenge one's clients with statements like "You have to change the 'people, places, and things' in your life" (this is a phrase that one often hears in self-help support groups and in traditional substance abuse treatment arenas). Again, even though this may ultimately be true, one has to prepare the way for this insight to develop in Jay's mind and experience by respecting where he is in the change process, specifically in regard to the influence of his male peers.

Two other stages of change are also relevant to this discussion. The first is the *action stage of change*, which is characterized by the client's active engagement in activities that will bring about change. Because Jay realizes the seriousness of being placed in adult probation, he is currently showing up for school and for counseling, and for his meetings with his probation officer. Therefore, Jay is in the action phase of change in this regard. To build rapport, the obvious thing for a counselor to do is to support his self-efficacy in regard to these positive behaviors and to emphasize Jay's autonomy and ability to make choices that will ultimately lead to his freedom from his current problems with probation.

The last stage not yet discussed is the *maintenance stage of change*. This stage is characterized by intrinsic motivation to sustain the changes that have been made thus far and to continue doing those behaviors that support one's long-term goals. Jay is not in the maintenance stage with any of his goals at the initiation of this counseling process. However, if he had presented in counseling as having maintained his part-time employment, for example, for a significant period of time (let's say that in Jay's case, this might be 6 months), then the counselor could congratulate him on this positive movement, support his self-efficacy in this area, and explore how he was able to make this change in the past in the hopes that there will be client-directed strategies that he could use again to change current troubling behaviors.

As we have seen, the stages of change and motivational interviewing approaches, both developed in the addiction studies field, provide an excellent guide for Jay's counselor to facilitate rapport building and ultimately positive behavior change. This section is obviously only an introduction to this process. An in-depth description of the application of these models in working with substance-abusing adolescents is beyond the scope and purpose of this chapter; however, there are sources in the literature that will provide interested readers with further information in this area (e.g., Baer & Peterson, 2002; Monti, Barnett, O'Leary, & Colby, 2001; Tober, 1991). To date, I found no sources for the application of these approaches specifically with males or females; therefore, whenever possible, gender-specific examples have been provided in this section to emphasize the applicability and adaptability of these models to work with substance-abusing boys.

Lastly there are two additional sources that will be helpful for interested readers to develop knowledge and skills in rapport building with this population. The first is a book chapter by Kiselica (2001) that describes strategies to aid in developing a therapeutic relationship with school-age boys. Kiselica's chapter highlights several specific "male-friendly" approaches to working with boys in general, such as rethinking the traditional 50-minute time frame for counseling and the face-to-face office setting that can leave traditional boys feeling "a bit like a fish out of water" (p. 47). Using alternative time schedules and settings, and appropriate self-disclosure and humor, for example, can help relieve some of the constraints of the traditional counseling setting for these boys. The other source that may be helpful with this population is an article by Hanna, Hanna, and Keys (1999) that provides specific strategies for working with adolescents who present as "defiant" and "aggressive." The authors provided "fifty strategies" that are practical and easily adaptable to a variety of theoretical approaches.

INTERVENTIONS

As with the beginning of the prior section on establishing rapport, this section begins with a caveat. The term *interventions* in this section does not refer to individual versus group versus family interventions. Nor does it refer to empirically validated treatment models that are a multimodal combination of these interventions. An intervention in this section means a clinical strategy that one can employ in working with substance-abusing boys. It is worth noting that there are excellent sources in the literature that describe family- and community-based intervention models for adolescent substance abusers (Henggeler, Pickrel, & Brondino, 1999; Liddle, 1999; Liddle et al., 2001; Sheidow & Henggeler, in press).

Having the ability to recognize gender-specific issues and subsequently create appropriate interventions requires a certain mind-set by the clinician, in much the same way that a culturally competent counselor has a mind-set that picks up on the relevance of ethnocultural factors with each client. In this mind-set, one is open and vigilant throughout the assessment and treatment process in regard to recognizing important cultural- and gender-specific information. Consequently, one is able to have a better sense of how to tailor interventions to "fit" with the gender and cultural characteristics of one's clients and their families.

To help create this mind-set, consider the gender role strain paradigm proposed by Pleck (1981, 1995; cited in Brooks & Good, 2001). This paradigm assumes that

> 1.) gender role norms are often inconsistent and contradictory, 2.) a large proportion of gender role norms are violated frequently, 3.) social condemnation and stressful psychological consequences commonly follow role violations, and 4.) many characteristics and behaviors prescribed by gender role norms are psychologically dysfunctional. (Brooks & Good, p. 9)

Similarly, Levant (2001b) described seven traditional norms of masculinity that may apply to Jay's case: "1.) avoidance of all things feminine, 2.) restrictive emotionality, 3.) toughness and aggression, 4.) self-reliance, 5.) achievement and status, 6.) non-relational attitudes toward sexuality, and 7.) fear and hatred of homosexuals" (p. 424).

Thinking in terms of Jay's case, to what gender role norms might Jay be prescribing? How do these norms play out in his life? How might a traditional substance abuse intervention be tailored with the gender role strain in mind?

Woven throughout our look at the stages of change model and the MI approach presented above was the example of how Jay's attempts at not drinking alcohol and his male friends' comments about his being "a wimp" affected his decision making about drinking alcohol. There is an underlying assumption that this language of being a "wimp" (or not) somehow had some saliency for Jay. Specifically, the male role socialization process (initiating gender role norms) has an influence on why boys (and in this case, Jay) choose to abuse substances. In short, Jay wants to be seen as a strong, tough, self-reliant male among his peer group, and he is afraid that his male peers will judge him to be "less than" if he doesn't drink. Perhaps they have taken it a step further and called him a "wussy" for not standing up to the rules of probation (implying that his choice not to drink with them makes him somehow more feminine than they are). Comments like these can have great sway on Jay's decision making.

If we assess that this could be a possibility, then we need to tailor our interventions in a way that is developmentally sensitive to the male socialization process. In other words, if there is saliency there for Jay, then we can tap into it, and find the areas where his intrinsic motivation for change lies.

As was noted above, the salient issue is that Jay does not want to be belittled by his peers. Let's consider five well-known substance abuse counseling strategies and tailor them in a gender-specific way to fit with Jay's situation with his peers. The five strategies are (a) managing thoughts of using substances, (b) managing emotions, (c) refusing offers to use substances, (d) dealing with family and interpersonal problems, and (e) building a recovery support system (Daley & Marlatt, 2006).

Managing Thoughts of Using Substances

Jay has expressed that he has tried not to drink alcohol with his friends; however, they "razz" him when he refuses to drink with them. What are the thoughts that go through his mind at that point? "This is bullshit! I should be able to drink with them.... I can't have a good time with these guys if I don't drink ... and I'm sick and tired of them calling me a wuss!" At this point, one could talk with Jay about the ways that our thoughts influence our decisions to drink or not (how thoughts influence behaviors) and explore the beliefs behind the thoughts. Subsequently, one may begin to see the gender role norms that influence Jay's thinking. Perhaps the larger gender-influenced beliefs behind his thoughts are that "guys are supposed to drink heavily together ... that's what men do to have a good time."

There are many ways to go from here based on one's theoretical preferences, but essentially from a gender-based perspective, one will need to educate Jay about the male socialization process using age-appropriate language, emphasizing how traditional male role expectations about drinking can limit one's freedom of choice (an issue salient to Jay), and find appropriate ways to develop discrepancy between role expectations and what Jay wants to be like as a man. Is it true that "all men" drink heavily to have fun? Perhaps having the client look for evidence of this in real life can be powerful and informative. With Jay's case, he may also be limiting himself in his artistic expression, because of traditional male role expectations. Being artistic is another salient issue for Jay, and he may be better able to talk about this male socialization process through the content of artistic expression versus drinking behaviors. Once the process becomes clearer for Jay, then it can be applied to the content issue of "drinking like a man."

The underlying substance abuse recovery process that the counselor needs to make explicit is that Jay is learning to monitor his thoughts about drinking alcohol. Self-awareness about the influence of one's thoughts is key, and once he has this awareness, then when he starts to think about drinking again, he can respond to these thoughts with counterstatements and reminders about why he is choosing not to drink in that moment.

Managing Emotions

Regulating one's affect may be the single most difficult task for someone who is trying to avoid relapsing to substance-abusing behaviors. For boys, the inability to manage emotions is seen as a symptom of something larger happening within this specific developmental transition, perhaps as a symptom of the "crisis of boyhood" that Levant has so adeptly described (2001a). Levant wrote,

> By the time a boy enters school he has learned to hide and feel ashamed of two important sets of emotions: those that express vulnerability in one way or another (fear, sadness, loneliness, hurt, shame, and disappointment) and those that express neediness, caring, or connection to others. As a result boys become deeply alienated from themselves and from those closest to them, from whom they feel they must hide their shameful sense of vulnerability and neediness. (2001a, pp. 355–356)

In addition to this "crisis of boyhood," Jay has had no male role models who could have helped to foster healthy management of his emotional states and his subsequent behaviors. Additionally, Jay's peers were a major influence when he was a young boy around the ages of 12 to 16, a difficult developmental time period that was compounded by the absence of his father. The group of males that Jay affiliated with became the place where he learned about being a male. Anger and aggressive behaviors predominated this period of his life, perhaps because he was initiated by a group of boys rather than by an adult male role model(s) like his father, a teacher, or a coach. His father is trying to do this now as part of his own recovery, but Jay is not open to this at this point.

According to the gender role strain paradigm, "social condemnation" follows violation of the gender norms. Perhaps this behavior by Jay's father of reaching out and talking about his feelings and desires would contradict a traditional gender role norm that men should not express vulnerable emotions to other men. Because Jay has not been taught about expressing feelings, he could possibly feel uncomfortable because his father would be violating this norm. At that same time, there is part of him that may desperately need for his father to be there for him to coach him on how to manage his emotional life. Lastly, not only has he learned to stuff his emotions through the male socialization process, but he has also become accustomed to numbing any feelings other than anger through using substances.

The task with "managing emotions," then, will be to help Jay recognize when he is having feelings, accept what he is feeling, understand the causes of his feelings (often erroneous beliefs systems), and learn how to cope with his emotional states. This understanding about how negative (and sometimes positive) emotional states can lead to substance abuse will be vitally important as he attempts to address his substance abuse issues. Based on what was previously discussed, knowing and accepting that one has feelings can be particularly difficult for substance-abusing males.

Physical activity can be particularly helpful in coping with emotions. Getting onto the basketball court or out into the field to throw a baseball or football back and forth can really facilitate rapport building and dialogue, which can reinforce the value of counseling as a way to build a structured, safe outlet for practicing the expression of one's emotions to another human being.

Refusing Offers to Use Substances

This strategy is obviously related to managing thoughts and emotions. However, there is a reason that it is being discussed separately and after the other two. Identifying those times in the social context when one will need to refuse the offer to use substances is more difficult without having at least a preliminary understanding and acknowledgment of the importance of one's thoughts and feelings in this process.

This counseling strategy manifests as a skills-training exercise. Role plays and rehearsals are excellent ways to build one's skills in drink refusal. Incorporating gender-specific strategies with this intervention happens in the creative way that the counselor sets up the role play. For example, if the counselor is playing the role of the person offering the alcohol or other drug, then they have the opportunity to test the client's ability to deal with gender-influenced issues, such as the one discussed earlier about peers, alcohol expectancies, and male role expectations. This role play would teach Jay refusal skills that he can use in the face of being emotionally upset with his peers perceiving him as a "wimp."

Dealing With Family and Interpersonal Problems

From the assessment of Jay, two overarching potentially problematic areas have been identified that can be a focus for treatment interventions: peer affiliations and family instability. The first step in dealing with family and interpersonal problems is to know where the conflicts arise. We have discussed at length conflicts with Jay's peers. We will now focus on salient family issues that Jay will need to address at some point in the counseling process, keeping in mind the importance of the stages of change model that was discussed earlier and emphasizing readiness to change.

One conflict that has arisen recently in Jay's family has been over Jay's father trying to return to his family after a long absence due to his own addiction. Jay's father wants to assume the traditional male role of "head of household," whereas Jay has felt like the "man of the house" since his father left. Complicating this is the fact that Jay's mother has been the actual head of household by maintaining steady employment, providing for her sons' basic needs, and so on. Yet, as a woman, she does not feel that these vital activities have been respected by her sons or her estranged husband.

As Jay progresses through counseling, one hopes that he will be able to identify this family conflict as a real problem for him in terms of his emotional stability. Assuming that we get to this point, the next step is for Jay to take a look at his part in this conflict. What part has he played? First, he has been ambivalent about his father participating in family counseling. If his father became a part of the family therapy process, then Jay would need to acknowledge that his father might be "officially" back in the family. Secondly, Jay has denied the severity of his father's addiction. This can happen for a variety of reasons, such as (a) Jay would have to admit to others that his father was "an addict," (b) Jay fears that his father's addiction would remove the culpability factor from his father's behavior, and (c) Jay potentially would lose his perceived status as "man of the house" if his father were to return in full force to the home.

Once we have laid out what Jay's role is in the conflict, then it is time to encourage Jay to face these conflicts directly. If we have had some success in having Jay identify his feelings, then we are at an advantage in teaching Jay how to express his feelings directly to his loved ones. This would obviously be a major step, and one would assume that Jay would be in the action stage of change at this point in terms of addressing his substance abuse issues.

Building a Recovery Support Network

Admittedly, this active task of building a recovery support network assumes that individuals are in the preparation, action, or maintenance stages of change. It will require sustained effort and motivation to do this. For Jay, associating with substance-abusing peers (and not having non-substance-abusing peer supports) has been a way of life.

The first gender-influenced barrier to building a support network is getting over the idea that asking for help is somehow a weakness for a man.

At this point, Jay will be more familiar with the male socialization process and understand this dynamic more fully than when he began counseling. One can support Jay's self-efficacy in being able to identify supportive people in his life and find organizations that may support his goals.

Additionally, Jay really lacks an understanding that he has strengths that can be translated into successes. One can provide feedback to Jay that he appears to be an intelligent and creative individual, with significant artistic ability, and that he can have a charming personality at times. These are qualities of individuals that most people naturally want to help. It is just a matter of identifying these supportive people and organizations and moving past the gender-based barrier regarding asking for help.

SUGGESTIONS FOR FUTURE TRAINING AND RESEARCH

Much research is needed in several key areas relevant to substance abuse counseling with boys. First, research studies specific to sex and gender variables in the substance abuse and addiction research arena are few and far between relative to other variables involved in assessment and treatment interventions. In fact, it is only recently that the U.S. government began to require that grant proposals include both male and female participants in federally funded research studies regarding substance abuse and addiction.

Given the troubling statistics presented in the beginning of this chapter about adolescent male substance abuse, one might ask, "Why are we not doing more research about boys and young men?" Studies from both sides of the nature versus nurture contingencies are welcomed. We may find that adolescent males *are* more biologically vulnerable to substance abuse than females; or perhaps we will find out that this substance abuse crisis among boys is a symptom of Levant's (2001a) "crisis of boyhood." Either way, the substance abuse prevention and treatment fields will be advancing.

For example, although altering genetics (biological determinants) is not within the realm of counseling, providing information about genetic risk factors (such as a family history of alcohol dependence) can be helpful in both prevention and early intervention work for substance abuse issues (providing a fact about the risk involved in choosing to drink abusively at an early age) and in treatment for substance dependence (providing validation that one may have an inherited predisposition for an illness in much the same way that one would inherit a predisposition for developing atherosclerosis or diabetes).

Alternatively, with "initiation" of use, or "experimental" use of substances, happening primarily in adolescence, we need to know more about the specific environmental factors for boys that are increasing their risk for developing substance abuse problems. Addressing environmental risk factors for substance abuse is something that we can concretely do in counseling. In fact, several interventions presented above (e.g., refusing offers to use substances, dealing with family and interpersonal problems, and building a recovery support system) are focused on altering the environmental risk factors (the others were focused on how the adolescent male substance abuser responds to the environment, e.g., managing thoughts of using and managing emotions).

The second key area for more research relevant to substance-abusing boys is in understanding their motivations for change and/or their motivations to continue abusing substances. One of the key factors influencing motivation may very well be the influence of male role expectations about drinking behaviors, about being a sexual man, and/or about being masculine in general. To date, I found no sources for the application of motivational interviewing specifically with males or females. Gender-based research in this area would contribute greatly to our understanding about how to work with the motivational factors specific to adolescent males (and females).

Third, the highest rates of substance abuse among all age groups in the United States occur among males who are moving through the transition phase from late adolescence into young adulthood, that is, from boyhood into manhood. Specifically, in the *National Survey on Drug Use and Health*, 18- to 25-year-old males represented the highest percentage of persons aged 12 or older who met the criteria for alcohol dependence or abuse in the past year (Office of Applied Studies, 2003, 2004, 2005b). Clearly, this is our highest-risk group in the United States. We need to focus our research and training activities to help this vital population of young men.

Lastly, it is unfortunate that gender and cultural issues (which are obviously intertwined) can be overlooked in the process of providing assessments and treatment. This is a training issue. Counselor educators must train students to demonstrate gender- and culture-specific rapport-building and intervention strategies that offer "many avenues of entry" into their client's world.

Many substance abuse counselors who work with adolescent males will tell you that working with this population—specifically, developing empathy and building rapport with these boys—can be a challenging task. This chapter strove to create a gender-sensitive mind-set and to present the process of tailoring basic substance abuse counseling strategies in a gender-sensitive way to meet the needs of boys. Additionally, by discussing a few of the basic adjustment issues of this population and exploring the potential underlying gender-based meanings of their substance-abusing behaviors, it is hoped that the aim of creating greater therapeutic empathy with this population was achieved. Greater empathy leads to strong rapport building, which leads to creating collaborative and effective interventions that will have meaning for this population of boys.

REFERENCES

American Psychiatric Association. (2000). *Diagnostic and statistical manual of mental disorders: Text revision* (4th ed.). Washington, DC: Author.

Baer, J. S., & Peterson, P. L. (2002). Motivational interviewing with adolescents and young adults. In W. R. Miller & S. Rollnick (Eds.), *Motivational Interviewing: Preparing people for change* (2nd ed., pp. 320–332). New York: Guilford.

Brooks, G. R., & Good, G. E. (2001). Introduction. In G. R. Brooks & G. E. Good (Eds.), *The new handbook of psychotherapy and counseling with men: A comprehensive guide to settings, problems, and treatment approaches* (pp. 3–21). San Francisco: Jossey-Bass.

Childress, A. R. (2006). What can human brain imaging tell us about vulnerability to addiction and to relapse? In W. R. Miller & K. M. Carroll (Eds.), *Rethinking substance abuse: What the science shows, and what we should do about it* (pp. 46–60). New York: Guilford.

Daley, D.C. , E. Marlatt, G. A. (2006). *Overcoming your alcohol or drug problem: Effective recovery strategies: Therapist guide* (2nd ed.). New York: Oxford University Press.

Dowdall, G. W., & Wechsler, H. (2002). Studying college alcohol use: Widening the lens, sharpening the focus. *Journal of Studies on Alcohol* (Suppl. No. 14), 14–22.

Hanna, F. J., Hanna, C. A., & Keys, S. G. (1999). Fifty strategies for counseling defiant, aggressive adolescents: Reaching, accepting, and relating. *Journal of Counseling and Development, 77*, 395–404.

Hasin, D, Hatzenbuehler, M., & Waxman, R. (2006). Genetics of substance use disorders. In W. R. Miller & K. M. Carroll (Eds.), *Rethinking substance abuse: What the science shows, and what we should do about it* (pp. 61–77). New York: Guilford.

Henggeler, S. W., Pickrel, S. G., & Brondino, M. J. (1999). Multisystemic treatment of substance abusing and dependent delinquents: Outcomes, treatment fidelity, and transportability. *Mental Health Services Research, 1*(3), 171–184.

Henggeler, S. W., Schoenwald, S. K., Borduin, C. M., Rowland, M. D., & Cunningham, P. B. (1998). *Multisystemic treatment of antisocial behavior in children and adolescents.* New York: Guilford.

Henggeler, S. W., Schoenwald, S. K., Borduin, C. M., Rowland, M. D., & Cunningham, P. B. (2002). *Serious emotional disturbance in children and adolescents: Multisystemic treatment.* New York: Guilford.

Hesselbeck, V. M., & Hesselbeck, M. N. (2006). Developmental perspectives on the risk for developing substance abuse problems. In W. R. Miller & K. M. Carroll (Eds.), *Rethinking substance abuse: What the science shows, and what we should do about it* (pp. 97–114). New York: Guilford.

Isenhart, C. (2001). Treating substance abuse in men. In G. R. Brooks & G. E. Good (Eds.), *The new handbook of psychotherapy and counseling with men: A comprehensive guide to settings, problems, and treatment approaches* (pp. 246–262). San Francisco: Jossey-Bass.

Johnston, L. D., O'Malley, P. M., Bachman, J. G., & Schulenberg, J. E. (2006). *Monitoring the Future national survey results on drug use, 1975–2005: Volume 1. Secondary school students* (NIH Publication No. 06-5883). Bethesda, MD: National Institute on Drug Abuse.

Kiselica, M. S. (2001). A male-friendly therapeutic process with school-age boys. In G. R. Brooks & G. E. Good (Eds.), *The new handbook of psychotherapy and counseling with men: A comprehensive guide to settings, problems, and treatment approaches* (pp. 43–58). San Francisco: Jossey-Bass.

Levant, R. F. (2001a). The crises of boyhood. In G. R. Brooks & G. E. Good (Eds.), *The new handbook of psychotherapy and counseling with men: A comprehensive guide to settings, problems, and treatment approaches* (pp. 355–368). San Francisco: Jossey-Bass.

Levant, R. F. (2001b). Desperately seeking language: Understanding, assessing, and treating normative male alexithymia. In G. R. Brooks & G. E. Good (Eds.), *The new handbook of psychotherapy and counseling with men: A comprehensive guide to settings, problems, and treatment approaches* (pp. 424–443). San Francisco: Jossey-Bass.

Liddle, H. A. (1999). Theory development in a family-based therapy for adolescent drug abuse. *Journal of Clinical Child Psychology, 28*(4), 521–532.

Liddle, H. A., Dakof, G. A., Parker, K., Diamond, G. S., Barett, K., & Tejeda, M. (2001). Multidimensional family therapy for adolescent drug abuse: Results from a randomized clinical trial. *American Journal of Drug and Alcohol Abuse, 27*(4), 651–688.

Meyers, K., Hagan, T. A., Zanis, D., Webb, A., Frantz, J., Ring-Kurtz, S., et al. (1999). Critical issues in adolescent substance use assessment. *Drug and Alcohol Dependence, 55*, 235–246.

Miller, W. R., & Rollnick, S. (1991). *Motivational interviewing: Preparing people to change addictive behavior.* New York: Guilford.

Miller, W. R., & Rollnick, S. (2002). *Motivational interviewing: Preparing people for change* (2nd ed.). New York: Guilford.

Monti, P. M., Barnett, N. P., O'Leary, T. A., & Colby, S. M. (2001). Motivational enhancement for alcohol-involved adolescents. In P. M. Monti, S. M. Colby, & T. A. O'Leary (Eds.), *Adolescents, alcohol, and substance abuse: Reaching teens through brief interventions* (pp. 145–182). New York: Guilford.

Moos, R. H. (2006). Social contexts and substance use. In W. R. Miller & K. M. Carroll (Eds.), *Rethinking substance abuse: What the science shows, and what we should do about it* (pp. 182–200). New York: Guilford Press.

Office of Applied Studies. (2003). *Results from the 2002 National Drug Survey on Drug Use and Health: National findings* (DHHS Publication No. SMA 03-3836, NSDUH Series H-22). Rockville, MD: Substance Abuse and Mental Health Services Administration.

Office of Applied Studies. (2004). *Results from the 2003 National Drug Survey on Drug Use and Health: National findings* (DHHS Publication No. SMA 04-3964, NSDUH Series H-25). Rockville, MD: Substance Abuse and Mental Health Services Administration.

Office of Applied Studies. (2005a). *Treatment Episode Data Set (TEDS): 1993–2003. National admissions to substance abuse treatment services* (DASIS Series: S-29, DHHS Publication No. SMA 05-4188). Rockville, MD: Substance Abuse and Mental Health Services Administration.

Office of Applied Studies. (2005b). *Results from the 2004 National Drug Survey on Drug Use and Health: National findings* (DHHS Publication No. SMA 05-4062, NSDUH Series H-28). Rockville, MD: Substance Abuse and Mental Health Services Administration.

Pleck, J. H. (1981). *The myth of masculinity.* Cambridge, MA: MIT Press.

Pleck, J. H. (1995). The gender role strain paradigm: An update. In R. Levant & W. S. Pollack (Eds.), *A new psychology of men* (pp. 11–32). New York: Basic Books.

Prochaska, J. O., DiClemente, C. C., & Norcross, J. C. (1992). In search of how people change: Applications to addictive behavior. *American Psychologist, 47*(9), 1102–1114.

Sheidow, A. J., & Henggeler, S. W. (in press). Multisystemic therapy with substance using adolescents: A synthesis of the research. In N. Jainchill (Ed.), *Understanding and treating adolescent substance use disorders.* Kingston, NJ: Civic Research Institute.

Tober, G. (1991). Motivational interviewing with young people. In W. R. Miller & S. Rollnick (Eds.), *Motivational interviewing: Preparing people to change addictive behavior* (pp. 248–259). New York: Guilford.

10

Finding Inner Peace in a Homophobic World

Counseling Gay Boys and Boys Who Are Questioning Their Sexual Identity

MARK S. KISELICA, MARYANN MULÉ,
AND DOUGLAS C. HALDEMAN

Most boys want to fit in. They want to be accepted by others, and they want others to see them as being "normal." So, they pick up on cues from the world around them about what it means to be a boy and a man, and they try to live up to those expectations. More often than not, the messages they receive about masculinity are that a boy must be strong, he must be self-reliant, and above all else, he had better *not* be a fag. But there is no credible research suggesting that a boy can choose his sexual orientation. Either he is straight or he is gay or he is bisexual. But if he isn't heterosexual, he faces a social world that is potentially hostile and dangerous: On the playground, in the hallways, and sometimes even at home, he will hear the word *fag* as the ultimate nasty epithet.

What is it like for a boy who is attempting to survive in this environment to have questions about his sexual orientation? Where can he go and to whom can he turn for help in a culture that is still largely heterocentric and homophobic? If he determines that he is gay, what are the risks he faces if he reveals his sexual orientation to himself and to others? What are the benefits he will discover and the challenges he will face if he can become a truly integrated member of the gay community? How can a professional counselor help him during his journey to manhood? The purpose of this chapter is to answer these questions by describing the adjustment difficulties of gay boys and boys who are questioning their sexual orientation, and to describe the process of helping these boys to clarify their identity, reveal their sexual orientation to themselves and others, and achieve peace and acceptance within themselves during the transition to adulthood.

IDENTITY DEVELOPMENT FOR GAY BOYS DURING ADOLESCENCE

The great developmental psychologist, Erik Erikson (1987), theorized that one of the key challenges of adolescence is the development of a stable identity. During this period of development, a boy attempts to establish a clear and consistent identity in the face of conflicting messages he receives from others about who he should be. The teenager experiences a psychological struggle as he tries to sort through these messages and his inner feelings related to them. If he resolves this struggle successfully, then he will enter early adulthood with an emerging sense of his social, political, religious, career, and sexual identity. If he fails in this task, however, he will be confused about who he really is, and he will be uncertain about the role he will play in terms of the relationships he has with others.

The identity formation process is complicated for a boy who is questioning his sexual orientation because society gives him the strong message that he cannot have questions about his sexuality and that it is not OK to be gay. Although he may have a sense that he is a gay, many people and institutions in his life are likely to tell him that there is only one acceptable form of sexual orientation, and that orientation is heterosexuality. Faced with these conflicting messages between his internal and external world, he is likely to be scared to admit to himself and to others that he is gay, and to experience confusion, depression, and a loss of his sense of self (Shannon & Woods, 1991; Slater, 1988). Yet, if he is to ever experience an authentic ownership of who he really is, and some semblance of the relief and peace of mind that come with that ownership, he must come to terms with his homosexuality and form an identity that he can live with. Gradually acknowledging his gay orientation to himself and to others is referred to as the *coming-out process* (Gluth & Kiselica, 1994).

It is our contention that the coming-out process is crucial for the development of a healthy identity in gay youth. This thesis is supported by the positions of all of the major mental health associations, and is based on the scientific literature indicating that homosexual orientation per se is not pathological, but rather a normal variant of the human experience. No credible research suggests that being gay is a choice, or that it can be changed through psychotherapy or other means. Moreover, same-sex attraction is not "the problem" that must be fixed in order for gay boys to feel better about their lives. Rather, we view "the problem" as the detrimental effects of an antigay world on the emotional well-being and social adjustment of gay boys (Haldeman, 2006). And we recognize that mental health professionals can play a major role in resolving the real difficulties of boys who are gay by empathizing with the questions and hardships these boys are likely to experience, offering appropriate support for connecting with the gay community, understanding the coming-out process for gay youth, and practicing gay-affirmative counseling strategies with this population.

Before we review these topics, however, we must acknowledge that some boys are bisexual (experience sexual attraction toward both males and females) and others are transgendered (report that they "feel like a girl in a boy's body"). Although gay, lesbian, bisexual, and transgendered youth are all considered members of the community of sexual minorities, the process of counseling bisexual and transgendered boys warrants an in-depth discussion and special considerations that are beyond the scope of this chapter. Counselors interested in learning more about helping these populations are referred to several helpful publications pertaining to counseling bisexual individuals (Firestein, 2007; Potocz-niak, 2007; Smiley, 1997) and transgendered people (Carroll, Gilroy, & Ryan, 2002; Korell & Lorah, 2007; Mostade, 2006; O'Shaughnessy & Carroll, 2007).

THE CHALLENGES OF GAY AND QUESTIONING YOUTH

Boys who are questioning their sexual identity—that is, who are wondering if they might be gay while living in a heterosexual world—face the painful reality that even thinking about being gay is a violation of a pervasive heterosexual norm. Although they may hear gay-affirming messages while viewing a handful of major television shows, such as *Will and Grace* and *Queer Eye for the Straight Guy*, or the Logo Channel, which is a new lesbian and gay network from MTV, these positive images tend to be greatly overshadowed by the much more frequent, powerful, and ominous heterocentric norms that being gay is sick, homosexuality is a sin, and "queers" ought to be punished. A boy who thinks he might be gay realizes that he is likely to become the target of harsh judgments and might even become the victim of vicious ridicule and assault if he were to reveal his internal struggles to others. So, it is common for gay youth to struggle with self-acceptance, psychologically wall off their true self from the rest of the world, and socially isolate themselves from others (Hayes & Hagedorn, 2001). At the same time, the decision to hide an essential side of oneself from others can be emotionally draining for gay adolescents (George & Behrendt, 1987), in addition to preventing them from executing the normative developmental tasks of gay identity development.

The school setting can be an especially toxic environment for a gay or questioning boy. If he comes out, or even if he refrains from revealing his homosexuality but still appears to be a "fag," he is likely to be teased and bullied at some point, if not on a regular basis. He may feel that there are no safe harbors for him at school, and as a result, his academic performance may diminish, and he might drop out. One gay high school student shared this heart-wrenching account of the daily harassment he suffered at school:

> I just began hating myself more and more as each year the hatred toward me grew and escalated from just simple name calling in elementary school to having persons in high school threaten to beat me up, being pushed and dragged around the ground, having hands slammed in lockers and a number of other daily tortures. (GLSEN-CO, 2000, ¶ 25)

The type of living nightmare experienced by this young man is not rare. Research findings show that more than half of all gay teenagers fear harassment at school, and 97% report that their classmates have expressed antihomosexual attitudes (Sears, 1991). Nearly one fifth of gay students have been attacked due to their sexual orientation, and 80% suffer from a sense of severe social isolation (GLSEN-CO, 2000). Gay students are two to four and a half times more likely to skip school because of feeling unsafe en route to or at school than are other students (GLSEN-CO, 2000). Even straight students recognize that it is not safe to be a homosexual in the school setting: Gay students have been identified by their peers as the most likely victims of violence in their schools (GLSEN-CO, 2000).

Many children who feel threatened at school consider their homes to be a haven of safety where they can be themselves, receive much-needed emotional support from parents and siblings, and refortify themselves to face the outside world. Sadly, this may not be the case for a gay or questioning boy because his home may also be a potential arena for rejection and conflict. He may be all too aware of the fact that his family shares the fear and hatred of gays that are espoused by other members of society. Consequently, he may hold back from coming out to family members due to worries that he will be a disappointment to his parents and siblings, or due to fears that he will be abused, thrown out of his home, or forced into therapy to "cure" him of his homosexuality (Ben-Ari, 1995; Gerstel, Feraois, & Herdt, 1989). These fears are not uncommon, and they are not unfounded. In one study that included over 142 gay and bisexual boys, over two thirds of these youths were troubled about disclosing their sexual orientation to their family (D'Augelli & Hershberger, 1993). Nearly one fifth of gay males report that they have suffered physical violence at the hands of a family member as a result of their sexual orientation, and about one quarter report that they left home at least once because of conflicts about their sexual orientation with family members (GLSEN-CO, 2000). And some families continue to pressure their sons to undergo "conversion therapy" or "reparative therapy," which is the controversial practice of attempting to convert homosexuals into heterosexuals, even though there is no credible evidence to support the efficacy or safety for these treatments, and most psychologists consider the practice to be unethical (Johnson, 2005).

When disclosure to family members does occur, the reactions of the boy's family members are crucial to his well-being. If his family is supportive of the young man, he is likely to move forward in the coming-out process with a greater sense of optimism and happiness. But such support appears to be rare. In one study of gay youth, 89% of the participants indicated that their parents would not be likely to accept their homosexuality (Edwards, 1996). Negative family reactions, including emotional detachment, fears of estrangement, and a general lack of understanding, are common (Saltzburg, 2004). After disclosure, family relations can become strained, and the boy may feel as though he is drowning in a sea of turmoil. The news about his sexual orientation is usually experienced negatively and is followed by long-term distress for the family. Many parents report going through stages of shock, denial, guilt, and anger before accepting their gay son (Robinson, Walters, & Skeen, 1989). But some never reach any level of acceptance and can, at best, only acknowledge that their son is gay (Ben-Ari, 1995).

The last bastion of hope for some people who have been turned away by their school and their families is the church. But gay boys who have been raised according to some religious doctrines are unlikely to receive a warm welcome in many religious communities. For example, historically many organized Christian denominations have played a central role in maintaining homophobic social attitudes, because of espousing the doctrine that homosexuality is a sin that must be condemned. In order to achieve true salvation, the "sinner" must repent his evil ways and return to God's plan for him, which means he must shed his homosexual orientation and make his place in this world by taking a wife and having a family. Religious traditions that deliver these types of teachings leave "the gay adolescent to feel ashamed, alone, rejected, and abandoned by God" and by his church community (Barber & Mobley, 1999, p. 162). Although a growing number of churches now promote tolerance for gay members, our experiences with counseling gay boys are that many still feel like outsiders in their church communities.

So, a gay boy who receives support from his family, attends a school that is a gay-affirming environment, and is a member of a church community that truly welcomes him is likely to accept himself and thrive. By comparison, a gay youngster who experiences condemnation and rejection at every turn faces tremendous odds that he will emerge from his adolescent years confused about who he is and suffering from numerous psychic wounds and social difficulties. Indeed, gay youth are greatly overrepresented among children who drop out of school (GLSEN-CO, 2000); run away from home (Savin-Williams, 1994); become infected with a sexually transmitted disease (GLSEN-CO); abuse drugs (Ryan

& Hunter, 2003); are the victim of physical, verbal, and sexual abuse (GLSEN-CO); experience social isolation and homelessness (GLSEN-CO); and attempt and complete suicide (Macgillivray, 2004; Stone, 2003). Suicide is an especially vexing problem because it has been estimated that gay youth account for about one third of all adolescent suicides (Borowsky, Ireland, & Resnick, 2001). As a society, we have a moral obligation to fight the bigotry, rejection, and violence that are the root causes of these problems.

THE ROLE OF THE GAY COMMUNITY IN IDENTITY DEVELOPMENT

Although society at large can be a harsh place for boys who are gay or questioning their sexual orientation, the gay community offers its members a healing network of support that can assist young men who are grappling with an emerging gay identity. Whereas gay counselors are well acquainted with the gay community, heterosexual counselors tend to have a very limited understanding of the gay culture. Acquiring an understanding of this culture can be a tremendous asset to any counselor trying to help an adolescent gay client because the gay community is filled with resources and social outlets that can be used by young gay men to find a place of affirmation and belonging.

Heterosexual counselors are often surprised to learn that there is tremendous diversity within the gay community. Because heterosexual counselors tend to socialize with other heterosexuals, their opportunities to learn about the gay world are limited. Their understanding of this world is also affected by the adoption of the widespread stereotype that all gay men are sensitive, artistic, and effeminate. But gay men are much more varied and complex than that, which is a basic fact that straight counselors must grasp. In his informative description of this complexity, Haldeman (2006) reported that "some of us are indeed style conscious and spend our weekends perpetually redecorating, although at least an equal number spend their weekends watching sports and working on their cars" (p. 307). One might expect all gay men to be members of the Democratic Party because of its history of supporting liberal causes, yet there are traditional, conservative Republicans among the ranks of gay men. Some gay men are very public about their sexuality, celebrate the emerging visibility of gays in the media, and fight for legally recognized civil unions or gay and lesbian marriages, whereas others cringe at the thought of these practices.

Gay men vary, too, in the family structures they create for themselves; some stay single throughout adulthood, others choose partners for life, and an increasing number of gay men are becoming parents. And many gay men struggle with the same problems that straight men do, such as finding a romantic partner, having amicable relationships, and learning to be comfortable with the expression of tender feelings (Haldeman,

2006). Furthermore, many gay men, like their heterosexual counterparts, face intensified existential struggles about masculinity, largely due to the messages received early in life suggesting that homosexuality and masculinity are incompatible. The resolution of these complicated issues is even more crucial for gay men who are in primary long-term relationships with other men.

The gay community consists of people from all socioeconomic levels, and all racial and ethnic groups. Gay men of color may face particular challenges with a White-dominated gay culture, while at the same time experiencing rejection in their own cultural communities.

Why is the knowledge of this diversity important? Our clinical experiences with gay boys have taught us that socially isolated gay youth are often fearful that they won't be able to find a place that fits for them in the gay community. Swayed by the pervasive influence of stereotypes about gay men, a boy may believe that all gay men are highly feminized in their behavior, and that as a gay man, he will never lead a productive life or be in a satisfying long-term relationship. The gay community is sometimes seen as valuing a "hypermasculine" counterstereotype. If a boy does not measure up to these particular images of "the gay man," he may be reluctant to enter the gay world, even after he has reached the conclusion that he is a homosexual. So, by understanding the wonderful diversity among gay men, a counselor can help a gay boy searching for a connection with other gay males to learn that there are people and places with whom he would be a good fit.

A useful understanding of the gay world must go beyond a recognition of its diversity, however, to include a sense of its other strengths, which are numerous and noteworthy. Leaders of the gay movement have been tireless champions for equal rights and social justice. Gay pride festivals have become major social events to celebrate the beauty and interests of gay men. There are extensive gay support networks and numerous gay communities where one can be "out" in relative safety and with acceptance. Dozens of folk songs, websites, and chat rooms are dedicated to the subject of coming out. Counselors who know how to access these activities and resources can help a boy to explore and find his place in the gay community, which can be a powerful antidote to the destructive and painful effects of homophobia as he sorts his way through the coming-out process.

It is important for counselors to have an understanding of the availability of resources for gay and questioning youth in their areas. Counselors working in most urban areas have extensive resources from which to draw; in rural areas, however, the situation may be quite different. The same distinction goes for schools in various areas. Schools in large and medium-size metropolitan areas are more likely to have gay–straight alliances than are schools in rural areas. Additionally, the general social attitude toward gay and questioning boys and their families may be more challenging for counselors working in rural areas. This may make the accessing of resources even more critical.

MODELS OF GAY IDENTITY DEVELOPMENT
AND THE COMING-OUT PROCESS

According to sexual identity development theorists, one of the major developmental challenges all people face is the task of establishing a sexual identity. This developmental task tends to be more complicated for individuals who are gay, lesbian, and bisexual because they recognize that their emerging identities vary from the dominant heterosexual norm. Consequently, it can be very difficult for these individuals to admit their sexuality to themselves and to others. With regard to gay boys and men, *coming out* refers to a process in which a boy or man acknowledges to himself and to others that he is gay (Gluth & Kiselica, 1994). Stage models of sexual identity development and the coming-out process have been proposed to explain some of the common experiences of nonheterosexuals as they attempt to define who they are as sexual beings. Counselors should have some understanding of these models in order to help a boy understand where he is in terms of his sexual identity and the difficulties he might face as he grapples with the coming-out process.

Although there are several models of sexual identity development pertaining to sexual minorities, we have limited our discussion to the homosexual identity model proposed by Cass (1979) because it is widely accepted in the field as a respected framework for understanding sexual identity development in gay boys and men. Although Cass described sexual identify development for both male and female homosexuals, we have focused our overview of her model on aspects of gay identity development. An overview and a critique of the Cass model follow.

Cass's Model

Cass (1979) proposed that ongoing interactions between a gay boy or man and his environment will trigger important reconsiderations of his sexual identity. He can react to these experiences by moving on to more advanced levels of sexual identity development, characterized by an increasing awareness and acceptance of himself as a gay male, or by becoming stuck in his current state of sexual identity awareness. Cass also emphasized that what occurs in a gay man's private world may not be expressed in his public life. For example, although he may privately accept his identity as a gay male, he may choose to maintain a public image of himself as a heterosexual.

Cass's model (1979) consists of six stages: Identity Confusion, Identity Comparison, Identity Tolerance, Identity Acceptance, Identity Pride, and Identity Synthesis. During the Identity Confusion stage, the individual develops a growing awareness of his homosexual feelings, but does not share these feelings with others due to societal prohibitions against homosexuality. If he responds to this conflict by denying his feelings, he will remain stuck in confusion about his identity, but if he decides to seek more information about gay life, he will move on to the Identity Comparison stage. In this second stage, the individual begins to accept that he is gay, but he may also experience tremendous social alienation. He may attempt to cope with these feelings by presenting himself as being heterosexual to others, while privately moving forward to absorb the reality that he is gay. During the Identity Tolerance stage, the person makes attempts to contact other gay individuals to find affirmation for his gay orientation. Positive experiences with other gay males will help him to accept his identity, whereas negative experiences could cause him to retreat from any further acceptance of his homosexuality. In stage 4, Identity Acceptance, the individual can fully acknowledge to himself that he is gay, and his contact with other gay males increases, even though he might keep his sexual identity private from heterosexuals. When the Gay Pride stage is reached (stage 5, or Identity Pride), the individual immerses himself in the gay culture, and he experiences tremendous joy and pride in being gay, as well as anger toward society for its homophobia. Some men become gay activists during this stage, and others become very antiheterosexual, limiting their relationships to only members of the gay community. In the final stage, Identity Synthesis, the individual merges his private and his public self and fully integrates his gay identity into his self-concept. Also, he can look at heterosexuals complexly and with more acceptance as he embraces the belief that sexual identity is not necessarily the primary factor in determining relationships with others.

Limitations and Contributions of Cass's Model

Authorities on the subject of gay identity development have criticized the Cass model (1979) on several grounds. Cass proposed that the highest stage of identity development entails being open with others about one's gay identity. This conjecture downplays the potential dangers of coming out in highly homophobic contexts (Ponterotto, Utsey, & Pedersen, 2006). Cass's model suggests that gay men develop their sexual identity in a linear fashion, moving sequentially from one stage to the next. However, some individuals may move through the stages in "back-and-forth, and up-and-down ways" (Troiden, 1989, p. 47). Other models emphasize different elements of the individual's identity and implicate the gay community more strongly in the identity development process than does Cass (Fassinger & Arseneau, 2006). Nevertheless, Cass's framework is useful for professionals counseling gay youth because it illuminates the significance of coming out for sexual minority individuals. Research has shown that most boys who are gay become aware of same-sex attraction between the ages of 10 and 11, and most reveal their sexual orientation to another person between the ages of 16 and 20 (D'Augelli & Hershberger, 1993; Sears, 1991). Thus, the odds are that a boy with a gay orientation who enters counseling will do so during the early to middle stages of his gay identity development, filled with confusion about who he is, afraid to discuss his sexual attraction to other males, and unsure of how he can safely explore the gay community. Cass's model provides a counselor with an understanding of these issues so that he or she can be prepared to empathize with the young man's feelings while guiding him toward a greater acceptance of himself as a gay individual.

A GAY-AFFIRMATIVE COUNSELING PROCESS

We recommend that mental health professionals practice a gay-affirmative counseling process with gay boys, the purpose of which is to complete the following therapeutic tasks: (a) Question and change (your) assumptions and language about gay males and heterosexuals, (b) establish a safe environment for the client, (c) respect the client's life experience, (d) investigate the client's issues, (e) encourage the client to explore the gay community as appropriate and to develop a support network, (f) teach the client skills for a successful adjustment, and (g) address family issues as they emerge.

Question and Change Your Assumptions and Language About Gay Males and Heterosexuals

Counselors who work with gay youth must become aware of their own stereotypes about gay males and work to eradicate their biases about this population. As was mentioned earlier in this chapter, for heterosexual counselors, this involves moving beyond stereotypical images of gay men and understanding the great diversity, complexity, beauty, and strengths of the gay community. Any counselor who believes that it is a sin to be gay or believes that homosexuality is a disease that can be cured should refer a gay or questioning client to another mental health professional. Heterosexual counselors will have to learn how to make adjustments in the language they use, which might reflect a heterosexual bias. For example, they must understand that the notion of parents is not limited to the traditional conceptions of a mother (woman) and father (man) because gay men are quite capable of raising children, and many gay couples do.

The client should be consulted as to what terminology best suits his own sense of identity. For most men and boys who acknowledge an erotic and affiliative attraction to other males, and are developing a certain degree of openness about this, the term *gay* is preferred. Some young people presently use the historically offensive term *queer* to indicate any variation in identity from heteronormativity, and to neutralize the term's former toxic power. The term *homosexual* is still sometimes used in general comparative discussions of sexual orientation, but is almost never applied to individuals because of its association with a former time in which "homosexuals" were considered to be mentally ill. Furthermore, some young people may identify as *bisexual*, which in youth may or may not be a transitional identifier. In any case, it is essential to ask the client how he identifies. If the client is uncertain and is questioning whether or not he may be gay, other adjustments in language use may be necessary during counseling.

First and foremost, the counselor should avoid language that clearly assumes the client is heterosexual. For example, "Is there someone special in your life?" is preferable to "Do you have a girlfriend?" The term *lifestyle* is to be avoided in descriptions of gay individuals or as a group because it incorrectly assumes that sexual orientation is chosen and trivializes the life experiences of gay men. Even more offensive is the demonstration of stereotypic beliefs regarding the lives of gay men and their relationships, as evidenced by ignorant and bigoted statements such as "Maybe you just haven't found the right girl yet" or, in reference to a gay male sexual relationship, "Which one of you is the man?" Above all, the counselor working with gay and questioning youth should strive to maintain a bias-free experience for clients in which they can freely explore the personal meanings of some potentially very confusing feelings.

Some gay and lesbian counselors may need to reflect on another bias referred to as *heterophobia*, which is fear or dislike of heterosexuals resulting from traumatic experiences perpetrated toward sexual minorities by the heterosexual world (Haldeman, 2006). Gay and lesbian counselors struggling with heterophobia might project their own issues with heterosexuals onto a gay or questioning boy and thereby thwart his attempts to develop healthy relationships with straight people, or encourage him prematurely to claim a gay identity. Just as straight counselors must monitor for any homophobic tendencies, gay and lesbian counselors must challenge themselves to be sure that their work is not affected by heterophobic bias.

Establish a Safe Environment for the Client

The counseling setting must be a safe place for gay and questioning boys "to speak openly about their experiences and to expect—at the very least—understanding and empathy in return" (Haldeman, 2006, p. 304). Using gay-sensitive language will be a good starting point in creating safety, but unless there are systemic, gay-affirming policies and messages in the environment, a gay or questioning youth is unlikely to approach a counselor for help. Consequently, in both school and agency settings, counselors must be advocates for policies that prohibit hate slurs and violence directed at a person or group's sexual orientation (Callahan, 2001; Hollander, 2000). Counselors also must support the creation and maintenance of gay–straight alliances, whose purpose is to promote the diversity and acceptance of every individual (Hollander, 2000). Each professional counselor should become familiar with the supports already in place for the gay community and advertise these within the community agencies, schools, and private practices in which he or she works (Israel & Selvidge, 2003). All surrounding visual and auditory information that counselors provide should challenge the traditional definitions of sexuality and sexual orientation that are the recognized norm (Carroll & Gilroy, 2001). School counselors should support the adoption of history lessons and have books pertaining to the gay experience in educational curricula (Muñoz-Plaza, Quinn, & Rounds, 2002). Lastly, no matter where a counselor works, he or she should encourage all other staff members to promote the safety and individuality of every person. Related to this ideal, the counselor can post a sign on his or her door that reads, "SAFE ZONE: This space respects all people regardless of sexual orientation, ethnic background, age, ability, and gender."

Respect the Client's Life Experience

Overlapping with the principle of creating safety, the counselor must always respect the client's life experience. For example, if the counselor is heterosexual, he or she must be careful not to draw too many parallels between his or her experience and that of the client, because the client might get the impression that the counselor is minimizing if not missing altogether the unique experience of what it is like to be a gay or questioning boy in a heterosexual world (Haldeman, 2006). The counselor especially must be careful not to normalize bullying as being "normal kids' stuff" with a gay or questioning boy because the extreme harassment some gay boys experience, or even those who are perceived or assumed to be gay, can be a living hell (Haldeman, 2006). Instead, the counselor should always try to understand the perspective of the youth, showing an acute sense of empathy and unconditional positive regard (Lemoire & Chen, 2005). Most of all, the counselor must affirm the young man and welcome the questions he has about his sexuality and the gay community.

Investigate the Client's Issues

One of the crucial decisions a gay boy must make is whether or not he should reveal his sexual orientation to others. Related to his dilemma associated with coming out, it is imperative that counselors never direct an adolescent in what to do. Instead, the counselor should explore with the client how he feels about coming out by asking the adolescent questions that will help him to clarify what he hopes to achieve by telling other people about his sexual orientation, anticipate the reactions of others to this disclosure and the impact of those reactions on him, and plan for how he intends to respond to their reactions (Lemoire & Chen, 2005). During the discussion of these issues, it can be helpful to teach the client the difference between being a "closeted" (private) and an "open" or "out" (public) gay person, and the pros and cons of each way of relating to the world (Barber & Mobley, 1999).

The young person who is truly questioning his sexual orientation presents particular challenges for the counselor. With such individuals, it is especially critical not to make inferences or assumptions about his sexual identity, or to use these as a basis for influencing the client, but to allow the client to develop a sense of identity on his own with facilitation from the counselor. Just as a homophobic counselor reaction that would recommend conversion therapy is inappropriate, so a knee-jerk encouragement to "come out of the closet and get on with it" is also ill advised. Rather, the counselor should inquire deeply and thoughtfully of the client what he questions about his sexual self—and in this domain, questions about the individual's erotic fantasy life and autoerotic behavior are crucial. Is the boy truly confused about his erotic attractions to both sexes? Is his experience of attraction to other males generalized, or is it localized on one particular person? Does he endorse a primary erotic response to other males, but is he afraid of the consequences if he does come out as gay? These are some of the many questions that counselors working with questioning boys need to explore in depth.

Some gay boys from different racial and ethnic backgrounds have cultural issues that can complicate the coming-out process. For example, sometimes Asian American and African American families view being gay as a White phenomenon. Thus, Asian American and African American boys might be rejected by their cultural communities for engaging in a "White lifestyle." Yet, these same boys may be targets of racism in White communities (Barber & Mobley, 1999), and therefore can find it difficult to create a home for themselves in the gay community, which is largely White (Haldeman, 2006). Furthermore, gay identity can interact with racial identity in unique ways:

> For example, a Black gay male with a conformity ego status tends to devalue his own racial group while idealizing Whites. Thus, for him, interaction in the White gay community is more comfortable and even preferable to being with Black gays or heterosexuals. The perspective changes when this Black gay male enters into the immersion/emersion ego status. He now idealizes his own racial group and devalues and denigrates Whites. At this time, he would tend to reject the larger White gay community. (Barber & Mobley, p. 171)

Cutting across racial and ethnic lines is the problem of trauma, which is an especially widespread and salient issue with gay youth that must be sensitively investigated by the counselor. Haldeman (2006) warned that nearly all gays "have experienced some kind of trauma related to harassment, abuse, discrimination, or violence in their lives" (p. 305). Furthermore, "If a gay client has experienced chronic depression or anxiety or has become intimacy avoidant in relationships, it is possible that there is unresolved trauma in the client's background" (Haldeman, 2006, p. 306). Thus, when these symptoms are present, the counselor should ask the boy to describe any experiences of harassment and assaults he might have experienced. Because these forms of abuse can cause a boy to hate himself for being gay, the counselor should assess for signs of internalized homophobia and help the boy to understand the sources of these beliefs and their impact on how he feels about himself (Barber & Mobley, 1999). Furthermore, because the school environment can be an especially venomous place for a gay youth, the counselor must discuss with the boy any harassment issues he has faced at school and help the boy to figure out ways to be safe in his school surroundings. When it is clear that the school provides either implicit or explicit condoning of gay bashing, then the counselor must become an advocate for social justice with the school system on the young man's behalf. (For extensive pertinent discussions of this approach to counseling, see Chen-Hayes, 2000, 2001.)

An examination of trauma can also lead to a discussion of the strength required to cope with it. It is true that when a young man comes out as gay, he relinquishes the possibility of heterosexual privilege in a homophobic culture. At the same time, he gains the unparalleled benefit of being truly himself, and thus discovers the source of strength he will need his entire life as a gay man in American society, coping with obstacles of all magnitudes. Above all, the "takeaway message" should be that what needs changing is our heterocentric and sometimes homophobic society, not the gay individual.

Although a counselor should never underestimate the degree to which sexual orientation concerns can affect a young man's life, the counselor also should never assume that all of the problems a gay adolescent is dealing with are focused on his sexual orientation (Pearson, 2003). Also, in some cases, a gay boy seeking counseling may have no interest in discussing his sexual orientation but wants to discuss other concerns. Thus, the counselor should be prepared to discuss gay issues with the client as much as the boy needs to, while remaining ready to discuss other challenges that would be experienced by any adolescent (Pearson), such as making friends, clarifying a career direction, and succeeding in school. Additionally, counselors need to be attentive to collateral mental health issues that may have nothing to do with the client's questions about sexual orientation.

Help the Client to Explore the Gay Community and Develop a Support Network

Earlier in this chapter, we encouraged counselors to learn about the gay community in order to assist a boy who is ready to explore that world as part of the process of clarifying his sexual identity and developing a support network. A word of caution related to that suggestion is in order. Although we endorse the idea of helping boys with an emerging gay identity to learn about the world of gay men, counselors must be careful not to push a boy into the gay culture until it is clear that the youngster has admitted to himself that he is gay, and that he is ready to learn more about the gay community. It is also prudent for counselors to bear in mind that the parents of some boys will strongly object to this practice as being a legitimate subject in counseling and might even punish a boy for exploring the gay world. For this reason, at the start of counseling, the counselor must establish with the family that all communications between the client and the counselor are confidential, except in cases in which there is a duty to break confidentiality, such as when a boy reveals that he has been sexually abused or there is a serious threat to harm himself or someone else. Under the protection of this confidentiality, a boy can safely explore the gay community, and the counselor's role during this exploration is to help the young man to clarify his emotional and cognitive reactions to what he learns about the diverse world of gay men.

Fortunately, there are numerous healthy websites available that can help a boy to learn about the gay culture and answer important questions he might have about his sexual identity. Here are a few excellent sites to which a counselor can direct a gay youth:

- OutProud, the National Coalition for Gay, Lesbian, Bisexual & Transgender Youth (n.d.), serves the needs of these young men and women by providing advocacy, information, resources, and support. The goal of OutProud, whose website is http://www.outproud.org, is to help queer youth become happy, successful, confident, and vital gay, lesbian, and bisexual adults. It can help gay youth with the following questions: How do I know if I'm gay? What does it mean to practice "safer sex"? How do I come out to my parents? OutProud also furnishes a list of high-quality books pertaining to gay youth.
- The National Youth Advocacy Coalition (n.d.), which is dedicated to improving the lives of gay, lesbian, bisexual, transgender, and questioning youth, operates a website, http://www.nyacyouth.org, which contains links to several talklines and hotlines, and to local support groups and church congregations that are welcoming to the sexual minority community.
- The website http://www.freetobeme.com (Freetobeme.com, n.d.) emphasizes information and tools to help youth understand homosexuality and same-sex attraction; help, support, and alternatives for youth who are or wonder if they are gay or lesbian; helpful information for friends and acquaintances of gay and lesbian youth; and resources for those who work with youth who are or wonder if they might be gay or lesbian.
- The GLBT National Help Center (2005) operates a website (http://www.glnh.org/index2.html) and a toll-free number (1-800-246-7743) gay youth can call for confidential support and counseling.

- The Trevor Project (2007) also operates a website, http://www. thetrevorproject.org, and toll-free numbers (1-866-488-7386 and 1-800-850-8078) for gay youth, with a particular emphasis on preventing suicide and helping gay boys who are in a crisis.
- The website http://www.teenwire.com, sponsored by Planned Parenthood Federation of America (1999–2007), provides information in both English and Spanish regarding youth sexuality. The "Archive" section includes specific articles pertaining to, but not limited to, the topics of coming out to friends, understanding varying sexual orientations, and comparing worldviews about being gay. Inquiries that youth have pertaining to safe sex practices, developing healthy sexual relationships, and general issues concerning sexual identity are addressed in a question-and-answer format.

The counselor can process with the young man his reactions to these websites. While doing so, the counselor should bear in mind that boys tend to have unfettered access to the Internet and spend hours surfing the Net. In our clinical experiences, gay boys (like straight boys!) are adept at finding pornographic websites that portray the sexual objectification of people. In our discussions with gay boys in counseling, some have told us that they consider the Internet to be a safe place for them to learn about gay sex. But we have learned from these boys that much of what they discover is not of a healthy nature. Thus, the counselor must discuss with a gay boy what lies out there on the information superhighway, and encourage him to think about the fact that sexual objectification is a problem that cuts across sexual orientations. The counselor and the boy can compare the different ways that gay sexual relationships are addressed between constructive sites, such as OutProud.org and teenwire.com, and pornographic ones. Engaging a boy in these discussions can help him to distinguish safe and healthy forms of gay sexual relations from those that are potentially dangerous and unhealthy. It is especially important that the young man know how to protect himself from becoming infected with a sexually transmitted disease (STD), such as HIV/AIDS, which has been a resurgent problem among young men in the gay community. Educating him about the prevention and transmission of, and testing for, STDs is crucial, particularly if he is ready to become sexually active (Gluth & Kiselica, 1994).

One of the wonderful features about the gay-support websites mentioned above is that they contain guidance about how a gay boy can link up with other youths who have questions about their sexual identity, as well as information about finding local gay support groups and organizations. Thus, a gay youngster can use these resources to help him develop a support network consisting of other gay youth. But the support network need not be limited to other gay individuals because there are many enlightened heterosexuals whose hearts are completely open to their gay sons and brothers. For example, research has established that about three quarters of gay youth reveal their sexual identity to a trusted friend and about a third to a caring family member, and these individuals have reacted to the disclosure in a supportive manner (D'Augelli & Hershberger, 1993). Many schools now have special student organizations consisting of many straight students, known as *gay–straight alliances,* whose purpose is to create communities of caring for all individuals, regardless of one's sexual orientation. Several professional organizations, such as the American Counseling Association, the American School Counselor Association, and the American Psychological Association— the memberships of which are largely heterosexual—have issued either position statements or practice guidelines whose aim is to support gay individuals and to suggest gay-sensitive approaches to helping the gay population. Thus, a large number of heterosexual lay and professional people are eager to welcome and help gay youth during their transition to adulthood. We recommend that counselors assist their gay clients to cautiously seek out these compassionate heterosexuals with the goal of adding them to a young man's support network. A gay young man who can construct a support system in both the gay and mainstream worlds will have multiple oases of safety he can turn to when he needs the healing benefits of acceptance, companionship, and affection.

Finding a supportive spiritual community can be another vital part of a support network for a gay boy. Because many ministers and the members of their congregations teach that homosexuality is a sin, gay boys often feel that there are no safe outlets for them to explore and define their spiritual beliefs. Some gay young men develop a reactive hostility toward organized religion as a result of these teachings. To help offset these negative consequences, the counselor who works with gay youth must get to know local church communities and their respective stands on homosexuality. Guiding a boy to a minister and church community that are identified as "open and affirming"—meaning that the faith community actively encourages lesbian, gay, bisexual, and transgender members, and generally supports gay rights and gay civil unions and/or marriages—can be an important step in helping the young man in his spiritual growth and his longing for a place in a caring community. It should also be emphasized, however, that many gay boys and men seek and achieve spiritual growth without participating in any organized religion. These latter individuals may have a need to discuss their spiritual issues without being directed to a faith community.

Teach the Client Skills for a Successful Adjustment

It takes a tremendous amount of skill to succeed with the challenges of being a gay boy in a heterocentric world. In order to prepare a gay youngster for these challenges, Barber and Mobley (1999) recommended that counselors teach gay youth important coping skills. Cognitive restructuring can be used to transform negative self-talk and self-deprecating impressions that have been internalized from a homophobic society about being gay into positive self-statements and affirming images about a gay sexual orientation. Assertiveness training can provide a gay young man with tactics to confront heterosexism and homophobia. And through role-play rehearsal, a gay boy can practice establishing friendships with other gay males, coming out to others, and developing support networks (Barber & Mobley, 1999).

Address Family Issues as They Emerge

A positive reaction by parents to a son's disclosure that he is gay can boost his self-esteem and help him to counteract any homophobic perceptions he might have about himself. Conversely, negative reactions can be an assault to the young man's self-esteem and intensify his internalized homophobia (Coleman, 1981–1982). According to DeVine (1984), family reactions can vary across time, and families tend to go through various adjustments as they attempt to deal with the issue of homosexuality. Prior to disclosure, family members may have no idea that a member of their family is gay, or they may suspect that he is but choose not to discuss the matter. After the gay member comes out to his family, it is common for family members, particularly parents, to experience guilt and anger, and to cope with the disclosure by insisting that their gay son keep his sexual identification a secret from others. However, some families are able to move beyond these initial reactions, accept their son's sexual orientation, and fully integrate the fact that they have a gay son into their sense of themselves as a family, while supporting their son's decision to be open about his sexual identity with the extended family and the outside world (DeVine, 1984).

In light of these considerations, it is clear that family counseling can be vital in helping family members move toward acceptance, stability, and harmony following a son's decision to come out to them. So, if a client has begun the process of coming out to his family, the counselor should explore with the boy the possibility of engaging his family in counseling to assist everyone with the process of adjusting to the impact of his sexual orientation on the family. Coenen and Kiselica (2000) have suggested that problem-solving communication training is an ideal framework for counseling families when one of its members is gay. In brief, this approach to counseling consists of four stages. During stage 1, the engagement stage, the counselor has separate meetings with the gay son and his parents, helping both parties to air their reactions to the disclosure and empathizing with those reactions. The skills-building stage follows, during which family members are taught how to reflect each other's perspectives and to engage in problem-solving strategies for evaluating and implementing various potential solutions to issues that might arise. As son and parents consider different alternatives, the counselor may have to help parents to unlearn myths about gay men (e.g., the parents did something "wrong," and that is why their son is gay) by teaching them how to use cognitive restructuring of those stereotypes. While the family negotiates its issues during stage 3, the conflict resolution stage, inappropriate behavior (e.g., screaming and blaming) is interrupted and labeled, instruction is provided, appropriate behavior is modeled, and the family is required to replay certain exchanges using appropriate skills. In the final stage of counseling, disengagement, the family becomes more adept at utilizing its skills, and the counselor gradually reduces his or her input and guidance until the counseling process is terminated.

The Internet can be a fabulous tool while helping the families of gay youth. Parents, Families and Friends of Lesbians and Gays, known as PFLAG (n.d.), maintains the website http://www.pflag.org. PFLAG promotes the health and well-being of gay, lesbian, bisexual, and transgender persons, their families, and their friends through the following: support, to cope with an adverse society; education, to enlighten an ill-informed public; and advocacy, to end discrimination and to secure equal civil rights. PFLAG provides opportunity for dialogue about sexual orientation and gender identity, and acts to create a society that is healthy and respectful of human diversity. PFLAG meetings are universally known for their warmth and support, as well as being an excellent resource for family members wishing to educate themselves about the subjects of sexual orientation and gender identity. The numerous national chapters of PFLAG make their meetings accessible to almost everyone, even those living in rural areas. We also recommend http://www.bidstrup.com/parents.htm (Bidstrup, 2000). The purpose of this website is to help parents of gay youth with their questions and worries about their son's homosexuality. It is superb! Counselors can encourage parents and other family members to visit these sites to learn accurate information about gays, dispel myths about this population, and find support as they assist their son with his coming-out process.

Summary

Helping a gay youth to cope with the process of coming out to himself and others is a complicated process that involves the completion of numerous therapeutic tasks. In the following case study, we illustrate these tasks through a gay-friendly approach to counseling with a boy named "Luke." Luke and the other people described in this case study are not particular people but a composite of many different people we have helped in counseling by using the gay-affirmative strategies that are described in this chapter. Any similarities between the individuals mentioned in this case study and an actual person are purely coincidental.

GAY-AFFIRMATIVE COUNSELING
WITH LUKE: A CASE STUDY

Luke was a White, 16-year-old high school student who started dropping in to see his school counselor, Mr. K., during the early part of his junior year. Luke was the middle child in a middle-class, Roman Catholic family consisting of him, his parents (Mr. and Mrs. B.), his three brothers, and his one sister. Luke was an above-average student who maintained A and B grades, and he was a reporter for his school paper. He was 5 feet 9 inches tall, and he was considerably chunky, weighing approximately 210 pounds.

Luke liked to hang out in Mr. K.'s office before and after school and sometimes during his study periods. During his initial contacts with Mr. K., Luke presented himself as a cheerful, happy-go-lucky person who loved to chat about his fellow students and school events. During some of those early visits, Luke spent part of the time discussing his relationship with another boy, named Ted. Initially, Luke made only passing comments about Ted as he jumped rapidly from one subject to the next. However, as time went by, it became clear that Luke was very preoccupied about Ted, expressing a passionate interest in Ted that soon became the dominant focus of his conversations. Luke was fascinated with Ted and idolized him for his intelligence, good looks, athletic talents, and admirable interpersonal skills. Because Luke was enamored with Ted and so sensitive to the slightest responses Ted made to Luke, Mr. K. hypothesized that Luke might be experiencing a homosexual attraction to Ted, so Mr. K. did everything in his power to empathize with Luke's experience and tried to become for Luke his mirror on life.

About 6 weeks into the school year, Mr. K.'s suspicions were confirmed one afternoon when Luke closed the door to Mr. K.'s office, sat in the chair next to Mr. K.'s desk, and, in a shaking voice, asked Mr. K. if the two of them could discuss "a problem." In a very receptive and gentle manner, Mr. K. encouraged Luke to state what was on his mind, at which point Luke blurted out, "I'm gay." Mr. K. responded by admitting to Luke that he had suspected Luke was gay, had been very concerned for Luke because he sensed Luke was troubled, and thanked Luke for sharing this highly personal news with him. Subsequently, a rambling river of information and feelings poured out of Luke, including his accounts of when he first felt attracted to boys, the difficulty he had had trying to decide to whom he could reveal his sexual identity, the antigay values of his parents and brothers, and his tortured attraction to Ted. Mr. K. listened to Luke with a compassionate expression on his face for about 30 minutes until the buzzer sounded over the school intercom system, indicating that it was time for a change of classes. At that instant, Mr. K. told Luke that it was perfectly understandable that he was upset and confused by all the things that were racing through his mind, and he invited Luke to come back either after school or the next day so he could discuss what it was like for him to reveal his sexual orientation to Mr. K. and to say anything else that might be on his mind.

Luke took up Mr. K. on his offer, showing up at his office after the end of the last class period. Mr. K. welcomed Luke back into his room, and offered him a snack as the two discussed the session they had had earlier that day. This time, Mr. K. did most of the talking, praising Luke for his courage in coming out to Mr. K., assuring Luke that anything he told Mr. K. would be kept in the strictest of confidence (except for "duty-to-warn" exceptions), and predicting for Luke that he might experience relief yet quite a few ups and downs emotionally as he considered his next step now that he had revealed his sexual orientation to another person. At the end of the session, Mr. K. gave Luke his home numbers and informed him that he could call Mr. K. if he were ever in a crisis. Mr. K. admitted that, as a heterosexual, he couldn't possibly know how difficult it must be for Luke to live with the fears he had related to his sexual identity questions, but he would do everything in his power to understand Luke's experience. Mr. K. also promised Luke that he would be there for him for as long as he needed Mr. K.'s support.

For the rest of the school year, Luke visited Mr. K. every day and sometimes two or three times a day. Luke used Mr. K. as the secure base upon which he would build his support network as he attempted to clarify his feelings about being gay and identify the people in his world to whom he would reveal his sexual identity. One of the first things Mr. K. did to foster that process was to have a frank discussion with Luke about his own sexual orientation and prior struggles with homophobia. Mr. K. informed Luke that he was a heterosexual and that he had worked for many years to become aware of and overcome his own irrational fears and biases about gays that had once been a part of his worldview. Luke appreciated Mr. K.'s honesty about these issues, which prompted the two of them to engage in numerous, intimate conversations about the pejorative messages each of them had received about gays during their formative years. These discussions unveiled a considerable amount of hatred that Luke had for himself. Consequently, Mr. K. explained to Luke how antigay messages can be so cruel and persistent that gay boys and men sometimes begin to apply these harmful messages to themselves. He urged Luke to consider that the same process had occurred inside Luke, and he taught Luke some methods for restructuring his homophobic self-statements. Mr. K. also told Luke that he genuinely felt proud to know Luke, and that he enjoyed Luke's company.

Mr. K. broached the subject of safe sex with Luke. Although Luke was not ready to engage in sex with another male, he often had urges to do so. Therefore, Mr. K. talked with Luke about AIDS and other STDs, accentuating the use of condoms as a highly reliable practice for preventing STD infection. He also encouraged Luke not to rush into any sexual relationships until he was emotionally ready to do so, encouraging Luke to think about developing close emotional relationships first.

Mr. K. regularly checked with Luke to determine if he was the target of ridicule or abuse by others, and indeed, this was often the case, even though Luke had not yet come out to anyone except Mr. K. Luke had slightly effeminate qualities, and other boys his age had picked up on this and periodically taunted him for them. For example, they started a ritual during which they would surround him, call him "Shaky Luke," push him back and forth, and then douse him with water, talcum powder, or soda. He typically responded to these bullying tactics by giggling and wrestling some of the boys to the ground, which allowed him to have physical contact with them. During their analyses of these incidents, Mr. K. helped Luke to see that he had mixed feelings about them. For example, although he hated the harmful intent of the boys' name-calling, he also liked wrestling with them because it gave him an opportunity to have close physical contact with some of the boys to whom he was sexually attracted. Mr. K. affirmed Luke's desire to be close to other males, but he also challenged Luke to see the self-defeating dynamic he was enabling with these other boys. He informed Luke that it would be possible to experience the type of intimacy he wanted with boys like Ted and the other boys who taunted him, but that such closeness could be achieved only if and when Luke was ready to investigate the community of gay men.

Luke admitted that he was keenly interested in learning more about the gay culture, but he was afraid about what might happen if that interest were to be discovered by others. Mr. K. responded by explaining the difference between being a closeted and an openly gay male, and informed Luke that gay men vary as to when and how much they are willing to reveal their sexual orientation to the outside world. Based on these discussions, Luke decided to explore some helpful websites for gay youth, and through one of those sites, he identified a chat room where he was able to talk with other gay boys and lesbian girls about his concerns and questions. When it was clear to Mr. K. that Luke was ready to explore gay life even further, he contacted a local community counselor who ran a special counseling center for gay youth. Toward the end of the academic year, Luke made a couple of visits to the center and he started to attend a support group there.

Over the course of the summer months between his junior and senior year, Luke continued to visit the gay youth center, and he called Mr. K. from time to time to update him about how things were going. By the time the summer was over, Luke had made two important decisions. First, he wanted to change the way he related to boys in his school. Second, although he was not ready to reveal his sexual orientation to any of the other students at his school, he was determined to inform his parents and siblings because he wanted them to know the truth about him before he went away to college.

In light of these goals, Mr. K. continued to support Luke with his school-related issues. For example, he taught Luke assertiveness strategies to use with other boys when they taunted him. Specifically, instead of enabling the abuse by giggling and "wrestling," Luke learned to yell, "Knock it off!" and to quickly walk away. This strategy deterred most of his assailants from bullying him any further, although one especially sadistic boy was determined to keep Luke as one of his targets, so he raised the level of abuse directed toward Luke. That boy began to use a malicious tone as he called Luke a *fag* and a *queer.* One day, he pushed Luke into the school pool, and pressed Luke's head underwater for so long that Luke nearly passed out. When this happened, Mr. K. arranged for a meeting between a vice principal, Luke, and his assailant. In the supportive presence of these two men, Luke told the other boy that he wanted the abuse to stop, and the vice principal affirmed that desire by warning the other student that he would face serious disciplinary actions should he ever threaten or cause bodily harm to Luke again. He also told the bully that the verbal taunting had to stop as well. Although these warnings marked the end of physical harm to Luke, from time to time the other boy still made nasty comments to Luke when he sensed he could get away with doing so, but the frequency and intensity of his barbs dramatically declined.

Meanwhile, Mr. K. supported Luke with his goal of coming out to his family. The two discussed how and when he would make a revelation to his family, and practiced how he would go about doing so. Luke decided that he would tell his mother first because he felt she would not "freak out" at the news, even though it might upset her. When she later responded to his disclosure with concern yet support, he decided that he would then tell his father. Before he took this step, however, Luke was concerned that his father might reject him. So, Mr. K. asked Luke if he could invite his mother in for a consult to suggest to her that they consider going for family counseling to address the changes and conflicts in their family that might result from further disclosure. Luke agreed to this plan, and the two of them met with Mrs. B. to consider this plan of action. During that meeting, Mrs. B. explained to Mr. K. how concerned she was for her son, fearing that he would face a difficult life because he was gay. Mr. K. empathized with and validated these fears, stating that he was concerned for Luke, too, because he was well aware of how tough the world can be on a gay male, yet he was confident that Luke could find his place in life, especially if he were able to enlist the support of his family. On that note, Mr. K. told Mrs. B. about a psychologist, Dr. R., at a local mental health center who was especially skilled at helping families that had a gay member, and he asked Mrs. B. if she would like to have that person's number. Mrs. B. accepted this information, and then she and Luke discussed how they would go about telling Mr. B. that Luke was gay. The two decided that they would prefer to tell Mr. B. first and then, after he had adjusted to the news, tell the rest of his immediate family.

The next 4 months were extremely stressful for Luke. Initially, his father did not take the news about Luke's sexual orientation well, responding by becoming emotionally distant from both Luke and his wife. Mrs. B. gave her husband one week to allow the news to settle in, and then she asked her husband to go with her and Luke for counseling. Reluctantly, he agreed, and the three of them went to see Dr. R. It was during these sessions that Mr. B. explained that his biggest concern about Luke's sexuality was that the family might be ostracized because of Luke's sexual orientation. He was also troubled by Luke's "choice" because being "queer" was not acceptable to the Catholic Church. No matter how upset Mr. B. became during the first couple of family sessions, Dr. R. always empathized with his feelings, while observing that he sensed Mr. B. still cared deeply about his son's well-being. Dr. R. also educated Mr. and Mrs. B. about homosexuality, explaining the inherent nature of sexual orientation. Dr. R. helped Mr. and Mrs. B. and Luke to negotiate a plan of action that they all could live with. According to this plan, Luke agreed to keep his sexual orientation private for the remainder of his high school years, while his parents adjusted to the realization that their son was gay. As part of that adjustment process, Mr. and Mrs. B. promised Luke that they would contact organizations like PFLAG to learn more about the life of families who have a gay son. After that time, Luke and his parents would reevaluate when and to whom they would reveal the news about Luke. By January of his senior year, Luke and his parents were relating to each other pretty well, and his sexual orientation was less of a source of concern to them.

Another issue that was addressed during Luke's senior year was his choice of a college. As Luke spent more time exploring the gay community and talking with other gay youth at the community center, he realized that he wanted to find a college or university that had an accepting attitude toward gays. After researching this matter carefully, he decided to attend a school in New York City, where he would major in journalism and gradually try to integrate himself into a nearby gay community.

By the time Luke graduated from high school, things had improved greatly for him although they were far from being perfect. He was feeling more comfortable with himself as a gay person, but he still yearned for closer ties with other people who were like him, which was one of the reasons he was eager to go away to college. He felt better about his relationships with his fellow students, yet he was still leery about letting anyone who wasn't a trusted friend know about his sexual orientation. He was getting along fine with his parents, but he still felt uneasiness between him and his father, and he longed for a day when he would inform the rest of his family about his sexuality. As he looked toward the future, however, he was confident that that day would come, and he anticipated a time when he could be more completely out and accepted for who he truly was, a gay man who cared for the people he loved and treasured their love in return.

CONCLUSION

Luke's experiences illustrate the complicated and stressful challenges that are associated with the coming-out process. They also demonstrate that supportive counseling can make a huge, positive difference for a gay boy who is struggling to come to terms with his emerging sexual identity in the face of abuse by peers and potential rejection from his family. We encourage counselors to use the gay-affirming strategies we have described in this chapter to help other boys who are like Luke to move forward with their sexual identity development. At the same time, we hope that counselors can see from Luke's case study that gay boys and men often have the experience of moving two steps forward, followed by one step backward because our homophobic world constantly throws up roadblocks in their way. Counselors must recognize and be prepared to deal with these realities so that they can be caring anchors for their gay clients as they travel on the road to inner peace and acceptance.

We acknowledge that the case study presented in the chapter depicted just one individual who cannot be considered representative of all gay youth. Luke happened to be White and a good student who enjoyed writing for the school paper. However, as was mentioned earlier in this chapter, there is great diversity within the gay community. Counselors must be prepared for the possibility that any boy who walks into his office could be gay, and understand that a boy's gay identity intersects with other salient aspects of his identity to form a complex sense of his self-concept.

In order to better prepare counselors for the process of working with gay youth, we support the continued coverage of gay issues in counseling courses. Historically, there was a concern among some multicultural scholars that attention directed to gay concerns would divert attention away from devoting enough emphasis on issues pertaining to race and ethnicity (Nuttal, Webber, & Sanchez, 1996). However, there currently appears to be a growing consensus that the study of the special concerns of gay men warrants consideration within the broader umbrella covering diversity education and social justice counseling (Lassiter & Barret, 2007). We welcome this movement and encourage counselor educators to include the topic of counseling gay boys and men in their curricula.

The American Psychological Association (2000) has developed "Guidelines for Psychotherapy With Lesbian, Gay and Bisexual Clients." This document is an important resource for counselors working with gay and questioning boys, providing useful considerations for treatment with this group as well as the scientific literature base on which they are founded. The document is available online at http://www.apa.org, and should be required reading for all secondary school counselors and psychologists.

We have identified some of the particular challenges that gay and questioning boys face in their struggle to form a cohesive sense of identity— a significant element of which is sexual orientation. It cannot be overemphasized that, despite considerable progress in public attitudes about homosexuality and gay people, young gay men still face considerable obstacles in the process of navigating a heterocentric culture. For some, both school and home may be stressful or even hostile environments. The value of adult allies, both heterosexual and lesbian or gay, cannot be overestimated. In the sometimes challenging but mostly rewarding process of helping a young gay or questioning boy to come to terms with himself, you have the opportunity to offer a safe haven, emotional support, education about sexual orientation, and information about community resources. You have the opportunity to become an invaluable ally, whose positive impact on the young man may be lifelong.

REFERENCES

American Psychological Association, Division 44/Committee on Lesbian, Gay and Bisexual Concerns Joint Task Force on Guidelines for Psychotherapy with Lesbian, Gay and Bisexual Clients. (2000). Guidelines for psychotherapy with lesbian, gay and bisexual clients. *American Psychologist, 57,* 1060–1073.

Barber, J. S., & Mobley, M. (1999). Counseling gay adolescents. In A. M. Horne & M. S. Kiselica (Eds.), *Handbook of counseling boys and adolescent males: A practitioner's guide* (pp. 161–178). Thousand Oaks, CA: Sage.

Ben-Ari, A. (1995). The discovery that an offspring is gay: Parents', gay men's, and lesbians' perspectives. *Journal of Homosexuality, 30,* 89–122.

Bidstrup, S. (2000). *Resources for the parents of gay, lesbian, bisexual and transgendered youth.* Retrieved July 2, 2007, from http://www.bidstrup.com/parents.htm

Borowsky, I. W., Ireland, M., & Resnick, M. D. (2001). Adolescent suicide attempts: Risks and protectors. *Pediatrics, 107,* 485–493.

Callahan, C. J. (2001). Protecting and counseling gay and lesbian students. *Journal of Humanistic Counseling, Education & Development, 40*(1), 5–11.

Carroll, L., & Gilroy, P. J. (2001). Teaching "outside the box": Incorporating queer theory in counselor education. *Journal of Humanistic Counseling, Education & Development, 40*(1), 49–58.

Carroll, L., Gilroy, P. J., & Ryan, J. (2002). Counseling transgendered, transsexual, and gender-variant clients. *Journal of Counseling and Development, 80,* 131–138.

Cass, V. C. (1979). Homosexual identity formation: A theoretical model. *Journal of Homosexuality, 4*(3), 219–235.

Chen-Hayes, S. F. (2000). Social justice advocacy with lesbian, bisexual, gay, and transgendered persons. In J. Lewis & L. Bradley, (Eds.), *Advocacy in counseling: Counselors, clients, & community* (pp. 89–98). Greensboro, NC: Caps Publications (ERIC/CASS).

Chen-Hayes, S. F. (2001). Systemic anti-oppression strategies for school counselors as allies affirming queer children, youth, and families of multiracial experience. In K. Kumashiro (Ed.), *Troubling intersections of race and sexuality: Queer students of color and anti-oppressive education* (pp. 163–178). Lanham, MD: Rowman & Littlefield.

Coenen, M. E., & Kiselica, M. S. (2000). When homosexuality is the issue: Family counseling. *Directions in Mental Health Counseling, 10*, 51–62.

Coleman, E. (1981–1982). Developmental stages of the coming out process. *Journal of Homosexuality, 7*(2/3), 31–43.

D'Augelli, A. R., & Hershberger, S. L. (1993). Lesbian, gay, and bisexual youth in community settings: Personal challenges and mental health problems. *American Journal of Community Psychology, 21*, 421–448.

DeVine, J. L. (1984). A systematic inspection of affectional preference orientation and the family of origin. *Journal of Social Work and Human Sexuality, 2*(2/3), 9–17.

Edwards, W. J. (1996). A sociological analysis of an invisible minority group: Male adolescent homosexuals. *Youth & Society, 27*, 334–335.

Erikson, E. H. (1987). *A way of looking at things: Selected papers from 1930 to 1980*. New York: Norton.

Fassinger, R., & Arseneau, J. (2006). "I'd rather get wet than be under that umbrella": Differentiating the experiences and identities of lesbian, gay, bisexual and transgender people. In K. Bieschke, R. Perez, & K. DeBord (Eds.), *Handbook of counseling and psychotherapy with lesbian, gay, bisexual and transgender clients* (2nd ed., pp. 19–49). Washington DC: APA Books

Firestein, B. (Ed.). (2007). *Becoming visible: Counseling bisexuals across the lifespan*. New York: Columbia University Press.

Freetobeme.com. (N.d.). *Free to be me: Becoming the person I want to be*. Retrieved July 2, 2007, from http://www.freetobeme.com

George, K. D., & Behrendt, A. E. (1987). Therapy for male couples experiencing relationship problems and sexual problems. *Journal of Homosexuality, 14*, 77–88.

Gerstel, C. J., Feraois, A. J., & Herdt, G. (1989). Widening circles: An ethnographic profile of a youth group. *Journal of Homosexuality, 17*, 75–92.

GLBT National Help Center. (2005). *GLBT National Help Center: Serving the gay, lesbian, bisexual, & transgender community*. Retrieved July 2, 2007, from http://www.glnh.org/index2.html

GLSEN-CO. (2000). *Just the facts: A summary of important statistics about gay and lesbian youth*. Retrieved March 21, 2007, from http://www.glsenco.org/Educators/Administrators/just_the_facts.htm

Gluth, D. R., & Kiselica, M. S. (1994). Coming out quickly: A brief counseling approach to dealing with gay and lesbian adjustment issues. *Journal of Mental Health Counseling, 16*, 163–173.

Haldeman, D. C. (2006). Queer eye on the straight guy: A case of gay male heterophobia. In M. Englar-Carlson & M. A. Stevens (Eds.), *In the room with men: A casebook of therapeutic change* (pp. 301–318). Washington, DC: American Psychological Association.

Hayes, B. G., & Hagedorn, W. B. (2001). Working with the bisexual client: How far have we progressed? *Journal of Humanistic Counseling, Education & Development, 40*(1), 11–21.

Hollander, G. (2000). Questioning youths: Challenges to working with youths forming identities. *School Psychology Review, 29*(2), 173–179.

Israel, T., & Selvidge, M. M. D. (2003). Contributions of multicultural counseling to counselor competence with lesbian, gay, and bisexual clients. *Journal of Multicultural Counseling and Development, 31*, 84–98.

Johnson, A. (2005, July 13). Most gays, psychologists reject conversion. Retrieved March 25, 2007, from http://www.msnbc.msn.com/id/8543982

Korell, S. C., & Lorah, P. (2007). An overview of affirmative psychotherapy and counseling with transgender clients. In K. J. Bieschke, R. M. Perez, & K. A. DeBord (Eds.), *Handbook of counseling and psychotherapy with lesbian, gay, bisexual, and transgender clients* (2nd ed., pp. 271–288). Washington, DC: American Psychological Association.

Lassiter, P. S., & Barret, B. (2007). Gay and lesbian social justice: Strategies for social advocacy. In C. C. Lee (Ed.), *Counseling for social justice* (2nd ed., 31–50). Alexandria, VA: American Counseling Association.

Lemoire, S. J., & Chen, C. P. (2005). Applying person-centered counseling to sexual minority adolescents. *Journal of Counseling and Development, 83*, 146–154.

Macgillivray, I. K. (2004). Gay rights and school policy: A case study in community factors that facilitate or impede educational change. *International Journal of Qualitative Studies in Education, 17*(3), 347–370.

Mostade, J. (2006). Affirmative counseling with transgendered persons. In C. C. Lee (Ed.), *Multicultural issues in counseling: New approaches to diversity* (3rd. ed., pp. 303–316). Alexandria, VA: American Counseling Association.

Muñoz-Plaza, C., Quinn, S. C., & Rounds, K. A. (2002, April–May). Lesbian, gay, bisexual and transgender students: Perceived social support in the high school environment. *High School Journal*, 52–63.

National Youth Advocacy Coalition. (N.d.). *National Youth Advocacy Coalition.* Retrieved June 30, 2007, from http://www.nyacyouth.org

Nuttal, E. V., Sanchez, W., & Webber, J. J. (1996). MCT theory and implications for training. In D. W. Sue, A. E. Ivey, & P. B. Pedersen (Eds.), *A theory of multicultural counseling and therapy* (pp. 123–138). Pacific Grove, CA: Brooks/Cole.

O'Shaughnessy, T., & Carroll, L. (2007). Coming to terms with gender identity: Counseling transgender students. In J. A. Lippincott & R. B. Lippincott (Eds.), *Special populations in college counseling: A handbook for mental health professionals* (pp. 49–60). Alexandria, VA: American Counseling Association.

OutProud. (N.d.). *OutProud: Be yourself.* Retrieved June 30, 2007, from http://www.outproud.org

Parents, Families and Friends of Lesbians and Gays (PFLAG). (N.d.). *PFLAG.* Retrieved June 30, 2007, from http://www.pflag.org

Pearson, Q. M. (2003). Breaking the silence in the counselor education classroom: a training seminar on counseling sexual minority clients. *Journal of Counseling and Development, 81*, 292–300.

Planned Parenthood Federation of America. (1999–2007). *Teen Wire.* Retrieved June 30, 2007, from http://www.teenwire.com

Ponterotto, J. G., Utsey, S. O., & Pedersen, P. B. (2006). *Preventing prejudice: A guide for counselors, educators, and parents* (2nd ed.). Thousand Oaks, CA: Sage.

Potoczniak, D. J. (2007). Development of bisexual men's identities and relationships. In K. J. Bieschke, R. M. Perez, & K. A. DeBord (Eds.), *Handbook of counseling and psychotherapy with lesbian, gay, bisexual, and transgender clients* (2nd ed., pp. 119–145). Washington, DC: American Psychological Association.

Robinson, B. E., Walters, L. H., & Skeen, P. (1989). Response of parents to learning that their child is homosexual and concern over AIDS: A national study. *Journal of Homosexuality, 18*, 59–80.

Ryan, C., & Hunter, J. (2003). Clinical issues with youth. In Substance Abuse and Mental Health Services Administration (Eds.), *A provider's introduction to substance abuse treatment for lesbian, gay, bisexual, and transgender individuals* (DHH Publication No. BKD392, pp. 99–103). Washington, DC: Substance Abuse and Mental Health Services Administration.

Saltzburg, S. (2004). Learning that an adolescent child is gay or lesbian: The parent experience. *Social Work, 49*(1), 109–118.

Savin-Williams, R. C. (1994). Verbal and physical abuse as stressors in the lives of lesbian, gay male, and bisexual youths: Associations with school problems, running away, substance abuse, prostitution, and suicide. *Journal of Consulting and Clinical Psychology, 62*(2), 261–269.

Sears, J. (1991). Educators, homosexuality, and homosexual students: Are personal feelings related to professional beliefs? *Journal of Homosexuality, 22*, 29–79.

Shannon, J. W., & Woods, W. J. (1991). Affirmative psychotherapy for gay men. *The Counseling Psychologist, 19*, 197–215.

Slater, B. R. (1988). Essential issues in working with lesbian and gay male youths. *Professional Psychology: Research and Practice, 19*, 226–235.

Smiley, E. B. (1997). Counseling bisexual clients. *Journal of Mental Health Counseling, 19*, 373–382.

Stone, C. B. (2003). Counselors as advocates for gay, lesbian, and bisexual youth: A call for equity and action. *Journal of Multicultural Counseling and Development, 31*, 143–155.

Trevor Project. (2007). *The Trevor Project.* Retrieved June 30, 2007, from http://www.thetrevorproject.org

Troiden, R. R. (1989). The formation of homosexual identities. *Journal of Homosexuality, 17*, 43–73.

11

"Boys Are Tough, Not Smart"

Counseling Gifted and Talented Young and Adolescent Boys

WILLIAM MING LIU, SAMUEL J. SHEPARD,
AND MEGAN FOLEY NICPON

Timothy is a precocious 12-year-old boy. Even when he was younger, he tended to comprehend school material well above his age. Although he was ready to enter school early and to skip several grades, his parents opted to keep him with his same-age peers. As a result, his curiosity and intellectual gifts caused him problems in the classroom and alienated him from his same-age peers. For instance, during snack time, Timothy would often punch a hole in the bottom of his paper cup to drink his punch. His intellectual gifts have not been fully assessed or tapped, he is often bored in his classroom, and his fidgety behavior is seen by teachers as attention deficits. He is constantly being sent to the principal's office and is in jeopardy of being suspended from school. His parents are considering attention deficit medication to reduce his disruptive behavior, with the hopes that he will not be suspended from school.

Timothy's case is familiar and not uncommon for those working with gifted and talented students. His case is complicated because Timothy is at the nexus of several intersecting issues about boys and school: gender, giftedness, and disruptive behaviors. Additionally, his problems in school are representative of a wider trend: Compared to girls, boys are not faring well in schools (Freeman, 2004; Kindlon & Thompson, 2000). Some professionals have speculated that boys are not succeeding in schools because schools are not "boy friendly," and that boys need more or a different type of encouragement than girls; that parental pressures and expectations create anxiety among boys that may depress achievement; that bullying creates a hostile academic environment; or that boys are not emotionally prepared for academic rigors (Alvino, 1991; Boyd, 1993; Czeschlik & Rost, 1994; Freeman; Kline & Short, 1991; Muir-Broaddus, 1995; Newman, Horne, & Webster, 1999; Roznowski, Reith, & Hong, 2000). Gifted boys may struggle with some or all of these problems, plus the unique challenges and stresses associated with giftedness. The purposes of this chapter are to raise awareness about the hardships of gifted and talented boys and to describe the process of counseling them. First, we define the terms *giftedness* and *talent*. Second, we discuss various adjustment and psychological issues that are common among gifted and talented boys. Finally, to illustrate therapeutic work with gifted boys, two case studies are presented. The first case study is focused on counseling, and the second on assessment.

DEFINITIONS OF GIFTEDNESS AND TALENT

Defining *giftedness* is a difficult task because the word has been assigned many different meanings in the professional literature. Previously, authors had defined giftedness according to single dimensions, such as leadership or academic potential (Awanbor, 1989; Kirk, 1972). Today, it is more likely that *giftedness* and *talent* refer to high levels of multiple abilities (e.g., intellectual, creative, physical, and psychosocial behaviors; Awanbor). Complicating the matter are variations in the definitions used in different states and educational institutions. For the purposes of this chapter, we employ the following definition, which is used in the educational system in Iowa:

> *"Gifted and talented children"* are those identified as possessing outstanding abilities who are capable of high performance. Gifted and talented children are children who require appropriate instruction and educational services commensurate with their abilities and needs beyond those provided by the regular school program. Gifted and talented children include those children with demonstrated achievement or potential ability, or both, in any of the following areas or in combination: 1). General intellectual ability, 2). Creative thinking, 3). Leadership ability, 4). Visual and performing arts ability, and 5). Specific ability aptitude. (Iowa Code 257.44, 2001)

In this chapter, the terms *giftedness* and *talent* are used synonymously, at times in tandem and at other times singularly. Common to almost all definitions of giftedness and talent is the idea that the individual must somehow be different from his or her peers—that the child must stand

out in some way. The nature of this difference can have profound implications across a number of domains in a boy's life. In some instances, a
boy's reaction to being (or being labeled as) different can have as much
to do with his adjustment as the difference itself. In addition, family,
social, and cultural factors can interact with these influences in a way
that casts the boy's gifts in a different light.

ADJUSTMENT ISSUES OF GIFTED
BOYS AND ADOLESCENTS

Some people may object to the idea of spending time worrying about
gifted and talented children, claiming that the practice of identifying
and supporting gifted education is elitist, discriminatory, and unnecessary (Colangelo & Davis, 2003). The reality is that being bright and
intellectually gifted does not always mean everything in life is easy. In
fact, the idea that giftedness should somehow lead to an easier or better
life can cause additional problems when issues do arise in the life of a
gifted child. Although much attention has been paid over the years to
the struggles of gifted girls (Hollinger, 1991; Kerr, 1997; McCormick &
Wolf, 1993), the experiences of gifted boys have been relatively overlooked. Specifically, although research has addressed gender differences
between boys and girls, the research has yet to explore masculinity or
masculine socialization in relation to academic performance among
gifted and talented boys.

Like all high-ability children, gifted and talented young and adolescent
boys may face a variety of adjustment issues throughout their development. In addition to problems common to all gifted and talented children, however, issues of psychological and physical development, and
masculinity and gender role identity, can interact with the experience
of giftedness in ways that create unique challenges for these boys. What
it means to be masculine in our society often has very little in common
with what it means to be gifted. In addition, men, like gifted young and
adolescent boys, are not supposed to have difficulties or display signs of
weakness, which further adds to the disconnection between the expectations placed on gifted boys and the reality of their adjustment in the
world. Finally, issues related to culture and race can also influence a
boy's experience of being gifted (Ford, 1993, 1996, 2000; McKenzie,
1986).

Although it is true that gifted boys experience the world in ways that
can lead to unique problems and difficulties, this does not mean that
they are any more susceptible to adjustment issues than other children.
For instance, Bartell and Reynolds (1986) found that fourth- and fifth-
grade gifted boys reported slightly lower self-esteem and higher levels of
depression than gifted girls, but the researchers concluded that overall,
there were no major differences between the groups of girls and boys.
Additionally, other research has shown that gifted children are at least

as well adjusted, if not better adjusted, than their nongifted peers, and that they are no more at risk for social or emotional problems (Bain & Bell, 2004; Neihart, 1999; Roznowski et al., 2000). Nevertheless, it is still important for clinicians, school psychologists, and other mental health providers to be aware of the unique issues and challenges faced by gifted young and adolescent boys.

One of the most common challenges in the field of giftedness is the task of ensuring that children have stimulating and challenging coursework, so that boredom and the problems associated with it do not arise. For gifted young and adolescent boys, boredom with average grade-level work can manifest itself in a variety of ways, such as acting out in ways that are disruptive to the class or simply losing interest in school altogether (Plucker & McIntire, 1996). As a result, it is possible that some gifted and talented young and adolescent boys are diagnosed with attention deficit hyperactivity disorder (Hartnett, Nelson, & Rinn, 2004). Behaviors that are disruptive in the classroom may sometimes mask a boy being unchallenged and academically understimulated. Additionally, school systems differ in their willingness and ability to identify gifted students and provide them with appropriately challenging coursework. As a result, some gifted young and adolescent boys may suffer the dual misfortune of having their talents go unrecognized while simultaneously being labeled as a troublemaker or an underachiever (Williams, 2001).

Underachievement is a paradoxical outcome for some gifted and talented young and adolescent boys. Given their potential, why would they underperform and fail to achieve? *Underachievement* or *underperformance* may be defined as having a high capacity or aptitude but low level of effort on academic tasks (Ford, 1992). And there may be a number of different reasons for subpar performance, none of which can singularly predict underachievement. For one, young and adolescent boys faced with unrelenting parental pressure to perform may experience small failures as catastrophic. Consequently, they may learn to avoid certain tasks over time (Alvino, 1991). In addition, internal and external expectations toward perfectionism could paralyze young and adolescent boys (Alvino, 1991). Finally, another contributing factor may be the misattribution of academic success. Some gifted and talented young and adolescent boys have a poor understanding of their abilities and thus have poorly integrated their abilities into their sense of self. As a result, they attribute their achievement to external factors such as luck, but internalize failures (Dweck, 1986).

Adding to the academic challenges of gifted boys is the emerging trend of kindergarten redshirting. Analogous to the sports practice of holding an athlete out of competition for a year in order to save his eligibility for a time when he is more physically prepared, kindergarten redshirting refers to parents who delay their son's entrance into kindergarten by a year to give him extra time to mature (Kerr & Foley Nicpon, 2003). The redshirting of boys, even at this early stage in their education, is often influenced by parental ideas that their sons will be better served by being taller, stronger, and more able to compete both physically and academically throughout their schooling.

For gifted boys, kindergarten redshirting can be especially harmful. The reality is that gifted children actually benefit from the company of older children who are more similar to them in mental age. Kerr and Foley Nicpon (2003) pointed out that, because of their tendency to learn to read earlier and be more socially and emotionally advanced than average boys, gifted boys are better suited to enter kindergarten at a younger age. Opting to delay a gifted boy from school entry can result in constant boredom with coursework that he has already mastered. In addition, peer relations could be difficult because of the inability of younger classmates to think at his level and appreciate and share his interests. Problems with peer relations can be difficult for any student, and can lead to teasing and bullying. Holding back gifted boys only makes them potentially more "out of sync" (i.e., asynchronous development) with their classmates, which may exacerbate these problems. Although parents and teachers are typically concerned with gifted boys being bullied and picked on, gifted boys have also been shown to bully other children (Peterson & Ray, 2006), and some feel that bullying by the gifted may be more likely in the cases of boys who have been redshirted. Kerr and Cohn (2001) argued that a gifted boy who has been delayed might take advantage of his physical maturity by bullying or bossing around classmates as an outlet for his frustration and boredom.

Asynchronous development has been used to refer to both the gap in mental age that may exist between gifted children and their chronological peers and the disparity between a gifted child's intellectual abilities and his or her physical and emotional maturity (Silverman, 2002). As a result of their intellectual talents, gifted young and adolescent boys have access to ideas that they may not be able to handle emotionally, such as current events and issues of social justice, moral and ethical dilemmas, and issues surrounding their own mortality (Robinson, 1996; Silverman, 1994). This can cause undue emotional stress and confusion. In addition, thinking about the world in a way that is different from how peers of the same age think can cause frustration and feelings of isolation for these boys when they attempt to find friends who share their interests and ideas.

Related to this idea of enhanced moral and ethical awareness is the tendency for gifted young and adolescent boys to have a heightened level of emotional sensitivity (Edmunds & Edmunds, 2005; Hébert, 2002). For gifted young and adolescent boys, this often means an increased awareness of the feelings of others, as well as an increased sensitivity to criticism. This sensitivity can be difficult for any child to deal with, as it can have profound implications for socialization and peer relations. For young and adolescent boys, this situation is particularly challenging, as increased emotionality is largely incompatible with traditional conceptions of masculinity (Levant, 1992). Gifted young and adolescent boys may also feel the need to hide or repress any feelings of loneliness, uncertainty, or fear, as society teaches boys that these emotions are unacceptable for men (Pollack, 1998). Hébert (2002) cautioned that gifted young and adolescent boys who grow up experiencing criticism and ridicule in a culture that does not value male sensitivity may choose to withdraw emotionally from those around them, which can lead to more serious psychological problems in the future.

Even without the issue of emotional sensitivity, gifted young and adolescent boys may find that it is difficult to fully reconcile their giftedness (or being labeled as gifted) with their ideas of a prototypical masculine boy. The idea of being "smart" or "brainy" has little to do with traditional male stereotypes such as leadership, sexuality, aggression, and assertiveness. By adolescence, most realize that talent in athletics is far more rewarded and encouraged in males than academic giftedness. In some cases, young and adolescent boys may perceive their abilities to be shunned by their peers, and come to view their talents as nothing more than a social handicap. Some studies have even identified gifted children who choose to take efforts to hide their abilities from their peers, such as dropping out of honors classes or extracurricular activities (Coleman & Cross, 1988; Rimm, 2002). This practice seems to be most common in the adolescent years, when there is often an increased emphasis on popularity and social standing.

These issues have implications for the socialization and peer relations of gifted boys. Thinking about and experiencing the world in a different way or at a different pace than age-mates can decrease the likelihood of finding common ground. Often, gifted young and adolescent boys have interests and hobbies that are not appealing to other children their same age (Robinson, 1996). Even their taste in common interests, such as movies, books, and video games, may be vastly different than that of their peers, which makes forming friendships more difficult. For instance, gifted young and adolescent boys may prefer movies with more mature themes and plots, but it is also possible that they prefer shows and entertainment that appeal to younger children. In either case, their tastes and aesthetics are asynchronous to those of their same-age peers. Furthermore, gifted young and adolescent boys can certainly benefit from the companionship of other gifted boys, but such like-minded peers are not always easy to find. Because of this, gifted young and adolescent boys may often make friends with older children whose interests and passions are likely to be more in line with their own (Kerr & Cohn, 2001). Alternatively, some gifted young and adolescent boys may simply prefer to spend time alone or to find companionship in books.

Gifted young and adolescent boys who fail to successfully navigate the potential pitfalls in their social and academic realms may be at risk for additional difficulties. Threats to a gifted boy's or adolescent's self-esteem or to his gifted identity may lead to deviant behavior and even violent acting out. Although gifted young and adolescent boys appear to be no more prone to delinquency than their peers (Neihart, 2002), there are nevertheless unique factors that can contribute to these behaviors in gifted children about which clinicians should be aware. For example, some gifted young and adolescent boys may suffer from comparisons to an older sibling or another high-achieving student, and begin to experience humiliation and resentment as a result (Kerr & Cohn, 2001). If a boy or adolescent perceives that his role as a gifted child has been assumed or overshadowed by another, he may feel a diminished sense of self-worth and choose to channel both his anger and his abilities into deviant or antisocial pursuits. In addition, gifted young and adolescent boys who feel rejected because of their gifts or their heightened sensitivity may withdraw emotionally, and as a result develop feelings of indifference or even dislike for those around them. Eventually, these attitudes can lead to harmful or even antisocial behaviors. It is important that clinicians be able to consider these influences when working with delinquent or high-risk gifted young and adolescent boys to adequately address the root causes of problem behaviors and implement appropriately tailored solutions (Seeley, 2003).

Finally, racial, cultural, and social factors have also been thought to exert an influence on gifted young and adolescent boys (Hébert, 2002). In addition to problems related to interpreting their giftedness with regard to ideas of masculinity, these young and adolescent boys can also feel pressure to view their abilities in light of racial and cultural conceptions of intelligence and the values placed on giftedness. Additionally, educators may have low academic expectations for culturally diverse boys and be less likely to identify gifted behaviors in racial and ethnic students (Frasier, 1997). Achievement is also linked with access to resources. Low access to educational, health, and developmental facilities has been shown to hinder achievement and limit opportunity (Begoray & Slovinsky, 1997).

Different cultural groups may have varying ideas about what it means to be gifted (Peterson, 1999), and may also have different expectations for (or reactions to) young and adolescent boys who have been labeled as gifted. Social factors, such as poverty and low socioeconomic status (McKenzie, 1986), make the identification of giftedness difficult and decrease the likelihood that appropriate resources will be available at home or in underfunded school systems. In addition, Ford and Harris (1995) pointed out that economically disadvantaged minority children may be pressured by their nongifted peers not to do well academically. For gifted young and adolescent boys living in dangerous and underprivileged neighborhoods, issues surrounding giftedness can take a necessary backseat to concerns such as safety, survival, and making ends meet. Language barriers can also stand in the way of the identification and expression of giftedness in young and adolescent boys from other cultures.

Most of the research that has been done in this area involves the experience of gifted African American children. Of primary concern to many gifted boys is the peer pressure they feel from other Black students to underachieve. Gifted African American students who receive high grades may be looked down upon and accused of "acting white" by taking on the characteristics and value system of the majority culture (Ford, 2002; Ford, Harris, & Schuerger, 1993). As a result, gifted Black students may intentionally underachieve or choose not to participate in gifted programs that might otherwise be a positive influence in their lives.

The research on gifted Asian American students has focused on identification issues, with only a few studies devoted to the social and emotional needs of these students (Plucker, 1996). One such study, a case report of a gifted Chinese American boy, highlighted conflicts that may arise because of different ethnic identities and levels of assimilation or acculturation between parents and their gifted child (Plucker, 1994). This boy found it especially challenging to exist and interact in two cultural contexts, and as a result withdrew socially both at school and at home. Issues surrounding vocational planning must also be considered when working with gifted Asian American boys. As Plucker (1996) noted, in Asian American families, career directions are often determined by the family, which tends to favor careers in math, science, and business. A gifted child's individual interests and abilities, which are often rewarded and reinforced by school personnel, may be perceived as being ignored by the family, which can be a source of conflict between a gifted Asian American boy and his parents.

Research on gifted Hispanic boys is also scarce. Kerr and Cohn (2001) described gifted Hispanic boys as frequently coming from patriarchal families that encourage traditional gender roles of male dominance, strength, and courage. Gifted Hispanic boys may have difficulty living up to this "machismo ethic" (p. 264), which demands that they demonstrate their manhood through physical strength and dominance. In examining how different cultural groups define giftedness, Peterson (1999) found that many Hispanic participants emphasized artistic talent, humility, and service to the community. This conception of giftedness may cause conflict for academically gifted boys as they attempt to balance opportunities to develop their talents and pursue their interests with obligations to provide for their families and communities and avoid competitive and self-serving behaviors.

Summary

This brief review on gifted and talented young and adolescent boys suggests that the definitions of giftedness and talent are multidimensional and vary by geography. This definitional variation may make identifying gifted and talented young and adolescent boys difficult depending on the school or educational context. Additionally, for some gifted and talented young and adolescent boys, academic success or the prospect of academic achievement may present them with a situation of masculine conflict and strain. To academically achieve is not considered masculine, but to not succeed may also be a masculine failure. One possible result for some young and adolescent boys may be to avoid the situation altogether by underperforming and underachieving. Another consideration for counselors is the impact of culture, race, and ethnicity with a boy's giftedness and talent. Sometimes, it is not so much a matter of whether a boy has gifts and talent but whether the capacity exists to nurture, support, and identify his giftedness. Because of contextual situations (schools and teachers) and available resources, some racial and ethnic young and adolescent boys are never given a full opportunity to actualize their talents.

CASE STUDIES

To illustrate some of the concepts reviewed in this chapter, we present two case studies. The first case study features a 17-year-old Korean college student in a counseling situation that occurs regularly in college and university counseling centers. We describe the presenting issue and the processes of developing rapport, intervening, and terminating counseling with the student. The second case study involves a 13-year-old White male who was previously diagnosed with ADHD. In this second case, we discuss the presenting issue, assessment procedures and observations, and results and recommendations related to the boy. We have added this assessment case because evaluations have become a normal part of the lives of many gifted and talented boys. Psychological assessments are used to ascertain their academic potential and psychological profile, and/or determine comorbid issues such as attention deficit or conduct-related problems. Pseudonyms are used, and both case studies end with a case analysis, which highlights important points about psychotherapeutic work with gifted boys.

Counseling Case

Presenting Issue

Shin is a 17-year-old second-year student at a Midwestern university. He was born and raised in Korea, where he graduated from high school after completing the 10th grade. He subsequently enrolled at university as an early entrance student at the age of 16. Shin chose to major in history after much contemplation as to whether or not this was the best educational route to take. He has a perfect grade point average (4.0) and participates in the university's honors program. Shin has regular contact with his parents in Korea; his father is a professor at a major national university, and his mother is a homemaker. Shin has no siblings.

Shin sought counseling at the onset of his spring semester after experiencing a number of significant stressors, including the declining mental health of his mother, the death of a close friend, and the choosing of a major. He reported that, during times of stress, he isolates himself and becomes overly consumed with studying. Although there is a significant amount of internal and external pressure on Shin to succeed in school, he recognizes that he often compromises his social life with excessive studying. When he lost his friend, he struggled over the fact that he often did not accept invitations to socialize with her, which led him to question the purpose of school, the true meaning of life, and the reason for his existence. This was further complicated by the fact that Shin feels he has few, if any, close friends at university; he is minimally involved in campus activities.

Shin's second area of concern focused mainly on family and cultural issues. Shin's mother is diagnosed with a mental illness about which he believed that he and his father were "in denial," especially regarding the severity and chronic nature of her illness. Shin felt that cultural and societal issues precluded his family's ability to address the issue openly and honestly. A related concern was the pressure that Shin feels about his educational and professional future. He recognizes the need to carry on his family's honor and to be successful enough to take care of his aging parents. Shin said that he feels a pull between what he wants to do in life versus what he is expected to do. Although he has chosen history as a major, he does not feel supported in this choice unless he attends law school as his next educational step. In light of this background information, Shin's stated goals for therapy were to (a) openly and honestly process his mother's mental illness and his role in the family; and (b) open up more in his interpersonal relationships.

Rapport and Interventions

Rapport was established with Shin by being attentive and responsive to several cultural, psychosocial, developmental, and academic factors that were salient for him. As rapport developed, Shin elaborated on the pressure he feels to be in more social relationships, as well as in a romantic relationship, while in college. In Shin's opinion, these demands are cultural and societal. As the only child in his family, he feels the need to marry in order to carry on his family name, and peers often say that he should be in a relationship as "part of the college experience." Shin is conflicted because he openly does not want to be in a relationship. The counselor examined Shin's belief system and how this influences his feelings about relationships. His fears about not being accepted by his family and peers if he does not have a heterosexual relationship were strong, as was the belief that he has limited time to adequately devote to building a relationship. Shin feels like his need to be academically minded precludes him from establishing deep, personal relationships with others. Shin and the counselor talked about his use of studying as a way to "excuse" developing relationships due to a possible fear about not being accepted for his thoughts, beliefs, and feelings. The counselor and Shin identified ways that Shin could connect with peers on campus who have similar interests and belief systems. Role play and modeling were used to help Shin feel confident to pursue these paths. The counselor gave Shin assignments to engage in social activities that varied from week to week.

As rapport continued to develop, Shin and the counselor began to discuss racial identification issues and cultural stereotypes that he feels exist on the university campus. Shin disclosed that he felt a strong need to be a representative of his ethnic group. He thinks about this pressure often and feels that it influences the academic stress that he experiences. Since coming to campus, some of Shin's own biases have been challenged (e.g., people who are gay are dysfunctional), and this has helped him think differently about the Korean student stereotype that he faces (e.g., poor English ability, always studying). For example, Shin's beliefs about sexual orientation have changed since he has become friends with his roommate, who identifies himself as gay.

During our sessions, the counselor also addressed Shin's past and present reactions to his mother's mental illness. Supportive, empathetic listening and psychoeducation were used to help increase Shin's knowledge about and comfort with mental illness. Shin said that he vacillates between feeling like he "got a raw deal" and feeling guilty for "feeling sorry for [himself]." Shin relayed that the cultural and family expectations are that he will be taking care of his parents in later years. Because of these expectations, Shin feels both overt and covert pressure to choose a different major, such as premedicine, or to pursue law school after the completion of his undergraduate studies because these are thought to be "respectable careers." Although he believes that he wants to become a historian, he is fearful about approaching the issue with his father. Through role play and extensive discussion, Shin became more comfortable with examining how to communicate better with his father about his future and his mother's mental illness.

As the therapeutic relationship developed, Shin disclosed that he worries almost all day, every day. Several interventions were suggested and attempted, including flooding, cognitive reframing, exposure with response prevention, analyzing the rationale for the worry, relaxation, breathing, and exercise. Shin found that he has difficulty relaxing or taking time to run, meditate, or read casually because this takes away from study time. However, the more Shin incorporated self-healing activities into his daily routine, the more he realized that having a more balanced approach to studying actually enhanced his productivity.

Termination

The concluding sessions focused on identifying ways that Shin would successfully make the transition back to Korea for the summer. This involved spending quality time with his mother, setting times to have one-on-one communication with his father, and reconnecting with old friends. The counselor focused on normalizing the need for privacy regarding family issues and how that is different from "being in denial." Positively, Shin said that he was more accepting of the nature and course of his mother's illness. He also identified ways that he could better connect with the university community upon his arrival to campus in the fall and what factors may make this easy or difficult for him.

Case Analysis

Shin's case reveals the important and complex intersections of masculinity (heterosexual relationships and reconsidering his homophobia), Asian cultural values and expectations (filial piety), and psychological and emotional maturation (developing close relationships). All of these issues are compounded by Shin's giftedness, which sometimes situates him apart from his peers. The counseling had to focus on these various issues, because all of them were significant stressors for Shin. The counselor addressed Shin's cultural values and worldview as a way to develop rapport, and normalized his emotions surrounding his mother's mental illness. Counseling also addressed the presenting issues of his mother's mental illness and his major choice, but also addressed collateral needs such as peer and social support. By preparing Shin for his trip to Korea and his eventual return, Shin was given tools to understand his family pressures and also coping strategies.

Assessment Case

Presenting Issue

Zach is a 13-year-old Caucasian student who was evaluated at the University of Iowa's Belin-Blank Assessment[1] and Counseling Clinic. Zach had a long history of being viewed as very bright, yet also displaying symptoms of depression and ADHD. This complicated presentation was recently compounded after the discovery of a tumor on his left adrenal gland. While Zach was being treated for ADHD and depression, his parents wanted him to be reassessed to determine (a) whether Zach's educational needs were being adequately met, and (b) if he truly met the diagnostic criteria for ADHD. As Zach matured, his parents suspected that depression was probably a more fitting diagnosis for Zach's behavioral and emotional symptoms.

At the time of the evaluation, Zach was an eighth-grade dual-enrolled student (home schooled with local middle school enrollment). He had been accelerated one year (he moved from sixth to eighth grade), and his parents wondered what would be the best educational environment for high school the following year. According to his parents, Zach's whole-grade acceleration had been a positive experience; he had also benefited from his school's talented and gifted program and outside enrichment classes. Zach's parents further said that he is aware of his high intelligence but does not "live up to his potential." He reportedly did not enjoy school and often displayed behavioral problems. He had a history of mood swings, stealing from his parents, lying about his behavior, and difficulty accepting responsibility. In addition, he had always struggled with fine-motor activities and writing, reportedly putting down only the minimum amount possible on assignments. He had received accommodations in the past that allowed him to use a computer to complete work. Zach was a strong writer when using a computer; however, he had ongoing problems with completing work neatly and on time. Socially, Zach had some friends at his church, but few at school.

The diagnostic picture for Zach was further complicated by the discovery of a tumor on his left adrenal gland earlier in the year. Reportedly, Zach had chronic high blood pressure for 3 years leading up to the diagnosis, but physicians could not find the cause. The tumor was not found until blood work revealed that Zach had dopamine levels that were 10 times the typical amount in boys his age. Apparently, the surgeon was unable to remove the tumor in its entirety, so Zach remained under close observation. He had to eat a restricted diet, and he experienced headaches and migraines, on a frequent basis. Positively, Zach enjoyed reading science fiction, learning about wars in history, and playing video games. He was interested in animals and played bass in the school's orchestra.

Assessment Procedures and Observations

In an attempt to answer the questions initially posed by Zach's parents, the psychologist administered various assessment instruments, including tests of cognitive ability, memory, fine-motor acuity, achievement, attentiveness and impulsivity, auditory processing, and executive functioning. General rating scales and those specific to ADHD were also administered to Zach, his parents, and his teachers. Clinical interviews and behavioral observations also provided insight into his strengths and vulnerabilities. Zach initially was hesitant to begin the testing process; he was more interested in reading his book than he was in interacting with the examiners. Zach did warm up over time, and, once comfortable, his activity level and behavior needed to be redirected more frequently. During our interview, Zach commented several times that his "brain thinks too fast for [his] words." He said that he is much better at typing out his papers than he is at writing them. Zach mentioned that counseling and the recent addition of a psychotropic medication to his treatment regimen had helped to improve his mood.

Results and Recommendations

The information obtained from the comprehensive evaluation was invaluable in answering the questions posed by Zach's parents. For example, results confirmed that Zach's academic and psychosocial presentation was quite complex. On the one hand, Zach's verbal and nonverbal cognitive abilities were extremely well developed; less than one tenth of 1% of students his age scored higher on the administered ability measure.

This performance validated the decision by Zach's parents and teachers to accelerate Zach one grade. On the other hand, Zach's fine-motor, memory, and written language skills were surprisingly less advanced. Whereas Zach's processing speed on visual-spatial tasks was extremely fast, his speed of processing on a task that combined fine-motor skill and visual scanning abilities was weak. His memory skills overall were lower than what would be expected given his overall IQ, and he had particular difficulty recalling information in the absence of recognition cues and encoding and retrieving nonverbally presented information. Furthermore, Zach struggled with paper-and-pencil tasks, and his written expression achievement was not at expected levels in light of his sophisticated verbal reasoning and knowledge. These extremely large intraindividual skill discrepancies likely translate into frustration on the part of Zach and the educators who understandably expect him to demonstrate, based upon his verbal and nonverbal precocity, advanced skills in all academic areas. It was the psychologist's belief that Zach's processing and academic difficulties need as much attention as his academic strengths in order for him to make a successful transition into high school.

The second major question posed was whether or not Zach met diagnostic criteria for ADHD and depression. The answer to this question remained tenuous. Zach did exhibit some motor impulsivity on a test of executive functioning, yet on a second measure of attention, impulsivity, and concentration, his style of responding was quick yet accurate. Behavioral rating scale reports were consistent with elevated hyperactivity and inattention symptoms, yet the predominant symptoms reported were consistent with those associated with dysthymia, or a low-grade depression that is present in adolescents for more than one year. Although Zach's depressive symptoms seemed to have improved tremendously with the support of psychotherapy and psychotropic medication, it was likely that the low activation, limited effort, and distractibility symptoms that are commonly associated with depression would remain. If Zach had an attention deficit disorder, it was thought to be secondary to his diagnosis of depression.

Based on these results, some recommendations were offered to Zach's parents and teachers. First, it was suggested that the results of the evaluation be shared with professionals from Zach's school so that considerations could be made regarding initiating special services through an Individualized Education Plan (IEP) or 504 Plan. These accommodations would address all of the symptoms that are present in students with fine-motor difficulties, written language delays, and attention difficulties. Tutoring for Zach was also suggested, as well as having a contact person at school to help him initiate organizational and time management strategies. The psychologist stressed that Zach's areas of academic strength should continue to be fostered so that he would experience academic success, which would likely boost his self-esteem.

He was an extremely bright student whose talents were rare and needed to be cultivated for continued growth.

Given Zach's extremely variable performance on memory tasks, coupled with his complicated medical history, it was important to recommend that Zach be evaluated by a neurologist to rule out any neurological causes for this pattern. Additionally, the psychologist recommended that Zach's psychotropic medication regimen be revisited in light of the assessment results and that psychotherapy services continue.

To help with inattentive symptoms, several accommodation recommendations were made, including "chunking" his workload into short segments and providing him breaks upon completing smaller demands, which would be a particularly useful strategy for writing assignments. With large projects, it was suggested that an adult assist Zach in writing down all the necessary steps toward reaching his desired objective. Each day, Zach and the adult could check off each completed step, as well as make plans for accomplishing any remaining steps.

The evaluation team recognized that Zach would be expected to complete a higher number of written projects once he entered high school. Given his fine-motor difficulties, these demands could increase his frustration and lead to a greater reluctance to complete such tasks. The team recommended that Zach's teachers be aware of this possibility and take measures to structure and streamline the amount of work he must complete without reducing exposure to challenging material. For example, his teachers could require him to complete only the more difficult questions for a given assignment, which would confirm his understanding of the material without compromising efficiency. In addition, his teachers could allow for extra time to copy information and/or reduce the need to copy from a blackboard or whiteboard. Also, voice recognition software or dictation options, if available through the school or at home, could be used to reduce the amount of writing Zach was required to complete. Finally, the psychologist recommended that Zach answer essay questions orally or with a word processor instead of in handwritten format.

Case Analysis

The masculinity issues for Zach are subtle but present. Similar to other young adolescents, he enjoys video games and reading, and he aspires to perform well. But unlike many of the other boys, Zach has several physical problems that limit his capacity to engage in physical play. Additionally, he is often singled out for individual attention and outside-the-classroom assistance, which only draw attention to his limitations. Consequently, he is limited in his engagement and socialization with other boys, and his understanding about "boy norms" may be truncated. He understands that he can achieve highly in many areas unlike his peers. One possible consideration for counselors is Zach's asynchronous development, which places him with age-dissimilar peers. Although positive in respect to academic challenges, he may also face masculine socialization pressures for which he is unready (e.g., physical challenges or athleticism). Additionally, given his medical condition, he is likely to experience significant frustrations with his inability to perform equally well across all domains. Zach is at risk to view himself as a failure, especially if his teachers do not understand his difficulties and if they fail to support him.

CONCLUSION

This chapter has been focused on the issues counselors must understand as they work with gifted and talented young and adolescent boys. Gifted and talented young and adolescent boys tend to experience unique masculine problems, which often put them in double-bind situations. For some of these young and adolescent boys, academic achievement is not considered masculine, but once they achieve and succeed, they invite additional expectations and pressures, which allow no room for failure. In response to being in such a bind, underperforming or underachievement may become a meaningful coping response to unrealistic expectations by parents and teachers.

Another issue addressed in this chapter is the duty of counselors to understand a complex array of factors that can affect any gifted boy or adolescent. Demographic and contextual variables, such as race, ethnicity, culture, and socioeconomic status, are often linked to whether or not resources are available to gifted boys and to the level of familiarity a gifted boy and his family may have with educational systems and testing situations. Being able to recognize the influence of these variables on the adjustment of gifted boys is crucial. Counselors also must know how to assist gifted boys with the developmental tasks of understanding oneself as gifted, achieving emotional maturity, and cultivating satisfying peer relationships. Finally, counselors must integrate an awareness of how the masculine socialization process and pressures to conform to traditional notions of what it means to be a man may be related to a gifted boy's or adolescent's difficulties. Furthermore, counselors must be aware that the well-intentioned evaluations and expectations of a gifted boy's parents and teachers, such as academically redshirting a boy, can have unintended consequences—such as boredom in school.

This chapter was not meant to be a comprehensive description of all potential issues faced by gifted and talented young and adolescent boys. Instead, we focused on addressing the most salient concerns counselors should be aware of when working with this population. The two case studies illustrated the complexity that is involved in working with gifted and talented young and adolescent boys, and they provided suggestions for how counselors may respond. We hope that our recommendations will help counselors to better identify and respond to the interplay of masculinity and giftedness issues that highly talented boys experience from day to day.

NOTE

1. The Connie Belin & Jacqueline N. Blank International Center for Gifted Education and Talent Development was established at the University of Iowa by the State of Iowa Board of Regents in June 1988. For more detailed information, please see http://www.education.uiowa.edu/belinblank/ (Belin-Blank Center, n.d.).

REFERENCES

Alvino, J. (1991). An investigation into the needs of gifted boys. *Roeper Review*, *13*(4), 174–181.

Awanbor, D. (1989). Characteristics of gifted and talented children and problems of identification by teachers and parents. *International Journal of Educational Development*, 9, 263–269.

Bain, S. K., & Bell, S. M. (2004). Social self-concept, social attributions, and peer relationships in fourth, fifth, and sixth graders who are gifted compared to high achievers. *Gifted Child Quarterly*, *48*(3), 167–178.

Bartell, N. P., & Reynolds, W. M. (1986). Depression and self-esteem in academically gifted and nongifted children: A comparison study. *Journal of School Psychology*, *24*, 51–61.

Begoray, D., & Slovinsky, K. (1997). Pearls in shells: Preparing teachers to accommodate gifted low income populations. *Roeper Review*, *20*(1), 45–49.

Belin-Blank Center. (N.d.). *The Connie Belin & Jacqueline N. Blank International Center for Gifted Education and Talent Development*. Retrieved July 2, 2007, from http://www.education.uiowa.edu/belinblank/

Boyd, R. (1993). Gender differences in gifts and/or talents. *International Journal of Educational Research*, *19*, 51–64.

Colangelo, N., & Davis, G. A. (2003). Introduction and overview. In N. Colangelo & G. A. Davis (Eds.), *Handbook of gifted education* (3rd ed., pp. 3–10). Boston: Allyn & Bacon.

Coleman, L. J., & Cross, T. L. (1988). Is being gifted a social handicap? *Journal for the Education of the Gifted*, *11*, 41–56.

Czeschlik, T., & Rost, D. H. (1994). Socio-emotional adjustment in elementary school boys and girls: Does giftedness make a difference? *Roeper Review*, *16*(4), 294–298.

Dweck, C. S. (1986). Motivational processes affecting learning. *American Psychologist*, *41*, 1040–1047.

Edmunds, A. L., & Edmunds, G. A. (2005). Sensitivity: A double-edged sword for the preadolescent and adolescent gifted child. *Roeper Review*, *27*, 69–77.

Ford, D. Y. (1992). Determinants of underachievement as perceived by gifted, above-average, and average Black students. *Roeper Review*, *14*(3), 130–136.

Ford, D. Y. (1993). An investigation of the paradox of underachievement among gifted black students. *Roeper Review*, *16*(2), 78–84.

Ford, D. Y. (1996). *Reversing underachievement among gifted Black students*. New York: Teachers College Press.

Ford, D. Y. (2000). The office for civil rights and non-discriminatory testing, policies and procedures. *Roeper Review*, *23*(2), 109–112.

Ford, D. Y. (2002). Racial identity among gifted African American students. In M. Neihart, S. M. Reis, N. M. Robinson, & S. M. Moon (Eds.), *The social and emotional development of gifted children: What do we know?* (pp. 155–163). Waco, TX: Prufrock Press.

Ford, D. Y., & Harris, J. J. (1995). Underachievement among gifted African American students: Implications for school counselors. *School Counselor, 42,* 196–203.

Ford, D. Y., Harris, J. J., & Schuerger, J. M. (1993). Racial identity development among gifted black students: Counseling issues and concerns. *Journal of Counseling & Development, 71,* 409–417.

Frasier, M. M. (1997). Gifted minority students: Reframing approaches to their identification and education. In N. Colangelo & G. A. Davis (Eds.), *Handbook of gifted education* (2nd ed., pp. 498–515). Boston: Allyn & Bacon.

Freeman, J. (2004). Cultural influences on gifted gender achievement. *High Ability Studies, 15,* 7–23.

Hartnett, D. N., Nelson, J. M., & Rinn, A. N. (2004). Gifted or ADHD? The possibilities of misdiagnosis. *Roeper Review, 26*(2), 73–76.

Hébert, T. P. (2002). Gifted males. In M. Neihart, S. M. Reis, N. M. Robinson, & S. M. Moon (Eds.), *The social and emotional development of gifted children: What do we know?* (pp. 137–144). Waco, TX: Prufrock Press.

Hollinger, C. L. (1991). Facilitating the career development of gifted young women. *Roeper Review, 13,* 135–139.

Iowa Code 257.44. (2001). Gifted and talented children defined. Retrieved July 20, 2006, from http://www.legis.state.ia.us/IACODE/2001/257/44.html

Kerr, B. A. (1997). *Smart girls: A new psychology of girls, women and giftedness.* Scottsdale, AZ: Gifted Psychology Press.

Kerr, B. A., & Cohn, S. J. (2001). *Smart boys: Talent, manhood, & the search for meaning.* Scottsdale, AZ: Great Potential Press.

Kerr, B. A., & Foley Nicpon, M. (2003). Gender and giftedness. In N. Colangelo & G. A. Davis (Eds.), *Handbook of gifted education* (3rd ed., pp. 493–505). Boston: Allyn & Bacon.

Kindlon, D., & Thompson, M. (2000). *Raising Cain: Protecting the emotional life of boys.* New York: Ballantine.

Kirk, S. A. (1972). *Educating exceptional children.* Boston: Houghton Mifflin.

Kline, B. E., & Short, E. B. (1991). Changes in emotional resilience: Gifted adolescent boys. *Roeper Review, 13*(4), 184–188.

Levant, R. F. (1992). Toward the reconstruction of masculinity. *Journal of Family Psychology, 5,* 379–402.

McCormick, M. E., & Wolf, J. S. (1993). Intervention programs for gifted girls. *Roeper Review, 16,* 85–87.

McKenzie, J. (1986). The influence of identification practices, race and SES on the identification of gifted students. *Gifted Child Quarterly, 30,* 93–95.

Muir-Broaddus, J. E. (1995). Gifted underachievers: Insights from the characteristics of strategic functioning associated with giftedness and achievement. *Learning and Individual Differences, 7,* 189–206.

Neihart, M. (1999). The impact of giftedness on psychological well-being. *Roeper Review, 22,* 10–17.

Neihart, M. (2002). Delinquency and gifted children. In M. Neihart, S. M. Reis, N. M. Robinson, & S. M. Moon (Eds.), *The social and emotional development of gifted children: What do we know?* (pp. 103–112). Waco, TX: Prufrock Press.

Newman, D. A., Horne, A. M., & Webster, C. B. (1999). Bullies and victims: A theme of boys and adolescent males. In A. M. Horne & M. S. Kiselica (Eds.), *Handbook of counseling boys and adolescent males: A practitioner's guide* (pp. 313–340). Thousand Oaks, CA: Sage.

Peterson, J. S. (1999). Gifted—through whose cultural lens? An application of the postpositivistic mode of inquiry. *Journal for the Education of the Gifted, 22,* 354–383.

Peterson, J. S., & Ray, K. E. (2006). Bullying and the gifted: Victims, perpetrators, prevalence, and effects. *Gifted Child Quarterly, 50,* 148–168.

Plucker, J. A. (1994). Issues in the social and emotional adjustment and development of a gifted, Chinese American student. *Roeper Review, 17,* 89–94.

Plucker, J. A. (1996). Gifted Asian-American students: Identification, curricular, and counseling concerns. *Journal for the Education of the Gifted, 19,* 315–343.

Plucker, J. A., & McIntire, J. (1996). Academic survivability in high-potential, middle school students. *Gifted Child Quarterly, 40,* 7–14.

Pollack, W. (1998). *Real boys: Rescuing our sons from the myths of boyhood.* New York: Henry Holt.

Rimm, S. (2002). Peer pressures and social acceptance of gifted students. In M. Neihart, S. M. Reis, N. M. Robinson, & S. M. Moon (Eds.), *The social and emotional development of gifted children: What do we know?* (pp. 13–18). Waco, TX: Prufrock Press.

Robinson, N. M. (1996). Counseling agendas for gifted young people: A commentary. *Journal for the Education of the Gifted, 20,* 128–137.

Roznowski, M., Reith, J., & Hong, S. (2000). A further look at youth intellectual giftedness and its correlates: Values, interests, performance, and behavior. *Intelligence, 28,* 87–113.

Seeley, K. (2003). High risk gifted learners. In N. Colangelo & G. A. Davis (Eds.), *Handbook of gifted education* (3rd ed., pp. 444–451). Boston: Allyn & Bacon.

Silverman, L. K. (1994). The moral sensitivity of gifted children and the evolution of society. *Roeper Review, 17,* 110–116.

Silverman, L. K. (2002). Asynchronous development. In M. Neihart, S. M. Reis, N. M. Robinson, & S. M. Moon (Eds.), *The social and emotional development of gifted children: What do we know?* (pp. 31–37). Waco, TX: Prufrock Press.

Williams, C. (2001). Parents fret most about struggles of gifted boys. *Times Educational Supplement, 4440,* 6–11.

Index